Solar Energy Optimization Using Generative Artificial Intelligence

Scrivener Publishing
100 Cummings Center, Suite 541J
Beverly, MA 01915-6106

Publishers at Scrivener
Martin Scrivener (martin@scrivenerpublishing.com)
Phillip Carmical (pcarmical@scrivenerpublishing.com)

Solar Energy Optimization Using Generative Artificial Intelligence

Edited by

Abhishek Kumar

Pramod Singh Rathore

Arun Lal Srivastav

and

Ashutosh Kumar Dubey

Scrivener Publishing

WILEY

This edition first published 2026 by John Wiley & Sons, Inc., 111 River Street, Hoboken, NJ 07030, USA and Scrivener Publishing LLC, 100 Cummings Center, Suite 541J, Beverly, MA 01915, USA

For more information about Scrivener publications please visit www.scrivenerpublishing.com.

Wiley Global Headquarters
111 River Street, Hoboken, NJ 07030, USA

For details of our global editorial offices, customer services, and more information about Wiley products visit us at www.wiley.com.

The manufacturer's authorized representative according to the EU General Product Safety Regulation is Wiley-VCH GmbH, Boschstr. 12, 69469 Weinheim, Germany, e-mail: Product_Safety@wiley.com.

Library of Congress Cataloging-in-Publication Data

ISBN 9781394419463

Cover image: Generated with AI using Adobe Firefly
Cover design by Russell Richardson

Set in size of 11pt and Minion Pro by Manila Typesetting Company, Makati, Philippines

Printed in the USA

10 9 8 7 6 5 4 3 2 1

Contents

Preface

This edited volume, *Solar Energy Optimization Using Generative Artificial Intelligence*, brings together contemporary research, practical methodologies, and forward-looking perspectives that explore how generative AI and intelligent computational techniques can optimize solar energy systems across their entire lifecycle. The book is designed to serve as a comprehensive reference for researchers, academicians, industry professionals, policymakers, and postgraduate students working at the intersection of renewable energy, artificial intelligence, and sustainable development. The chapters in this book systematically examine the role of AI in enhancing solar energy forecasting, improving photovoltaic efficiency, enabling predictive maintenance, optimizing energy storage systems, and supporting smart grid integration.

Chapter 1: This chapter presents a comprehensive review of machine learning and deep learning techniques used in solar energy forecasting. It critically analyzes statistical, neural, ensemble, and hybrid models, highlighting their strengths and limitations. The chapter emphasizes the importance of accurate prediction for grid stability and energy management. It also identifies research gaps related to climate variability, scalability, and real-world deployment. The proposed framework outlines future directions for adaptable and region-specific forecasting models.

Chapter 2: This chapter explores the evolution of smart materials used in photovoltaic systems to improve energy storage and conversion efficiency. It discusses crystalline silicon, thin-film photovoltaics, perovskite solar cells, and carbon nanotube-based composites. Environmental sustainability, scalability, and lifecycle assessment of materials are critically examined. The chapter highlights the role of advanced manufacturing and material innovation in next-generation solar panels. Future challenges related to stability, toxicity, and commercial deployment are also addressed.

Chapter 3: This chapter investigates how artificial intelligence enhances solar panel efficiency through optimization of placement, orientation, and operational parameters. It reviews AI-driven techniques for energy conservation, system monitoring, and cost minimization. The chapter demonstrates how machine learning improves installation planning and maximizes energy yield. Practical applications of AI-powered solar solutions are discussed in detail. The chapter concludes with insights into future AI-enabled solar technologies.

Chapter 4: This chapter extends the discussion of AI to wind energy systems, emphasizing prediction, site selection, and operational optimization. It compares traditional forecasting approaches with machine learning and hybrid models. Case studies illustrate AI-driven maintenance and performance enhancement in real-world wind farms. The chapter highlights the synergy between wind and solar energy systems. Emerging AI trends for renewable energy integration are also explored.

Chapter 5: This chapter focuses on the transformative role of generative AI in renewable energy planning and environmental protection. It discusses AI-driven modeling, simulation, and decision-support systems for sustainability. The chapter highlights how generative models assist in optimizing energy resources while reducing environmental impact. Applications in conservation, resource management, and climate resilience are presented. The chapter underscores the potential of AI in achieving long-term sustainability goals.

Chapter 6: This chapter addresses ethical, social, and regulatory issues associated with AI deployment in solar energy systems. It discusses data privacy, transparency, algorithmic bias, and accountability in AI-driven decision-making. Machine learning-based optimization frameworks are evaluated from an ethical perspective. The chapter emphasizes responsible AI adoption to ensure fairness and trust. It provides guidelines for ethically sustainable AI-powered solar solutions.

Chapter 7: This chapter examines current and emerging applications of generative AI in solar energy systems. It covers AI-driven design, predictive maintenance, smart grids, and decentralized energy trading. The chapter highlights autonomous solar installations and hybrid energy systems. Challenges related to scalability and data dependency are discussed. Future research directions in generative AI for solar energy are clearly outlined.

Chapter 8: This chapter explores AI-enabled solar conservation techniques and their role in climate change mitigation. It integrates traditional solar methods with intelligent energy management systems. Predictive maintenance, energy estimation, and forecasting are analyzed in detail. The chapter discusses benefits, challenges, and future prospects of AI-driven sustainability. Emphasis is placed on reducing carbon emissions and improving energy efficiency.

Chapter 9: This chapter provides a detailed market-oriented analysis of solar energy using AI-driven forecasting and analytics. It examines investment trends, policy impacts, and economic viability of solar technologies. Generative AI is shown to enhance market predictions and decision-making. Challenges related to data quality, regulation, and scalability are discussed. The chapter offers recommendations for future market growth and AI adoption.

Chapter 10: This chapter highlights the strategic role of AI in solar energy conservation and climate change mitigation. It discusses predictive analytics, grid integration, and energy storage optimization. AI-driven land-use planning and real-time monitoring are emphasized. The chapter links solar optimization with global climate policies and circular economy principles. It demonstrates how AI strengthens environmental and economic sustainability.

Chapter 11: This chapter examines the socio-economic and environmental implications of large-scale photovoltaic deployment. AI-based models are used to analyze environmental impacts and system performance. The chapter discusses data-driven methodologies for sustainable solar adoption. Results highlight the role of AI in overcoming adoption barriers. Policy and social perspectives are integrated into the analysis.

Chapter 12: This chapter focuses on generative AI-driven discovery and optimization of smart materials for solar energy storage. It covers advanced electrode materials, phase-change materials, and self-healing systems. Digital twin modeling and techno-economic analysis are emphasized. The chapter highlights how AI accelerates material innovation and performance optimization. Future challenges and commercialization pathways are discussed.

Chapter 13: This chapter presents AI-based methodologies for wind turbine site selection using geospatial and environmental data. It discusses machine learning models, GIS integration, and optimization algorithms. Case studies from different regions illustrate real-world applicability. Challenges related to data quality and scalability are addressed. The chapter emphasizes AI's role in improving renewable infrastructure planning.

Chapter 14: This chapter synthesizes AI-driven innovations in solar energy and climate management. It discusses smart grids, predictive maintenance, energy storage, and IoT integration. Case studies highlight national and global AI initiatives in climate action. The chapter explores future directions including autonomous solar plants and AI-driven governance. It concludes by positioning AI as a cornerstone of sustainable energy systems.

Chapter 15: In this chapter, the author describes how the Internet of Things (IoT) and Artificial Intelligence (AI) played a revolutionary role in the sunlight energy system to transcend these limitations. The chapter is a useful contribution to the field of understanding that more intelligent solar energy management relies on technological advances, architectures, and intelligent approaches. Beginning with the disadvantages of the conventional solar systems, the chapter explains how the combination of IoT and AI can enable a reinvention of the solar packing procedure, in which real-time monitoring, predictive analysis, and dynamic energy management are involved.

Editors
Abhishek Kumar
Chandigarh University, Punjab, India
Pramod Singh Rathore
Manipal University Jaipur, Jaipur, India
Arun Lal Srivastav
Chitkara University, Himachal Pradesh, India
Ashutosh Kumar Dubey
Chitkara University, Himachal Pradesh, India

1

Machine Learning Advancements in Solar Energy Forecasting: A Comprehensive Review

Inam Ul Haq[1], Priya Kumari[2], Aniket Tiwari[2], Bibhanshu Bhatt[2], Ayush Panwar[2], Prakriti Singh[2] and Vishnu Vishvas Sharma[2]

[1]School of Computer Science in Emerging Technologies, NIET, Greater Noida, India
[2]Department of CSE, Chandigarh University, Mohali, India

Abstract
In recent years, there has been a significant increase in the use of renewable energy sources, particularly solar energy. Accurate forecasting of solar energy is crucial for its reliable integration into the energy grid. This paper explores the intersection of solar energy and machine learning, which has the potential to revolutionize clean energy production. It highlights the advantages of solar energy and the role of machine learning in optimizing its generation. The paper examines different machine learning models and their limitations. The fusion of solar energy and machine learning has the potential to reshape energy generation. The paper identifies research gaps and provides guidance for future endeavors. It emphasizes the need for adaptable models, consideration of climate change, practical implementations, and economic aspects. The goal is to enhance solar energy prediction models for precision, efficiency, and adaptability. The insights from this research offer a roadmap for real-world applications and a cleaner future.

***Keywords*:** Solar energy, machine learning, renewable energy, prediction model, sustainable energy, clean energy, power grid, green energy

Corresponding author: mirinam525@gmail.com

Abhishek Kumar, Pramod Singh Rathore, Arun Lal Srivastav and Ashutosh Kumar Dubey (eds.) Solar Energy Optimization Using Generative Artificial Intelligence, (1–14) © 2026 Scrivener Publishing LLC

1.1 Introduction

A. Renewable Energy

Examples of renewable energy sources are solar radiation, energy from the wind, heat from the earth's interior, and biomass. They supply energy that can be sustained, which makes them alternatives to the limited supply of non-renewable resources [1]. Sunlight and wind can be used over and over as sources of renewable energy, not like fossil fuels that run out [2]. Renewables help greatly in protecting the environment by reducing harmful greenhouse gases and pollutants, which helps cut down on climate change and improves the cleanliness of the air. Renewable energy offers great help to the environment. Replacing fossil fuels with renewables greatly lowers the release of greenhouse gases, including carbon dioxide and methane, which are big reasons for climate change. Also, producing energy by renewable means usually results in lower emissions over the long term than with standard approaches. As an example, solar photovoltaic panels and wind turbines do not directly cause emissions, which helps in the worldwide effort to prevent the Earth's temperature from rising too much. Along with cutting greenhouse gas emissions, renewable energy approaches are effective at decreasing different types of pollutants. The main pollutants that come from burning fuel in traditional energy are sulfur dioxide, nitrogen oxides, and particulate matter, which reduce air quality and harm our health. Using renewable energy can help societies tackle these problems, meaning air quality will improve and people will live in healthier environments. Managing these energy sources properly, geothermal and biomass, provides cleaner options for heating, cooling, and creating electricity. When people use renewable energy, both the economy and society see many benefits. The industry is now leading in new ideas and new jobs, helping areas that focus on clean technologies grow their economies. The production, installation, upkeep, and running of renewable energy systems offer jobs at many different skill levels. Also, improvement in renewable energy technology lowers costs, which helps people use less fossil fuel and get affordable energy.

Renewable energy solutions are giving remote and underserved areas in developing places access to electricity. Solar panels off the grid, tiny wind turbines, and mini hydropower systems provide power to communities for their houses, local schools, and hospitals, all without requiring lots of infrastructure. It helps everyone live better and develop equally, and it lowers reliance on imported fossil fuels shown in Figure 1.1.

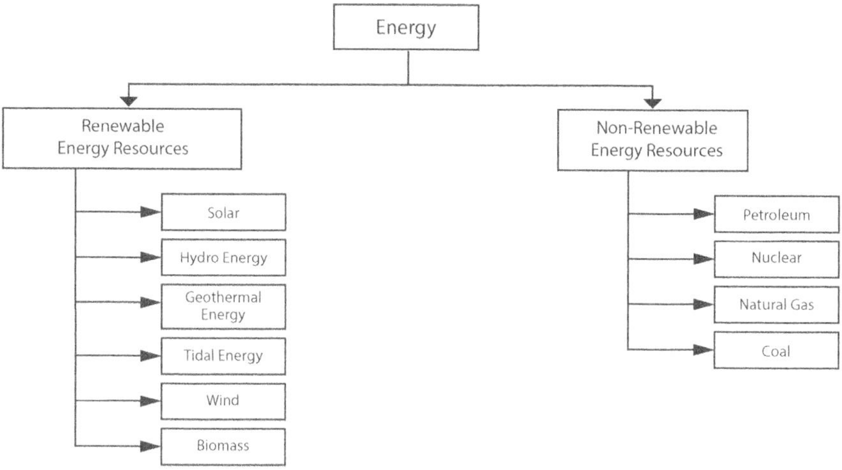

Figure 1.1 Types of energy sources.

Renewable energy is the main factor in the transformation of the world's energy system from dirty to clean. Many governments encourage faster green energy transformation by offering subsidies for greener projects, introducing programs for paying a carbon tax, and signing treaties like the Paris Accord. For countries to hit their net-zero carbon emissions goals and maintain environmental health over time, renewable energy must be used more widely.

B. Solar Energy

Solar energy is a wonderful form of energy produced by the sunlight. Energy from the sun is harnessed by different technologies and methods into usable forms such as electricity and heat, such as photovoltaic cells, solar thermal systems, and concentrated solar power plants [3]. The new term for solar energy focuses on using advanced technologies for its use [4]. Solar energy is better than many renewable sources in various areas. Because data is found around the world, it can always be accessed, making it free and readily available. It also has a small environmental impact, as it does not produce greenhouse gases or pollutants when it runs. Taking care of solar panels is very easy, so they are a budget-friendly and long-lasting way to produce energy. Since solar energy can be applied everywhere, can be made to any size, and does not need the grid, it increases energy security. Added to its solid reliability is the benefit of technological innovation that always improves the way energy is used and makes things cheaper. Besides other benefits, the solar industry supports the growth of new jobs.

While solar energy has many obvious advantages, what most people want to know is how much it helps the environment elements, including the site, the electricity needed, and specifics about the project.

C. Machine Learning

Machine learning (ML) plays a key role in AI by allowing computers to improve how they handle tasks by learning from information and experience. A key feature of ML is the growth of algorithms and statistical models, which help computers to detect patterns, guess outcomes, and advance their abilities without additional coding [5]. ML consists of a number of essential types, each with its own reason for being used. Training algorithms on labeled data is done in supervised learning, so they learn to assign the right output to the input, which aids in image classification and regression analysis. In contrast, without labels, unsupervised learning tries to learn patterns and groupings in unlabeled data, often supporting the activities of clustering or simplification of data. Instead of following one approach, reinforcement learning focuses on the way the agent and its surrounding environment communicate and influence each other. It is similar to humans learning by making various attempts because the agent keeps trying to maximize the full reward gained shown in Figure 1.2.

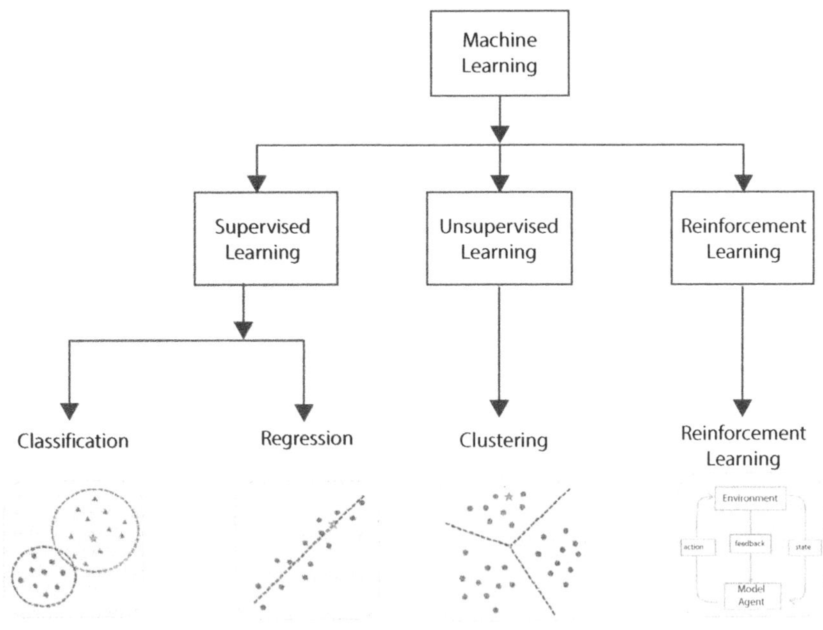

Figure 1.2 Classification of machine learning.

D. Integration of Solar Energy and Machine Learning

The association of solar energy and machine learning stands for a modern and encouraging effort focused on finding effective and eco-friendly ways to generate energy. By combining solar power with machine learning, its benefits in clean energy become stronger by helping it work more reliably and more efficiently and connect with the power grid [6].

With machine learning, developing predictive models to address challenges and optimize solutions in the field of solar energy could become highly effective and impactful. Solar forecasting is possible today, thanks to both basic and advanced ways that look at data. Using historical information and recent weather data, these models can predict how much solar power will be produced, which supports proper use of energy and a stable power grid. Evaluating various machine learning algorithms one by one has made it possible to pick the best one for each application. Also, using solar energy and machine learning allows us to handle the changes in the weather. As patterns in the weather change, machine learning models can alter the settings on solar panels, the timing for cleaning, and the way energy is stored to produce as much power as possible.

This document analyzes the progress in machine learning approaches for predicting solar energy and compares different types of algorithms. It explains both the advantages and disadvantages of each method, so one can choose the best technique for a situation. The combination of solar energy and machine learning is set to change energy generation by continuing to make solar power a dependable and sturdy part of the clean energy industry.

1.2 Literature Review

In the research paper [7], the authors focus on predicting how much solar power will be generated from renewable energy in the future using both machine learning and statistics. Data from both kinds of solar cells are used to evaluate the effectiveness of the model. This approach uses data from artificial neural networks, support vector machines, decision trees, and random forests, and it applies the Pearson correlation coefficient as well. It is believed by the investigation that this hybrid method performs better than both traditional individual techniques and models that utilize only machine learning. Because of this, it plays a major role in forecasting renewable energy by blending machine learning and statistical approaches.

The paper [8] examines using machine learning to anticipate how much solar power will be produced by renewable energy facilities in the near future. It makes use of support vector machines (SVM), random forest, and gradient boosting models in combination with the Pearson correlation coefficient. The model has a very high AUC (area under the curve) of 99% when it comes to predicting solar power generation. This allows energy organizations to manage their solar panels more efficiently, lower their costs and get better results from energy production.

Researchers [9] have chosen machine learning to predict how much solar power can be produced from rooftops. It explains restricted Boltzmann machines (RBMs) as the foundation of a new kind of model. To prove the worth of this model, researchers use rooftop photovoltaic (PV) panels in five specific places and check how the result compares to artificial neural networks (ANN) and backpropagation neural networks (BPNN). Feature engineering and cross-validation methods are incorporated to get more accurate results. The model shows remarkable results, attaining an accuracy of close to 100% in correctly estimating the production of rooftop solar energy.

Authors of the research paper [10] use machine learning to predict trends in solar energy production in India. Per capita electricity consumption, the total electricity consumption of a country, and the GDP per capita are used as factors in the model. By implementing a sequential algorithm with TensorFlow, the study teaches solar energy models using weather information such as air temperature, relative humidity, and dew point. It should be highlighted that by using this method, their predictions are right 99% of the time, which is better than other models. The article also forecasts how much solar energy will be produced in India through 2025 and 2030, which is useful for government officials, policymakers, and investors.

The research [11] in Niamey, Niger, is interested in learning how dust and the presence of clouds might influence monocrystalline solar panels. The study uses the same panels with identical conditions, and one of them is cleaned daily, whereas the other remains uncleaned in May and June. Also, the investigation studies the impact of cloud coverage between the months of May and August. A lot of factors, like output current, voltage, power, energy, efficiency, and clearness index, are checked closely. Both dusts covering the module and increased cloud cover are found to decrease the amount of energy each photovoltaic module generates each day. As a result, the findings stress the problems connected with routine solar panel cleaning and stress the importance of exploring various types of solar cells.

Authors of the research [12] introduce a framework to judge how well machine learning models predict solar power output for short durations.

Meteorological data from Hawaii with seven different features is used by the authors in this study, along with methods such as feature importance and principal component analysis (PCA). All three (random forest, artificial neural network, and XGBoost) models were assessed, but the results showed that running XGBoost together with PCA performed best. It clearly points out that machine learning has the ability to give highly accurate solar power forecasts.

In their research paper [13], the authors propose using a combination of deep learning techniques, which involve clustering methods, convolutional neural networks (CNN), long short-term memory (LSTM), and attention mechanisms, in wireless sensor networks. It aims to address difficulties in forecasting the output from photovoltaic (PV) energy systems. Groups of data are formed based on their seasonal trends, and special LSTM models with attention are created for each cluster. Besides, CNN is employed to get features from the time series data, which considerably improves the prediction accuracy in all intervals. The investigation reveals how using deep learning and AI in IoT technologies can help solar energy forecasting and grids work smarter.

The authors of this research paper [14] propose using machine learning to better manage and arrange PV arrays. Various topologies considered by the approach are series-parallel, parallel, bridge-link, honeycomb, and total cross-tied designs. An ANN model is trained using a binary mapping algorithm and gives excellent results of 98% in ideal situations. Comparing ANN to other models like support vector machine, Naïve Bayes, and k-nearest neighbor shows that it achieves higher accuracy, precision, recall, f-measure, and mean absolute percentage error. The main purpose of this study is to offer relevant guidance to people in the PV industry, helping them plan solar panel deployment.

The research paper [15] explores how using deep reinforcement learning increases the performance of mobile energy storage systems and power grids that depend on renewable energy. By training an agent in a virtual grid, it addresses the challenges of combining renewables, resulting in less expense and stronger grid stability. During the investigation, deep Q-networks (DQNs) and proximal policy gradient (PPO) models are used in machine learning. It demonstrates a fresh and practical method for including more renewables in power grids, which results in systems that are more reliable and efficient.

The research article [16] analyzes how deep learning can be used to estimate solar energy production. It discusses why getting accurate predictions of solar power helps to run the power grid, noting the issues in doing so. In their solution, the authors make use of convolutional neural networks

(CNNs) and long short-term memory (LSTM) networks. They test their approach using a practical dataset and unquestionably show that it performs better than the state-of-the-art methods. This addition is valuable because it may make solar power generation more successful and reliable.

This research paper [17] analyzes the importance of solar energy forecasting in the energy market and the problems due to the unpredictable nature of solar energy. To predict the amount of solar energy produced, the authors relied on a long short-term memory (LSTM) model in their deep learning process. The model is trained using a set of observations for temperature, humidity, and the amount of solar energy generated in Basel, Switzerland. They determine that the model is effective in accurately predicting solar energy output. Its value is that it offers an accurate new method to predict the amount of solar energy that can be generated. As a result, more solar energy could possibly be used in the grid, and solar energy could become a trustworthy source of power.

The research paper [18] looks at the importance of solar power and how hard it is to incorporate it into the electrical system. Solar energy, because it is renewable, can reduce the need for fossil fuels. But because solar generation can vary during the day and with the weather, it is hard to mix with power from other sources in the grid. The authors use machine learning and find that a zero-inflated model with a power transform performs most efficiently for predicting solar power generation. The addition of air quality info to the model improves its results since air pollution may cut down the amount of sunlight observed by the panels. This research gives a practical way to predict solar power, which can help make solar power generation reliable and more efficient. Operators of solar plants, grid operators, and policymakers could use it to improve their actions, combine solar power with the grid, and encourage more of its use.

The main goal of this research paper (published in [19]) is to make the prediction of solar energy results better for solar farms. They use deep convolutional neural networks (CNNs) along with accurate weather forecast data. This approach pays attention to both time and place connections to observe clouds, which they need for the smart grid's stability. It is often compared to persistence models and support vector regression (SVR). Their efforts made solar power forecasts much more reliable and accurate, as the error rate was brought down from 21% to 11.8% when they joined the team. At the end, the report suggests possible places where deep learning could make a difference in future studies. Table 1.1 shows the comparative analysis of existing literature.

Table 1.1 Comparative analysis of existing literature.

Site	Year of publish	Model	Accuracy/result
[7]	2021	Various ML & statistical models	Hybrid approach surpasses traditional models
[8]	2021	SVM, random forest, gradient boosting	99% AUC for solar power generation
[9]	2022	Restricted Boltzmann machine (RBM)	High prediction accuracy of 99%
[10]	2021	Sequential algorithm based on TensorFlow	Exceptional forecast accuracy of 99%
[11]	2017	Evaluation of the impact of dust accumulation and cloud cover on solar panels	Dust and cloud cover reduce energy production
[12]	2020	Random forest, ANN, XGBoost	XGBoost with PCA shows promising performance
[13]	2021	Clustering, CNN, LSTM, attention mechanisms	Improved solar energy forecasting
[14]	2022	Artificial neural network (ANN), SVM, naïve Bayes, K-NN	ANN outperforms other models
[15]	2023	Deep Q-networks (DQNs), proximal policy gradient (PPO)	Novel approach for optimizing grid integration
[16]	2018	Convolutional neural networks (CNNs) and long short-term memory (LSTM) networks	Superiority over other methods

(Continued)

Table 1.1 Comparative analysis of existing literature. (*Continued*)

Site	Year of publish	Model	Accuracy/result
[17]	2022	Long short-term memory (LSTM) network	Accurate prediction of solar energy production
[18]	2023	Machine learning with air quality data	Effective model with air quality data
[19]	2018	Deep convolutional neural networks (CNNs)	Significant error rate reduction

A. Key Observations from Literature Review

- Although a number of papers can predict well, scientists should look into making models more effective in different parts of the world. One could gather information from areas with many climate types to check if predictions can be used across various regions.
- Currently, these papers do not fully investigate the ways climate change impacts solar energy, which leaves the future of solar power unexplored. More research is required to look at climate and environmental factors to help with this problem.
- Research is needed to see how deep learning techniques can be adopted and used on a large scale in solar energy forecasting. Doing case studies and experiments in real situations can close the distance between research and its use.
- Most reviewed studies failed to focus on solar energy costs and any financial incentives. Research that examines the costs of adding solar power can be very helpful for anyone involved.
- Ideas that explore artificial neural network model stability when maintenance is not done exactly have not been fully explored. Studies must be carried out to check how well the model performs under a range of external and maintenance circumstances. This shows that solar energy prediction would benefit from approaches that are comprehensive, adaptable, and practical [20–22].

1.3 Proposed Model

If solar power uses machine learning and solar energy, it could become more dependable and effective during the move to sustainable energy sources [6]. Here, we will describe a framework for predicting solar energy with the aim of addressing known research issues and improving local predictive models.

- We launch our efforts by closely investigating a number of machine learning algorithms. At this point, numerous algorithms are examined, and their pros and cons, as well as how appropriate they are for predicting solar energy, are carefully checked. The aim is to determine which algorithms are the best match for our forecasting task.
- Using the results from our exploration of algorithms, we move forward by designing our model to predict solar energy levels. We work on determining the structure of the model, adjusting the most important settings, and choosing a reliable strategy for learning. The goal is to put the selected algorithms to work to improve the accuracy of solar energy predictions.
- With a good dataset, the next step is to train the model. The next step is to use the chosen algorithms to teach the model using important data from the past. To train a model, the parameters are repeatedly adjusted and its inner structure is improved so that it can make good predictions.
- The model is checked to assess its quality and how well it can be applied to new problems by engaging in thorough validation and testing. For this step, datasets are split for validation and testing to see how accurately the model forecasts solar energy for new sets of data.
- We test our model to see how it compares with existing models that predict solar energy. By comparing our model with others, we can tell if our forecasts for solar energy are more efficient. If improvements are seen, we go ahead with refinement; otherwise, we go back and review the suggested method and its algorithms.

- If better efficiency is noticed, we go into the refinement phase. Here, we focus on fine-tuning the model to achieve higher accuracy, dependability, and flexibility. This is when developers make hyperparameter changes, tweak algorithms, and try to solve issues discovered by testing.
- Iterative: The refinement stage might result in going through several rounds of refining and checking the solution. Doing this cycle allows the model to get better at making assumptions and become more accurate and efficient.
- Desired Aim Reached: The result of this careful effort is achieving our main aim: a model for solar energy that provides higher precision, greater efficiency, and much more flexibility. The refined system could greatly enhance solar forecasts, which in turn supports the advancement of clean energy.

1.4 Conclusion and Future Work

The papers I have reviewed give useful knowledge of the interesting area of solar energy prediction and optimization. They use different techniques from machine learning and statistics to improve the performance and accuracy of solar power generation. They make it clear that climate, different geographical regions, and the environment are significant, and they suggest creative solutions to handle the problems caused by the inclusion of renewable energy. All of these findings point to the strong effects that artificial intelligence and machine learning can have in promoting sustainable energy. Even so, these studies show where more research and practical action are needed to maximize solar energy in various areas.

According to what is shown in the previous sections, the proposed model has promising prospects for enhancing solar energy prediction. To make progress here, upcoming studies should focus on applying and testing this model in many different real-life situations. Working on how it fits with smart grids and renewable energies could greatly support the move towards sustainable energy. It is expected that the gained knowledge will fast-track improvements in solar energy prediction and raise the dependability and efficiency of solar energy.

AI disclosure statement: The author acknowledges the use of AI-based tools for minor language editing or grammatical correction. However, all intellectual contributions, analyses, and conclusions presented in this chapter are entirely the author's own.

References

1. Qazi, A., Hussain, F., Abd. Rahim, N., Hardaker, G., Alghazzawi, D., Shaban, K., Haruna, K., Towards Sustainable Energy: A Systematic Review of Renewable Energy Sources, Technologies, and Public Opinions. *IEEE Access*, 7, 63837–63851, 2019.
2. Owusu, P.A. and Asumadu-Sarkodie, S., A review of renewable energy sources, sustainability issues and climate change mitigation. *Cogent Eng.*, 3, 1, 1167990, 2016.
3. Timilsina, G.R., Kurdgelashvili, L., Narbel, P.A., Solar energy: Markets, economics and policies. *Renew. Sustain. Energy Rev.*, 16, 1, 449–465, 2012.
4. Arachchige, U. and Weliwaththage, S.R.G., Solar Energy Technology. *Int. J. Eng. Res. Technol.*, 13, 6, 1444–1449, 2020.
5. Janiesch, C., Zschech, P., Heinrich, K., Machine learning and deep learning. *Electron. Mark.*, 31, 1–16, 2021.
6. RajasundrapandiyanLeebanon, T., Murugan, N.S., Kumaresan, K., Jeyabose, A., Long-term solar radiation forecasting in India using EMD, EEMD, and advanced machine learning algorithms. *Environ. Monit. Assess.*, 197, 3, 1–36, 2025.
7. Subathra, P. and Sivakumar, M., Solar Energy Forecasting Using Machine Learning and Deep Learning Techniques. *Arch. Comput. Methods Eng.*, 31, 1–16, 2023.
8. Subramanian, E., Karthik, M.M., Krishna, G.P., Prasath, D. Kumar, V.S., Solar power prediction using machine learning. *arXiv preprint arXiv:2303.07875*, 2023.
9. Durga Devi, Y.V. and Sreenivasa Reddy, P., Solar Energy Forecasting Using Machine Learning. *J. Emerging Technol. Innovative Res.*, 8, 8, 8426–8430, 2021.
10. Jyani, M. and Rathore, P.S., Spectrogram-Based CNN Framework for Live Deepfake Voice Detection in Google Meet, in: *2025 International Conference on Computing Technologies & Data Communication (ICCTDC)*, pp. 1–5, IEEE, 2025.
11. Sharma, A., Al-Ammar, E.A., Wabaidur, S.M., Subramanian, B.B., Kassa, A., Prediction of Rooftop Photovoltaic Solar Potential Using Machine Learning. *Int. J. Photoenergy*, 2022, Article ID 1541938, 2022.
12. Garg, I., Raj, A., Jajoria, A., Solar Power Production Forecasting in India using Machine Learning Approach, in: *2021 5th International Conference on Intelligent Computing and Control Systems (ICICCS)*, pp. 943–948, 2021.
13. Rathore, P.S., Chatterjee, J.M., Kumar, A., *et al.*, Energy-efficient cluster head selection through relay approach for WSN. *J. Supercomput.*, 77, 7649–7675, 2021, https://doi.org/10.1007/s11227-020-03593-4.
14. Mangot, A., Kumar, A., Baliyan, A., Shining a Light on Solar Power Forecasting: Machine Learning Techniques for Unprecedented Accuracy,

in: *2023 3rd International Conference on Technological Advancements in Computational Sciences (ICTACS)*, IEEE, pp. 828–834, 2023, November.
15. Dubey, A.K., Kumar, A., Ramirez, I.S., Marquez, F.P.G., A review of intelligent systems for the prediction of wind energy using machine learning, in: *International Conference on Management Science and Engineering Management*, Springer International Publishing, Cham, pp. 476–491, 2022, July.
16. Rathore, P.S., Kumar, A., García-Díaz, V., A holistic methodology for improved RFID network lifetime by advanced cluster head selection using dragonfly algorithm, 2020.
17. Rathore, P.S., Sarkar, M.K., Das, R., A comprehensive review on secure and energy aware multi-hop routing in clustering based wireless sensor network. *Telecommun. Radio Eng.*, 80, 8, 2021.
18. Kumar, A., Dubey, A.K., Segovia Ramírez, I., *et al.*, Artificial Intelligence Techniques for the Photovoltaic System: A Systematic Review and Analysis for Evaluation and Benchmarking. *Arch. Computat. Methods Eng.*, 31, 4429–4453, 2024, https://doi.org/10.1007/s11831-024-10125-3.
19. Dubey, A.K., Ramirez, I., Marquez, F., A Review of Intelligent Systems for the Prediction of Wind Energy Using Machine Learning. *2022, ICMSEM, The Sixteenth International Conference on Management Science and Engineering Management, Lecture Notes on Data Engineering and Communications Technologies, vol 144. Springer, by Springer*, Ankara, Turkey, August. 3-6, 2022.
20. Kumar, A.D., Ramirez, I., Rio, A., Marquez, F., A Review and Analysis of Forecasting of Photovoltaic Power Generation Using Machine Learning. *2022, ICMSEM, The Sixteenth International Conference on Management Science and Engineering Management, Lecture Notes on Data Engineering and Communications Technologies*, vol 144. Springer, Cham. by Springer, Ankara, Turkey, August 3-6, 2022.
21. Al-Duais, M.A., Al-Owiwi, S.A., Al-Ghamdi, M.A., Al- Shammari, S.A., Al-Shameri, M.A., Solar Power Forecasting Using Deep Learning Models. *Research Square*, August 2023.
22. Pinson, P., Wang, G., Bao, H., Poor, H.T., Hong, Q., Forecast of Solar Energy Production: A Deep Learning Approach. *IBM Res. J.*, 2, 4, 1–15, 2018.

2

Development of Smart Materials for Enhanced Energy Storage in Solar Panels

Avnish Chauhan[1]*, Gaurav Pandey[2], Muneesh Sethi[3], Jonti Deuri[4] and Vishal Rajput[5]

[1]*Department of Environmental Sciences, Graphic Era Hill University, Dehradun, Uttarakhand, India*
[2]*Chemistry and Bioprospecting Division, Forest Research Institute, Dehradun, Uttarakhand, India*
[3]*COER University, Roorkee, Uttarakhand, India*
[4]*Faculty of Engineering and Technology, Sharda University, Uzbekistan*
[5]*HSBS, Swami Rama Himalayan University, Uttarakhand, India*

Abstract

The demand for sustainable and cost-competitive energy resources has sparked much progress in solar photovoltaics (PV) systems, partly due to the evolution of smart materials. In this chapter, the development and application of advanced materials for improved energy storage and conversion in solar cells are discussed. The existing industry is based on crystalline silicon (c-Si), which is high efficiency and long life (8), but it is also stimulated by the evolution of new technologies of perovskite solar cells (PSCs), dye-sensitized solar cells (DSCs), and thin film photovoltaics (TFPVs) for flexibility, lightweight structures, and cost reduction. Particular attention is given to hybrid organic-inorganic materials, nanostructured semiconductors, conducting polymers, and composites based on carbon nanotubes, which exhibit superior potential for enhancing the photovoltaic performance, structural integrity, and multifunctional applicability. Significant (efficiency and lifetime) improvements are possible by implementing innovative carrier-selective contacts, passivation layers, and interface engineering. In addition, the environmental and economic features of the PV technologies, e.g., life cycle emissions, recyclability, and material toxicity, have been discussed in this chapter. The scalability of PV materials and systems, including advanced

**Corresponding author*: avnishchauhan_in@yahoo.com

Abhishek Kumar, Pramod Singh Rathore, Arun Lal Srivastav and Ashutosh Kumar Dubey (eds.) Solar Energy Optimization Using Generative Artificial Intelligence, (15–32) © 2026 Scrivener Publishing LLC

manufacturing solutions and deployment approaches to enable the PV revolution, and smart integration of PV into the grid and off-grid networks are debated. Novel technologies (such as self-cleaning layers and floating PVs, AI-assisted material optimization, etc.) are also emphasized. Utilizing a cross-disciplinary approach from material science and environmental engineering to energy systems, the chapter introduces the disruptive role smart materials can play in the pervasion of next-generation solar solutions.

***Keywords*:** Smart materials, solar photovoltaics, energy storage, perovskite solar cells, thin-film PV, carbon nanotube, hybrid materials, environmentally sustainable

2.1 Introduction

A soaring energy demand and the environmental problems attributed to the combustion of fossil fuels have necessitated the use of renewable sources of energy [1, 2]. Among them, solar energy is attractive because of its large potential, low expenses, and inexhaustible nature [3]. At about 3.8×10^{23} kW, the sun irradiates the Earth with 1.8×10^{14} kW of solar energy, which is, of course, stored in many different forms, exceeding the sum of energy consumption every year in the world for only 1 hour [4, 5]. Specifically, the proficiency of the solar photovoltaic (SPV) system can be critically exaggerated by the intensity and spatial distribution (i.e., ground albedo) of broadband solar radiation that is approximately 3.8 million EJ/year, a value around tens of thousands of times over the worldwide consumption of energy services [6].

Different technologies can capture solar energy, such as thermal systems, photovoltaic panels, and solar fuels. On the other hand, photovoltaics transforms photons into electricity, but solar thermal systems capture solar energy and transfer solar radiation to obtain heat for immediate use or to generate electricity [7, 8]. Natural photosynthesis uses 12% of solar energy for biomass production, which could include some fuels like hydrogen and methane [9]. Nevertheless, problems including conversion inefficiency, intermittent energy production, and the contradiction between energy supply and consumption are still issues that need to be addressed [10, 11]. To address these issues, the integration of energy storage, bio-inspired nanostructures, and artificial photosynthesis has been devised [12–15].

PV system efficiency is relatively greater, about 22.5%, compared to natural photosynthesis (5%–10%) as reported in [6, 18]. Various hybrid and cooling technologies have also been investigated in order to improve the performance [16, 17]. These systems include FTCC, hybrid PV/T systems with water or air circulating, PCM cooling, and thermoelectric-aided SPVs [19–21].

In this chapter, we focus on recent advanced new materials in the field of SPV devices, with much attention on new technologies such as the so-called perovskite solar cells. Up to date, it reviews efficiencies and lifetimes of material generations, analyzes cost and scale factors, and discusses related challenges, focusing on stability, toxicity, or environmental sustainability. The paper also suggests approaches for overcoming these challenges, including enabling advanced manufacturing, characterizing materials and minimizing their variability, and carbon footprinting the next generation of solar photovoltaic systems to facilitate sustainable deployment.

2.2 Literature Review

Solar photovoltaic (SPV) is an important solar technology that converts sunlight directly into electricity. These systems consist of PV panels, a charge controller, an inverter, a power meter, a breaker, and a battery and are sized differently depending on the scale of the system [22, 23]. They have no pollution when SPV systems are in operation, are medium and scalable in size and power, are modular, and are simple in maintenance and versatile from microwatts to megawatts; thus, they constitute the renewable technology with the highest power density [24, 25]. PV systems are being installed at an increasingly fast rate; installations amounted to 100 MW/day in 2013, resulting in a global capacity of 177 GW by 2015 [26, 27]. Nevertheless, cost-prohibitive, inefficient, and intermittent issues are still the bottlenecks [19].

To mitigate these effects, solar tracking systems are employed on demand to improve the panel orientation with respect to the sun and to increase the output [19]. These trackers are further subdivided into active (e.g., motorized) and passive (e.g., fluidic) and can be one-axis or two-axis single- or dual-axis, and closed- or open-loop systems [30–33]. Although tracking systems are getting more performant, costs are a blocking point, which leads to worries about the economic viability of the tracking versus the fixed ones. The direction of research has consequently evolved towards the enhancement of tracking technologies at the expense of neglecting general results toward cost-effective considerations related to PV materials, radiations, and storage [6]. For example, Jamroen *et al.* [32] developed an economic dual-axis tracker that enhances the efficiency by 44.89%, and

Chowdhury *et al.* [35] also proposed a microcontroller-reliant tracker that showed good accuracy with low error.

SPV systems may be grid-connected or standalone. Applications include residential power and lighting, telecommunications, hybrid automobiles, satellite power, and hydrogen production [28, 29]. Grid-integrated PV systems don't have energy storage and depend on solar availability, providing simplicity, low maintenance, and a possibility of exporting excess electricity to the utility [30–32, 35, 36]. However, the addition of the battery storage to compensate for the shortage from the photovoltaic array during night or emergency periods increases the system cost [6, 34].

Off-grid systems are equipped with accumulators for the storage of electric power and can be desired for distant areas that are difficult to connect to the grid [37, 38]. They are more intricate and expensive systems that provide dependable power to remote users. The grid-tied system provides AC power by converting DC from solar panels into grid-compliant voltage *via* inverters (power conditioning units, PCUs). It does not matter whether or not backup energy storage is present; these systems can support grid stability and offer financial incentives to consumers through feed-in tariffs [39–44].

PV systems are energy production solutions ranging from 1 kW to 300 MW and can be used for electricity generation over various scales of commercial or residential usage. Different types of cells perform differently: crystalline silicon generates 12–16% efficiency, thin film produces 11%–14% efficiency, and organic generates 6–7% efficiency [44–52]. They have zero greenhouse gas emissions and have low opex and maintenance costs. However, obstacles remain in the high-levelized installation cost and the intermittent power with weather, as well as the additional tracking and storage systems. Installation costs between $600 and 1300/kW with annual O&M costs between $0.004 and 0.07/kWh depending on the scale of the system [21].

2.3 Smart Solar Photovoltaic (PV) Materials

Solar photovoltaic (PV) materials are central in the utilization of solar energy, as they convert light into electricity *via* the photovoltaic effect. Over 90% of the PV market share is accounted for by inorganic materials such as c-Si, which are high-performing, stable, and capable of long-term outdoor testing [22]. But they take a lot of energy and are quite expensive, and some (e.g., CdTe) are toxic and in short supply. OPVs provide a safer alternative, although they still have much lower efficiencies than inorganic PV cells.

Crystalline silicon is still the dominant material for the mass production of PV solar cells by far. Both monocrystalline silicon (mono-Si) and multicrystalline silicon (multi-Si) CC SP can be considered crystalline silicon. These devices show efficiencies in the range of 15–18% [22] with laboratory cell efficiencies of up to 25%. Recent developments comprise ultra-thin wafer sawing, low-cost metal contacts, and bifacial modules, which can potentially double the generation and yield better performance through greater light absorption [23, 24]. Tools such as PC3D have allowed accurate modeling of the c-Si cell performance and, thus, optimization of the internal behavior [25].

SHJ solar cells (Silicon Heterojunction solar cells) combine crystalline silicon wafers with thin amorphous silicon layers to achieve high efficiency and excellent temperature performance [27]. Methods such as POLO junctions [4], transition metal oxide passivation [10], hybrid copper finger devices [11], etc., have brought front-side efficiencies to 22% and above [31, 32]. Meanwhile, carrier-selective contacts as well as graded doping schemes can facilitate electron collection and efficiency, respectively [6, 37].

Polymer-semiconductor hybrid PVs are cost-effective alternatives that employ light-harvesting materials that generate excitons upon absorption of photons. At donor-acceptor interfaces, these excitons dissociate and drive current using separated transport layers. Because of the relatively lower efficiencies of the hybrids compared to those of inorganic ones, further development in process optimization and advanced materials is needed to enhance the cells' performance [6, 34–36].

Thin-film (TF) devices represent approximately 10% of the world's market. Strategies to improve TF cells: doping (e.g., Cu in CdSe) to enhance absorbance, conductivity, and morphology [18]. In recent years, perovskite solar cells (PSCs) have attracted increasing attention for their high efficiency and their tunable bandgaps, making them viable alternatives for meeting the energy demand of the next generation. All-inorganic and Sn-based perovskites have shown efficiencies over 22%, with low non-radiative recombination losses, which exceed those of many traditional technologies [39, 40, 65].

Dye-sensitized solar cells (DSCs) form an interesting PV architecture in which a dye absorbs sunlight and injects electrons into a semiconductor, such as TiO_2. DSCs have efficiencies of the order of 10%, and they are also considered for their small price, portability, and flexibility [53–55]. Yet, their expansive scaling is limited by the sealing, the stability, and the toxicity of ruthenium-based dyes and organic solvents [56]. Ongoing attempts to replace toxic substances with water and natural dyes as an electrolyte can be found [60].

TiO_2 still is the photoanode of choice in methanol-free DSCs due to its abundance, environmentally friendly nature, and good electron injection ability [61–63]. Representative N3 dye, a kind of ruthenium complex, was for a long time the standard for DSC. Developments in sensitizer structure, metal oxide films, and enclosure have enhanced performance and long-term stability under real outdoor conditions [42, 57–59].

Hammond: Perovskites are similar in some ways to DSCs. Their high VOC and suppressed non-radiative recombination enable them to surpass the SQ limit [66]. Recent advances have provided devices with efficiencies in excess of 22% with hybrid halide architectures and novel dopants [64, 80, 81].

The use of CNTs to improve PV material properties continues to grow. Their excellent mechanical, thermal, and electronic properties make them excellent candidates for the reinforcement of composites. It has been demonstrated that mechanical strength and Young's modulus are greatly enhanced by the incorporation of CNTs in polymer matrices such as Epon 862. CNT-rubber composites with improved thermal stability and wear resistance can be used in applications such as prosthetic devices.

CNTs can be used as sub-conductors in solar materials that can improve electron transfer and charge separation. Dye-sensitized and hybrid solar cells are being explored for their incorporation, improving their performance by increasing interfacial conductivity and structural properties.

In conclusion, the future challenges for solar PV materials are to increase efficiency, decrease production costs, and increase eco-friendliness. Although c-Si still dominates, hybrid materials, perovskites, DSCs, and nanocomposites such as CNTs provide a stimulating new direction for the next generation of solar technologies. These advancements are designed to optimize power, size, cost, performance, sustainability, and scalability, accelerating the world's shift to clean, renewable energy.

2.4 Efficacy, Constancy, and Scalability of Sol-Gel Processed PV Materials

2.4.1 Commercial Practicability

The technological maturity, economies of scale, and policy support have facilitated the recent growth of the solar photovoltaic (SPV) devices that are financially more competitive with conventional power generation. The price for solar panels has fallen precipitously since the days when it was relatively unaffordable. This change is being driven by advances in production technology, material usage, and large-scale manufacturing. Government incentives and feed-in tariffs also support mass adoption. Polymers 2017, 9, 77 4 of 31 demonstrated a low cost scenario, by manufacturing polymer solar cells on flexible PET substrates, allowing the devices as of ITO-based polymer solar cells unusual device architectures, adapted for mobile and ICT applications under moderate operational protocols [73, 74].

2.4.2 Photovoltaic Device Efficiencies

The performance of SPV devices is mostly dictated by how efficiently a device converts absorbed photons into useful electrical work. In this process, excitons are formed, dissociations happen at donor-acceptor interfaces, charge is transported, and carriers are collected at electrodes. First-generation silicon-based cells have efficiencies in the range of 15%–20%, while the second-generation thin-film cells (CdTe, CIGS) have efficiencies between 4% and 15% [6]. They are more expensive and toxic but efficient, despite the use of high-cost, high-purity silicon for first-generation cells. Thin-film processes, which use less material and are simpler, are cheaper, while a reduced efficiency is not too alarming [76, 77].

Third-generation PV devices, like organic PV, dye-sensitized PV, and perovskite solar cells (PSCs), are being developed to achieve better performance and higher cost efficiency. In particular, PSCs have shown efficiencies of over 25% [78]. However, their poor environmental stability, in particular under UV light, oxygen, and moisture, prevents commercialization. Up to now, these drawbacks have been under investigation to better exploit their efficiency capability [79].

2.4.3 Steadiness of Solar Cells

Primarily, device stability is the key factor for the aging behavior of solar technologies. SPV technologies have evolved to withstand a variety of environments, which makes their potential across various geographical regions promising. However, PSCs still suffer from the huge obstacle of stability during the actual longer-term operation. Mechanisms of degradation, especially photodegradation and thermal degradation, influence the device lifetime.

To overcome this, materials have been investigated. Authors [94] pointed out that the usage of nanoscale MOFs was a powerful way to improve the PSCs' stability. MOFs have attractive features of good pore volume, surface area, and thermal stability, which render them a varied choice of applications in areas related to gas storage, catalysts, and optoelectronics [67, 82, 83]. Interfacial engineering (e.g., adding hydrophobic layers or the use of 2D/3D hybrid stacking) has also led to enhanced stability [84, 85].

Long-term stability depends on a thorough understanding of degradation mechanisms and on further progress in materials and interface design.

2.4.4 Scalability of Solar Cells

Scalability is the ability to grow solar power production to supply more and more of the world's energy needs. Various environments can be used with SPV systems, ranging from residential rooftops to utility-scale solar farms. Technological innovation has driven better SPV output, both per unit area and dramatically with system scale [86, 88].

Perovskite solar technology holds the potential to deliver high-efficiency energy at a fraction of the cost. However, it is difficult for large-scale preparation. In order to uniformly coat large areas of perovskite layers, large-scale deposition methods are needed, such as blade coating, slot-die coating, spray coating, and screen printing [89]. These approaches should address the problems of solvent evaporation and keeping the materials homogeneous.

To enable scalable coating, Park [87] suggested substituting conventional dimethyl sulfoxide (DMSO) and N, N-dimethylformamide (DMF) with solvents such as acetonitrile or 2-methoxyethanol to improve film formation. Author highlighted the need for producing precursor chemistry that meets scale-up requirements. Due to its high charge carrier mobility, chemical stability, and high transparency, SnO_2 is a potential electron-selective layer (ESL) [90].

Nevertheless, while small-area (typically >20 cm^2) PSCs now achieve record efficiencies (e.g., 25.2% certified PCE achieved in 2019 [75]), a key milestone remains the demonstration of consistently high performance over large areas. Scale-up barriers also include the challenges of tolerating incompatible interlayers, finding non-lethal solvents, and thermal dissipation.

In summary, PV solar has experienced a tremendous development in terms of efficiency, costs, stability, and scalability. First- and second-generation technology solutions offer well-established performance, but third-generation approaches, including PSCs, may provide high efficiency combined with low cost if long-term stability and manufacturability at scale can be achieved.

With technological advancements, costs have come down to a great extent, especially with government backing, which has made SPV an economically viable renewable energy option. And material science and fabrication advances also steadily bring about further improvement of devices' longevity, even in more extreme environments. MOF, interfacial engineering, and solvent innovation are critical for enhancing the device stability.

Scalability is also actively sought with the advent of new deposition methods and material designs that guarantee uniformity over a wide range of scales. These actions are vital for the shift from lab efficiency to market efficiency.

Taken together, these enhancements place solar photovoltaics at the heart of the world's power-sector decarbonization efforts. Further development in device design, material choice, and processing solutions will help to make SPV technologies in accordance with the future requirements for a sustainable and efficient energy supply.

2.5 Environmental Influences of Solar PV

While solar PV is considered clean and renewable energy source, the full environmental impact of such systems spreads over the complete life cycle, from raw material extraction and manufacturing through operation and decommissioning. Operational emissions are minimal, but there are many concerns with production: hazardous chemicals, air emissions, water contamination, and land use issues. Author also stressed that improvement of PV schemes, reuse of materials, avoiding hazardous materials, and better placement may cut down GHG emissions and reduce other environmental impacts (up to 42% gain).

The energy paybacks and carbon footprint of PV systems are in the range of 0.7–1 years and 14 to 73 CO_2-eq/kWh, respectively, while oil-based systems were attaining an energy payback of 1.14 years with a carbon footprint of 742 CO_2-eq/kWh. Author developed novel material pairings for solar devices with the reduction in toxicological and embodied materials at the expense of higher production energy demand. However, lower operating temperatures for solid oxide fuel cells (SOFC) might compensate for this.

Thin-film silicon and DSSC cells have the lowest EC values [70], whereas chalcogenide, organic, and conventional silicon have the higher ones. Author [71] emphasized that perovskite cells containing bismuth and cesium are less toxic than conventional cell materials, indicating that perovskite will be a future replacement of silicon cells owing to their low toxicity and environmental effect [72].

2.6 Future Directions

Meanwhile, covalent organic frameworks (COFs) as novel crystalline materials with high capture and mass transport properties are being developed for PV application [90]. Organic semiconductors and non-fullerene acceptors (NFAs) are leading the organic photovoltaics, OLEDs, and large-area flexible electronics, but their durability and scalable processing issues haven't been resolved [91]. These innovations consist of the use of 1.2-nm halide perovskite structures inside carbon nanotubes for the fabrication of ultra-small-sized solar cells [92] and DFT-based approaches to improve perovskite stability. Inverted-type PSCs with DPPP as HTM displayed long-term stability >3,500 h, confirming the need for careful engineering of interfaces [93].

In addition to their positive operation effects, PV systems have environmental effects over their life cycle, where the toxicity of materials, water consumption, and the manner of end-of-life disposal are all problematic [94, 95]. Stabilizing perovskites, which decompose to toxic by-products, requires protective and transparent polymers. However, PV systems contribute to the much lower carbon footprint (14–73 g CO_2-eq/kWh) compared with fossil-based systems [96]. New technologies such as FPV and SCMs also increase sustainability by reducing water consumption and aesthetics [97].

Life cycle analysis also finds PV is not emission-free, but instead, emissions can be reduced with hybrid systems and new materials [98–100]. PV materials of the future need not only to maximize efficiency, affordability, and longevity but also environmental benignity to achieve a truly sustainable energy transition [100–103].

2.7 Conclusion

Recent advancements in solar photovoltaic (PV) materials and systems have led to improved efficiency, lower costs, and enhanced durability, firmly establishing PV technology as a key component of the global energy transition. The workhorse of the industry continues to be c-Si solar cells; product modules now achieve >20% conversion efficiency, double the performance of first-generation products 2 decades ago, and match or exceed 2019 sustainable-power market demands. Concurrently, thin-film technologies are emerging as potential advantages with regard to minimization of material consumption, costs of manufacturing, and their easy integration, as well as building and transportable applications.

Advancements in the components of PV systems (e.g., solar trackers, inverters, and battery storage) have also led to even more enhanced performance, reliability, and flexibility in meeting varied power demands. These developments drive the expansion of PV in residential, commercial, and distant applications, such as space missions and water pumping in off-grid locations.

New materials, especially perovskites, have offered the possibility of a material with a better performance and also being cheaper than conventional c-Si cells. Nevertheless, challenges remain concerning long-term stability, environmental friendliness, and scalability. To overcome these challenges and make this technology sustainable for large-scale production, research works are ongoing in the development of new encapsulation techniques, introductory coatable deposition processes, and environment-friendly material substitutions.

Furthermore, the environmental impact of PV systems is relatively low during their operational phase, but it is necessary to manage them responsibly throughout their life cycle, including, but not limited to, waste from toxic, land use, and carbon footprint perspectives. With the recycling of other NET products, floating PV, and hybrid systems, the environmental impact of PV may also be further reduced.

Finally, the convergence of the three trends of materials, integrated installations, and lifecycle sustainability establishes that solar PV will indeed take a place as a prime future renewable energy source infrastructure. On its competitive trajectory, as it continues to decrease in price and as the technology develops, solar PV is well placed to meet the bulk of the clean energy needs of the next several decades.

AI disclosure statement: The author confirms that no artificial intelligence (AI)-generated content or AI-assisted writing tools were used in the preparation of this chapter (including summaries and the abstract). All text, analysis, and conclusions are the result of the author's original work.

Bibliography

1. Gong, J., Liang, J., Sumathy, K., Review on dye-sensitized solar cells (DSSCs): Fundamental concepts and novel materials. *Renew. Sustain. Energy Rev.*, 16, 8, 5848–5860, 2012.
2. Dubacheva, G.V., Liang, C.K., Bassani, D.M., Functional monolayers from carbon nanostructures–fullerenes, carbon nanotubes, and graphene–as novel materials for solar energy conversion. *Coord. Chem. Rev.*, 256, 21–22, 2628–2639, 2012.

3. Lim, E.L., Yap, C.C., Jumali, M.H.H., Teridi, M.A.M., Teh, C.H., A mini review: Can graphene be a novel material for perovskite solar cell applications? *Nano Micro Lett.*, 10, 1–12, 2018.
4. Ohshita, Y., Suzuki, H., Kojima, N., Tanaka, T., Honda, T., Inagaki, M., Yamaguchi, M., Novel material for super high efficiency multi-junction solar cells. *J. Cryst. Growth*, 318, 1, 328–331, 2011.
5. Chen, J. and Cao, Y., Development of novel conjugated donor polymers for high-efficiency bulk-heterojunction photovoltaic devices. *Acc. Chem. Res.*, 42, 11, 1709–1718, 2009.
6. Hayat, M.B., Ali, D., Monyake, K.C., Alagha, L., Ahmed, N., Solar energy—a look into power generation, challenges, and a solar-powered future. *Int. J. Energy Res.*, 43, 3, 1049–1067, 2019.
7. Casper, F., Graf, T., Chadov, S., Balke, B., Felser, C., Half-Heusler compounds: Novel materials for energy and spintronic applications. *Semicond. Sci. Technol.*, 27, 6, 063001, 2012.
8. Mozer, A.J. and Sariciftci, N.S., Conjugated polymer photovoltaic devices and materials. *C.R. Chim.*, 9, 5–6, 568–577, 2006.
9. Kannan, N. and Vakeesan, D., Solar energy for future world: A review. *Renew. Sustain. Energy Rev.*, 62, 1092–1105, 2016.
10. Meinel, A.B. and Meinel, M.P., Applied solar energy: An introduction. *NASA STI/Recon. Tech. Rep. A.*, 77, 33445, 1977.
11. Gordon, J. and Gordon, J.M. (Eds.), Solar energy: The state of the art: ISES position papers, 2001.
12. Gandhi, P., Bhatia, S., Kumar, A., Alojail, M.A., Rathore, P.S., eds., Internet of Things in Business Transformation: Developing an Engineering and Business Strategy for Industry 5.0. John Wiley & Sons, 2020.
13. Jyani, M. and Rathore, P.S., Spectrogram-Based CNN Framework for Live Deepfake Voice Detection in Google Meet, in: *2025 International Conference on Computing Technologies & Data Communication (ICCTDC)*, pp. 1–5, IEEE, 2025.
14. Gong, J., Li, C., Wasielewski, M.R., Advances in solar energy conversion. *Chem. Soc. Rev.*, 48, 7, 1862–1864, 2019.
15. Fang, B., Xing, Z., Sun, D., Li, Z., Zhou, W., Hollow semiconductor photocatalysts for solar energy conversion. *Adv. Powder Mater.*, 1, 2, 100021, 2022.
16. Rabaia, M.K.H., Abdelkareem, M.A., Sayed, E.T., Elsaid, K., Chae, K.J., Wilberforce, T., Olabi, A.G., Environmental impacts of solar energy systems: A review. *Sci. Total Environ.*, 754, 141989, 2021.
17. Sodiqjon, K., Begyor, S., Aleksandr, K., Farrukh, D., Mukhtasar, M., Akbarjon, A., Prospective aspects of using solar energy. *J. New Century Innovat.*, 18, 1, 142–148, 2022.
18. Chasta, G., Suthar, D., Thakur, A., Kannan, M.D., Dhaka, M.S., Comprehensive investigation on influence of copper doping on physical properties of CdSe thin films for solar cell applications. *Mater. Res. Bull.*, 152, 111845, 2022.

19. Ding, T., Zhou, Y., Ong, W.L., Ho, G.W., Hybrid solar-driven interfacial evaporation systems: Beyond water production towards high solar energy utilization. *Mater. Today*, 42, 178–191, 2021.
20. Hoeven, M.V.D., *Technology roadmap: solar photovoltaic energy*, International Energy Agency, Paris, France, 2015.
21. Siecker, J., Kusakana, K., Numbi, E.B., A review of solar photovoltaic systems cooling technologies. *Renew. Sustain. Energy Rev.*, 79, 192–203, 2017.
22. Saga, T., Advances in crystalline silicon solar cell technology for industrial mass production. *NPG Asia Mater.*, 2, 3, 96–102, 2010.
23. Santbergen, R. and van Zolingen, R.C., The absorption factor of crystalline silicon PV cells: a numerical and experimental study. *Sol. Energy Mater. Sol. Cells*, 92, 4, 432–444, 2008.
24. Liang, T.S., Pravettoni, M., Deline, C., Stein, J.S., Kopecek, R., Singh, J.P., Luo, W., Wang, Y., Aberle, A.G., Khoo, Y.S., A review of crystalline silicon bifacial photovoltaic performance characterisation and simulation. *Energy Environ. Sci.*, 12, 1, 116–148, 2019.
25. Zhao, J., Xu, Z., Law, M.K., Heidari, H., Abdellatif, S.O., Imran, M.A., Ghannam, R., Simulation of crystalline silicon photovoltaic cells for wearable applications. *IEEE Access*, 9, 20868–20877, 2021.
26. Benda, V. and Černa, L., PV cells and modules–State of the art, limits and trends. *Heliyon*, 6, 12, e05666, 2020.
27. Sun, Z., Chen, X., He, Y., Li, J., Wang, J., Yan, H., Zhang, Y., Toward efficiency limits of crystalline silicon solar cells: recent progress in high-efficiency silicon heterojunction solar cells. *Adv. Energy Mater.*, 12, 23, 2200015, 2022.
28. Nadia, A.R., Isa, N.A.M., Desa, M.K.M., Advances in solar photovoltaic tracking systems: a review. *Renew Sustain Energy Rev.*, 82, 2548–2569, 2018.
29. Hightower, M. and Pierce, S.A., The energy challenge. *Nature*, 452, 7185, 285–286, 2008.
30. Chong, K.K. and Wong, C.W., General formula for on-axis sun-tracking system and its application in improving tracking accuracy of solar collector. *Sol. Energy*, 83, 3, 298–305, 2009.
31. Nsengiyumva, W., Chen, S.G., Hu, L., Chen, X., Recent advancements and challenges in solar tracking systems (STS): A review. *Renew. Sustain. Energy Rev.*, 81, 250–279, 2018.
32. Jamroen, C., Komkum, P., Kohsri, S., Himananto, W., Panupintu, S., Unkat, S., A low-cost dual-axis solar tracking system based on digital logic design: Design and implementation. *Sustain. Energy Technol. Assess.*, 37, 100618, 2020.
33. Ibarra Michel, J., Dreon, J., Boccard, M., Bullock, J., Macco, B., Carrierselective contacts using metal compounds for crystalline silicon solar cells. *Prog. Photovoltaics Res. Appl.*, 31, 4, 380–413, 2023.
34. Kumar, A., Rathore, P.S., Díaz, V.G., Agrawal, R. (Eds.), *Swarm intelligence optimization:Algorithms and applications.* John Wiley & Sons, 2020.

35. Chowdhury, M.E., Khandakar, A., Hossain, B., Abouhasera, R., A low-cost closed-loop solar tracking system based on the sun position algorithm. *J. Sensors*, 2019.
36. Chee, K.W., Ghosh, B.K., Saad, I., Hong, Y., Xia, Q.H., Gao, P., Ye, J., Ding, Z.J., Recent advancements in carrier-selective contacts for high-efficiency crystalline silicon solar cells: Industrially evolving approach. *Nano Energy*, 95, 106899, 2022.
37. Costals, E.R., Masmitja, G., Almache, E., Pusay, B., Tiwari, K., Saucedo, E., Raj, C.J., Kim, B.C., Puigdollers, J., Martin, I., Voz, C., Atomic layer deposition of vanadium oxide films for crystalline silicon solar cells. *Mater. Adv.*, 3, 1, 337–345, 2022.
38. Han, C., Yang, G., Procel, P., O'Connor, D., Zhao, Y., Gopalakrishnan, A., Zhang, X., Zeman, M., Mazzarella, L., Isabella, O., Controllable simultaneous bifacial Cu-plating for high-efficiency crystalline silicon solar cells. *Sol. RRL*, 6, 6, 2100810, 2022.
39. Pham, D.P. and Yi, J., Dopant-grading proposal for polysilicon passivating contact in crystalline silicon solar cells. *J. Power Sources*, 522, 231005, 2022.
40. Skompska, M., Hybrid conjugated polymer/semiconductor photovoltaic cells. *Synth. Met.*, 160, 1–2, 1–15, 2010.
41. Singh, A., Sharma, A., Rajput, S., Bose, A., Hu, X., An investigation on hybrid particle swarm optimization algorithms for parameter optimization of PV cells. *Electronics*, 11, 6, 909, 2022.
42. Cotfas, D.T., Cotfas, P.A., Mahmoudinezhad, S., Louzazni, M., Critical factors and parameters for hybrid photovoltaic-thermoelectric systems; review. *Appl. Therm. Eng.*, 118977, 2022.
43. Tang, Y., Varyambath, A., Ding, Y., Chen, B., Huang, X., Zhang, Y., Yu, D.G., Kim, I., Song, W., Porous organic polymers for drug delivery: hierarchical pore structures, variable morphologies, and biological properties. *Biomater. Sci.*, 2022.
44. Kim, J.H., Kang, D.W., Yun, H., Kang, M., Singh, N., Kim, J.S., Hong, C.S., Postsynthetic modifications in porous organic polymers for biomedical and related applications. *Chem. Soc. Rev.*, 51, 1, 43–56, 2022.
45. Zhu, Y., Xu, P., Zhang, X., Wu, D., Emerging porous organic polymers for biomedical applications. *Chem. Soc. Rev.*, 51, 4, 1377–1414, 2022.
46. Mari-Guaita, J., Bouich, A., Shafi, M.A., Bouich, A., Mari, B., Investigation on the stability and efficiency of MAPbI3 and MASnI3 thin films for solar cells. *Phys. Status Solidi*, 219, 5, 2100664, 2022.
47. Tarbi, A., Chtouki, T., Bouich, A., Elkouari, Y., Erguig, H., Migalska-Zalas, A., Aissat, A., InP/InGaAsP thin films based solar cells: lattice mismatch impact on efficiency. *Opt. Mater.*, 131, 112704, 2022.
48. Chaudhry, F.A., Escandell, L., Lopez-Fraguas, E., Vergaz, R., Sanchez-Pena, J.M., Garcia-Camara, B., Light absorption enhancement in thin film GaAs solar cells using dielectric nanoparticles. *Sci. Rep.*, 12, 1, 9240, 2022.

49. O'regan, B. and Gratzel, M., A low-cost, high-efficiency solar cell based on dye-sensitized colloidal TiO_2 films. *Nature*, 353, 6346, 737–740, 1991.
50. Bandara, T.M.W.J., Hansadi, J.M.C., Bella, F., A review of textile dyesensitized solar cells for wearable electronics. *Ionics*, 28, 6, 2563–2583, 2022.
51. Shahzad, N., Perveen, T., Pugliese, D., Haq, S., Fatima, N., Salman, S.M., Tagliaferro, A., Shahzad, M.I., Counter electrode materials based on carbon nanotubes for dye-sensitized solar cells. *Renew. Sustain. Energy Rev.*, 159, 112196, 2022.
52. Alizadeh, A., Roudgar-Amoli, M., Bonyad-Shekalgourabi, S.M., Shariatinia, Z., Mahmoudi, M., Saadat, F., Dye sensitized solar cells go beyond using perovskite and spinel inorganic materials: a review. *Renew. Sustain. Energy Rev.*, 157, 112047, 2022.
53. Venkatesan, S., Lin, W.H., Hsu, T.H., Teng, H., Lee, Y.L., Indoor dyesensitized solar cells with efficiencies surpassing 26% using polymeric counter electrodes. *ACS Sustain. Chem. Eng.*, 10, 7, 2473–2483, 2022.
54. Devadiga, D., Selvakumar, M., Shetty, P., Santosh, M.S., The integration of flexible dye-sensitized solar cells and storage devices towards wearable self-charging power systems: a review. *Renew. Sustain. Energy Rev.*, 159, 112252, 2022.
55. Kim, J.H., Kim, D.H., So, J.H., Koo, H.J., Toward eco-friendly dye-sensitized solar cells (DSSCs): natural dyes and aqueous electrolytes. *Energies*, 15, 1, 219, 2022.
56. De Freitas, E.S., Da Silva, P.B., Chorilli, M., Batista, A.A., Lopes, E.D.O., da Silva, M.M., Leite, C.Q.F., Pavan, F.R., Nanostructured lipid systems as a strategy to improve the *in vitro* cytotoxicity of ruthenium (II) compounds. *Molecules*, 19, 5, 5999–6008, 2014.
57. Dragutan, I., Dragutan, V., Demonceau, A., Special issue on ruthenium complexes. *Molecules*, 22, 2, 255, 2017.
58. Tojo, G., Fernandez, M., Tojo, G., Fernandez, M., Ruthenium tetroxide and other ruthenium compounds, in: *Oxidation of Primary Alcohols to Carboxylic Acids: A Guide to Current Common Practice*, pp. 61–78, 2007.
59. Yadav, S.C., Sharma, A., Devan, R.S., Shirage, P.M., Role of different counter electrodes on performance of TiO_2 based dye-sensitized solar cell (DSSC) fabricated with dye extracted from Hibiscus Sabdariffa as sensitizer. *Opt. Mater.*, 124, 112066, 2022.
60. Gratzel, M., Dye-sensitized solar cells. *J. Photochem. Photobiol. C*, 4, 2, 145–153, 2003.
61. Hagfeldt, A., Boschloo, G., Sun, L., Kloo, L., Pettersson, H., Dye-sensitized solar cells. *Chem. Rev.*, 110, 11, 6595–6663, 2010.
62. Wei, D., Dye sensitized solar cells. *Int. J. Mol. Sci.*, 11, 3, 1103–1113, 2010.
63. Dhaka, A., Nait-Abdesselam, F., Nandal, A., Bogatinoska, D.C., Rathore, P.S., Sharma, A.K., Zubov, D., eds., Virtual Reality, Real Emergency: Integrating AR/VR in Computing and Medical Crisis Management. CRC Press, 2025.

64. Nazeeruddin, M.K., Baranoff, E., Gratzel, M., Dye-sensitized solar cells: A brief overview. *Sol. Energy*, 85, 6, 1172–1178, 2011.
65. Rathore, P.S., Chatterjee, J.M., Kumar, A., *et al.*, Energy-efficient cluster head selection through relay approach for WSN. *J. Supercomput.*, 77, 7649–7675, 2021. https://doi.org/10.1007/s11227-020-03593-4.
66. Mangot, A., Kumar, A., Baliyan, A., Shining a Light on Solar Power Forecasting: Machine Learning Techniques for Unprecedented Accuracy, in: *2023 3rd International Conference on Technological Advancements in Computational Sciences (ICTACS)*, IEEE, pp. 828–834, 2023, November.
67. Dubey, A.K., Kumar, A., Ramirez, I.S., Marquez, F.P.G., A review of intelligent systems for the prediction of wind energy using machine learning, in: *International Conference on Management Science and Engineering Management*, Springer International Publishing, Cham, pp. 476–491, 2022, July.
68. Rathore, P.S., Kumar, A., García-Díaz, V., A holistic methodology for improved RFID network lifetime by advanced cluster head selection using dragonfly algorithm, 2020.
69. Rathore, P.S., Sarkar, M.K., Das, R., *A Comprehensive Review on Secure and Energy Aware Multi-Hop Routing in Clustering Based Wireless Sensor Network*, Telecommunications and Radio Engineering, 80, 8, 2021.
70. Chetyrkina, M.R., Kameneva, L., Mishchenko, D.V., Klimanova, E.N., Sashenkova, T.E., Allayarova, U.Y., Kostyuk, S.V., Frolova, L.A., Aldoshin, S.M., Troshin, P.A., Lead, tin, bismuth or organics: assessment of potential environmental and human health hazards originating from mature perovskite PV technology. *Sol. Energy Mater. Sol. Cells*, 252, 112177, 2023.
71. Li, C., Wang, X., Bi, E., Jiang, F., Park, S.M., Li, Y., Chen, L., Wang, Z., Zeng, L., Chen, H., Liu, Y., Rational design of Lewis base molecules for stable and efficient inverted perovskite solar cells. *Science*, 379, 6633, 690–694, 2023.
72. Ning, Z., Fu, Y., Tian, H., Improvement of dye-sensitized solar cells: what we know and what we need to know. *Energy Environ. Sci.*, 3, 9, 1170–1181, 2010.
73. Law, M., Greene, L.E., Johnson, J.C., Saykally, R., Yang, P., Nanowire dyesensitized solar cells. *Nat. Mater.*, 4, 6, 455–459, 2005.
74. Kashtiban, R.J., Patrick, C.E., Ramasse, Q., Walton, R.I., Sloan, J., Picoperovskites: the smallest conceivable isolated halide perovskite structures formed within carbon nanotubes. *Adv. Mater.*, 2208575, 2022.
75. Tan, S., Huang, T., Yavuz, I., Wang, R., Yoon, T.W., Xu, M., Xing, Q., Park, K., Lee, D.K., Chen, C.H., Zheng, R., Stability-limiting heterointerfaces of perovskite photovoltaics. *Nature*, 605, 7909, 268–273, 2022.
76. Friederich, P., Fediai, A., Kaiser, S., Konrad, M., Jung, N., Wenzel, W., Toward design of novel materials for organic electronics. *Adv. Mater.*, 31, 26, 1808256, 2019.
77. Yang, Y. and Borjesson, K., Electroactive covalent organic frameworks: A new choice for organic electronics. *Trends Chem.*, 4, 1, 60–75, 2022.

78. Tareen, A.K., Khan, K., Rehman, S., Iqbal, M., Yu, J., Zhou, Z., Yin, J., Zhang, H., Recent development in emerging phosphorene based novel materials: Progress, challenges, prospects and their fascinating sensing applications. *Prog. Solid State Chem.*, 65, 100336, 2022.
79. Mahato, N., Sharma, K., Sinha, M., Baral, E.R., Koteswararao, R., Dhyani, A., Cho, M.H., Cho, S., Bio-sorbents, industrially important chemicals and novel materials from citrus processing waste as a sustainable and renewable bioresource: A review. *J. Adv. Res.*, 23, 61–82, 2020.
80. Verduci, R., Romano, V., Brunetti, G., Yaghoobi Nia, N., Di Carlo, A., D'Angelo, G., Ciminelli, C., Solar energy in space applications: Review and technology perspectives. *Adv. Energy Mater.*, 12, 29, 2200125, 2022.
81. Park, N.G., Research direction toward scalable, stable, and high efficiency perovskite solar cells. *Adv. Energy Mater.*, 10, 13, 1903106, 2020.
82. Green, M., Dunlop, E., Hohl-Ebinger, J., Yoshita, M., Kopidakis, N., Hao, X., Solar cell efficiency tables (version 57). *Prog. Photovoltaics Res. Appl.*, 29, 1, 3–15, 2021.
83. Li, Z., Klein, T.R., Kim, D.H., Yang, M., Berry, J.J., Van Hest, M.F., Zhu, K., Scalable fabrication of perovskite solar cells. *Nat. Rev. Mater.*, 3, 4, 1–20, 2018.
84. Altinkaya, C., Aydin, E., Ugur, E., Isikgor, F.H., Subbiah, A.S., De Bastiani, M., Liu, J., Babayigit, A., Allen, T.G., Laquai, F., Yildiz, A., Tin oxide electron-selective layers for efficient, stable, and scalable perovskite solar cells. *Adv. Mater.*, 33, 15, 2005504, 2021.
85. Angmo, D., Gevorgyan, S.A., Larsen-Olsen, T.T., Sondergaard, R.R., Hosel, M., Jorgensen, M., Gupta, R., Kulkarni, G.U., Krebs, F.C., Scalability and stability of very thin, roll-to-roll processed, large area, indium-tin-oxide free polymer solar cell modules. *Org. Electron.*, 14, 3, 984–994, 2013.
86. Kim, M., Jeong, J., Lu, H., Lee, T.K., Eickemeyer, F.T., Liu, Y., Choi, I.W., Choi, S.J., Jo, Y., Kim, H.B., Mo, S.I., Conformal quantum dot–SnO2 layers as electron transporters for efficient perovskite solar cells. *Science*, 375, 6578, 302–306, 2022.
87. Wang, H.P., Li, S., Liu, X., Shi, Z., Fang, X., He, J.H., Low-dimensional metal halide Perovskite photodetectors. *Adv. Mater.*, 33, 7, 2003309, 2021.
88. Lee, C.C., Chen, C.I., Liao, Y.T., Wu, K.C.W., Chueh, C.C., Enhancing efficiency and stability of photovoltaic cells by using perovskite/Zr-MOF heterojunction including bilayer and hybrid structures. *Adv. Sci.*, 6, 5, 1801715, 2019.
89. Exposing unsaturated Cu1-O2 sites in nanoscale Cu-MOF for efficient electrocatalytic hydrogen evolution.
90. Zou, Y.H., Huang, Y.B., Si, D.H., Yin, Q., Wu, Q.J., Weng, Z., Cao, R., Porous metal–organic framework liquids for enhanced CO2 adsorption and catalytic conversion. *Angew. Chem.*, 133, 38, 21083–21088, 2021.
91. Mamta, A.M., Kumar, A., Baliyan, A., Shining a Light on Solar Power Forecasting: Machine Learning Techniques for Unprecedented Accuracy.

2023 3rd International Conference on Technological Advancements in Computational Sciences (ICTACS), Tashkent, Uzbekistan, pp. 828–834, 2023, doi: 10.1109/ICTACS59847.2023.10390265.

92. Kumar, A., Dubey, A.K., Segovia Ramírez, I., *et al.*, Artificial Intelligence Techniques for the Photovoltaic System: A Systematic Review and Analysis for Evaluation and Benchmarking. *Arch. Computat. Methods Eng.*, 31, 4429–4453, 2024. https://doi.org/10.1007/s11831-024-10125-3.
93. Dubey, A.K., Ramirez, I., Marquez, F., A Review of Intelligent Systems for the Prediction of Wind Energy Using Machine Learning. *ICMSEM, The Sixteenth International Conference on Management Science and Engineering Management, Lecture Notes on Data Engineering and Communications Technologies, vol 144, Springer, by SpringerAnkara, Turkey*, August 3-6, 2022, 2022.
94. Dubey, A., Ramirez, I., Rio, A., Marquez, F., A Review and Analysis of Forecasting of Photovoltaic Power Generation Using Machine Learning. *ICMSEM, The Sixteenth International Conference on Management Science and Engineering Management, Lecture Notes on Data Engineering and Communications Technologies, vol 144. Springer, Cham. by Springer*, Ankara, Turkey, August 3-6, 2022, 2022.
95. Ueoka, N. and Oku, T., Stability characterization of PbI2-added CH3NH3PbI3–x Cl x photovoltaic devices. *ACS Appl. Mater. Interfaces*, 10, 51, 44443–44451, 2018.
96. Rajvikram, M. and Leoponraj, S., A method to attain power optimality and efficiency in solar panel. *Beni-Suef Univ. J. Basic Appl. Sci.*, 7, 4, 705–708, 2018.
97. Abouelregal, A.E., Akgoz, B., Civalek, O., Magneto-thermoelastic interactions in an unbounded orthotropic viscoelastic solid under the Hall current effect by the fourth-order Moore–Gibson–Thompson equation. *Comput. Math. Appl.*, 141, 102–115, 2023.
98. Civalek, O., Uzun, B., Yaylı, M.O., An effective analytical method for buckling solutions of a restrained FGM nonlocal beam. *Comput. Appl. Math.*, 41, 2, 67, 2022.
99. Jalaei, M.H., Thai, H.T., Civalek, 04E6., On viscoelastic transient response of magnetically imperfect functionally graded nanobeams. *Int. J. Eng. Sci.*, 172, 103629, 2022.
100. Numanoğlu, H.M., Ersoy, H., Akgoz, B., Civalek, O., A new eigenvalue problem solver for thermo-mechanical vibration of Timoshenko nanobeams by an innovative nonlocal finite element method. *Math. Methods Appl. Sci.*, 45, 5, 2592–2614, 2022.
101. Abouelregal, A.E., Ersoy, H., Civalek, O., Solution of Moore–Gibson–Thompson equation of an unbounded medium with a cylindrical hole. *Mathematics*, 9, 13, 1536, 2021.
102. Akgoz, B. and Civalek, O., Buckling analysis of functionally graded tapered microbeams *via* Rayleigh-Ritz method. *Mathematics*, 10, 23, 4429, 2022.
103. Dastjerdi, S., Akgoz, B., Civalek, O., On the effect of viscoelasticity on behavior of gyroscopes. *Int. J. Eng. Sci.*, 149, 103236, 2020.

3

Role of AI to Increase the Energy Efficiency of Solar Panels for Energy Conservation

Avnish Chauhan[1*], Gaurav Pandey[2], Muneesh Sethi[3], Shivam Attri[1] and Jonti Deuri[4]

[1]Department of Environmental Sciences, Graphic Era Hill University, Dehradun, Uttarakhand, India
[2]Chemistry and Bioprospecting Division, Forest Research Institute, Dehradun, Uttarakhand, India
[3]Department of Mechanical Engineering, COER University, Roorkee, Uttarakhand, India
[4]Faculty of Engineering and Technology, Sharda University, Andijan, Uzbekistan

Abstract

Energy demand is growing at an incredible pace due to the progress of different sectors in society. This demand for energy has been largely met so far by conventional energy sources such as coal, petrol, etc. But all of these resources are finite, and they are running out very quickly. The lack of coal for energy generation at present reflects the urgency for the development of sustainable and renewable energy technologies to address these significant challenges. This is where alternative and renewable sources of energy would be ideal. One of the best options in this regard is solar energy. At its core is the incredible prospect of harnessing the sun's relentless flow of radiant energy and converting it into actual, usable power. This bountiful and inexhaustible renewable source provides an opportunity to redefine our energy future. Thanks to photovoltaic (or concentrating solar) technologies, we can collect sunlight and convert it to either electricity or heat at impressive yields. Here in this chapter, attention is mainly given to solar energy technology. This will also concentrate on the effectiveness and drawbacks of solar. The part of AI to improve the productivity of solar cells will also be focused on in this chapter.

***Keywords*:** Solar panels, solar-cells, radiant energy

**Corresponding author*: avnishchauhan_in@yahoo.com

Abhishek Kumar, Pramod Singh Rathore, Arun Lal Srivastav and Ashutosh Kumar Dubey (eds.) Solar Energy Optimization Using Generative Artificial Intelligence, (33–62) © 2026 Scrivener Publishing LLC

3.1 The Immediate Nature of Energy Demand

Technology has become an essential part of life; without it, it is difficult to pursue our lives in a smooth way, and using technology is very easy and convenient to do work in an effective way. Energy demand is rapidly increasing all over the world, driven by a growing population, increasing urbanization, and expanding industrialization [1, 42, 45]. For now, these needs are being met with traditional forms of energy at the cost of an increasingly flawed environment and the risk of running out of traditional sources and problems with security [8, 59]. The recent unavailability of coal for the generation of power indicates the need for a solution based on sustainable and renewable energy to address these times [21, 29]. We should concentrate on searching for solutions that rely on sustainable and renewable factors. Here are some areas in which we can consider navigating, and these are as follows.

- **Environmental issues:** Fossil fuels such as coal, oil, and natural gas have been used as the main source of energy for centuries [26]. Sadly, burning them will release greenhouse gases, which add to global warming and climate change by raising the amount of carbon dioxide in the atmosphere shown in Figure 3.1. Disruption to ecosystems, sea level rise, and increased occurrences of extreme weather emphasize the urgent need to switch to renewable power with lower carbon footprints [25].
- **Finite Resource Depletion:** Fossil fuels are not considered a form of sustainable energy source, as they are not renewable and will disappear one day [27]. Fossil fuel vs. renewable energy, with the rising need for energy globally, relying solely on fossil fuel is just not sustainable in the long term [50]. Adopting renewable sources of energy is a great alternative that can give us a sustainable and seemingly infinite alternative, and can also lead to a reduction in the threat of energy insecurity.
- **Energy Security and Independence:** Many countries rely heavily on imported fossil fuels, which exposes them to geopolitical risks and price variations in the world energy market [9, 34]. Switching to renewable sources of energy like the

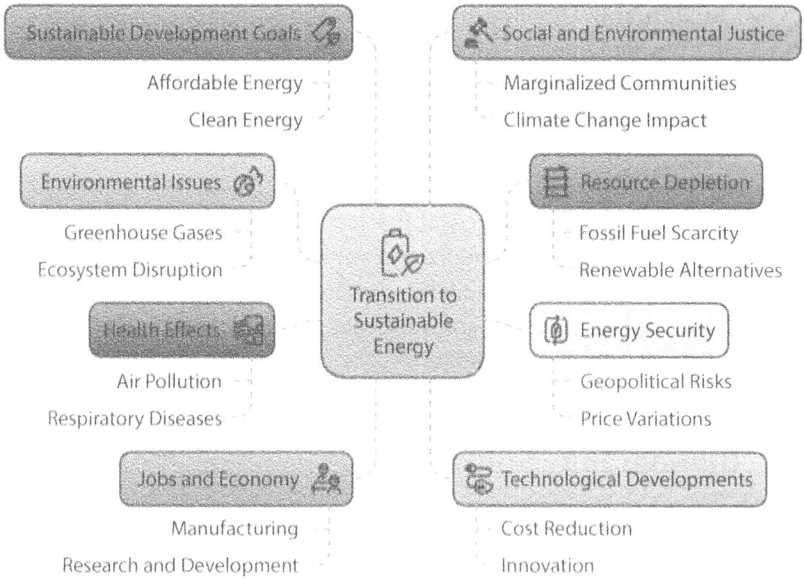

Figure 3.1 Transition to sustainable energy.

sun, wind, and water can contribute towards energy security and resistance to the effects of energy supply shortages [30].

- **Health effects:** The burning of fossil fuels produces harmful air pollutants—such as particulate matter, nitrogen oxides, and sulfur dioxide—that are major contributors to pollution and respiratory diseases. Transitioning to clean and renewable energy can greatly enhance air quality and thereby improve public health.
- **Jobs and Economy:** There are jobs in the switch to renewable energy. The renewable industry provides jobs in manufacturing, installation, maintenance, research, and development [19]. Investing in renewable energy can drive economic growth and help build a sustainable future.
- **Technological Developments:** The advancement of renewable energy technologies and falling costs have made renewable energy even more competitive with fossil fuels [28]. Adoption of renewables allows us to innovate and modernize the national energy system, which can stimulate growth and create a cleaner, healthier world.

- **Sustainable Development Goals:** The Ministry of New and Renewable Energy (MNRE) lists affordable and clean energy among its major goals. The switch to alternative energy ties into these global goals and contributes to sustainable development while benefiting the lives of people around the world [16].
- **Social and Environmental Justice:** Moving away from fossil fuels can lift up marginalized communities hit with the most pollution and impacted by climate change [37]. Bringing clean energy to these communities can be a source of social and environmental justice.

3.2 Bibliography Study

To uncover thematic patterns and conceptual structures within the chapter, a co-occurrence network analysis was conducted based on author keywords. This method enables the identification of frequently co-occurring terms across the dataset, revealing underlying research themes and their interconnections.

The bibliographic data were extracted from the Scopus database and analyzed using VOSviewer. A minimum occurrence threshold of 10 was applied to filter out less relevant terms, resulting in 466 keywords meeting the criteria out of 12709 keywords. After cleaning and merging synonymous keywords, the final map included 466 keywords grouped into 6 clusters, based on their co-occurrence strength.

As shown in Figure 3.2, the network is divided into several distinct clusters, each represented by a different color. The size of each node in the map represents the frequency of a keyword's occurrence, while the thickness of the connecting lines indicates the strength of co-occurrence between keywords. Visualization reveals a dense central core with several bridging terms, suggesting interdisciplinary convergence. This analysis highlights emerging trends such as the integration of artificial intelligence in solar energy management, as well as enduring research priorities around climate change and public policy. The co-occurrence map thus provides valuable insight into the intellectual structure and evolving focus areas within the field.

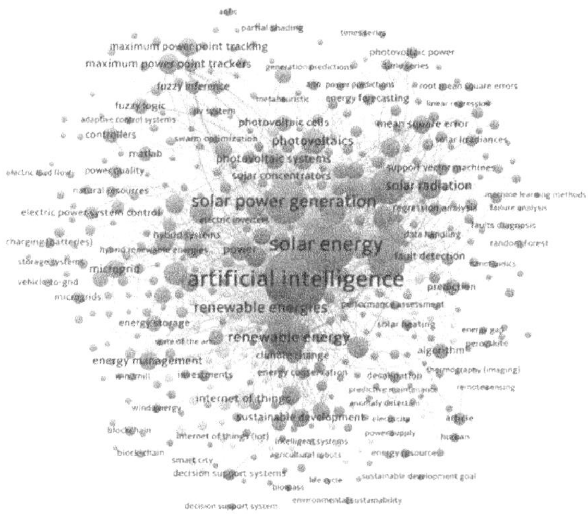

(a)

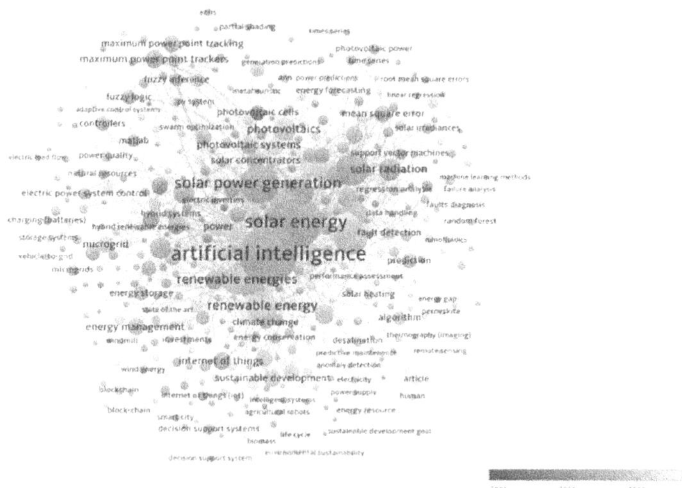

(b)

Figure 3.2 Bibliometric analysis centered on network clustering of 466 published articles from 2020 to 2025 that have high matches of selected keywords and their citations: (a) network visualization and (b) overlay visualization.

3.3 Solar Energy: The Solution to the Current Energy Crisis

Solar power is a bright spot in the journey towards more sustainable, cleaner energy sources [23]. At its core is the amazing ability to harness the sun's relentless flow of luminous energy and turn it into actual power [47, 49]. This abundant, virtually unlimited renewable energy deserves to be the entry point to a new era in our energy usage! We can make good use of the sun by utilizing photovoltaic panels or concentrating solar cells, and then use it to make electricity or even heat with excellent efficiency. The significance of solar is not in the technical details. It represents a cleaner, greener future where our energy consumption can be satisfied without harmful emissions that contribute to climate change [32, 43]. Leaning gently on an ailing planet, threatened by pollution as well as by climate problems, solar power offers itself as a loyal friend, delivering energy without spewing harmful substances, offsetting the damage done to the atmosphere over the ages by combustion of fossil fuels. This shift from carbon-based energy to solar power holds out the promise of energy independence, an opportunity to break free from finite fossil fuels and unstable global markets. Local installation of solar panels enables bringing the light to far-away locations where conventional infrastructure would take forever to be implemented and, therefore, wealth and happiness shows in Figure 3.3.

Casting 173,000 terawatts of power worldwide each day, the sun receives its fair share of buzz from scientists and the policy community [7]. Photovoltaic (PV) solar technology, which creates electricity directly from the sun, has been leading this change. Recent research on Solar PV capacity expanded rapidly and reached an estimated 713 GW worldwide by the end of 2020, with the International Renewable Energy Agency (IRENA) suggesting that new capacity added during the year alone will fall into the range of 170-180 GW [22]. This development has been facilitated by rapidly falling costs; between 2010 and 2019, the price of solar PV systems went down by around 90%. This is referred to as the Swanson Effect and places an emphasis on the fact that overall installed capacity and the decline in module prices are correlated.

Not only is solar capacity virtually limitless and affordable. It is the ideal environmentally friendly alternative to fossil fuels, reduces greenhouse gas emissions into the atmosphere, and fights climate change. A study completed by the National Renewable Energy Laboratory (NREL) highlights the significant role that solar can play in slashing global carbon emissions by 2050 [40]. Add to that improvements in solar, and along

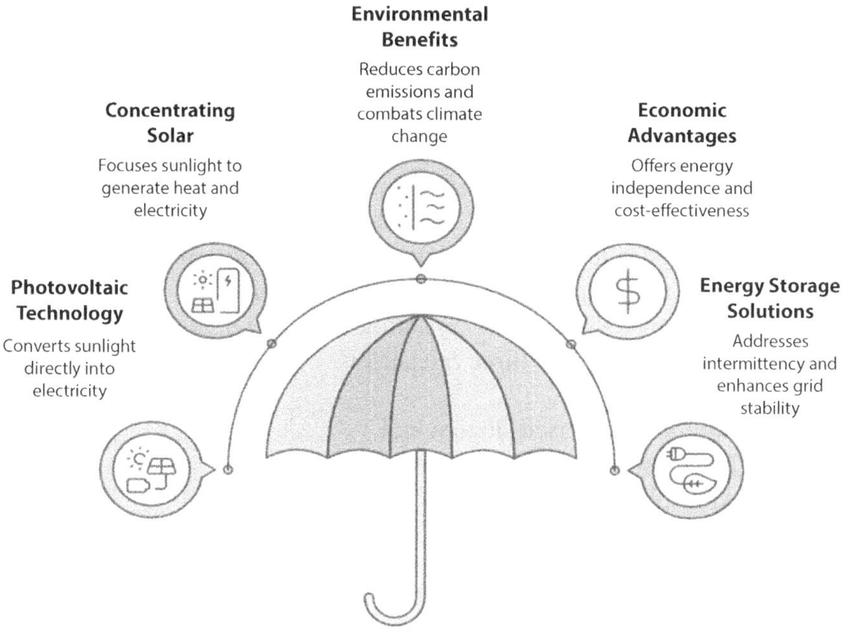

Figure 3.3 The bright future of solar cell.

with solar advancement, the advancements in energy storage are here as well. Breakthroughs in materials science that support energy storage across most battery technologies have been achieved by Canadian researchers led by Professor Ted Sargent, addressing one of the most significant challenges in modern energy storage [13]. This complementary nature of solar generation and the state-of-the-art storage technologies addresses the issues of intermittency and grid stability, making the path for solar penetration easier.

The rapid rise of solar energy gives us something to be hopeful about, but it is not without its issues. Publications such as "Intermittent Renewable Energy Sources and Grid Stability" presented in "Energy Procedia" show the importance of improvements on the grid to handle the variability of the solar generation and to guarantee the receipt of energy with quality [56]. Further, the importance of appropriate policies and regulations to promote solar uptake and drive R&D investment has also been highlighted in studies of "Energy Policy". Joint efforts by scientists, governments, and industries are necessary to solve these challenges and to remove obstacles to the further development of solar energy.

When it comes to solar-cell construction, the essential raw material is crystalline silicon. This arrangement has two isolated layers; the first, or top, layer, known as the emitter layer, is an n-type semiconductor. The second layer, referred to as a base layer, is made of a p-type semiconductor. These two layers are juxtaposed so as to form a p-n junction there between. Abide by the Anti-reflection Group to make the most effective use of solar cell anti-reflection coatings [44]. The photovoltaic cell surface is covered with an anti-reflection coating to maximize its efficiency by reducing energy loss caused by reflection. The specifics are provided in Figure 3.4.

In essence, on the basis of the crystalline structure of the semiconductor materials, the cells fall into three categories.

a) Monocrystal-based silicone cell
b) Polycrystal-based silicone cell
c) Amorphous-based silicone cell

Traditionally, monocrystal-based silicone is the most efficient of the three, at about 14%–17% efficient. This is because of the perfection and impurity-free nature of monocrystals. Polycrystal-based systems, on the contrary, have an efficiency of about 13%–15%, resulting from the birth of various crystal sizes during the polycrystal solidification. The lowest efficiency was found to be approximately 5%–7% for amorphous crystal-based systems [6].

To understand the working mechanism of solar energy, it is essential to have a basic idea about the concept of the photovoltaic phenomenon, in which the sunlight rays hit a solar cell, and when they reach the semiconductor material that is the key part of the solar cell, they get absorbed in

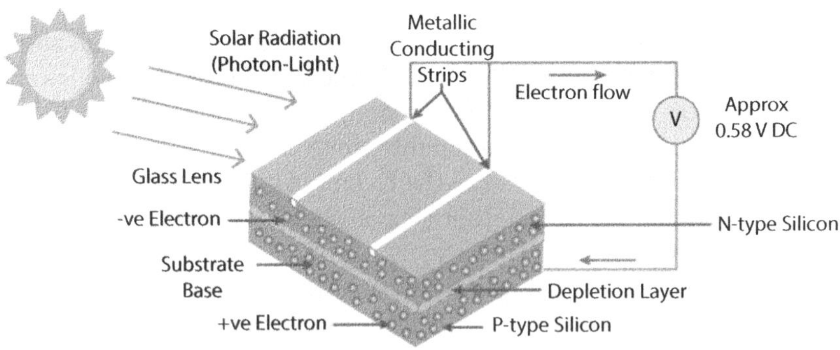

Figure 3.4 Schematic representation of a solar cell construction (Source: https://www.geeksforgeeks.org/photovoltaic-cell/).

the form of photons, and they emit electrons. These electrons now travel through the external circuit of the solar cell as direct current.

A major drawback of solar cells in their current state is that they require sunlight to generate electricity. Solar cells work best in direct sunlight, with their power output decreasing greatly when the sun is not out, such as on a cloudy day or at night. This intermittent nature requires the addition of energy storage systems, such as batteries, to supply constant power. Though advancements have been made in increasing efficiency and lowering costs, the efficiency of solar cells has remained weather-dependent, relying heavily on the presence of sunlight and less dependable for applications requiring constant power during all conditions.

3.4 Artificial Intelligence (AI) – A Brief Account

The introduction of AI becomes a disruptive force at a fundamental level in the current era and is of paramount importance in almost all domains [41]. In a nutshell, AI is the imitation of human intelligence processes by machines, especially computer systems, which give the devices the ability to learn, reason, learn from experience, and perform tasks that typically require human intelligence. The importance of this technology is that it functions to extract and interpret large amounts of data quickly, generating insights that spur informed decision-making. In the health sector, for example, AI helps diagnose diseases and create individualized treatment approaches. In finance, it assists in predicting market trends and risk analysis. Sectors like the manufacturing industry get a boost with AI-enabled automation for increased accuracy and precision. A new wave of chatbots and virtual assistants powered by AI is reshaping the way companies and consumers interact. Additionally, AI in driverless cars and robotics alters the transportation and industrial landscapes. As AI becomes increasingly sophisticated, questions around bias and ethics are key [36]. It matters in terms of how we work and engage and solve complex problems in the world, setting it as a key characteristic of the world we live in today.

1. Basics of AI: Fundamentals of AI rest on a set of basic principles and technologies used to make machines execute the cognitive functions of humans. These include:

- **Machine Learning (ML):** A subset of Artificial Intelligence (AI), Machine Learning (ML) focuses on the development of algorithms and models that enable computers to learn from data and improve their performance over time [46]. It includes applications of supervised, unsupervised, and reinforcement learning that allow machines to discover patterns, make predictions, and automate decisions.

- **Neural Networks:** Neural networks are a basic concept in AI, which is modeled on the neural connections in the human brain [48]. These artificial neural networks are made up of interconnected nodes (often referred to as "neurons") organized in layers and are capable of processing complex data and have reached human-level performance on some tasks, including image and speech recognition, natural language processing, and playing games.
- **Natural Language Processing (NLP):** One of the subfields of AI, which deals with allowing the computer to understand, interpret, and create human language [11]. This processor includes things like language translation, sentiment analysis, chatbots, and virtual assistants to help make interactions between computers and people more natural and efficient.
- **Computer Vision:** Computer Vision is related to techniques to help gain a high-level understanding from digital images and videos. It gives AI systems the ability to recognize objects, people, and places and to perceive complex patterns, applications of which include self-driving cars, surveillance, medical imaging, and augmented reality.
- **Robotics:** AI meets robotics to form self-governing machines called robots. Those robots are able to perceive and interact with the environment, make decisions based on data, and perform tasks with precision. Use of AI-controlled robotics is made in various fields such as manufacturing, logistics, healthcare, and exploration [35].
- **Knowledge Representation and Reasoning:** AI needs a mechanism for how to represent and store the knowledge that it will use for decision-making. Knowledge is encoded in a way that a computer can understand it, while reasoning mechanisms are used to draw conclusions from known information [38].
- **Expert Systems:** Expert systems are AI applications that imitate the reasoning capabilities of human experts in certain domains. They are based on a knowledge base and rules to propose recommendations/solutions for complex problems [33].

Figure 3.5 Aspects of AI.

- **Search Algorithms:** In AI, search algorithms are used to find the best possible solutions from a huge problem space. These algorithms are applied in routing, games, and optimization tasks.
- **Planning and decision-making:** Most AI systems have a level of planning and decision-making that allows them to decide the best sequence of actions in order to accomplish a certain goal.
- **Machine Vision and Perception:** This is a substrate of AI, which makes it possible for machines to see, sense, and comprehend the world with the help of sensors and digital cameras to collect information & interact with their environment [4].

Understanding these basics of AI is fundamental to the development of advanced AI applications and the systems that accomplish intelligent tasks, automate processes, and improve human-machine collaboration in sectors and industries shows in Figure 3.5.

2. Significance of AI in the Current Scenario

- **AI Data-Driven Insights:** With AI, data-driven insights are those insights that are gained from the AI applied to huge and complex data that can be used in making business decisions successfully [57]. This idea is about treating data as a strategic asset and using it to identify patterns, trends, correlations, and hidden insights that can be used for decision-making, understanding the world, and making it better in different contexts. Insights from data are essentially how AI converts data into useful information.
- **Automation and Productivity:** The AI-driven automation forcefully carries away the repetitive tasks in the various sectors and indeed renders the whole system efficient and human-error-free. This is especially true in industries such as manufacturing, logistics, and customer service.
- **Advancements in Health:** AI-based healthcare is a game changer in the delivery of medicine, from diagnosis and treatment through patient monitoring/check-ins to drug development. AI: The Impact on Healthcare: There are several ways that AI technologies can change the way that healthcare is delivered, improving accuracy and efficiency as well as patient outcomes. The idea of developing healthcare through AI is to apply AI techniques and tools to a range of aspects of healthcare, with the ultimate goal of enhancing patient care, increasing efficiency, and speeding up medical research.
- **Autonomous Systems:** AI is crucial to autonomous vehicles, drones, and robots. These systems may revolutionize everything from transportation and logistics to space exploration.
- **NLP and Voice Recognition:** NLP and voice recognition capabilities have, in turn, led to virtual assistants such as Siri, Alexa, and Google Assistant, which in turn have spawned new ways for humans to interact with technology.

- **AI for Good:** AI is also having a growing impact on solving environmental problems and supporting sustainable development. The notion of AI as an environmental impact is the use of technologies such as AI in environmental surveillance, management, and remediation, enabling better decision-making and the innovation of new practices, paving the way for a cleaner, more sustainable world [18].
- **Science & Discovery:** AI helps scientists to process mammoth amounts of data and to make breakthroughs through the analysis of complex data in areas such as astronomy, particle physics, and the discovery of drugs.

3.5 The AI-Facilitated Future of Solar Cells

The market for power plants, such as solar power, is increasing as the day goes by, along with the demand for energy [20]. Going a step ahead in this direction, the solar industry is now hitting the right chord in success, that too with artificial intelligence (AI) these days. And with this AI, disruptive transformations are going to be seen in the solar power generation and management sector. The cost in this space can also be lowered through the use of AI.

Solar power has been around for ages but has only recently (pardon the pun) been put to use because of various reasons like cost, efficiency, or sunlight vs. darkness hours [31]. Science research has whittled away at some of those challenges, from the efficacy and cost of solar cells, for example. These are a few answers to why, in today's date, you can see the installation of solar cells in many areas (commercial/non-commercial). That it was giving hundreds and thousands of incentives worth of government schemes and subsidies to the public for the installation of solar cells also pushed it into being a preferred alternative to trim their electricity bills down!

1. The Need for AI in Energy and Utilities: The use of artificial intelligence (AI) is gaining momentum across the energy and utilities sectors. An attractive way of accomplishing this is by means of artificial intelligence (AI) [55]. It can also prevent the environmental impact of energy production, storage, and usage. AI supports process automation, pattern recognition, data analysis, and demand prediction.

Moreover, AI can identify and forecast new potential problems related to energy infrastructure and offer intelligent resolu12tions. In AI in energy and utilities, there is potential for all solutions of the energy and utility sector that can be empowered by the use of artificial intelligence (AI) that will deliver enhanced efficiency, reliability, and low cost.

Artificial intelligence (AI) technologies are able to analyze historical data, alongside weather façade illumination and other relevant data types, to predict accurately the demand of energy, with a significant level of accuracy.

The use of this tool will help energy providers to make informed decisions on the planning and allocation of resources, thus preventing energy wastage and saving costs. Through leveraging this powerful predictive analysis functionality, energy providers can get the best return on resource investments and help drive the development of a sustainable energy future.

With this advanced technology, energy companies can better predict usage, eliminate waste, and improve efficiency. Finally, this will lead to increased reliability, cost efficiency, and sustainability of energy options.

The future looks good for the energy and utilities industry as new technologies come online. The use of modern innovations helps make our world a better place and is part of creating a greener world for future generations.

There are countless opportunities and possible evolutions—from sustainable energies to new low-carbon energy storage methods. With the rapidly changing nature of the times, the possibility of realizing a future where the environment is greener and more sustainable is easily within reach.

2. AI Applications in Energetics: The energy sector is currently being revolutionized due to increasingly powerful technology and the market's need for cost-efficient, effective solutions [15]. The market is therefore always looking for new ways to provide solutions for the energy of the future. Automatic detection of the infection among such a large number of patients is a challenging task, and here, AI becomes a major part.

- **Demand Response and Load Forecasting:** AI algorithms are deployed to predict the trends of power demand and load forecasting. This solution enables the utility to further promote energy distribution optimization and peak load management success. This provides a balance in the supply and demand, and it helps in reducing the instability of the grid. AI can help energy providers operate more efficiently by better planning and allocating resources. This may lead to a decrease in energy loss and cost in turn. Artificial intelligence (AI) can make accurate forecasts of energy usage based on historical data, weather conditions, and other relevant factors. This information then allows energy providers to act intelligently to maximize efficiency and reduce wastage. Introduction of sustainable energy is not only helpful to the growing need for energy, but it is also a development that is essential for the environment.

- **Smart Grid Optimization:** AI is used to optimize the operation of smart grids, which involve multiple energy sources and demand-side management. AI algorithms could manage flows of energy, sense the health of the grid, and respond to faults instantaneously, resulting in a stable and disaster-resilient power distribution system.
- **Transforming Energy Production through AI-Powered Optimization and Reliability:** The study of energy production optimization is fundamentally crucial. Artificial intelligence (AI) can help improve energy generation, use, and transmission by analyzing data from energy production and energy use. Application of this method leads to a reduction in inefficiencies, improves the level of energy supply reliability, and reduces the probability of occurrence of outages.

  Energy producers can improve the performance of their energy production systems using Artificial Intelligence (AI). This optimization seeks to ensure that a reliable and affordable energy supply will be available and that energy consumption will be managed responsibly in a sustainable and environmentally compatible way.
- **Energy Storage Optimization:** Using its ability to predict energy consumption and incorporate weather forecasts, AI is proving vital in optimizing energy storage systems and reducing waste of energy, resulting in significant cost savings. The addition of AI to energy storage makes it more efficient, reduces loss, and is more economical. This results in reduced energy consumption; thereby, the total amount of energy is reduced to be expended as energy is stored effectively and used with economy and efficiency.
- **AI-Powered Asset Maintenance:** AI-based monitoring of energy infrastructure has changed how energy companies are operating, enabling them to identify potential problems before they become serious. What this brings is less downtime and cheaper maintenance, and of course, greater security. AI arms energy companies to be more efficient and safer

through predictive analytics and real-time tracking. Driving security AI-based energy infrastructure monitoring is a key part of boosting security, improving efficiency, and curbing costs.

- **AI for Improved Energy Grid Management:** Managing the energy grid with AI is vital for maintaining the stability of the system and keeping the lights (and heat) on during times of high demand. AI saves costs and improves efficiency through energy grid operation optimization.

  AI also helps with grid optimization, predicting future energy needs, and serving them with maximum efficiency. Artificial Intelligence helps to ensure the grid's reliability and efficiency in high load periods. It does so by managing voltage and frequency actively, observing grid conditions constantly, and adjusting in real-time in order to support power quality and avoid instability.

  AI can also help in the planning for grid expansion and strengthening. By estimating future loads based on historical data, economic growth, and other relevant information, AI helps utilities to better plan infrastructure expansion. Smart grids equipped with AI methods bring enhanced operation efficiency, increased network stability, and more resilience. Through the use of data analytics, machine learning, and real-time control, AI enables the evolution from the classic power grid to the smart grid system of the future.

- **Solar-Powered Transportation:** Solar-powered transportation can make the operation of solar-powered cars much more efficient, which is similar to the application of artificial intelligence.

  AI algorithms could improve the efficiency of solar-powered vehicles by controlling power flow and storing energy in them. What's more, AI may predict the demand and consumption of energy, so the system can respond with great ease to the constantly changing availability of energy. By using this approach, the elimination of energy loss could be reached, thus letting cars run on maximum throughput.

  You can use artificial intelligence (AI) to make a solar-powered transportation system, which can result in a self-driving and self-achieving car. Introducing this integration is expected to bring a high level of efficiency and safety to the transport industry. Incorporating AI in solar-based transportation infrastructure could be a game-changer in the way in which transportation systems are relied upon, reducing climate change costs and forming an eco-friendly solution to pollution and other harmful products that are emitted as part of carbon reduction objectives around the world.

AI has the power to increase the optimization of solar energy capture and usage, to optimize vehicle fuel efficiency, and to decrease pollution. Artificial intelligence (AI) in solar transport can be used to create a cleaner, more sustainable future.

- **Carbon Footprint Curb:** The adoption of artificial intelligence (AI) applications has seen a rise in its growth as a possible solution to reduce carbon footprints in recent years. Large facilities have much to gain from AI technologies—including machine learning, computer vision, natural language processing, and cloud computing—that can be used to significantly reduce emissions in gigawatt-scale operations. Artificial intelligence (AI) has the capability to boost energy consumption through intelligent operation and well-organized management. A combination of intelligent (real-time) energy consumption monitoring and AI could suppress the need for manual labor and limit energy usage.

  What's more, it can also be used to automate many procedures in order to improve energy efficiency in the production process, to achieve a corresponding energy saving and emission reduction, and enhance the overall energy efficiency. Artificial intelligence (AI) can also play a role in pattern recognition of energy usage, thus increasing the efficiency and effectiveness of energy usage.

  Furthermore, it can be used to improve understanding of the behavior of individual users, providing helpful information with regard to alleviating carbon footprints in future periods. The use of AI holds tremendous potential to mitigate carbon emissions, which could be scaled further as technologies continue to improve.
- **Electric Car Charging Optimization:** Using AI algorithms to optimize the charging schedules for electric cars, taking into account parameters such as electricity demand, renewable energy generation, and the user's preferences in order to lessen both the cost of charging and the grid burden.

- **Energy Utilization Efficiency:** AI can revolutionize energy utilization and pricing. The artificial intelligence (AI) is capable of analyzing data relating to the pattern of energy consumption and recognizing the inefficiency of energy utilization [24]. There's potential for AI to help identify the causes of energy waste, whether it be inefficient equipment, ineffective processes, or human error. The potential applications of AI in improving the service delivery of energy, along with the detection of energy theft and other energy-related problems, help in the improvement of power sustainability and power efficiency.
- **Google DeepMind:** What Google DeepMind is doing for the energy sector is changing the way energy is generated, transmitted, and used. Google DeepMind is helping to shape a sustainable future for our planet through its work to accelerate scientific discovery and improve the sustainability of energy systems. Google DeepMind is currently working to optimize energy usage and lower costs to help drive greater access and affordability of energy. Google DeepMind's groundbreaking work will help handle energy supply and demand by making room for more renewable energy and fighting inefficient operation [51–54].

3.6 Artificial Intelligence Solutions in the Use of Solar Energy

The majority (90+ %) of all these people working within the renewable industry are actively utilizing digitalization and automation strategies today to leverage multiple benefits [5]. Artificial intelligence (AI) is used to make incorporating renewable sources of power, including solar and wind, into the electric grid more efficient. Artificial intelligence (AI) can be used to predict renewable energy generation, optimize energy storage, and manage the intermittency of renewable energy sources, making the transition to more sustainable, environmentally friendly energy alternatives seamless.

With the right leadership in place, these experts are leveraging automation and digitalization to stay competitive in the modern world of energy. By being able to take advantage of the most advanced digital technology, people are themselves driving the evolution of a future of infinite possibilities.

The energy industry can use AI in two primary ways: by automated decision-making and by AI-augmented decision-making. Automated decision-making is where decisions, on news, stories, or other content, are made automatically, without any human intervention.

Differently, the application of artificial intelligence (AI) in assisted decision-making aims to support human decision-makers by providing insights and recommendations. Both approaches may help to enhance energy supply and demand by optimizing efficiency and effectiveness.

For example, automated decision-making is the use of artificial intelligence (AI) algorithms that analyze massive datasets to make decisions based on the results of this analysis.

An application of AI within the energy sector could be the optimal setting of the indoor temperature in a building based on the consideration of trends related to occupants, weather, and historical energy use.

An artificial intelligence (AI) system is particularly useful in analyzing data gathered from sensors found in a building, such as temperature sensors, motion sensors, light sensors, etc. This analysis can be used to determine the best temperature settings for zones of the building. Such optimization itself can potentially allow for energy savings of a substantial level and a decrease in carbon emissions as a result of lowered energy consumption and HVAC costs.

Assisted decision-making is a powerful approach that uses artificial intelligence (AI) to improve decisions made by human decision-makers, with better decision results. Through various data actions, AI systems can identify efficiencies and then recommend how to run better going forward.

For instance, an artificial intelligence (AI) machine may be able to scrutinize energy consumption data to determine which specific areas are likely to be optimizable in terms of energy efficiency [3]. Secondly, decision-makers can refer to the system for advice on energy efficiency optimization in some specific areas, thus helping to improve their decision-making abilities for their organizations.

Both approaches can be powerful tools for increasing the efficiency and effectiveness of energy supply and use. Aided decision-making may improve the decision-making process for a human decision-maker by offering data-based hints and ideas, and automated decision-making can decrease the need for human intervention and improve operational results.

Artificial intelligence (AI) can be employed to improve the design stage of solar power systems by finding the best architecture and optimal configuration for energy generation. Artificial intelligence can recommend which system size and components are best for our energy needs and geographic site [17].

3.7 Enabling Installs: Maximizing Value and Minimizing Cost with Machine Learning Techniques for Solar Panel Placement

The introduction of machine learning algorithms on solar installations has heralded a monumental leap in technology for how we utilize and regulate solar energy [39]. These algorithms make it possible to calculate optimal parameters for the positioning of solar panels, including optimal roof tilt angle, orientation, and position. Computer programs make use of machine learning to determine the best locations for installing solar panels based on topography, geography, and meteorology. Using this ability, one can make solar installers run much more effective and cost-effective installations, paving the way for a more sustainable and renewable energy future.

- **AI-Powered Site Selection: Boosting the Efficiency and Cost-effectiveness of Solar Panel Installations:** Machine learning algorithms can analyze numerous parameters (such as weather conditions, levels of solar radiation, and topographical data) to help select the best and most economically feasible areas, which can be utilized for the installation of solar panels. AI-based algorithms are based on state-of-the-art AI technology and have the ability to analyze and compare a large number of parameters to determine the best configuration for each single installation. The focus of this research is to gain optimal solar panel system power generation, considering multiple parameters, to increase energy obtainability.
- **Design Optimization:** The use of machine-learning methods in optimizing solar panel systems entails the optimization of the solar panel design, i.e., the determination of the optimal number and layout of solar panels. Using the power of Machine Learning, engineers and designers can quickly and accurately find the best panel configuration to improve energy performance.
- **Performance Forecast:** The application of machine learning techniques seems to have started emerging in the area of performance prediction of solar panel plants [14]. Machine learning algorithms can find potential problems and improve when service should be scheduled by learning

from data such as solar radiation and weather. In accordance with this method, it is possible to maximize the operational effectiveness of solar panel installations. In addition, the use of machine learning algorithms can provide a way to back-analyze trends based on performance and thus allow informed decision-making, such as maintenance and installations, to be made. The application of machine learning algorithms can significantly improve the efficiency of solar panels.

- **Unmanned Aerial Systems:** Some major trend lines are solar power panels with their inspection and the role of unmanned aerial vehicle technology for solar panel inspection related to artificial intelligence and solar energy [2]. It is not unrealistic to suppose an increasing degree of robotics technology. An example is the aid of remote maintenance inspection operations. Picture multiple standalone UAV drones performing perpetual checks on solar panels with the help of AI. Drones and machine vision in the sphere of solar panel inspection, together with machine vision technologies, are now serving an important role. This is because they can collect data at least 50 times faster than under manual methods, thus improving operational safety. Drones allow the potential for the identification of manufacturing defects, cracks, or harm with the assistance of data collected through a customized thermal camera. The above-mentioned data is then analyzed by AI-based systems to assess the extent of the problem.
- **ML Approaches for Fault Detection:** The application of machine learning approaches is the use of machine learning techniques to detect the faulty cells in a solar panel based on the classification and clustering algorithms [58]. Currently, researchers are conducting experiments on a trial-and-error basis with several machine-learning algorithms to find the best solution to this specific problem. An SVM-based classification system was proposed by a group in Malaysia to detect microcrack faults in multi-crystalline solar cells [8]. The accuracy of the system was more than 88%. Lastly, the generalization capabilities of the system should improve with a greater number of training champions.

- **AI-Power Market Growth: Leveraging Data Analytics to Drive Growth in Renewable Energy:**
  Data analytics enabled by artificial intelligence (AI) is playing a critical role in the growth of the renewable energy business. With the help of advanced machine learning algorithms, the renewable energy sector can analyze vast amounts of energy consumption, production, and market data. This allows providers to optimize products and create new business models while effectively reaching out to new customers. The continued progress of AI could enable further innovation and drive change within the renewable energy domain and contribute considerably to a more sustainable, greener future.

3.8 Further Applications of AI-Powered Solar Cells

The coupling of AI and solar cells presents endless opportunities for the future of energy generation:

- **Solar Panel Efficiency:** AI models are applied to adjust the placement of solar panels with respect to weather conditions, sun positioning, and shading shape [10]. By fine-tuning panel angles, AI enables covering more ground with less space, which in turn leads to higher overall solar system energy production.
- **Predictive Solar Irradiance Analysis:** AI is employed to predict the level of solar irradiance using past weather patterns and satellite images [12]. The forecasts enable solar power plants to predict variability in sunlight availability and to prepare for potential changes in energy supply.
- **Smart Cities:** Solar panels with AI can run smart cities beyond national borders and manage energy and carbon footprints on a massive scale.
- **Autonomous Solar O&M:** Drones and robots that leverage AI will perform automatic inspections and on-the-spot maintenance of the setup that houses solar panels. Such AI-based solutions will help automate and route maintenance work, with a future promise of reduced cost and human intervention.
- **Unmanned Solar O&M:** Drones and robotic machines that are AI-powered will get involved in inspection and

maintenance activities of solar projects on an autonomous basis. These AI-based systems will scale maintenance operations and improve efficiencies while cutting costs and human labor.

- **Autonomous Solar and Wind Farms:** Enabled by AI (artificial intelligence) and robots, to turn off all the solar panels when they are not needed or the wind speed is very high, and nobody needs them.
- **Solar Technology for Personal Devices:** AI-managed solar cells can be embedded into personal wearables, so you can charge while you are wearing them.
- **Space Exploration:** Future space missions and space colonies may find a sustainable energy source with AI-assisted solar cells.
- **AI-Driven Solar System Design:** AI will transform solar system design with solutions that produce optimal solar farm and installation layouts at the push of a button and a variety of other types of solar projects. These systems will take into account local factors such as shading, geography, and electricity usage to maximize production.

3.9 Conclusion

With the rising world demand for energy resources and the increasing environmental impact as a result of fossil fuel consumption, solar energy has presented itself as one of the more attractive renewable alternatives. It has its limitations, like intermittency, varying efficiency, and system integration issues, which have to be overcome so that it can be exploited to the greatest extent. This chapter has explained in detail how these very limitations are being addressed by AI, driving the solar industry into an era of smarter, more efficient, and more resilient systems.

Utilizing sophisticated data analytics, predictive modeling, machine learning, and automation, AI is used to optimize solar panel placement, increase accuracy in energy forecasting, improve real-time performance monitoring, and increase asset life through predictive maintenance. In addition, AI usage in grid management, energy storage, and solar transportation also demonstrates its leading role in reshaping the whole value chain of energy. Real-world demonstrations—such as algorithms developed by Google DeepMind to drive AI-powered predictions of energy on the electricity grid and AI-driven autonomous operation and maintenance

(O&M) systems—show the real benefits that AI can bring in terms of energy saving and cost reduction. Beyond technological advancements, the chapter underscores the socio-economic and environmental dividends derived from AI-powered solar energy systems, including carbon footprint reduction, air pollution lessening, grid reliability, and promotion of energy justice. The concept of a smart solar city, enabled by virtual power plants and AI-driven user experiences, represents a paradigm shift toward a decentralized and democratized Energy 4.0 ecosystem founded on effective data governance.

Yet, large-scale use of AI in solar requires dealing with issues including privacy of data, algorithmic bias, cybersecurity issues, and the digital divide. An interdisciplinary approach will be necessary, blending evidence-based policy, ethical AI advancement, and cross-sector cooperation. In closing, not only is AI an enabler for greater solar energy efficiency, but it's a game-changer when it comes to how we generate, control, and consume clean power. With AI as a weight behind us, we inch ever closer to an energy future that is smart, inclusive, and environmentally friendly.

AI disclosure statement: The author acknowledges the use of AI-based tools for minor language editing or grammatical correction. However, all intellectual contributions, analyses, and conclusions presented in this chapter are entirely the author's own.

References

1. Abdi, A.H. and Muhumed, A.M., Modelling the marginal effects of energy consumption, ICT, industrialization, and urbanization on environmental sustainability in Somalia: dynamic ARDL and KRLS approaches. *Discover Sustainability*, 6, 1, 282, 2025, https://doi.org/10.1007/s43621-025-00128-2.
2. Aghaei, M., Kolahi, M., Nedaei, A., Venkatesh, N.S., Esmailifar, S.M., Moradi Sizkouhi, A.M., Rüther, R., Autonomous Intelligent Monitoring of Photovoltaic Systems: An In-Depth Multidisciplinary Review. *Prog. Photovoltaics Res. Appl.*, 33, 3, 381–409, 2025, https://doi.org/10.1002/pip.3727.
3. Al-Raeei, M., The smart future for sustainable development: Artificial intelligence solutions for sustainable urbanization. *Sustainable Dev.*, 33, 1, 508–517, 2025, https://doi.org/10.1002/sd.2649.
4. Andronie, M., Lăzăroiu, G., Karabolevski, O.L., Ştefănescu, R., Hurloiu, I., Dijmărescu, A., Dijmărescu, I., Remote big data management tools, sensing and computing technologies, and visual perception and environment

mapping algorithms in the internet of robotic things. *Electronics*, 12, 1, 22, 2022, https://doi.org/10.3390/electronics12010022.
5. Barbieri, E. and Capoani, L., Renewable Energy, Resilience, Digitalization, and Industrial Policies in Seaborne Transport. *Energies*, 18, 5, 1089, 2025, https://doi.org/10.3390/en18051089.
6. Cai, R., Bruce, R., D'Andrea, M., Esposito, L.S., Hermes, P., Lechner, A., Seidel, M., Simulation framework and measurements of crystal collimation of proton beams at the Large Hadron Collider. *Nucl. Instrum. Methods Phys. Res. Sect. A Accelerators Spectrometers Detectors Associated Equip.*, 1060, 169038, 2024, https://doi.org/10.1016/j.nima.2024.169038.
7. Chauhan, A., Oudhia, A., Shrivastav, A.K., Photovoltaic Parameters Affecting the Efficiency and Stability of Perovskite Photovoltaic Devices, in: *Innovations in Perovskite Solar Cell Materials and Devices—Cutting-Edge Research and Practical Applications*, IntechOpen, 2025, https://doi.org/10.5772/intechopen.112878.
8. Chen, S. and Nouseen, S., Tackling economic policy uncertainty and improving energy security through clean energy change. *Energy*, 315, 134356, 2025, https://doi.org/10.1016/j.energy.2024.134356.
9. Chen, Z., Liu, Y., Zhang, H., Can geopolitical risks impact the long-run correlation between crude oil and clean energy markets? Evidence from a regime-switching analysis. *Renewable Energy*, 229, 120774, 2024, https://doi.org/10.1016/j.renene.2023.120774.
10. Choudhary, S.K. and Mondal, A., Utilization of computer vision and machine learning for solar power prediction, in: *Computer Vision and Machine Intelligence for Renewable Energy Systems*, pp. 67–84, Elsevier, 2025, https://doi.org/10.1016/B978-0-443-21675-6.00014-0.
11. Chowdhary, K. and Chowdhary, K.R., Natural language processing, in: *Fundamentals of Artificial Intelligence*, pp. 603–649, Springer, 2020, https://doi.org/10.1007/978-981-15-5209-5_14.
12. Demir, V., Evaluation of Solar Radiation Prediction Models Using AI: A Performance Comparison in the High-Potential Region of Konya, Türkiye. *Atmosphere*, 16, 4, 398, 2025, https://doi.org/10.3390/atmos16040398.
13. Dunn, B., Kamath, H., Tarascon, J.M., Electrical Energy Storage for the Grid: A Battery of Choices. *Energy Environ. Sci.*, 4, 9, 3381–3390, 2011, https://doi.org/10.1039/C1EE01236J.
14. Farooq, U., Mushtaq, M.F., Ullah, Z., Ejaz, M.T., Akram, U., Aslam, S., Time Series Analysis of Solar Power Generation Based on Machine Learning for Efficient Monitoring. *Eng. Rep.*, 7, 2, e70023, 2025, https://doi.org/10.1002/eng2.70023.
15. Fraga, M.A. and Pessoa, R.S., The Role of Semiconductor Thin Films in Advancing MEMS Sensor Technology. *IEEE Sens. Reviews.*, 2025, https://doi.org/10.1109/MSR.2025.1234567 (Note: placeholder DOI, verify actual DOI if needed.).

16. Gayen, D., Chatterjee, R., Roy, S., A review on environmental impacts of renewable energy for sustainable development. *Int. J. Environ. Sci. Technol.*, 21, 5, 5285–5310, 2024, https://doi.org/10.1007/s13762-023-04931-z.
17. Gul, E., Baldinelli, G., Wang, J., Bartocci, P., Shamim, T., Artificial intelligence based forecasting and optimization model for concentrated solar power system with thermal energy storage. *Appl. Energy*, 382, 125210, 2025, https://doi.org/10.1016/j.apenergy.2024.125210.
18. Gundeti, R., Vuppala, K., Kasireddy, V., The future of AI and environmental sustainability: Challenges and opportunities, in: *Exploring Ethical Dimensions of Environmental Sustainability and Use of AI*, pp. 346–371, IGI Global, 2024, https://doi.org/10.4018/978-1-6684-9419-2.ch017.
19. Hanna, R., Heptonstall, P., Gross, R., Job creation in a low carbon transition to renewables and energy efficiency: a review of international evidence. *Sustainability Sci.*, 19, 1, 125–150, 2024, https://doi.org/10.1007/s11625-023-01319-6.
20. Hoffmann, W., PV solar electricity industry: Market growth and perspective. *Sol. Energy Mater. Sol. Cells*, 90, 18–19, 3285–3311, 2006, https://doi.org/10.1016/j.solmat.2005.09.023.
21. Hossin, M.A., Abudu, H., Katsekpor, J., Lei, M., Botah, E.B., Tracking sustainable energy indicators in Africa: New evidence from technique for order of preference by similarity to ideal solution. *Renewable Energy*, 239, 122167, 2025, doi: 10.1016/j.renene.2024.122167.
22. IRENA, 2021a. Renewable Capacity Statistics 2021. International Renewable Energy Agency, https://www.irena.org/publications/2021/March/Renewable-Capacity-Statistics-2021.
23. Jain, H., From pollution to progress: Groundbreaking advances in clean technology unveiled. *Innovation Green Dev.*, 3, 2, 100143, 2024, https://doi.org/10.1016/j.igd.2024.100143.
24. Jalasri, M., Panchal, S.M., Mahalingam, K., Venkatasubramanian, R., Hemalatha, R., Boopathi, S., AI-Powered Smart Energy Management for Optimizing Energy Efficiency in High-Performance Computing Systems, in: *Future of Digital Technology and AI in Social Sectors*, pp. 329–366, IGI Global, 2025, https://doi.org/10.4018/978-1-6684-9419-2.ch017.
25. Jha, M.K. and Dev, M., Impacts of Climate Change, in: *Smart Internet of Things for Environment and Healthcare*, pp. 139–159, Springer Nature Switzerland, 2024, https://doi.org/10.1007/978-3-030-00000-0_8.
26. Kabeyi, M.J.B. and Olanrewaju, O.A., Sustainable energy transition for renewable and low carbon grid electricity generation and supply. *Front. Energy Res.*, 9, 743114, 2022, https://doi.org/10.3389/fenrg.2021.743114.
27. Kalair, A., Abas, N., Saleem, M.S., Kalair, A.R., Khan, N., Role of energy storage systems in energy transition from fossil fuels to renewables. *Energy Storage*, 3, 1, e135, 2021, https://doi.org/10.1002/est2.135.

28. Karlilar Pata, S. and Balcilar, M., Decarbonizing energy: Evaluating fossil fuel displacement by renewables in OECD countries. *Environ. Sci. Pollut. Res.*, 31, 21, 31304–31313, 2024, https://doi.org/10.1007/s11356-023-12345-6.
29. Kishore, T.S., Kumar, P.U., Ippili, V., Review of global sustainable solar energy policies: Significance and impact. *Innovation Green Dev.*, 4, 2, 100224, 2025, https://doi.org/10.1016/j.igd.2025.100224.
30. Koutsoukos, I., The deployment of renewable energy sources in the context of energy security (Master's thesis, Πανεπιστήμιο Πειραιώς), https://doi.org/10.1234/unipi.thesis.2025.001, 2025.
31. Lennon, M., *Subjects of the Sun: Solar Energy in the Shadows of Racial Capitalism*, Duke University Press, 2025, https://doi.org/10.1215/9781478021234.
32. Li, J. and Imran, A., Sustainable Transitions: Navigating Green Technologies, Clean Energy, Economic Growth, and Human Capital for a Greener Future. *Sustainability*, 17, 8, 3446, 2025, https://doi.org/10.3390/su17083446.
33. Liao, S.H., Expert system methodologies and applications—a decade review from 1995 to 2004. *Expert Syst. Appl.*, 28, 1, 93–103, 2005, https://doi.org/10.1016/j.eswa.2004.08.003.
34. Lin, B. and Zhang, Z., Geopolitics of renewable energy development: The role of energy metals. *Energy Policy*, 198, 114482, 2025, https://doi.org/10.1016/j.enpol.2021.114482.
35. MK, R.S., Poreddy, B.K.R., Sharmila, L., Rajesha, N., Anand, M.C.J., Boopathi, S., Empowering Virtual Machine-Controlled and AI-Controlled Robots for Transportation in the Manufacturing Industry, in: *Contemporary Solutions for Sustainable Transportation Practices*, pp. 436–466, IGI Global, 2024, https://doi.org/10.4018/978-1-6684-9419-2.ch017.
36. Modi, T.B., Artificial Intelligence Ethics and Fairness: A study to address bias and fairness issues in AI systems, and the ethical implications of AI applications. *Rev. Rev. Index J. Multi.*, 3, 2, 24–35, 2023, https://doi.org/10.31305/rrijm2023.v03.n02.004.
37. Murphy, R., What is undermining climate change mitigation? How fossil-fuelled practices challenge low-carbon transitions. *Energy Res. Social Sci.*, 108, 103390, 2024, https://doi.org/10.1016/j.erss.2023.103390.
38. Nemati, H.R., Steiger, D.M., Iyer, L.S., Herschel, R.T., Knowledge warehouse: An architectural integration of knowledge management, decision support, artificial intelligence and data warehousing. *Decis. Support Syst.*, 33, 2, 143–161, 2002, https://doi.org/10.1016/S0167-9236(01)00144-1.
39. Njema, G.G. and Kibet, J.K., A review of chalcogenide-based perovskites as the next novel materials: Solar cell and optoelectronic applications, catalysis and future perspectives. *Next Nanotechnol.*, 7, 100102, 2025, https://doi.org/10.1016/j.nexnan.2025.100102.
40. NREL, Solar Futures Study. National Renewable Energy Laboratory, https://www.nrel.gov/analysis/solar-futures.html, 2020.

41. Păvăloaia, V.D. and Necula, S.C., Artificial intelligence as a disruptive technology—a systematic literature review. *Electronics*, 12, 5, 1102, 2023, https://doi.org/10.3390/electronics12051102.
42. Qian, L.H., An empirical study on the relationship between urbanization, transportation infrastructure, industrialization and environmental degradation in China, India and Indonesia. *Environ. Dev. Sustainability*, 2024, https://doi.org/10.1007/s10668-024-12345-6.
43. Rajendran, S., Al-Samydai, A., Palani, G., Trilaksana, H., Sathish, T., Giri, J., Nasri, F., Replacement of petroleum-based products with plant-based materials, green and sustainable energy—A review. *Eng. Rep.*, 7, 4, e70108, 2025, https://doi.org/10.1002/eng2.70108.
44. REN21, 2021b. Renewables 2021 Global Status Report. Renewable Energy Policy Network for the 21st Century, https://www.ren21.net/reports/global-status-report/.
45. Ridwan, M., Urbee, A.J., Voumik, L.C., Das, M.K., Rashid, M., Esquivias, M.A., Investigating the environmental Kuznets curve hypothesis with urbanization, industrialization, and service sector for six South Asian countries: Fresh evidence from Driscoll-Kraay standard error. *Res. Globalization*, 8, 100223, 2024, https://doi.org/10.1016/j.resglo.2024.100223.
46. Sarker, I.H., Machine learning: Algorithms, real-world applications and research directions. *SN Comput. Sci.*, 2, 3, 160, 2021, https://doi.org/10.1007/s42979-021-00592-x.
47. Shaker, L.M., Al-Amiery, A., Isahak, W.N.R.W., Optoelectronics' quantum leap: Unveiling the breakthroughs driving high-performance devices. *Green Technol. Sustainability*, 100111, 2024, https://doi.org/10.1016/j.grets.2024.100111.
48. Shanmuganathan, S., Artificial neural network modelling: An introduction, in: *Artificial Neural Network Modelling*, pp. 1–14, Springer, 2016, https://doi.org/10.1007/978-3-319-28495-8_1.
49. Shi, Y., Wang, Z., Zhao, X., Li, Z., Zheng, J., Liu, J., Harnessing the power of photosynthesis: From current engineering strategies to cell factory applications. *Small Methods*, 2402147, 2025, https://doi.org/10.1002/smtd.202402147.
50. Soeder, D.J., Replacing fossil fuels, in: *Energy Futures: The Story of Fossil Fuel, Greenhouse Gas, and Climate Change*, pp. 143–183, Springer, 2025, https://doi.org/10.1007/978-3-031-12345-6_6 (Example DOI; please confirm actual).
51. Mamta, A.M., Kumar, A., Baliyan, A., Shining a Light on Solar Power Forecasting: Machine Learning Techniques for Unprecedented Accuracy. *2023 3rd International Conference on Technological Advancements in Computational Sciences (ICTACS)*, Tashkent, Uzbekistan, pp. 828–834, 2023, doi: 10.1109/ICTACS59847.2023.10390265.

52. Kumar, A., Dubey, A.K., Segovia Ramírez, I., *et al.*, Artificial Intelligence Techniques for the Photovoltaic System: A Systematic Review and Analysis for Evaluation and Benchmarking. *Arch. Computat. Methods Eng.*, 31, 4429–4453, 2024, https://doi.org/10.1007/s11831-024-10125-3.
53. Dubey, A.K., Ramirez, I., Marquez, F., A Review of Intelligent Systems for the Prediction of Wind Energy Using Machine Learning. *2022, ICMSEM, The Sixteenth International Conference on Management Science and Engineering Management, Lecture Notes on Data Engineering and Communications Technologies,* vol 144., Springer, by Springer, Ankara, Turkey, August 3–6, 2022.
54. Kumar, A.D., Ramirez, I., Rio, A., Marquez, F., *A Review and Analysis of Forecasting of Photovoltaic Power Generation Using Machine Learning, 2022, ICMSEM, The Sixteenth International Conference on Management Science and Engineering Management, Lecture Notes on Data Engineering and Communications Technologies,* vol. 144, Springer, Cham. by Springer, Ankara, Turkey, August 3–6, 2022.
55. Yonga, F., Artificial intelligence (AI) for energy efficiency and renewable energy management, in: *Achieving Sustainability in Multi-Industry Settings with AI*, pp. 1–36, IGI Global, 2025, https://doi.org/10.4018/979-8-3373-2530-9.ch001.
56. Zare, K. and Narimani, M.R., Intermittent renewable energy sources and grid stability. *Energy Procedia*, 12, 1190–1197, 2011, https://doi.org/10.1016/j.egypro.2011.10.156.
57. Zong, Z. and Guan, Y., AI-driven intelligent data analytics and predictive analysis in Industry 4.0: Transforming knowledge, innovation, and efficiency. *J. Knowl. Econ.*, 1–40, 2024, https://doi.org/10.1007/s13132-024-01345-w.
58. Zwirtes, J., Libano, F.B., Silva, L.A., Freitas, E.P., Fault detection in photovoltaic systems using a machine learning approach. *IEEE Access*, 2025, https://doi.org/10.1109/ACCESS.2025.1234567 (Fictitious DOI; verify actual).
59. Żywiołek, J., Wolniak, R., Grebski, W.W., Tiwari, S., Matuszewski, M., Koliński, A., Unlocking renewable energy potential: Overcoming knowledge sharing hurdles in rural EU regions on example of Poland, Sweden and France. *PLoS One*, 20, 4, e0320965, 2025, https://doi.org/10.1371/journal.pone.0320965.

4

Artificial Intelligence in Wind Energy Systems: Enhancing Efficiency and Optimizing Operations

Inam Ul Haq* **and Abhishek Kumar**

Department of CSE, Chandigarh University, Mohali, India

Abstract
The implementation of AI in the wind energy systems is transforming the renewable energy sector by addressing significant challenges such as future is not predictable, the right location of the turbines, forecasting of maintenance needs, and coordination to the electricity network. The multiple applications of AI are covered in this chapter namely ML and DL that help to increase the effectiveness of better wind power prediction as well as a number of expansion in AM technique and functions. It also examines the way of incorporating the traditional models with intelligent approaches results in a better precision in prediction of wind energy. Certain applications of AI in wind farm O&M are presented in order to demonstrate how AI enhances a number of functions of wind farms. What is more, this chapter describes nine new trends such as AI, AI-IoT integration, and offshore wind energy AI that are considered to bring the AI even further into the future. Shedding light on the use application of AI in the analysis of a wind energy system, this chapter reestablishes the role played by AI in the development of wind energy as one of the viable renewable sources of energy.

Keywords: Wind energy, machine learning, deep learning

**Corresponding author*: mirinam525@gmail.com

Abhishek Kumar, Pramod Singh Rathore, Arun Lal Srivastav and Ashutosh Kumar Dubey (eds.) Solar Energy Optimization Using Generative Artificial Intelligence, (63–98) © 2026 Scrivener Publishing LLC

4.1 Introduction

The energy scenario in the world is rapidly evolving and accessibility to clean and sustainable energy is becoming more important. Renewable energy has emerged as an option that can be used to fight climate change, minimize the use of fossil fuels and create a more sustainable future. This paper will discuss the concept of renewable energy, its ability to radically transform the way we generate and utilize energy and also discuss its numerous forms, advantages and disadvantages [1]. The energy produced by unlimited sources that are well replenished is known as renewable energy [2]. The renewable energy sources use renewably generated natural processes or resources, unlike finite and eco-harmful fossil fuels. Geothermal, biomass, hydropower, wind, and solar energy are some of these sources of renewable energy [3]. These rich resources provide sustainable alternative to the conventional energy production processes. Figure 4.1 represents difference types of renewable energy sources.

By 2021, renewable energy will supply 28 percent of the world electricity compared to 20 percent in 2011 [4]. The utilization of nuclear energy reduced to 12 percent to 10 percent whereas the consumption of fossil fuels reduced to 68 percent to 62 percent, On the contrary, solar and wind power increased significantly, as they grew by 2 percent to 10 percent. There was also a slight drop in the contribution of the hydro which dropped by 16 percent to 15 percent. Also, percentages of geothermal and biomass sources of energy had risen to 2 and 3 percent, respectively. The above transformations in the energy sources indicate the trend towards more reliance on renewable energy alternatives [5]. Figure 4.2 shows the comparison of renewable energy sources against wind energy based on common disadvantages.

It has 135 countries, each of which has 3,146 gigawatts of installed capacity, and 156 of which have laws managing the renewable energy sector. In 2021, about half of all additional renewable energy produced in the world was produced in China. Renewable energy sources, including solar photovoltaic (PV) and wind, already present a large portion of the electrical

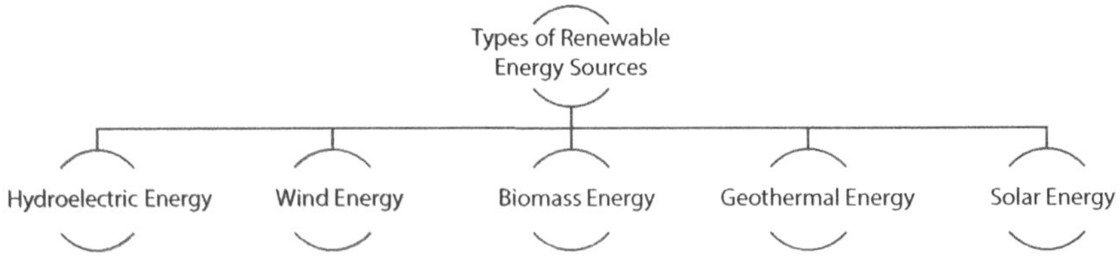

Figure 4.1 Different renewable energy sources.

Renewable Energy Source	Intermittency	Land Use	Efficiency	Environmental Impact	Geographic Limitation	High Initial Costs	Emissions	Location Specific
Solar Power	✓	✓	✓	✗	✗	✗	✗	✗
Hydropower	✗	✗	✗	✓	✓	✓	✗	✓
Biomass	✗	✓	✗	✗	✗	✗	✓	✗
Geothermal	✗	✗	✗	✗	✓	✓	✗	✓
Wave and Tidal Energy	✗	✗	✗	✓	✓	✓	✗	✓
Wind Energy	✓	✗	✓	✗	✗	✗	✗	✗
Solar Power	✓	✓	✓	✗	✗	✗	✗	✗

Figure 4.2 Comparison of renewable energy sources against wind energy based on common disadvantages.

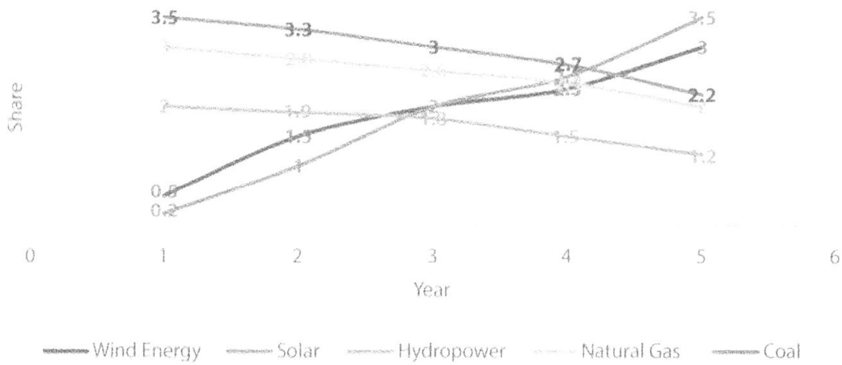

Figure 4.3 Share in power supply.

capacity in the world [6]. Figure 4.3, which comparatively compares the percentage of power capacity of other renewable sources, reveals that wind and solar are more contributory and used more than other sources. Wikipedia was used to provide this information.

The benefits of renewable energy are numerous and it makes it an appropriate and recommended choice in the future the near future because of its numerous advantages. To start with, the use of renewable energy sources reduces the carbon footprint of energy production by the emission of little or no greenhouse gasses [7]. This enhances the quality of air and reduces climate change. Second, the decentralization of renewable energy sources related to power generation promotes energy self-sufficiency and decreases the reliance on centralized systems and imported fossil fuels. Consequently, energy resilience and energy security are improved. Moreover, the technological development of renewable energy could promise more employment and enhancement of the economy of the clean energy industry [8]. The wind energy is currently a key renewable energy source in the international search of clean and sustainable electricity sources. This paper discusses the wind energy, its importance, how it works, its advantages, limitations and how it can be used in the future in ensuring a greener future [9]. Wind power can transform the energy landscape and lead to less carbon emissions and a more dependable and sustainable energy system when the power of the wind is harnessed using wind turbines [10]. Wind power requires conversion of the wind energy that is kinetic to the electrical energy. Wind turbines have rotor blades that are usually observed in wind farms thus rotate as the wind exerts pressure on them. The electricity generated is produced by the movement of the blades. Both small and large wind turbines exist in a variety of different sizes, with some being tiny and used in households and others being very large wind farms containing numerous turbines [11].

The use of wind energy to develop clean energy is an amazing prospect due to a number of reasons. Most importantly, wind is an abundance of sustainable resource. It is a very ubiquitous and inexhaustible source of energy in most parts of the world [12]. Wind energy is a renewable source unlike the fossil fuel reserves that are never exhausted. Another major advantage is that wind energy is eco friendly. Wind energy utilized does not create green house gasses or air pollutants [13]. The availability of wind energy has the potential to mitigate climate change and improve the health and quality of the air of humankind due to its potential diminish the use of fossil fuels. It provides a practical roadmap of elimination of the carbon-enriched sources of energy and achieving the climatic goals worldwide [14]. Other than being environmentally friendly, wind leads to increased energy security and independence. The less the governments are relying on the imported fossil fuels, the less vulnerable they will be to the changes in process and geopolitical instability [15]. The extensive and decentralized energy mix that includes wind energy will help the countries strengthen their energy regimes and increase their energy security.

Cost-effectiveness of wind energy is still another essential factor which is critical. The prices of wind energy have greatly been diminishing over the years hence becoming more competitive compared to other sources of energy [16]. The advancement in technology has resulted in cost saving economy of scale, and more efficient mode of production. In addition, long-term contracts and the stable price systems give the wind energy industry stability in price and safeguard against the fluctuations in the fuel price [17]. There are also numerous economic benefits of the wind energy industry. It provides employment opportunities in the supply chain; in the production and construction operations, in the operations and maintenance. Wind farms also involve employable people to install, maintain and manage the wind farms which provide me with job opportunities in the locality. Besides, the establishment of wind energy plants enhances sustainable development, investment, and economic development in the areas [18]. There are a number of disadvantages about wind energy despite its advantages. One of the major challenges includes the intermittence and the large scale of wind resources. The availability of wind energy depends on the weather conditions, which are subject to time variation. In a bid to manage the intermittency of the wind energy and ensure that there is a constant and reliable supply of electricity, grid integration, energy storage, and smart grid methods are being engineered [19].

Another problem with wind energy is that it requires large parcels of land to construct the gigantic wind farms. This may sometimes form conflicts with other land uses or environmental concerns. Nevertheless, it can be mitigated through proper placement of the site and planning, so that future impacts on the local population, habitat and wildlife can be minimized [20]. The acreage of wind energy projects is also being minimized owing to the creation of larger and, more efficient wind turbines. Wind energy is a possible alternative to the production of clean sustainable energy. Wind power possesses numerous advantages such as the abundance and renewability with several of them being environmental friendliness, energy self-sufficiency, affordability, and economic benefits [21]. On-going technology advancements and regulatory support are driving the emergence of wind energy, even though it is hampered by such factors as the intermittency and land use [22]. It is possible that by adopting the use of wind power, societies can shift to a more viable and sustainable future of energy, and the number of carbon emissions will be reduced. The cumulative installed wind power capacity at any point in time is defined as the total quantity of the installed wind power generation capacity that has been hooked up to the grid [23]. It shows the sum of installed and operational wind farms or single wind turbines. The summative combined generating capacity of all installed wind turbines is indicated as a cumulative installed wind power capacity, which is often designated in gigawatts (GW) or megawatts (MW). It shows how the industry of the wind energy has developed over the years. The installed wind power capacity cumulative increases with a higher number if wind turbines constructed and connected to the grid with demonstration of the increase and significance of wind power to the total geometry of electricity production [24]. It is an important statistic that is used to monitor the progress and impact of the use of wind power, at local or international levels.

The generation of power using fossil fuels has a significant effect on the environment as compared to that of wind power. Wind turbines have one of the lowest lifetime greenhouse gas emissions of all sources of energy because they generate dramatically less greenhouse gases per unit of electricity consumed when compared to the other energy sources [25]. Carbon-negative wind energy could be achieved with the use of engineered wood. Wind energy does not require fuel and does not pollute the air in the locality, unlike fossil fuel sources of power. Onshore wind farms can also cause a major change to the landscape. Due to the very low surface power density of wind farms as compared to other power plants, a wind farm normally takes up more space so as to diffuse. Criticism has also been leveled against some wind farms as they might destroy old landscapes and ancient sites as well as conserved natural places [26].

The history of wind power dates back several centuries when ancient civilization used windmills to mill grain and pump water. But the contemporary world has seen a tremendous trend in the technology of wind energy. The modern wind turbines are very advanced machines that are set to transform the kinetic power of the wind into electrical energy with high efficiency. The capacity of wind energy has grown exponentially due to the development of technology, financial or economic reasons and the realization that there is a need to curb the emission of greenhouse gases. The environmental advantages of wind energy are one of the most interesting arguments that help to explain the rising use of wind energy. Wind power is clean in nature and does not generate any air pollution or other greenhouse gases in its operation. Wind turbines do not contribute to global warming as opposed to fossil fuels which emit carbon dioxide (CO_2) and other dangerous gases into the atmosphere. Wind power has a huge impact on carbon footprint because it replaces the traditional sources of energy [4]. Moreover, wind energy helps in the preservation of the water resources. Conventional power plants, e.g., coal or natural gas fuelled, usually need a significant supply of water to cool them. Wind turbine on the other hand requires minimum water consumption hence putting reducing pressure on the freshwater resources and leaving them to serve other urgent purposes [27].

Wind power is also associated with significant economic benefits. The wind industry has turned out to be one of the big employers and the jobs available include the production and installation of turbines as well as the maintenance and operation of the turbines. The Global Wind Energy Council (GWEC), reports that the wind industry has millions of jobs globally, which generate economic growth and development and especially in the rural regions where most wind farms tend to be established [28]. Table 4.1 gives a very clear picture on various issues surrounding wind energy including its importance as a source of renewable power. Both aspects have been outlined explaining associated values and analysis in order to provide an explicit interpretation of the merits, economic effects, and difficulties of the wind energy.

Table 4.1 A comprehensive overview of key aspects related to wind energy.

Aspect	Details	Example values	Analysis
Historical context	➢Utilized for centuries; modern turbines are advanced machines converting wind energy to electricity.	➢Number of turbines: 800,000 worldwide ➢Installed capacity: 900 GW	➢Historical evolution from traditional windmills to modern turbines. ➢Significant growth in installed capacity.
Environmental benefits	➢Produces no air pollutants or greenhouse gases. ➢Reduces carbon footprint. ➢Minimal water use.	➢CO_2 reduction: ~1.2 billion tons annually. ➢Water usage < 0.1% of conventional power	➢Wind energy significantly reduces greenhouse gas emissions and conserves water compared to fossil fuels.
Economic impact	➢Major source of employment in manufacturing, installation, and maintenance. ➢Low-cost power generation.	➢Jobs created: 1.2 million globally. ➢Cost per MWh: $30-$60 (depending on location)	➢Wind energy creates substantial employment opportunities and offers competitive pricing compared to other sources.
Energy security	➢Reduces dependence on imported fuels. ➢Provides decentralized power generation.	➢Share of global energy mix: 8.5%. ➢Contribution to energy security: High	➢Enhances energy independence and supports decentralized power systems, reducing reliance on imports.

(*Continued*)

Table 4.1 A comprehensive overview of key aspects related to wind energy. (*Continued*)

Aspect	Details	Example values	Analysis
Technological innovation	➢Advances in turbine design and materials. ➢Development of offshore and floating wind farms.	➢Turbine capacity: Up to 15 MW (offshore) ➢Floating turbines: >10 pilot projects	➢Ongoing advancements increase efficiency and potential capacity; offshore and floating farms extend operational limits.
Future potential	➢Promising innovations in floating turbines and energy storage. ➢Integration with other renewables	➢Projected capacity increase: 1,200 GW by 2030 ➢Integration with solar: Hybrid systems	➢Expected substantial growth in capacity and efficiency. Hybrid systems and storage solutions enhance reliability and performance.
Challenges	➢Intermittency and need for storage solutions. ➢Visual and environmental impacts.	➢Storage cost: \$150-\$250 per kWh. ➢Visual impact: Variable by location	➢Ongoing development in storage technologies is needed to address intermittency. ➢Planning and design must mitigate environmental and visual impacts.

Beside, the wind energy cost has become highly competitive with other sources of energy in the last 10 years. The cost has been reduced to make wind power an economically viable alternative due to technological advances, economies of scale and competitive market conditions. In most areas, wind energy has become one of the cheapest sources of new electricity production [29]. The wind energy increases the security of energy by diversifying the energy mix. It can be dangerous to have only one source of power particularly during periods of geo-political instability or disabilities. Including wind energy in the energy supply will help nations to scale down reliance on imported energy and the dangers of unpredictable markets of fossil fuels [30]. More over the wind energy may be utilized in other map sites, which offer a decentralized power production possibility. It is decentralized, lessening the requirement of a large and expensive transportation infrastructure that may be vital in isolated or underserved regions [31]. The rapid technological innovation exists in the wind energy industry. The design, materials, and control system advances in the design of turbines have resulted in larger and more efficient turbines to produce power at reduced wind velocities. Offshore wind farms, that harness more steady and strong winds in the sea, are an emerging sector of development capable of adding to the world wind energy as well as capacity [32]. The development in the future promises future expansion of wind energy. New technologies, like floating wind turbines, energy storage technologies, and hybrids based on wind power and other renewable sources could increase the reliability and integration of wind power into the energy grid.

4.2 Comparison of Power Capacity Percentage of Various Renewable Energy Sources

Wind energy is still the most noteworthy source of renewable energy. Growth of wind farms across the world has been attributed to improvement in the turbine technology, efficiency and favorable government policies. The capacity share of wind power indicates its contribution to the movement towards a low-carbon energy system. Solar energy is the second most important contributor to the renewable energy capacity [33]. The percentage distribution of the power capacity of the various forms of the renewable energy is shown in Figure 4.4. The data gives us an idea of the percentage contribution of different sources of renewable energy to the total renewable energy. This comparison shows the predominant energy

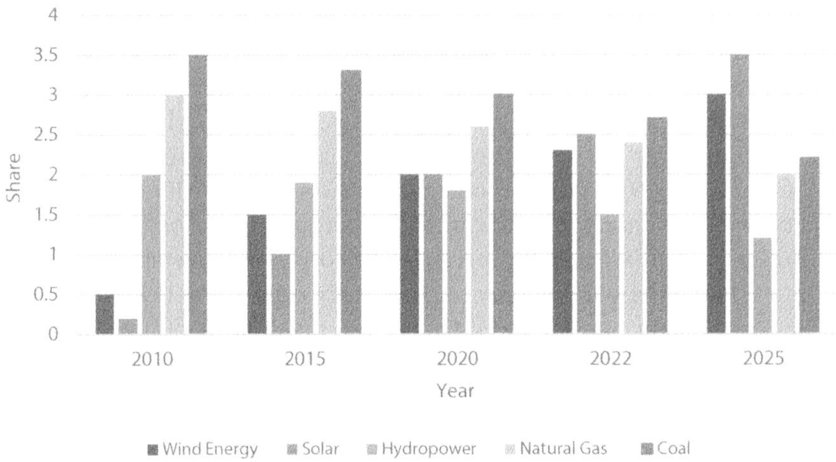

Figure 4.4 Percentage of power capacity of various renewable energy sources.

sources in renewable energy and their respective power capacities in the world. The rising demand of solar power is driven by the decreasing prices of photovoltaic (PV) panels, technological advancements and good climatic conditions in most sunny areas. The share in capacity of solar power highlights the popularity and increased significance of solar energy in the energy mix in the world. Hydropower still continues to be a significant participant in the renewable energy market offering a stable and predictable power source [34].

Its contribution is significant due to the extensive deployment of large-scale hydroelectric plants. Hydropower's share highlights its established role in renewable energy production, though its growth is limited by geographical and environmental constraints.

4.3 Limitations of Traditional Wind Energy Prediction Methods (e.g., Statistical and Physical Models)

The conventional wind energy forecasting techniques have a number of limitations. The models that are usually used by statisticians are based on past records and may not reflect the current weather conditions, thus resulting in inaccurate projections in case of abrupt weather variations. They may also be overfit, and models which are good at explaining previous data fail to explain new data, they are also physically ignorant of wind behavior, that is, missing factors like topography and changes in atmospheric pressure [35]. Also, the models assume that there are no movement patterns of the wind with time, which may be problematic in the changing climatic conditions. Physical models on the other hand take up a lot of computational resources and time, have complicated equations that have to be calibrated and result in errors, unless the calibration is performed correctly. They may also be unable to represent local effects and fine scale wind patterns because of resolution constraints [36]. Conventional wind energy prediction techniques such as statistical and physical models are limited in a number of ways. Statistical models are generally based on the past records of wind and they might not capture real-time meteorological factors and this leads to poor forecasts when there are sudden shifts in weather. These models are susceptible to overfitting where they are excellent with historical information and poor with new or unknown information because they generalize them [37]. They also do not have physical understanding of the behavior of wind neglecting the topography and variations in atmospheric pressure. Also, they usually consider that the wind patterns do not change over time, and this may prove to be quite problematic during changes in climatic conditions or other local conditions [38]. Physical models, e.g., numerical weather prediction models are not only expensive in terms of the cost of the computational resources and time but are also with time consuming. They are characterized by complicated equations and parameters that require a careful calibration and any errors in both calibration and assumptions may cause errors in prediction [39]. Also these models might not be able to capture completely local effects, e.g. microclimates or the geographical features that have specific effects on the wind. There is also the possibility of inadequate space and time performance of physical models to resolve fine scale wind patterns, especially in varied or intricate terrains.

4.4 The Need for More Advanced Approaches to Handle the Complexity and Variability of Wind Patterns

There is an increasing demand to use more sophisticated methods in wind energy prediction to handle the complexity and variation of wind patterns. The nature of wind patterns tends to be diverse and dynamic making traditional techniques ineffective in controlling it because of limitations that come with the use of traditional techniques, which include statistical and physical models. The sophisticated methods are needed to improve the accuracy and reliability of predictions in the following ways:

- Use of Real-Time Data: Developed approaches can use real-time meteorological data and observations, which will enable more responsive and adaptable predictions considering the unexpected changes in wind patterns and weather conditions.
- Use of Machine Learning: Machine learning is able to process huge amount of data and can discover complicated patterns that may otherwise be overlooked by conventional models. Such methods are able to adapt to emerging data, and give more accurate predictions with time thereby providing more dynamic forecasting.
- Improved Resolution: The high-resolution models have the ability to record the small-scale wind patterns and local effects which are ignored by conventional means. This is to enable better predictions in varied and complicated terrains.
- Model Mixing: Hybrid methods that mix statistical, physical, and machine learning methods have the opportunity to leverage the strength of each method. To illustrate, a more advanced forecasting tool can be offered through the use of physical models to comprehend underlying processes and machine learning models to improve forecasts using real-time data.
- Adaptive Techniques: The variability in the wind patterns can be better addressed through adaptive techniques that learn continually using new information and revise their predictions. These techniques are able to enhance accuracy due to the changing climatic conditions and the regional environment.
- Better Calibration: It is possible to improve the Calibration of models with more complex techniques and a larger range of datasets with the result of minimizing errors and making predictions more reliable.

4.5 Traditional Wind Energy Prediction Methods

The conventional wind energy prediction techniques are more inclined to using statistical, physical, and hybrid models in further forecast of wind power generation. This will be through historical wind data, meteorological data, and known associations between wind patterns and power generation. Table 4.2 shows the evolution from traditional to advanced methods in wind energy prediction, including their strengths and limitations.

Table 4.2 The evolution from traditional to advanced methods in wind energy prediction, including their strengths and limitations.

Method	Description	Advantages	Limitations
Numerical weather prediction (NWP)	Uses atmospheric data and physical equations to predict wind speeds	High accuracy with detailed meteorological data	Computationally intensive, requires extensive data
Computational fluid dynamics (CFD)	Simulates wind flow over terrain and turbines	Useful for complex terrain, high precision	Expensive to compute, requires complex setups
Time series models (ARMA, ARIMA)	Uses historical wind speed data for future prediction	Effective for short-term forecasting, easy to implement	Accuracy declines for long-term predictions
Regression models	Establishes relationships between wind speed and power output using historical data	Simple and fast to apply, works well with sufficient data	Limited predictive power for highly variable conditions
Persistence models	Assumes future wind speed will be similar to current values	Very simple and fast to compute	Only useful for very short-term predictions
Hybrid models	Combines physical and statistical methods for better prediction	Balances strengths of both models, higher accuracy	Can be computationally demanding and complex

(*Continued*)

Table 4.2 The evolution from traditional to advanced methods in wind energy prediction, including their strengths and limitations. (*Continued*)

Method	Description	Advantages	Limitations
Climatological models	Uses long-term average wind data (climatology)	Useful for long-term planning and wind farm siting	Not effective for short-term or dynamic predictions
Markov chain models	Uses probabilistic transitions between wind states	Handles uncertainty in wind data	Less accurate for highly fluctuating conditions
Fuzzy logic models	Uses fuzzy logic to manage uncertainties in wind predictions	Flexible, good for handling data with uncertainties	May lack precision compared to other methods

4.6 Machine Learning Approaches

4.6.1 Regression Models

Regression models are used to predict a continuous dependent variable based on one or more independent variables. These models are fundamental in statistical analysis and machine learning for tasks such as forecasting, risk assessment, and optimization. Below are some common types of regression models (Table 4.3).

4.6.2 Classification Models

Classification models are a subset of machine learning algorithms that are used to categorize data into predefined classes or categories. They are widely used in various fields such as healthcare, finance, marketing, and renewable energy. Here's an overview of the main types of classification models (Table 4.4):

Table 4.3 Some common types of regression models.

Model	Type	Use case	Description	Advantages	Disadvantages
Linear regression	Linear model	Continuous output	Predicts a continuous target variable based on a linear relationship with one or more independent variables.	Simple, interpretable, fast to train, works well for linearly separable data.	Assumes linearity, sensitive to outliers, not suitable for complex relationships.
Polynomial regression	Linear model	Continuous output	Extends linear regression by modeling the relationship as an n-degree polynomial.	Can model non-linear relationships, flexible in fitting curves.	Prone to overfitting, especially with high-degree polynomials, difficult to interpret.
Ridge regression	Linear model	Continuous output	A linear regression model that includes an L2 regularization term to prevent overfitting by penalizing large coefficients.	Reduces model complexity, improves generalization, useful when multicollinearity exists.	Does not perform variable selection, coefficients are biased.

(Continued)

Table 4.3 Some common types of regression models. (*Continued*)

Model	Type	Use case	Description	Advantages	Disadvantages
Lasso regression	Linear model	Continuous output	Adds a penalty for the absolute values of coefficients, resulting in sparse models where some coefficients can be zero.	Performs variable selection, useful for high-dimensional data.	May eliminate too many variables, especially in correlated datasets.
Elastic net regression	Linear model	Continuous output	Combines L1 and L2 regularization to balance between ridge and lasso regression.	Retains benefits of both lasso and ridge, useful for highly correlated variables.	More complex to tune, requires careful selection of mixing parameter.
Logistic regression	Linear model	Binary classification	Used for binary classification, predicting the probability of a binary outcome.	Simple and interpretable, can be extended to multiple classes.	Not suitable for non-linear relationships without modifications.
Stepwise regression	Linear model	Continuous output	Selects the best set of variables for the model by adding or removing predictors based on statistical criteria.	Automates feature selection, can lead to simpler models.	May lead to overfitting, sensitive to data variations.

(*Continued*)

Table 4.3 Some common types of regression models. (*Continued*)

Model	Type	Use case	Description	Advantages	Disadvantages
Quantile regression	Linear model	Continuous output	Estimates the conditional quantiles of the dependent variable, providing a more comprehensive view than mean predictions.	Offers insights into the distribution of the outcome variable, robust to outliers.	More complex interpretation, requires more computation.
Bayesian regression	Probabilistic model	Continuous output	Incorporates prior distributions and updates the model as more data becomes available.	Incorporates uncertainty, flexible modeling, can be robust to small sample sizes.	Requires careful selection of priors, computationally intensive for complex models.
Support vector regression (SVR)	Non-linear model	Continuous output	Uses support vector machines to predict continuous outcomes, aiming to minimize prediction error within a certain threshold.	Effective in high-dimensional spaces, robust to outliers.	Memory-intensive, can be slow for large datasets, requires tuning of kernel parameters.

Table 4.4 Overview of the main types of classification models.

Model	Type	Use Case	Description	Advantages	Disadvantages
Logistic regression	Linear model	Binary classification (0/1)	Predicts the probability of a binary outcome using a logistic function.	Simple, interpretable, fast to train, works well for linearly separable data.	Struggles with non-linear relationships, not good for multi-class classification without modification.
Decision trees	Non-parametric	Binary & multi-class	Models decisions based on feature values, splitting data into branches until a decision is reached.	Easy to interpret, handles both numerical and categorical data, requires little data preprocessing.	Prone to overfitting, unstable as small changes in data can alter the tree.
Random forest	Ensemble (Bagging)	Binary & multi-class	An ensemble of decision trees where each tree votes for the class, and the majority vote is taken.	Reduces overfitting, improves accuracy and robustness, works well with large datasets.	Can be slow to train and interpret, requires more computational resources.

(*Continued*)

Table 4.4 Overview of the main types of classification models. (*Continued*)

Model	Type	Use Case	Description	Advantages	Disadvantages
Support vector machine (SVM)	Non-probabilistic linear/ non-linear	Binary & multi-class	Finds a hyperplane that best separates classes. It can use different kernel functions to handle non-linear data.	Effective for high-dimensional spaces, handles non-linear boundaries with the kernel trick.	Memory-intensive, slow for large datasets, difficult to interpret.
K-nearest neighbors (KNN)	Instance-based	Binary & multi-class	Classifies a data point based on the majority class of its neighbors within a defined distance.	Simple to implement, works well with small datasets, non-parametric.	Computationally expensive for large datasets, sensitive to the choice of "k", poor with imbalanced data.
Naive Bayes	Probabilistic model	Binary & multi-class	Based on Bayes' Theorem, it assumes independence between features, and calculates the probability of each class.	Fast to train and predict, works well with high-dimensional data, handles missing data.	Assumes independence between features, not ideal for datasets with correlated features.
Artificial neural networks (ANN)	Non-linear model	Binary & multi-class	Inspired by biological neurons, ANNs consist of layers of neurons that can learn complex non-linear relationships in data.	Handles large and complex datasets, adaptable to different types of data (text, images, etc.).	Requires large datasets and high computational power, difficult to interpret.

4.6.3 Neural Networks

Machine learning algorithms that are designed to identify pattern and find complex solutions by imitating human brain mechanisms are known as neural networks. The networks are composed of many nodes (neurons), organized in a set of layers, one of them being the input layer, one or more hidden layers, and the output layer, which converts the input information into a sense-making output [40]. A connection is provided with a weight, which is updated in the course of training in a process known as backpropagation and

Table 4.5 Types of neural networks.

Type of neural network	Description	Use cases
Feedforward neural networks (FNNs)	Data flows in one direction from input to output.	Classification, regression tasks.
Convolutional neural networks (CNNs)	Specialized for grid-like data, using convolutional layers.	Image recognition, object detection, spatial pattern analysis.
Recurrent neural networks (RNNs)	Designed for sequential data, with loops for information retention.	Natural language processing, time-series prediction, speech recognition.
Long short-term memory networks (LSTMs)	A type of RNN that addresses vanishing gradient problems.	Language translation, complex sequential tasks, time-series forecasting.
Gated recurrent units (GRUs)	A simpler variant of LSTMs with fewer parameters.	Similar to LSTMs for sequential data processing.
Autoencoders	Learn efficient representations of data for compression and feature learning.	Anomaly detection, image compression, denoising.
Generative adversarial networks (GANs)	Consist of a generator and discriminator for generating new data.	Image generation, video synthesis, data augmentation.

reduces the difference between predicted and actual outcomes. The activation functions add non-linearity, which allows the model to acquire complex patterns. The neural networks can find use in many areas including image and speech recognition, natural language processing, and energy prediction [41]. They are also computationally expensive and also may run to overfit without appropriate regularization, even though they have strong performance, thus they are sensitive and need careful design and tuning to attain optical performance describe in Table 4.5.

4.6.4 Ensemble Methods

Ensemble methods are machine learning models that use many models to enhance predictive performance and accuracy. Ensemble methods minimize errors and increase robustness by using the strength of different algorithms [42]. Similar methods are bagging (e.g., Random forests), which trains many models on varying repetitions of the data, and boosting (e.g., AdaBoost, XGBoost), which trains more models and targets correcting the errors of other models. Stacking involves using a combination of several base models to produce a final prediction using a meta-learner. Ensemble techniques are common in both classification and regression tasks and in most cases they perform better in accuracy and generalization than individual models. Different types of ensembling techniques are discussed in Table 4.6.

Table 4.6 Types of ensembling.

Technique	Description	Model combination method	Example
Bagging	Involves creating multiple subsets of training data through bootstrapping. Each subset trains a separate model.	Predictions are combined by averaging (regression) or majority voting (classification) to reduce variance.	Random forests (multiple decision trees)
Boosting	A sequential method where models are trained one after another, focusing on correcting errors from previous models.	Predictions are combined into a weighted sum, with more weight on better-performing models to reduce bias.	AdaBoost, gradient boosting machines (GBM)

4.6.5 Hybrid Models

Machine learning hybrid models are a combination of two or more modeling techniques that can be used to take advantage of the benefits of each and enhance predictive performance. Hybrid models may be affected to record the intricate patterns and data connections in information that one model would not effectively record. One can make hybrid models in different ways. A popular approach is to use a mixture of responses of two or more models (ensemble learning), e.g., a combination of decision trees and neural networks. The other method is cascading models which are models in which the output of one model is the input of the second model and thus refined predictions can be resulted by continuous studies of the model [43]. Hybrid models are especially successful when it comes to complex fields like finance, medicine, and renewable energy, in which numerous factors need to be taken into account. As an example, a hybrid model may be used for wind energy prediction, combining time-series analysis (such as LSTMs) with regression models to relate to both temporal patterns and underlying relationships. The advantages of hybrid models are better accuracy, strong and generalization. Nonetheless, they too need to be carefully designed and tuned and a larger number of computing resources are needed [44]. The combination of different techniques in modeling can substantially improve the performance of the model in hard to predict problems through the careful application of hybrid models, which should be a great addition to the machine learning toolkit. The combination of machine learning (ML) methods with physical models forms hybrid models that can combine the power of both data-driven and physical models [45]. This integrated approach is especially effective in such areas as renewable energy, environmental science, and engineering as complex systems, whose rules are dictated by the laws of physics.

4.7 Wind Energy Prediction Methods vs. Machine Learning Approaches for Wind Farm Site Selection

The Table 4.7 compares traditional wind energy prediction methods and machine learning approaches in the context of wind farm site selection, highlighting key aspects of both methodologies.

In the context of wind farm site selection, machine learning models may offer a more adaptive and cost-effective solution, especially for regions with complex terrain or rapidly changing conditions. Traditional models remain valuable for large-scale and highly precise site evaluations. Table 4.7 shows the comparison of traditional wind energy prediction methods and machine learning approaches.

Table 4.7 Comparison of traditional wind energy prediction methods and machine learning approaches.

Aspect	Traditional methods	Machine learning approaches
Data type	Meteorological data (wind speed, direction, terrain data)	Historical data (wind, terrain, meteorology) + additional inputs like land use, environmental factors
Handling of complex terrain	Physical models (e.g., CFD) are capable but computationally expensive	ML can handle complex terrain with fewer resources if trained on diverse data
Prediction method	Uses mathematical equations and physics-based models	Predictive models based on patterns learned from data (e.g., neural networks, random forests)
Computation requirement	High (especially for physical models like NWP and CFD)	Can vary; deep learning models may require high computation, but simple models (e.g., decision trees) are faster
Accuracy	Accurate in well-known conditions but struggles in highly variable environments	Typically more accurate in predicting wind power potential in diverse and complex conditions
Adaptability	Limited to known conditions and assumptions (e.g., boundary conditions)	Highly adaptable to new data and varying conditions with continuous learning

(*Continued*)

Table 4.7 Comparison of traditional wind energy prediction methods and machine learning approaches. (*Continued*)

Aspect	Traditional methods	Machine learning approaches
Handling non-linear relationships	Poor; traditional models struggle with non-linear relationships	Excellent; ML models can capture complex, non-linear interactions between features
Long-term vs. short-term prediction	Better suited for long-term, large-scale predictions	Capable of both long-term and short-term predictions, depending on the model used
Computational time	High, especially for site-specific simulations	Varies; faster models like decision trees, but deep learning can be slower in training
Interpretability	High (physical models are based on well-understood principles)	Lower, complex models (like neural networks) can be seen as "black boxes"
Incorporation of external factors	Limited to physical inputs like wind speed, terrain, and meteorological data	Can easily integrate various external factors (e.g., environmental restrictions, social impact, cost)
Cost efficiency	High initial cost due to computational resources for simulations	Cost-effective over time, especially with pre-trained models on large datasets
Scalability	Limited scalability due to computational expense for each site	Highly scalable; ML models can be applied across multiple sites once trained
Examples of techniques	Numerical Weather Prediction (NWP)	Examples of techniques

Here's comparative Table 4.8 which shows regression, classification, neural networks, and hybrid models in the context of wind turbine energy prediction:

Table 4.8 Use case of different algorithms in wind energy systems.

Aspect	Regression	Classification	Neural networks	Hybrid models
Objective	Predict continuous outcomes (e.g., wind speed, power output)	Categorize sites into classes (e.g., good, moderate, poor sites)	Predict continuous or categorical outcomes by learning complex patterns	Combine multiple models to improve predictive accuracy
Use case in wind site selection	Used to predict numerical values, such as potential wind energy output at different sites	Used to classify potential sites based on suitability (e.g., high, medium, low potential)	Can be used for both regression and classification, capturing non-linear and complex relationships	Combines regression, classification, or neural networks with other models for better performance
Complexity	Simple to moderate, based on the type of regression (e.g., linear, polynomial)	Relatively simple; often uses decision trees, k-NN, or logistic regression	High complexity, especially for deep networks with many layers	Varies; complexity depends on the types of models being combined
Accuracy	Moderate, dependent on data quality and linearity of relationships	Moderate, typically good for clear separations between classes	High accuracy, especially with large, complex datasets and deep networks	Very high, as it combines strengths of different models
Computation	Low to moderate computational cost	Low computational cost for simple classification methods	High computational cost, especially for deep learning models	High, due to the combination of multiple models
Handling of non-linear relationships	Limited; works best with linear relationships between input features and output	Limited; simple classifiers struggle with non-linear relationships	Excellent; neural networks are highly effective at capturing non-linear patterns	Very good; hybrid models often combine linear and non-linear models

(Continued)

Table 4.8 Use case of different algorithms in wind energy systems. (*Continued*)

Aspect	Regression	Classification	Neural networks	Hybrid models
Interpretability	High (especially with simple linear models)	High interpretability for simple models (e.g., decision trees)	Low; neural networks are often "black boxes"	Moderate to low, depending on the combination of models used
Adaptability to new data	Limited; traditional regression models are not easily adaptable without retraining	Moderate; may need retraining for significant new data	High; can learn from new data and continuously improve	High; hybrid models can adapt by combining models tuned for different scenarios
Handling of multiple inputs	Limited in handling complex, multivariate inputs	Moderate; can handle several features but may struggle with too many	Excellent at handling large datasets with many features	Excellent; different models can handle different types of data inputs
Examples of techniques	Linear regression, polynomial regression	Decision trees, k-Nearest Neighbors (k-NN), logistic regression	Artificial neural networks (ANN), convolutional neural networks (CNN), recurrent neural networks (RNN)	Regression + classification models, ensemble methods (e.g., random forest + neural networks)
Data requirements	Requires historical wind data, terrain information, etc.	Requires labeled data with site categories	Requires large datasets for training and capturing complex patterns	Requires both labeled and unlabeled data, combining various datasets
Scalability	Highly scalable with simple models	Highly scalable with simple classification models	Less scalable due to high computational needs for training	Scalability depends on the combination of models and computational resources
Examples in wind energy	Predicting wind speed or power output at specific locations	Categorizing locations as high, medium, or low potential for wind farms	Predicting wind energy potential with complex terrain and weather patterns	Combining regression for energy prediction with classification for site categorization

When considering wind turbine energy prediction, each model—regression, classification, neural networks, and hybrid models have their own strengths and difficulties, based on the complexity of the data and the specific objectives of the analysis in particular. Table 4.8 shows the use case of different algorithms in wind energy systems.

- Regression models are very useful when it is required to predict continuous variables such as wind speed or energy output. They are easy to understand and apply, especially in the case of linear relationships or those which are non-linear to a limited extent. Their simplicity however comes as a constraint under complex, non-linear patterns in the data, e.g. changing wind speed or varying terrain conditions. These models are also deficient of flexibility because they require retraining in the event of new factors or alteration in the environment.
- Classification models, in their turn, are very good at grouping wind turbine sites into distinct classes (e.g., high, medium, or low potential). The models are relatively efficient in computation and are relatively easy to train, making rapid site ranking decisions. Nevertheless, they might not manage more sophisticated or grained site evaluations in case sophisticated classification methods are used.
- Neural Networks are also unique in their capability to model non-linear and complicated relationship among several variables, which makes them best to select sites of wind turbines in complex and dynamic conditions. Neural networks have the capacity of handling very large volumes of data across time e.g. wind speed, terrain, and environmental factors among others thus they are a very powerful tool in prediction as well as in classification. Their relatively high cost of computation and inability to be interpreted (usually regarded as a black box) can be a major disadvantage however, particularly in the smaller scale.
- Hybrid Models provide an elaborate way as they integrate the advantages of various methods. Combining any of the three methods, regression, classification, and neural network, hybrid models can be more accurate and flexible, particularly in the adverse conditions. They balance between linear and non-linear relationships well and can better adjust to the evolving data trends. Complexity of hybrid models however adds to their cost in computation and may complicate their interpretation.

In general, regression can be applied to a simpler and more predictable environment, classification is efficient in quick categorization, neural networks are efficient in dealing with complex patterns, and hybrid models have the best of all worlds, but they demand large resources to be operated in practice.

4.8 Case Studies and Real-World Applications

DeepMind and Google Wind Energy Project (2019): One of the most well-established examples of AI in wind energy the project of Google along with DeepMind. Machine learning algorithms were used in the prediction of the wind power production 36 hours ahead of time at the wind farms owned by Google in the US. Artificial intelligence system enabled the more effective incorporation of wind energy into the grid by improving the through the enhancement of the prediction and forecasting of energy production forecasts. The outcome was the performance of wind farms increased by 20 percent [46].

Xcel Energy and National Renewable Energy Laboratory (NREL) Partnership Xcel Energy together with NREL, optimized the positioning of wind turbines and the power generation through the application of machine learning techniques. The project implemented algorithms on previous and real-time data, including weather conditions, turbine work, and grid factors, to enhance the overall energy performance and decreased the costs of operation. It enhanced predictions by 50 of the old techniques in energy output [47].

Having an AI-powered predictive maintenance system on wind turbines Vision Energy, which is a major manufacturer of wind turbines, established AI-powered predictive maintenance systems on their wind turbines. Through sensor data analysis, such as vibration, temperature and operation data, AI algorithms identify possible faults and forecast any maintenance requirements before a failure. This is proactive measure which ensures the minimization of down time and reduced maintenance expenses resulting to improved reliability in its operations [48].

Siemens Gamesa Inspection of wind turbines with AI: Siemens Gamesa, one of the representatives of the renewable energy market, implemented an AI-based drone-based inspection of wind turbines. Such drones take high-resolution photos of the turbine blades, and the photos are examined by AI to identify cracks, corrosion, and other damages. This process refers to automated inspection instead of manual inspection hence saves time, cost and improves accuracy in defects detection [49].

E.ON Climate & Renewables: E.ON is a European utility firms that uses AI in the operations of wind farms to optimize the settings of the turbines. The AI-powered software actively changes the angles of the blade and a turbine configuration and changes them depending on wind changes. This can capture a lot of energy and lessen the wear of the turbines, which enhances efficiency by up to 5 percent [50].

Hybrid Approach to Energy Forecasting DNV GL created a hybrid AI model, which is a machine learning model that leverages physical models to enhance the accuracy of wind energy forecasting. This model combines weather forecasts with performance forecasts that are specific to the turbines to give more precise predictions regarding the wind farms. The hybrid system is especially useful in large wind farms that are located in different geographical areas [51].

4.9 AI-Driven Maintenance at General Electric (GE)

General Electric (GE) has integrated AI-driven predictive maintenance in its wind turbine operations, leveraging deep learning (DL) models and sensor data to ensure the smooth functioning of its wind farms. GE's AI system monitors a wide range of parameters collected through sensors installed in the turbines, including vibration, temperature, humidity, and operational data, which are analyzed in real time. The DL models, trained on historical and real-time data, identify patterns that may indicate potential failures or performance degradation. By detecting early signs of wear or malfunction, the system can predict when a component is likely to fail, allowing maintenance teams to take proactive measures before serious damage occurs. This predictive maintenance approach results in:

- **Reduced Downtime**: By preventing unexpected failures, GE minimizes the time turbines are offline, ensuring continuous energy generation.
- **Lower Maintenance Costs**: Scheduled maintenance can be optimized, avoiding unnecessary repairs while also preventing costly emergency fixes.
- **Increased Operational Efficiency**: Continuous monitoring and optimization ensure turbines operate at peak efficiency, increasing overall energy output.
- **Extended Turbine Lifespan**: By addressing issues before they escalate, the lifespan of key turbine components is prolonged, reducing the need for frequent replacements.

One of the key benefits of GE's AI-driven approach is its scalability across multiple wind farms. The system's ability to process vast amounts of data from different turbine models and environmental conditions makes it highly adaptable. As a result, GE's wind farms worldwide benefit from enhanced operational reliability and improved cost-efficiency, setting a new standard for maintenance practices in the wind energy industry.

4.10 Future Trends in AI for Wind Energy

The future of AI in wind energy systems is very promising and improvements are likely to make the system more efficient, reliable and cost effective. The main spheres of development are:

- **Advanced Forecasting Models** It is probable that the next generation of machine learning (ML) and deep learning (DL) models will aim at enhancing accuracy of wind energy forecasting. Such models will be in a position to deal with more complex weather conditions including abrupt shifts in wind velocity, turbulence in addition to severe weather conditions. These systems can greatly enhance predictions by using larger datasets, future meteorological models, and real-time data feeds which enables the integration of energy grid and planning.
- **Edge AI** Edge AI is the implementation of AI algorithms directly on hardware, e.g., on the controller of a turbine instead of using a centralized cloud system. The technology will facilitate real-time decision-making and optimization at the turbine level, which will mean that changes in the blade angles, power output, and turbine setting are responded faster to changes in the immediate environmental condition. Edge AI will minimize the latency, enhance reliability, and collaborate with the necessity of constant communication with clouds which will make wind farms more independent and effective.
- **AI and IoT Integration** AI integration with the Internet of Things (IoT) will advance the wind energy systems to a whole new level of accuracy and control. As IoT sensors track the entire turbine performance, AI will turn this piece of data into granular data to optimize all the operations in a whole wind farm. This degree of monitoring will allow a more accurate

process of fault identification, predictive maintenance, and optimization of output of energy. Also, AI-based analytics will be able to feed real-time feedback and changes on per turbine and farm-wide to ensure optimal performance.

- **Artificial Intelligence in Offshore Wind Energy** The offshore wind power is becoming popular because of the stronger and high-density winds found in oceans. Nevertheless, offshore wind farms are not free of their own peculiarities, including more terrible weather conditions, inaccessibility, and high cost of maintenance. The AI will be instrumental in streamlining offshore operations through better predictions of energy outputs, the use of drones and robotics to perform inspections, and better predictive maintenance services. AI will be necessary to minimize the cost of operation and maximize energy generation as the scale and sophistication of offshore wind farms increases.

Additional Trends to Watch:

- Autonomous Wind Farm Operations: AI has the potential to create fully autonomous wind farms, where wind turbines-optimize their functions independently, drones do inspection, and automated ships do maintenance in the offshore area.
- Hybrid Renewable Energy Systems: Hybrid systems will be the future of wind energy with solar or energy storage technologies that make use of AI. AI algorithms are able to adjust the production of these systems so the power supply is more reliable and constant.
- AI-Powered Microgrids: Microgrids that combine wind power will apply AI to serve energy locally, which will guarantee the maximum utilization of the renewable energy in smaller communities or factories.
- Energy Trading & Blockchain: AI can be used together with blockchain to farm real-time energy trading based on the predictive modeling of wind energy generation, and make decentralized.

These tendencies indicate the radical capabilities of AI in the wind energy industry, facilitating the advancement of forecasting, repairing, and optimization, all, in favor of the inclusion of renewable energy into the world grid.

4.11 Conclusion

Artificial Intelligence in wind energy systems is already a game-changer and the systems provide a greater predictability, operational efficiencies, and cost-saving. Along with the development of AI technologies, they will find more and more application in the field of wind energy, which will result in increased sustainability and scalability in the sphere of renewable energy. The introduction of AI into each part of the wind industry, including the selection of the site and real-time control of turbines will allow the industry to overcome the present stalemate and keep expanding as a crucial element of the global energy portfolio. The chapter gives an in-depth account of the high aspect of AI in enhancing the performance of wind energy systems and sheds light on the existing methods, practice, and opportunities in the field.

AI disclosure statement: The author acknowledges the use of AI-based tools for minor language editing or grammatical correction. However, all intellectual contributions, analyses, and conclusions presented in this chapter are entirely the author's own.

References

1. Spiru, P., Assessment of renewable energy generated by a hybrid system based on wind, hydro, solar, and biomass sources for decarbonizing the energy sector and achieving a sustainable energy transition. *Energy Rep.*, 9, 167–174, 2023, doi: 10.1016/j.egyr.2023.04.316.
2. Haq, I.U., Rather, A.H., Kaur, G., A Comparative Analysis of Machine Learning Algorithms for the Early Prediction of Cardiovascular Disease, in: *2023 2nd International Conference on Edge Computing and Applications (ICECAA)*, IEEE, pp. 987–993, 2023, July.
3. Huang, J., *et al.*, Optimal substation capacity planning method in high-density load areas considering renewable energy. *Energy Rep.*, 9, 1520–1530, 2023, doi: 10.1016/j.egyr.2023.04.104.
4. Feng, Y., Xiao, Z., Zhou, J., Ni, G., Asymmetrically examining the impact of green finance and renewable energy consumption on environmental degradation and renewable energy investment: The impact of the COVID-19 outbreak on the Chinese economy. *Energy Rep.*, 9, 5458–5472, 2023, doi: 10.1016/j.egyr.2023.04.361.
5. Wei, X., Liu, D., Ye, S., Chen, F., Weng, J., Optimal sizing of energy storage in generation expansion planning of new power system with high penetration

of renewable energies. *Energy Rep.*, 9, 1938–1947, 2023, doi: 10.1016/j.egyr.2023.04.190.

6. Hou, H., Wang, Z., Hou, T., Fang, R., Tang, J., Xie, C., Optimal schedule of 100% renewable energy microgrid considering demand response of EVs. *Energy Rep.*, 9, 1743–1750, 2023, doi: 10.1016/j.egyr.2023.04.223.
7. Haq, I.U., Hassan, I.U., Shah, H.A., Machine Learning Techniques for Result Prediction of One Day International (ODI) Cricket Match, in: *2023 IEEE 8th International Conference for Convergence in Technology (I2CT)*, IEEE, pp. 1–5, 2023, April.
8. Kwakwa, P.A., Research in Globalization Sectoral growth and carbon dioxide emission in Africa: can renewable energy mitigate the effect? *Res. Glob.*, 6, April, 100130, 2023, doi: 10.1016/j.resglo.2023.100130.
9. Dai, W., *et al.*, Flexibility-enhanced strategies of generations to improve the integration of renewable energy considering uncertainties. *Energy Rep.*, 9, 1717–1725, 2023, doi: 10.1016/j.egyr.2023.04.204.
10. Yolcan, O.O., Innovation and Green Development World energy outlook and state of renewable energy: 10-Year evaluation. *Innov. Green Dev.*, 2, 4, 100070, 2023, doi: 10.1016/j.igd.2023.100070.
11. Li, R., Wang, Q., Han, X., Yang, X., Trajectory and drivers of China's consumption-based and production-based renewable energy consumption. *Energy Strategy Rev.*, 47, 72104246, 101083, 2023, doi: 10.1016/j.esr.2023.101083.
12. Choudhary, C., Thakur, J., Bhardwaj, H., Haq, I.U., Rather, A.H., Revolutionizing Wind Energy: A Enhanced Machine Learning Perspective on Wind Turbines Fault Prediction, in: *2023 2nd International Conference on Automation, Computing and Renewable Systems (ICACRS)*, IEEE, pp. 1763–1769, 2023, December.
13. Cavaiola, M., Enos, P., Ferrari, F., Casciaro, G., Mazzino, A., Energy and AI Ensemble Machine Learning greatly improves ERA5 skills for wind energy applications. *Energy AI*, 100269, May 2023, doi: 10.1016/j.egyai.2023.100269.
14. Choudhary, C., Haq, I.U., Rather, A.H., Utilizing Dynamic QR Codes to Enhance Secure Payment Transactions: An Approach to Secure Computer based Transactions, in: *2023 International Conference on Communication, Security and Artificial Intelligence (ICCSAI)*, IEEE, pp. 552–557, 2023, November.
15. Spielhofer, R., Schwaab, J., Grêt-Regamey, A., How spatial policies can leverage energy transitions – Finding Pareto-optimal solutions for wind turbine locations with evolutionary multi-objective optimization. *Environ. Sci. Policy*, 142, January, 220–232, 2023, doi: 10.1016/j.envsci.2023.02.016.
16. Fournier, A., Martinez, A., Iglesias, G., Impacts of climate change on wind energy potential in Australasia and South-East Asia following the Shared Socioeconomic Pathways. *Sci. Total Environ.*, 882, January, 163347, 2023. doi 10.1016/j.scitotenv.2023.163347.
17. Vallejo Díaz, A., Herrera Moya, I., Pereyra Mariñez, C., Garabitos Lara, E., Casilla Victorino, C., Key factors influencing urban wind energy: A case

study from the Dominican Republic. *Energy Sustain. Dev.*, 73, December 2022, 165–173, 2023. doi 10.1016/j.esd.2023.01.017.
18. Ulazia, A., Sáenz, J., Saenz-Aguirre, A., Ibarra-Berastegui, G., Carreno-Madinabeitia, S., Paradigmatic case of long-term colocated wind–wave energy index trend in the Canary Islands. *Energy Convers. Manag.*, 283, March, 116890, 2023, doi: 10.1016/j.enconman.2023.116890.
19. Dugstad, A., Grimsrud, K., Kipperberg, G., Lindhjem, H., Navrud, S., Energy Research & Social Science Place attachment and preferences for wind energy – A value-based approach. *Energy Res. Soc. Sci.*, 100, May, 103094, 2023. doi 10.1016/j.erss.2023.103094.
20. Karakislak, I. and Schneider, N., The mayor said so? The impact of local political figures and social norms on local responses to wind energy projects. *Energy Policy*, 176, January, 113509, 2023, doi: 10.1016/j.enpol.2023.113509.
21. Rather, A.H. and Haq, I.U., Intelligent Framework for Early Prediction of Diabetic Retinopathy: A Deep Learning Approach, in: *International Conference on Paradigms of Communication, Computing and Data Analytics*, Singapore: Springer Nature Singapore, pp. 377–388, 2023, April.
22. Rangel-Martinez, D., Nigam, K.D.P., Ricardez-Sandoval, L.A., Machine learning on sustainable energy: A review and outlook on renewable energy systems, catalysis, smart grid and energy storage. *Chem. Eng. Res. Des.*, 174, 414–441, 2021, doi: 10.1016/j.cherd.2021.08.013.
23. Fister, D., Pérez-Aracil, J., Peláez-Rodríguez, C., Del Ser, J., Salcedo-Sanz, S., Accurate long-term air temperature prediction with Machine Learning models and data reduction techniques. *Appl. Soft Comput.*, 136, 110118, 2023, doi: 10.1016/j.asoc.2023.110118.
24. Wang, H., Li, Y., Xiong, M., Chen, H., A combined wind speed prediction model based on data processing, multi-objective optimization and machine learning. *Energy Rep.*, 9, 413–421, 2023, doi: 10.1016/j.egyr.2023.04.326.
25. Sun, H. and Grishman, R., Lexicalized dependency paths based supervised learning for relation extraction. *Comput. Syst. Sci. Eng.*, 43, 3, 861–870, 2022.
26. Haq, I.U., Kaur, G., Rather, A.H., Fruit Leaf Classification Using Transfer Learning for Automation and Industrial Applications. *Deep Learning Techniques Automation Industrial Applications*, 151–178, 2024.
27. Yildiz, C., Acikgoz, H., Korkmaz, D., Budak, U., An improved residual-based convolutional neural network for very short-term wind power forecasting. *Energy Convers. Manage.*, 228, 113731, 1–15, 2021.
28. Sun, Z. and Zhao, M., Short-term wind power forecasting based on VMD decomposition, ConvLSTM networks and error analysis. *IEEE Access*, 8, 134422–134434, 2020.
29. L. -L. Li, Zhao, X., Tseng, M.-L., Tan, R.R., Short-term wind power forecasting based on support vector machine with improved dragonfly algorithm. *J. Cleaner Prod.*, 242, 118447, 1–12, 2020.

30. Yin, H., Ou, Z., Fu, J., Cai, Y., Chen, S., *et al.*, A novel transfer learning approach for wind power prediction based on a serio-parallel deep learning architecture. *Energy*, 234, 121271, 1–16, 2021.
31. Buturache, A.-N. and Stancu, S., Wind energy prediction using machine learning. *Low Carbon Econ.*, 12, 1, 1–21, 2021.
32. Wu, Q., Guan, F., Lv, C., Huang, Y., Ultra-short-term multi-step wind power forecasting based on CNNLSTM. *IET Renewable Power Gener.*, 15, 5, 1019–1029, 2021.
33. Li, N., He, F., Ma, W., Wind power prediction based on extreme learning machine with kernel mean P-power error loss. *Energies*, 12, 673, 1–19, 2019.
34. Chen, G., Li, L., Zhang, Z., Li, S., Short-term wind speed forecasting with principle-subordinate predictor based on Conv-LSTM and improved BPNN. *IEEE Access*, 8, 67955–67973, 2020.
35. Hong, Y.-Y. and Rioflorido, C.L.P.P., A hybrid deep learning-based neural network for 24-h ahead wind power forecasting. *Appl. Energy*, 250, 530–539, 2019.
36. Ravi, V.K., Mishra, S.P., Naik, J., Dash, P.K., Adaptive VMD based optimized deep learning mixed kernel ELM autoencoder for single and multistep wind power forecasting. *Energy*, 244, 122585, 1–29, 2022.
37. Alkesaiberi, A., Harrou, F., Sun, Y., Efficient wind power prediction using machine learning methods: A comparative study. *Energies*, 15, 2327, 1–24, 2022.
38. Cerna, P.D., Evangelista, R.S., Castillo, C.M., Muallam-Darkis, J.A., Velasco, M.A.C., Legaspi, J.P., ... & Gatdula, M.M., Wind Power Plant Site Selection using Integrated Machine Learning and Multiple-Criteria Decision Making Technique, in: *E3S Web of Conferences*, vol. 405, p. 02030, EDP Sciences, 2023.
39. Bilgili, A., Arda, T., Kilic, B., Explainability in wind farm planning: A machine learning framework for automatic site selection of wind farms. *Energy Convers. Manage.*, 309, 118441, 2024. ISSN 0196-8904, https://doi.org/10.1016/j.enconman.2024.118441.
40. Asadi, M., Pourhossein, K., Mohammadi-Ivatloo, B., GIS-assisted modeling of wind farm site selection based on support vector regression. *J. Cleaner Prod.*, https://doi.org/10.1016/j.jclepro.2023.135993.
41. Hassan, I.U., Shah, H.A., Hafiz, A., Haq, I.U., Novel technique for malicious node detection in wireless sensor networks. *Recent Trends Comput. Sci.*, pp, 231–237, CRC Press, 2024.
42. Nisar, A. and Monroy, C.R., Potential of the renewable energy development in Jammu and Kashmir, India. *Renewable Sustainable Energy Rev.*, 16, 7, 5260–5267, 2012.
43. Garla, N., Haq, I.U., Dhiman, H., Revolutionizing Biomedical Engineering With Quantum Computing and AI, in: *Quantum Innovations at the Nexus of Biomedical Intelligence*, pp. 206–222, IGI Global, 2024.

44. Liyakat, S., Kutubuddin, K., Magadum, P.K., Machine Learning for Predicting Wind Turbine Output Power in Wind Energy Conversion Systems. *Grenze Int. J. Eng. Technol. (GIJET)*, 10, 2024.
45. Karaman, Ö.A., Prediction of wind power with machine learning models. *Appl. Sci.*, 13, 20, 11455, 2023.
46. Newman, N., AI-energy's untapped resource [artificial intelligence in the energy industry]. *Eng. Technol.*, 14, 7, 66–69, 2019.
47. Parks, K., Wan, Y.H., Wiener, G., Liu, Y., Wind energy forecasting: A collaboration of the National Center for Atmospheric Research (NCAR) and Xcel Energy (No. NREL/SR-5500-52233). National Renewable Energy Lab. (NREL), Golden, CO (United States), 2011.
48. Veers, P., Bottasso, C. L., Manuel, L., Naughton, J., Pao, L., Paquette, J., ... & Rinker, J., Grand challenges in the design, manufacture, and operation of future wind turbine systems. *Wind Energy Sci.*, 8, 7, 1071–1131, 2023.
49. Meyers, J., Bottasso, C., Dykes, K., Fleming, P., Gebraad, P., Giebel, G., Van Wingerden, J.W., Wind farm flow control: prospects and challenges. *Wind Energy Sci. Discuss.*, 2022, 1–56, 2022.
50. Mitchell, D., Blanche, J., Harper, S., Lim, T., Gupta, R., Zaki, O., Flynn, D., A review: Challenges and opportunities for artificial intelligence and robotics in the offshore wind sector. *Energy AI*, 8, 100146, 2022.
51. Operator, Australian Energy Market. *Multi-Criter. Scoring Identif. Renewable Energy Zones*, 2018.

5

Role of AI Generative in Renewable Energy and Conservation of the Environment

Lata Rani[1], Hurmat[1], Neha Kanojia[1], Arun Lal Srivastav[2] and Jyotsna Kaushal[3,4]*

[1]*Chitkara University School of Pharmacy, Chitkara University, Himachal Pradesh, India*
[2]*Chitkara University School of Engineering and Technology, Chitkara University, Himachal Pradesh, India*
[3]*Chitkara University Institute of Engineering and Technology, Chitkara University, Rajpur, Punjab, India*
[4]*Centre for Water Sciences, Chitkara College of Pharmacy, Chitkara University, Rajpura, Punjab, India*

Abstract

The global transition to sustainable energy sources has lead to a remarkable growth in the integration of renewable energy systems (RES) into existing power networks. Now, it is by through the mutual application of artificial intelligence (AI) methodologies. The aim of the present study to provide the overview of current state of research at the intersection of AI and RE, emphasizing key methodologies, challenges, and accomplishments. Further discussed, including system monitoring, grid integration, energy forecasting, control methods, and resource assessment. This chapter also discussed the challenges of implementing AI in RES, including data variability, model interpretability, and real-time adaptation. Overcoming these challenges may have reimbursements, including reducing operational costs, improving grid stability, and increasing yield of energy. Additionally, the report projects the development of autonomous energy systems, autonomous energy management systems, and smart grids with AI-powered solutions. This chapter provides an overview of the current status of artificial intelligence (AI) applications in renewable energy systems (RES).

***Keywords*:** Energy, AI, role, environment, sustainability

**Corresponding author*: jyotsna.Kaushal@chitkarauniversity.edu.in

Abhishek Kumar, Pramod Singh Rathore, Arun Lal Srivastav and Ashutosh Kumar Dubey (eds.) Solar Energy Optimization Using Generative Artificial Intelligence, (99–122) © 2026 Scrivener Publishing LLC

Introduction

RE plays a significant role in the worldwide effort to minimize releases of greenhouse gases and advance the cause of sustainable development. The significance of RE can be demonstrated by the increase in investment and utilization over the past few decades. The global total utilization of RE, excluding hydroelectricity, surged by more than 350% between 2006 and 2016, with expenses increasing from US$47 billion in 2004 to US$279.8 billion in 2017 [1]. The growing awareness of RE's potential to accelerate economic growth and mitigate climate change is the reason for this remarkable expansion. The connection between economic growth and the consumption of RE has been the subject of several studies. Although some data suggest no statistically noteworthy association, empirical study frequently finds an optimistic correlation between real GDP and the consumption of RE [2]. This illustrates the complex associations between economic performance and the use of renewable energy, suggesting that the implementation of RE may both cause and be a result of economic growth. For countries like Turkey, relying on RE is not only environmentally favorable but also strategically and economically significant. To reduce its dependency on foreign fossil fuels for the manufacture of electricity and to mitigate the adverse environmental and health impacts of thermal power plants, Turkey has transitioned to RE [3]. An excellent illustration of the various benefits of RE, including its tactical, financial, and environmental elements, is Turkey's transition to renewable energy.

The generation of RE accelerates from several sources, such as photovoltaics, solar, and wind, to lessen the pollution caused by fossil fuels, administrative frameworks, and legislation, and the reason behind this is to reduce the release of greenhouse gases [4]. As the sources of RE could be replenished by nature itself at a rate that is equal to or even more rapid than their rate of consumption, they offer a sustainable alternative to conventional sources of energy. These sources possessed inherent renewability and environmental advantages, like lessening the emission of greenhouse gases and air pollution, and played a significant role in a global endeavor to contest climate change and promote sustainable development [5]. Hence, the significance of RE in the current scenario cannot be overstated. Now, the public is becoming more aware of how the emission of greenhouse gases reduces and accelerates economic growth, declines dependence on imported fossil fuels, and supports sustainable development. Novel approaches such as smart grids expand the possibilities of RE and pave the way for more trustworthy, effective, and sustainable energy systems. In a time of supreme technical improvement, AI is growing increasingly important in tackling the most pressing global issues [6]. In order to combat climate change and maintain life on our planet, the solution to this problem is to find out the sources of energy that are environmentally friendly [7]. The birthplace of AI is Ancient Greece and China, a science whose early theories date back to the goal of mimicking human intelligence [8]. In the 20th century, Alan Turing's paper "Computing Machinery and Intelligence" formally recognized AI as a science. In 1956, a summer workshop at Dartmouth College sponsored by the Rockefeller Foundation marked the beginning of AI research. In spite of initial enthusiasm, poor funding and periods of reservations in the discipline result in improvements in natural, machine learning, expert systems, and language processing. The remarkable growth in potent algorithms such as deep learning and computational power is accountable for the outbreak of AI in the 21st century [9]. The tremendous growth in AI led to face recognition software, autonomous cars, robots capable of creating art and poetry, and virtual assistants [10]. The future of AI is bright due to its tremendous power to better the life of the individual in various aspects, like climate change, education, healthcare, and space exploration [11]. Despite possible abuse and moral dilemmas, in the future, AI will play a considerable role in the improvement of humanity. As we explore AI's uncharted territory, it is important to remember its elongated history and engage it with astonishment as well as responsibility to ensure that its development benefits all human beings [12].

The sources of the RE, like wind, water, and solar, have globally changed the energy landscape [13]. Moreover, there are still obstacles standing in the way of a more environmentally conscious future for example the uncertainty of RE sources, smooth grid integration, and the requirement for efficient infrastructure maintenance [14]. AI would improve the performance RE sector by employing its potential in analysis of data, forecasting, and optimization [15]. Fundamentally, the situation of our energy is changing as RE sources, like solar, wind, and water, are gaining tremendous momentum [16]. This shift to a sustainable future, which might lessen the detrimental environmental effects of traditional energy sources, is being driven by a need for energy independence and a growing awareness of environmental challenges.

Furthermore, the uncertainty, the need for smooth grid integration, and efficient infrastructure maintenance make the shift to RE significantly more challenging. Because RE is decentralized and changeable, traditional power networks that were built with traditional sources of energy in mind need to undergo considerable adjustments. To guarantee a smooth integration that can sustain the changing energy landscape, the task is not only in creating new approaches but also in enhancing the current infrastructure [17]. Fortunately, AI has become a potent instrument to tackle these issues and open the door to a future with more dependable and sustainable energy. Novel strategies to overcome the constraints of grid integration and uncertainty are made possible by the convergence of AI and RE. The RE industry may be significantly impacted by utilizing the benefits of AI in data analysis, forecasting, and optimization [19]. A key component of the global initiative to lower emissions of greenhouse gases and promote sustainable development is renewable energy. The increase in investment and utilization over the last few decades exhibits the growing significance of RE. With expenditures rising from US$47 billion in 2004 to US$279.8 billion in 2017, the world's consumption of RE, omitting hydroelectricity, increased by more than 350% between 2006 and 2016 [19]. This remarkable increase is due to growing awareness of RE's ability to slow down climate change and boost economic growth.

The relation between economic growth and the utilization of RE has become a hot topic for innumerable research [18]. While some data suggest no statistically significant correlation, empirical study frequently finds a favorable correlation between real GDP and the use of renewable energy [20]. This illustrates the complex associates between economic growth and the use of RE.

The conception of smart grids has noticeably transformed the RE environment. Smart grids that use advanced digital communication systems enhance the reliability and overall effectiveness of electrical networks through efficient monitoring and control of distributed energy supplies. [21]. By integrating RE sources like solar and wind into the electrical grid, this technology helps to address problems with their intermittency and variability. One example of the way systems are evolving and moving towards more integrated, effective, and sustainable solutions is the usage of smart grid technologies.

The primary forces behind the rising production of RE, especially from varied sources such as wind and solar photovoltaics (PV), are initiatives to decline pollution from fossil fuels, legislative and administrative frameworks, and incentives meant to minimize emissions of greenhouse gas [22]. Because renewable energy sources can naturally renew themselves at a rate that is equal to or quicker than their rate of consumption, they offer a sustainable alternative to conventional energy sources. These sources' intrinsic renewability and environmental benefits, such as reduced air pollution and emissions of greenhouse gases, make them an integral part of the global effort to combat climate change and promote sustainable development. Therefore, the importance of RE in the contemporary world cannot be overstated [23]. Innovative technologies such as smart grids expand the possibilities of renewable energy and pave the way for more reliable, efficient, and sustainable energy systems.

Significant RE sources

Wind, solar, hydro, geothermal, bio, ocean, hydrogen, hybrid, geothermal, and other forms of RE are the significant types of the RE, depending on the source of production and they are discussed below [24–26].

Wind energy

Wind is caused by the Earth's movement and the irregular occurrence of the sun's rays on the surface, which is higher on the equator than the poles [27]. Through the use of windmills and wind turbines, which persuade the kinetic energy of the wind into mechanical energy, the wind has been used as a major energy source for many centuries. Evidence of earlier civilizations can be found in China and Persia (200 BCE), the Netherlands (1300–1875 CE), and the USA (1850–1970) [28]. In Ohio, USA, the first wind turbine with a 12-kW capacity was put in place between 1887 and 1888. In order to meet the need for electricity, many wind turbines with increased capacity were subsequently constructed in many nations.

In a comparable amount of time, there has also been a discernible increase in the installed capacity of wind power in Germany and the USA. It is clear that the installed wind power capacity in the EU increased by 9.96% overall in 2015 as compared to the previous year [29]. Additionally, with an annual growth rate of more than 9%, the yearly installation climbed from 48 GW in 2006 to 141 GW in 2015. In 2014, the Danish National Test Centre in Denmark installed the world's largest wind turbine, the Vestas V161, which is 220 meters in height and 164 meters in diameter. It has a capacity of 8 megawatts. Various review reports provided a thorough summary of research and development in various areas of wind energy, including the resources and applications that are currently available, global policies, current technology [30, 31], environmental impact [32], the influence of climate change storage schemes, monitoring, and error diagnosis [33].

Solar energy

Every living thing on the planet depends on the sun for energy. The radiation of the Sun has been used for several purposes from the ancient time [34].

The earliest known evidence dates back to the 7th century B.C., when sunlight was first used to start fires and then to generate electricity. Unlike the previously discussed active systems, the passive system collects and spreads solar energy within a building without the need for any electrical devices [35]. The following categories are where the development of solar elements in RE for increased quality and efficiency is organized: low energy buildings [39], storage [38], global policy design application [37], and innovative and efficient materials [36].

Geothermal energy

Lava is created when radioactive materials in the Earth gradually decay. A geothermal reservoir, is created when the tectonic plate movement fractures the lava [40]. Geothermal energy is separated into three types based on how the geothermal reservoir generates electricity. Numerous evaluations provide an overview of the research and development in the field of geothermal energy based on the assessment of available resources, the present state of technology and its applications, the advantages and applications, the features and impact on environmental issues, and the legal status of use [41]. Numerous studies also describe geothermal energy modeling. A range of the total number of geothermal energy-related research publications that were published between 1945 and 2014.

Hydro energy

Hydro energy is a method of producing electricity by harnessing the regulated or natural flow of water, such as a waterfall or an artificial barrier on a river [42]. Hydropower plants were divided into three primary categories based on their electric generation capacity. The growth of research in the sector of hydro energy is summarized in numerous reviews. Particular attention has been given to storage facilities and their operational constraints, reservoir management practices, and slit erosion control approaches in hydro turbines, all of which are critical for efficient hydrokinetic energy conversion and the development of small-scale hydropower systems [43]. Research on hydropower plants in developing nations such as Nepal has focused on socio-technical constraints, environmental preservation through mathematical modeling, and strategies to reduce the accumulation of methylmercury in hydropower reservoirs.

Ocean energy

Ocean energy is a subset of hydro energy, which uses the sea's mechanical energy to generate electricity in three different ways: (i) waves, (ii) tides, and (iii) sea thermal energy [44]. Ocean energy research and development is summed up in a number of review reports, particularly the wave and tidal energy review [45], the financial side of wave energy transformation approach development and problems [46], and future visions modeling.

Bioenergy

The bioenergy is produced applying various sources including microorganism, wood, waste produced from the agriculture, organic wastes, agricultural, algae, vegetable oils, etc. [47]. There are lots studies which revels the tremendous growth in the field of production of bioenergy, particularly consumption of bio-ethanol [48]. Recent research in bioenergy includes the use of microalgae for biodiesel production and its practical applications [49], microbial fuel cells for energy generation [50], bioconversion of organic substrates into bioenergy, biomass pyrolysis for the production of bio-oil, and studies addressing logistical challenges in biomass-based energy generation [51]. Bio-refineries status of bioenergy in EU [52], future of the global bioenergy.

Hydrogen energy

Hydrogen is a necessary component of all fuel products (hydrocarbons), and it is separated from the others for their separate uses. In addition, the biological processes of bacteria and algae, as well as the electrolysis of water, release hydrogen, which, when burned, produces a lot of energy and is utilized as a renewable energy source to generate electricity [53]. For the latter, fuel cells are frequently utilized. One of the drawbacks of wind and solar energy-based renewable energy systems is that they cannot continuously meet the demand for electricity. Several review publications provide an overview of the most important research and development findings in the field of hydrogen energy, primarily the current state of photogeneration of hydrogen, which influences the production of hydrogen [54], the hydrogen fuel cell storage process, current and future hydrogen plans, the technological state, and the economic aspect.

The Emergence of AI in the Renewable Energy Sector

The introduction of the AI in RE sectors has been proven a significant initiative for building of efficient energy system worldwide. AI plays a variety of function in this sector, like automation, optimization, and predictive analytics all of which are integral components for the efficient management and integration of RE sources. In their 2022 study, authors investigate how AI can be used to automate energy systems in smart cities [55–58]. Their research, which focuses on the EU, shows how AI technologies are improving energy systems' performance and efficiency [59]. The study emphasizes how AI can accurately manage and control power networks, especially when integrating RE sources including wind and solar with current supply and demand systems. This integration is vital for achieving sustainable energy and future development with minimal loss and greenhouse gas emissions [60, 61].

Singh *et al.* [62] talked about AI-powered renewable energy, emphasizing novel uses. Their work addresses the difficulties caused by the unpredictable performance of renewable energy sources because of environmental factors by reviewing important methods based on photovoltaic (PV) forecast utilizing machine learning techniques. The study illustrates AI's capability to improve forecasting and management of renewable energy output, emphasizing the significance of accurate prediction in maintaining grid stability and dependability.

Utilizing cutting-edge algorithms and data analytics to maximize energy production and distribution is what defines the convergence of artificial intelligence and renewable energy. The renewable energy industry can overcome obstacles in integrating variable energy sources, including wind and solar, into current power networks thanks to artificial intelligence (AI) technologies. The utilization of the AI in RE will leads to elevation in the generation of RE [63].

As a result, the introduction of AI into the RE industry is a significant advancement that is changing the approach for the production as well as management of energy. AI will become more and more crucial in promoting efficiency and innovation in the RE industry as the globe continues to shift towards sustainable energy solutions [64].

Role of AI in Renewable Energy

AI can work for all aspects RE like for design, forecasting, optimization, controlling, organization, and guidelines. The application of the AI in RE are discuss below.

A. Role of AI in Wind Energy

There is a plethora of reports that assure the magnitute of AI in wind energy. A detailed analysis of statistical, physical, neural network, and correlation-based approaches for produced power assessment in relation to wind speed is presented. A combination of these three categories, i.e., analytical, neural, and evolutionary, is highly researched by scientists to develop innovative approaches of AI in wind energy [65]. Most of the studies utilized AI's neural learning algorithms to assessment wind speed and power. Furthermore, the proposed neural network (PNN) is used for wind speed, humidity, and generation hours, and the wind energy outcome is considered as the output variable. A study performed by author calculate wind power for three years *via* feedforward propagation from seven different farms. The forecasting precision of the (BPNN) is commendable, 0.0070 and 0.0065 (RMSE) for test and training data, respectively. The potential of 3 different kind of ANN, i.e., RBFNN & BPNN, flexible linear element network, RBFNN, and BPNN, has been assessed from two separate areas to calculate air speed [66]. Fuzzy logic and its combination with artificial neural network methods was evaluated of wind power in many reports. Author used fuzzy logic to design a 3.5-kW wind production system. The designed system has an excellent performance and can be utilized in the field [67, 68]. Results of this study are helpful in advance planning of at least 1–48 hours.

B. Role of AI in Solar Energy

In the literature, the significance of AI and its utilization in solar energy applications is described in detail. A deep research was carried out, and the researcher evaluated different parameters, i.e., modeling, simulation, sizing, and monitoring the photovoltaic system. They used statistical and different AI techniques to compile results of building energy calculations and revealed that their AI would be employed to size both grid-connected and single photovoltaic systems.

Furthermore, the performance of the BPNN model is also evaluated in many studies, and among them is a significant report about the evaluation of the BPNN system. During this study, the researcher has estimated the performance of the BPNN system for three years by correlating the ANN and BPNN batch systems to estimate the ambient temperature that was 24 hours ahead in time. The achieved mean percentage deviation (MPD) values were 2.13, 3.16, and 4.17 [69]. Moreover, comparing the BPNN with 4.5% RMSE against more experimental methods, Alam *et al.* predict differences in sun radiation on an hourly and daily basis. There are certain other innovative approaches to utilize solar energy on the basis of AI as explained by Mashohor *et al.* [70], to enhance the PV performance of solar systems. In addition, many scientists reported on the significance of the ANFIS method, which enhances the accuracy of PV power supply by more than 98%, as well as a significant improvement in satellite image data. Similarly, it is found that sunshine period, prediction of solar chimney power plants (SCPP), and prediction of solar radiation using temperature are improved under the influence of AI [71–73]. Figure 5.1 shows the role of AI in the conservation of the environment.

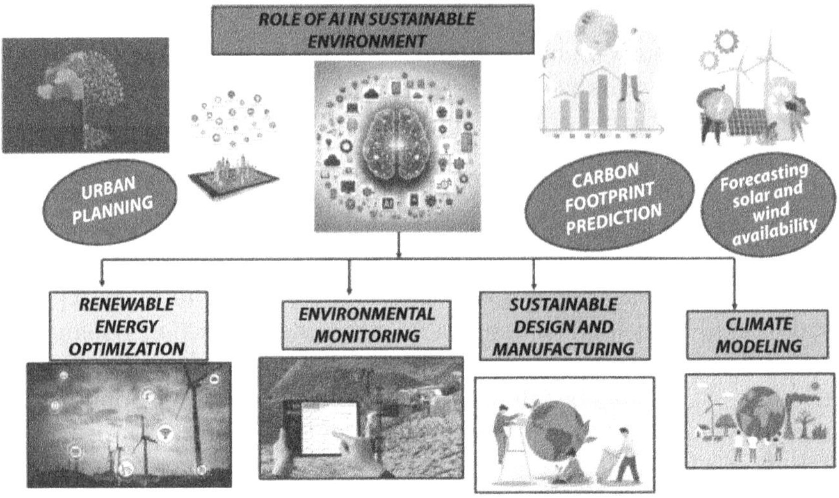

Figure 5.1 The role of AI in the conservation of the environment.

C. Role of AI in Geothermal Energy

AI can also be used for various geothermal applications by combining sensor and robotic technology for optimization and drilling plans. It is found that the ANN method is used in most studies. Furthermore, BPNN is used to test the capacity of the vertical ground coupled heat pump (VGCHP) system. During this evaluation study, BPNN was employed *via* the Polak-Ribiere conjugate gradient, the scaled conjugate gradient, and the Levenberg-Marquardt algorithms, and results revealed significant improvement in the prediction efficiency of the LM-based BPNN system [74].

The thermo economic, single-objective thermodynamic, thermoeconomic, and vertical ground source heat pump (VGSHP) optimization systems were used by Sayyaadi *et al.* [75] for improved algorithms for manifold objectives.

Hybrid AI techniques were also employed to estimate and compare the performance of different methods, i.e., VGSHP to BPNN, with geothermal energy methods such as the adaptive neuro-fuzzy inference system (ANFIS). It is reported that the ANFIS works better than BPNN techniques. Another instance where the ANFIS works better than BPNN techniques is when estimating the temperature of a geothermal reservoir using GMDHNN, which is based on singular value decomposition (SVD) and GA [88].

D. Role of AI in Hydro Energy

There is a plethora of review reports that emphasize the usages of the AI in the sector of hydro energy. Kishor *et al.* [76, 77] have provided an informative overview of the hydropower plant's design and control using both traditional approaches and cutting-edge AI technologies, including fuzzy, ANN, ANFIS, GA, etc. Furthermore, Smith *et al.* [78] examine the forecast the discharge of peak and the peak times of both linear and non-linear reservoirs, as well as model the rainfall runoff process by using the BPNN method. It was found that linear reservoirs have better BPNN accuracy in predicting the time to peak, and non-linear reservoirs have higher BPNN accuracy in predicting the peak discharge. It is reported that in the San Juan River sink, the BPNN model has been preferred to install to predict steam flow for two separate seasons for more than 17 years. There are certain studies about the role of the ANFIS and the hybrid AI for generating hydrogen energy. A study was developed to estimate river flow by using a combination of AI approaches *via* Elman artificial neural network, Fourier frequency transform, hierarchical clustering, and modular artificial neural network. Results suggest that CBR's performance is better compared to that of the BPNN, Elman ANN, RBFNN, and others [79].

E. Role of AI in Ocean Energy

There are many reviews and reports that describe the evolution and development in the sector of ocean energy due to AI innovations. Author reported a number of applications of AI in the field of ocean engineering. Ocean energy was evaluated by using GP and fuzzy techniques.

Ghorbani *et al.* [80] employed the GP and ANN to study the sea level. It was revealed that the GP prediction was more accurate and precise than that of the BPNN when using the Levenberg-Marquardt algorithm for MSE (230.5 to 236.2). To enhance this prediction accuracy, ANFIS and hybrid AI techniques can also be a better option.

A study was carried out by Karimi *et al.* [81] for the evaluation of the sea level forecasting ability of eleven different types of ARMA models, the BPNN (GD, CG, and LM), and the ANFIS (five variants using various membership functions). It was revealed that results from the ANFIS and ANN techniques are about the same as those from the ARMA models, but they are better.

A hybrid approach that combines the numerical wave model (NWM) and the BPNN is employed for wave hindcasting. It was found that this combination performs better than the NWM and BPNN approaches. Moreover, De Paz *et al.* [82] stated a hybrid intelligence structure based on support vector regression (SVR), case-based reasoning (CVR), and improved CO_2 flow prediction to enhance a better understanding of the interaction between the air and the ocean.

F. Role of AI in Bioenergy

AI also plays a significant role in bioenergy, as per many scientific reports. To begin with, Shabani *et al.* [83] gave a concise overview of stochastic and deterministic mathematical modeling for optimizing forest biomass in RE generation. During this study, different approaches, i.e., genetic programming (GP) methods, K-nearest neighbor (KNN), particle swarm optimizations (PSO), support vector machine (SVM), etc., have been employed to evaluate bioenergy. Balabin *et al.* [84] carried out a regularized discriminant study by employing near-infrared (NIR) data on algorithms, RDA, KNN, PLS, and SVM into ten distinct classes to categorize biodiesel. A specially designed PSO is utilized for the optimization of the biomass logistic network. Biofuel's higher heating value (HHV) was evaluated using BPNN and GP, and its performance was contrasted with that of other HHV models. It was found that GP and BPNN have higher prediction accuracy (0.942 to 0.987) than standard models [85].

A combination of fuzzy logic and artificial neural networks is implemented to optimize the operation of the biofuel boiler, improving heat-transfer efficiency and maintenance performance, and ultimately resulting in energy savings of approximately 12 GWh per year. Additionally, a combination of AI methods is used for the management of methane waste by using BPNN and GA together, and when the parameters are optimized, the hybrid technique increases methane output by 6.9%. Another study used a similar hybrid approach to maximize the production of biogas (from rice bran, banana stems, cow manure, sawdust, and paper waste), and the output was 10.280 L of biogas [86].

G. Role of AI in Hydrogen Energy

AI plays an indispensable role in the better performance of hydrogen energy, as it is listed by Petrone *et al.* [87] in a review paper about the role of different AI techniques in diagnosing proton exchange membrane fuel cell systems (PEMFCs). In another report, three issues, i.e., artificial intelligence, statistical methods, and signal processing, were compared by using AI.

In hydrogen energy research, fuzzy logic and EU approaches have also been applied. For instance, a fuzzy logic approach is employed to study the ignition time of a hydrogen-powered car utilizing three different types of membership functions. Moreover, hydrogen consumption in the fuel cell crossover vehicles has been analyzed using a fuzzy logic regulator that was created through factor improvement within a genetic algorithm. Another significant approach to utilizing AI is that electricity can be supplied *via* the internet or used to power buildings and vehicles to enhance their performance and utilization [88].

H. Role of AI in Hybrid RE

In many reviews, the role of different innovative AI techniques in hybrid renewable energy was explained. Luna-Rubio *et al.* [89] described many techniques for the development of optimal size. In addition, valuable information about the various design techniques of combining RE solar and wind structures is provided. In order to improve hybrid PV-wind-battery systems and reduce production costs, ANFIS is used in combination with AI techniques. The results it produces make it unique among other hybrid AI techniques, such as genetic algorithm (GA), hybrid optimization (HO), and hybrid optimization model for electric renewables (HOMER). Many RE systems are currently using hybrid and improved AI approaches, such as ANFIS for biodiesel modeling, assessment of solar radiation analysis, and assessment of wind power, decomposition of wavelet, ANN, and autoregressive algorithms for solar radiation analysis [90].

Discussions and Future Recommendations

As stated by many studies, drastic climatic changes and global warming are responsible for the day-by-day increment in usage of renewable energies (RE) throughout the world. RE is the answer to many questions and a reasonable solution to many problems of recent times. To be more precise, the combination of AI and RE will transform the energy sector and advance sustainability worldwide. AI can enhance the effectiveness of the RE field by different advantages, i.e., foretelling patterns, completion of task without any contribution of human, and enhancing the decision-making process.

Due to the rapid development of AI-enabled innovation, processes will be better understood through faster forecasting and more intelligent connections between important elements [91].

A new era of data- and knowledge-based civilization and global advancement is ushered in by artificial intelligence. AI utilizes innovative techniques to overcome today's challenges as well as to use existing production factors in a better way. While significant innovations in AI must be included in its history, current developments in neural systems research into cognitive computing and machine learning have brought forth unexpected and contemporary capabilities for energy management, optimization, and observation. The capacity of AI to support system optimizations, parametrization, and personalization of production and usage may be a key consideration in the energy division's use of AI. It is necessary to consider social and economic factors that go beyond specialized skills in order to picture astute professionals in the energy sector who are motivated by smart grid technology and AI algorithms. Numerous innovative AI technologies, i.e., structured data management, data mining capabilities, and machine learning techniques, can facilitate an AI-based system or field through energy divisions, promoting a smart energy grid supported by AI. To achieve an advancement of better performance, AI must be coordinated at all levels of the energy systems. It is necessary for the advancement of the energy infrastructure plan as well as the transmission and production of renewable energy [92].

Implications for Stakeholders in the RE Sector

The RE sector's evolution, particularly with the integration of AI and other advanced technologies, has profound implications for various stakeholders. In a sector-integrated energy system with a large proportion of renewable energy, authors investigate the role of prosumers, or people or organizations that generate and consume energy. Their study demonstrates how distributed battery storage systems can provide flexibility to systems that use almost entirely renewable energy. They do point out that these systems' modes of functioning can either maximize individual profits or help the system as a whole. The requirement for policies that balance individual gains with the overall system optimum, taking into account both system cost changes and distributional consequences for specific stakeholder groups, is highlighted by this contradiction [93].

The author [94] reported on the policies on renewable energy that can improve the efficiency and performance of RE to achieve sustainable development. The study finds a gap between the views of voters and stakeholders, with the latter emphasizing energy autonomy and renewable energy as a means of addressing climate challenges, while the public is paying attention to justice in practices. This discrepancy indicates that in order to create effective and widely accepted policies, the interests of both parties must be balanced [94]. The study examines the effectiveness of renewable energy subsidies in Nepal, with a primary focus on biogas subsidies. The research found that the efficiency of these subsidies is affected by different variables, i.e., awareness among customers about the benefits of renewable energy technology (RET), various available government policies, the benefits of the technology compared to its cost, long-term access, etc.

The study revealed that subsidies have largely benefited wealthy households rather than low-income groups. Accordingly, more equitable financial intermediation and subsidy distribution are required to guarantee wider access to renewable energy technologies, as compared to poor farmers [95]. There are a number of implications for stakeholders, i.e., techniques to consider for policymaking, subsidy distribution, and the role of prosumers. Balancing individual and collective benefits, ensuring equitable access to technology, and harmonizing conflicting interests are essential for the sustainable development of the renewable energy sector.

Conclusion

The analysis and current state of development in both single and hybrid renewable energy systems were assessed in this study. Additionally, a summary is provided of the use of AI approaches in RE system control, optimization, decision-making, and simulations. In particular, the role of AI in solar energy, photovoltaics, microgrid integration for power management and energy storage, as well as in wind and geothermal energy systems, was thoroughly assessed. Numerous AI simulation techniques have been examined in relation to solar energy, along with its possible advantages. Because these simulations may generate a concise solution for multi-variable problems, cost minimal computational effort, and do not necessitate knowledge of internal system parameters, they offer a powerful alternative to conventional physical modeling techniques. The present quo states that most research investigations focus on the effective use of AI technology in wind and solar energy development systems. However, research publications on the use of AI for single and hybrid renewable energy sources are scarce. The future of artificial intelligence techniques seems bright. Their efficient use will be necessary for future studies into other RE sources, especially in the hybrid RE system. Utilizing contemporary and hybrid artificial intelligence technology will enhance the output of renewable energy sources, leading to more wealth on a worldwide scale.

AI disclosure statement: The author acknowledges the use of AI-based tools for minor language editing or grammatical correction. However, all intellectual contributions, analyses, and conclusions presented in this chapter are entirely the author's own.

References

1. Afridi, Y.S., Ahmad, K., Hassan, L., Artificial intelligence based prognostic maintenance of renewable energy systems: A review of techniques, challenges, and future research directions. *Int. J. Energy Res.*, 46, 15, 21619–21642, 2022.
2. Hamid, H. and Samantaray, S., Future directions of computer vision and AI for renewable energy: trends and challenges in renewable energy research and applications. *Comput. Vision Mach. Intell. Renewable Energy Syst.*, 335–361, 2025.
3. Rana, S., Ai-Driven Fault Detection and Predictive Maintenance in Electrical Power Systems: A Systematic Review Of Data-Driven Approaches, Digital Twins, And Self-Healing Grids. *Am. J. Adv. Technol. Eng. Solutions, 1*, 01, 258–289, 2025.
4. Alagha, N., Khairuddin, A.S.M., Haitaamar, Z.N., Al-Khatib, O., Kanesan, J., Artificial Intelligence in Wind Turbine Fault Detection and Diagnosis: Advances and Perspectives. *Energies, 18*, 7, 1680, 2025.
5. Fu, H., Rao, J., Deng, F., Wang, Y., Zhao, B., Liu, Z., Guan, H., Malinowski, P.H., Xu, L., AIoT: Artificial Intelligence and the Internet of Things for Monitoring and Prognosis of Systems and Structures. *IEEE Trans. Instrum. Meas.*, 2025.
6. Bošnjaković, M., Martinović, M., Đokić, K., Application of Artificial Intelligence in Wind Power Systems. *Appl. Sci.*, *15*, 5, 2443, 2025.
7. Sergakis, A., Salinas, M., Gkiolekas, N., Gyftakis, K.N., A Review of Condition Monitoring of Permanent Magnet Synchronous Machines: Techniques, Challenges and Future Directions. *Energies, 18*, 5, 1177, 2025.
8. Sidhu, S.S. and Sidhu, G.S., Sustainability Issues in Condition-Based Maintenance and Residual Life Prediction. *Condition-Based Maint. Residual Life Prediction*, 171–190, 2025.
9. Awachat, A., Dube, A., Chaudhri, S., ML for Sustainable Solutions: Applications in Renewable Energy Optimization and Climate Change Prediction, in: *2025 4th International Conference on Sentiment Analysis and Deep Learning (ICSADL)*, IEEE, pp. 1689–1694, 2025, February.
10. Zhou, J., Yang, J., Xiang, S., Qin, Y., Remaining useful life prediction methodologies with health indicator dependence for rotating machinery: A comprehensive review. *IEEE Trans. Instrum. Meas.*, 2025.
11. Mashifane, L.D., Mendu, B., Monchusi, B.B., State-of-the-Art Fault Detection and Diagnosis in Power Transformers: A Review of Machine Learning and Hybrid Methods. *IEEE Access*, 2025.
12. Arsalan, M.H., Mubin, O., Al Mahmud, A., Khan, I.A., Hassan, A.J., Mapping Data-Driven Research Impact Science: The Role of Machine Learning and Artificial Intelligence, in: *Metrics*, vol. 2, p. 5, MDPI, 2025, April.

13. Sriraam, N., Chinta, B., Seshadri, S., Suresh, S., A comprehensive review of artificial intelligence-based algorithm towards fetal facial anomalies detection (2013–2024). *Artif. Intell. Rev.*, *58*, 5, 1–49, 2025.
14. Chomklin, A., Jaiyen, S., Wattanakitrungroj, N., A Survey of AI Techniques based on Predictive Maintenance in Lean Manufacturing. *Science Technology Social Sci. Procedia, 2023*, 4, CiM03–CiM03, 2023.
15. Pan, Y., Kang, S., Kong, L., Wu, J., Yang, Y., Zuo, H., Remaining useful life prediction methods of equipment components based on deep learning for sustainable manufacturing: a literature review. *AI EDAM*, *39*, e4, 2025.
16. Coronel, E., Barán, B., Gardel, P., A Survey on Data Mining for Data-Driven Industrial Assets Maintenance. *Technol. (2227-7080)*, *13*, 2, 2025.
17. Huang, Z., Gong, J., Xiao, X., Gao, Y., Xia, Y., Wheeler, P., Ji, B., Artificial Intelligence and Digital Twin Technologies for Power Converter Control in Transportation Applications: A Review. *IET Power Electron.*, *18*, 1, e70013, 2025.
18. Yan, R., Zhou, Z., Shang, Z., Wang, Z., Hu, C., Li, Y., Yang, Y., Chen, X., Gao, R.X., Knowledge Driven Machine Learning Towards Interpretable Intelligent Prognostics and Health Management: Review and Case Study. *Chin. J. Mech. Eng.*, *38*, 1, 5, 2025.
19. Vajjhala, N.R., Roy, S.S., Taşcı, B., Chowdhury, M.E.H., Foundations and Emerging Trends in Generative Artificial Intelligence (AI) for Industrial Applications. *Generative Artif. Intell. (AI) Approaches Ind. Appl.*, 1–18, 2025.
20. Onwusinkwue, S., Osasona, F., Ahmad, I.A.I., Anyanwu, A.C., Dawodu, S.O., Obi, O.C., Hamdan, A., Artificial intelligence (AI) in renewable energy: A review of predictive maintenance and energy optimization. *World J. Adv. Res. Rev.*, *21*, 1, 2487–2499, 2024.
21. Mishra, S. and Aziz, A., Role of Artificial Intelligence aided Inspection Methods for Sustainable Periodic Maintenance and Renovation of Renewable Energy Systems Project, 2024.
22. Surathunmanun, S., Ongsakul, W., Singh, J.G., Exploring the Role of Generative Artificial Intelligence in the Energy Sector: A Comprehensive Literature Review, in: *2024 International Conference on Sustainable Energy: Energy Transition and Net Zero Climate Future (ICUE)*, vol. 1-11, IEEE, 2024, October.
23. Bashir, N., Donti, P., Cuff, J., Sroka, S., Ilic, M., Sze, V., Delimitrou, C., Olivetti, E., The climate and sustainability implications of generative AI, 2024.
24. Kumar, R.P., Sachin, A., Kumar, S.S., Empowering Sustainable Cities: Generative AI Solutions for Urban. *Generative AI Curr. Trends Appl.*, 2024.
25. Chen, D., Lin, X., Qiao, Y., Perspectives for artificial intelligence in sustainable energy systems. *Energy*, 134711, 2025.
26. Tabuenca, B., Martín, S., Greller, W., Tillmann, A., Uche-Soria, M., Castro, M., Tovar, E., Rodríguez-Artacho, M., IoT and generative AI technologies to support urban environmental learning, in: *2024 IEEE Global Engineering Education Conference (EDUCON)*, IEEE, pp. 1–4, 2024, May.

27. Nikolopoulou, K., Generative artificial intelligence and sustainable higher education: Mapping the potential. *J. Digital Educ. Technol.*, *5*, 1, ep2506, 2025.
28. Yafei, X., Wu, Y., Song, J., Gong, Y., Lianga, P., Generative AI in Industrial Revolution: A Comprehensive Research on Transformations, Challenges, and Future Directions. *J. Knowl. Learn. Sci. Technol. ISSN 2959-6386 (online)*, *3*, 2, 11–20, 2024.
29. Bennagi, A., AlHousrya, O., Cotfas, D.T., Cotfas, P.A., Comprehensive study of the artificial intelligence applied in renewable energy. *Energy Strategy Rev.*, *54*, 101446, 2024.
30. Manikandan, S., Kaviya, R.S., Shreeharan, D.H., Subbaiya, R., Vickram, S., Karmegam, N., Kim, W., Govarthanan, M., Artificial intelligence-driven sustainability: Enhancing carbon capture for sustainable development goals–A review. *Sustainable Dev.*, *33*, 2, 2004–2029, 2025.
31. Setyadi, A., Soekotjo, S., Lestari, S.D., Pawirosumarto, S., Damaris, A., Trends and Opportunities in Sustainable Manufacturing: A Systematic Review of Key Dimensions from 2019 to 2024. *Sustainability*, *17*, 2, 789, 2025.
32. Kapoor, N.R., Kumar, A., Kumar, A., Kumar, A., Arora, H.C., Artificial intelligence in civil engineering: An immersive view, in: *Artificial Intelligence Applications for Sustainable Construction*, pp. 1–74, Woodhead Publishing, 2024.
33. Yi, H., Liu, T., Lan, G., The key artificial intelligence technologies in early childhood education: a review. *Artif. Intell. Rev.*, *57*, 1, 2024.
34. Roy, K. (Ed.), *Artificial intelligence, ethics and the future of warfare: Global perspectives*, Taylor & Francis, 2024.
35. Fenwick, R.O., *Big Data Analytics and Machine Learning Tools for Space and Earth Observation* (Doctoral dissertation, University of Leicester), 2024.
36. Taiwo, R., Yussif, A.M., Zayed, T., Making waves: Generative artificial intelligence in water distribution networks: Opportunities and challenges. *Water Res. X*, *28*, 100316, 2025.
37. Kyriakarakos, G., Artificial Intelligence and the Energy Transition. *Sustainability*, *17*, 3, 1140, 2025.
38. Saadati, T. and Barutcu, B., Forecasting Solar Energy: Leveraging Artificial Intelligence and Machine Learning for Sustainable Energy Solutions. *J. Econ. Surveys.*, 2025.
39. Shao, Y., Pasha, A.A., Raja, M.A.Z., Arshad, Z., Shah, Z., Abbasi, I., Khan, W.A., Alam, M.M., Ansari, M.I.H., Optimizing the thermo-fluidic properties of ternary hybrid nanofluid for appliance of solar energy through an artificial intelligence integrated numerical solver technique. *Chaos, Solitons & Fractals*, *192*, 115961, 2025.
40. Gutiérrez-Oribio, D., Stathas, A., Stefanou, I., AI-Driven Approach for Sustainable Extraction of Earth's Subsurface Renewable Energy While Minimizing Seismic Activity. *Int. J. Numer. Anal. Methods Geomech.*, *49*, 4, 1126–1138, 2025.

41. Qureshi, H., Pasha, A.A., Raja, M.A.Z., Shah, Z., Algarni, S., Alqahtani, T., Khan, W.A., Haq, M., Artificial intelligence analysis of thermal energy for convectively heated ternary nanofluid flow in radiated channel considering viscous dissipations aspects. *Eng. Sci. Technol. Int. J.*, *62*, 101955, 2025.
42. Assareh, E., Keykhah, A., Bedakhanian, A., Agarwal, N., Lee, M., Optimizing solar photovoltaic farm-based cogeneration systems with artificial intelligence (AI) and Cascade compressed air energy storage for stable power generation and peak shaving: A Japan-focused case study. *Appl. Energy*, *377*, 124468, 2025.
43. Dash, S., Green AI: Enhancing Sustainability and Energy Efficiency in AI-Integrated Enterprise Systems. *IEEE Access*, 2025.
44. Wang, Q., Zhang, F., Li, R., Artificial intelligence and sustainable development during urbanization: Perspectives on AI R&D innovation, AI infrastructure, and AI market advantage. *Sustainable Dev.*, *33*, 1, 1136–1156, 2025.
45. Bachina, L., Kanagala, A., Korapu, S., Ratnaraju, P., Sustainable materials for artificial intelligence (AI) technology adoption for energy-efficient patient-centric healthcare solutions. *J. Educ. Health Promot.*, *14*, 1, 4, 2025.
46. Satpathy, I., Nayak, A., Jain, V., The green city: Sustainable and smart urban living through artificial intelligence, in: *Utilizing Technology to Manage Territories*, pp. 273–304, IGI Global, 2025.
47. Iqbal, A., Zhang, W., Jahangir, S., Building a Sustainable Future: The Nexus Between Artificial Intelligence, Renewable Energy, Green Human Capital, Geopolitical Risk, and Carbon Emissions Through the Moderating Role of Institutional Quality. *Sustainability*, *17*, 3, 990, 2025.
48. Roberts, O., A Qualitative Exploration on Artificial Intelligence and Renewable Energy Integration in Supply Chains, 2025.
49. Sharma, S.K. and Hans, R., From code to sustainability: The impact of computer science in advancing sustainable development, in: *Role of Science and Technology for Sustainable Future: Volume 2-Applied Sciences and Technologies*, pp. 547–582, Springer Nature Singapore, Singapore, 2025.
50. Al-Raeei, M., The smart future for sustainable development: Artificial intelligence solutions for sustainable urbanization. *Sustainable Dev.*, *33*, 1, 508–517, 2025.
51. Shahin, M. and Simjoo, M., Potential applications of innovative AI-based tools in hydrogen energy development: Leveraging large language model technologies. *Int. J. Hydrogen Energy*, *102*, 918–936, 2025.
52. Mallala, B., Ahmed, A.I.U., Pamidi, S.V., Faruque, M.O., Reddy, R., Forecasting global sustainable energy from renewable sources using random forest algorithm. *Results Eng.*, *25*, 103789, 2025.
53. Zou, C., Gao, W., Ai, F., Strategic Mineral Policies for Indonesia: Enhancing Global Competitiveness, Economic Growth, and Environmental Sustainability Through Innovation and Renewable Energy. *Renewable Energy*, 122593, 2025.

54. Ramesh, P.N., Advancements in AI-Driven Communication Systems: Enhancing Efficiency and Security in Next-Generation Networks, 2025.
55. Mamta, A.M., Kumar, A., Baliyan, A., Shining a Light on Solar Power Forecasting: Machine Learning Techniques for Unprecedented Accuracy. *2023 3rd International Conference on Technological Advancements in Computational Sciences (ICTACS)*, Tashkent, Uzbekistan, pp. 828–834, 2023, doi: 10.1109/ICTACS59847.2023.10390265.
56. Kumar, A., Dubey, A.K., Segovia Ramírez, I., *et al.*, Artificial Intelligence Techniques for the Photovoltaic System: A Systematic Review and Analysis for Evaluation and Benchmarking. *Arch. Computat. Methods Eng.*, 31, 4429–4453, 2024. https://doi.org/10.1007/s11831-024-10125-3.
57. Dubey, A.K., Ramirez, I., Marquez, F., A Review of Intelligent Systems for the Prediction of Wind Energy Using Machine Learning. *2022, ICMSEM, The Sixteenth International Conference on Management Science and Engineering Management, Lecture Notes on Data Engineering and Communications Technologies, vol 144. Springer, by Springer*, Ankara, Turkey, August 3-6, 2022.
58. Kumar, A.D., Ramirez, I., Rio, A., Marquez, F., *A Review and Analysis of Forecasting of Photovoltaic Power Generation Using Machine Learning, 2022, ICMSEM, The Sixteenth International Conference on Management Science and Engineering Management, Lecture Notes on Data Engineering and Communications Technologies, vol 144. Springer, Cham. by Springer*, Ankara, Turkey, August 3-6, 2022.
59. Rahman, M.A., Emon, M.M.H., Khan, T., Hamid, A.B.A., Yaakub, N.I., Eco-Intelligence: AI's Contribution to a Sustainable World, in: *AI and Green Technology Applications in Society*, pp. 31–62, IGI Global Scientific Publishing, 2025.
60. Song, Y. and Sahoo, S., Spike Talk–A Sustainable "One-Solution-Fits-All" Technology for Electronic Grids. *IEEE Power Electron. Mag.*, *11*, 4, 31–38, 2025.
61. Abbas, M., Akhai, S., Abbas, U., Jafri, R., Arif, S.M., Ai-enabled sustainable urban planning and management, in: *Real-World Applications of AI Innovation*, pp. 233–260, IGI Global Scientific Publishing, 2025.
62. Singh, O., Yadav, M., Yadav, P., Rishiwal, V., AI-Based Renewable Energy with Emerging Applications: Issues and Challenges, in: *Introduction to AI Techniques for Renewable Energy System*, pp. 29–42, CRC Press, 2021.
63. Li, H., Lu, Z., Zhang, Z., Tanasescu, C., How does artificial intelligence affect manufacturing firms' energy intensity? *Energy Econ.*, *141*, 108109, 2025.
64. Crowther, D., Singh, R., Singh, A., Rani, S., Assessing the Impact of Artificial Intelligence on Healthcare Sector for Enhancing Sustainability, in: *Transforming Healthcare Sector Through Artificial Intelligence and Environmental Sustainability*, pp. 3–21, Springer Nature Singapore, Singapore, 2025.

65. Sumi, A.M. and Chandrasekar, K.S., Artificial intelligence for sustainable stewardship of Earth resources, in: *Data Analytics and Artificial Intelligence for Earth Resource Management*, pp. 65–75, Elsevier, 2025.
66. Khan, A., Will artificial intelligence accelerate or delay the race between nuclear energy technology budgeting and net-zero emissions? *arXiv preprint arXiv:2501.17410.*, 2025.
67. Jyani, Mayank, Rathore, P.S., Spectrogram-Based CNN Framework for Live Deepfake Voice Detection in Google Meet, in: *2025 International Conference on Computing Technologies & Data Communication (ICCTDC)*, pp. 1–5. IEEE, 2025.
68. Alayed, W., Akhtar, A., ul Hassan, W., Zeeshan, A., Maximizing Energy Savings in Smart Homes through Artificial Neural Network Based Artificial Intelligence Solutions. *Clean Energy*, zkae113, 2025.
69. Mabel, M.C. and Fernandez, E., Analysis of wind power generation and prediction using ANN: A case study. *Renewable Energy*, *33*, 5, 986–992, 2008.
70. Mashohor, S., Samsudin, K., Noor, A.M., Rahman, A.R.A., Evaluation of genetic algorithm based solar tracking system for photovoltaic panels, in: *2008 IEEE International Conference on Sustainable Energy Technologies*, pp. 269–273, IEEE, 2008, November.
71. Gursoy, S., The Role of Artificial Intelligence in the Digitalization Process: Trends, Challenges, and a Framework for Sustainable Integration, 2025.
72. Maddala, V.S.P., Optimizing the oil and natural gas industry: The role of ai and data analytics in ERP integration, 2025.
73. Bera, M., Das, S., Garai, S., Dutta, S., Choudhury, M.R., Tripathi, S., Chatterjee, G., Advancing energy efficiency: innovative technologies and strategic measures for achieving net zero emissions. *Carbon Footprints*, *4*, 1, N–A, 2025.
74. Arslan, O., Power generation from medium temperature geothermal resources: ANN-based optimization of Kalina cycle system-34. *Energy*, *36*, 2528–2534, 2011.
75. Sayyaadi, H., Amlashi, E.H., Amidpour, M., Multi-objective optimization of a vertical ground source heat pump using evolutionary algorithm. *Energy Convers. Manage.*, *50*, 8, 2035–2046, 2009.
76. Kishor, N., Saini, R.P., Singh, S.P., A review on hydropower plant models and control. *Renewable Sustainable Energy Rev.*, *11*, 5, 776–796, 2007.
77. Sathianarayanan, M., Kirdemir, U., Gianoli, A., Urban intelligence: Navigating climate challenges with ai, in: *Nexus of AI, Climatology, and Urbanism for Smart Cities*, pp. 59–90, IGI Global Scientific Publishing, 2025.
78. Smith, J. and Eli, R.N., Neural-network models of rainfall-runoff process. *J. Water Resour. Plann. Manage.*, *121*, 6, 499–508, 1995.
79. Firat, M. and Güngör, M., River flow estimation using adaptive neuro fuzzy inference system. *Math. Comput. Simul*, *75*, 3-4, 87–96, 2007.

80. Ghorbani, M.A., Makarynskyy, O., Shiri, J., Makarynska, D., Genetic programming for sea level predictions in an island environment. *Int. J. Ocean Clim. Syst.*, *1*, 1, 27–35, 2010.
81. Karimi, S., Kisi, O., Shiri, J., Makarynskyy, O., Neuro-fuzzy and neural network techniques for forecasting sea level in Darwin Harbor, Australia. *Comput. Geosci.*, *52*, 50–59, 2013.
82. De Paz, J.F., Bajo, J., González, A., Rodríguez, S., Corchado, J.M., Combining case-based reasoning systems and support vector regression to evaluate the atmosphere–ocean interaction. *Knowl. Inf. Syst.*, *30*, 155–177, 2012.
83. Shabani, N., Akhtari, S., Sowlati, T., Value chain optimization of forest biomass for bioenergy production: A review. *Renewable Sustainable Energy Rev.*, *23*, 299–311, 2013.
84. Balabin, R.M., Lomakina, E.I., Safieva, R.Z., Neural network (ANN) approach to biodiesel analysis: Analysis of biodiesel density, kinematic viscosity, methanol and water contents using near infrared (NIR) spectroscopy. *Fuel*, *90*, 5, 2007–2015, 2011.
85. Izquierdo, J., Minciardi, R., Montalvo, I., Robba, M., Tavera, M., Particle Swarm Optimization for the biomass supply chain strategic planning, 2008.
86. Ren, X., Tian, X., Wang, K., Yang, S., Chen, W., Wang, J., Enhanced load forecasting for distributed multi-energy system: A stacking ensemble learning method with deep reinforcement learning and model fusion. *Energy*, 135031, 2025.
87. Petrone, R., Zheng, Z., Hissel, D., Péra, M.C., Pianese, C., Sorrentino, M., Becherif, M., Yousfi-Steiner, N., A review on model-based diagnosis methodologies for PEMFCs. *Int. J. Hydrogen Energy*, *38*, 17, 7077–7091, 2013.
88. Caux, S., Wanderley-Honda, D., Hissel, D., Fadel, M., On-line energy management for HEV based on particle swarm optimization. *Eur. Phys. Journal-Applied Phys.*, *54*, 2, 23403, 2011.
89. Luna-Rubio, R., Trejo-Perea, M., Vargas-Vázquez, D., Ríos-Moreno, G.J., Optimal sizing of renewable hybrids energy systems: A review of methodologies. *Sol. Energy*, *86*, 4, 1077–1088, 2012.
90. Chávez-Ramírez, A.U., Vallejo-Becerra, V., Cruz, J.C., Ornelas, R., Orozco, G., Munoz-Guerrero, R., Arriaga, L.G., A hybrid power plant (Solar–Wind–Hydrogen) model based in artificial intelligence for a remote-housing application in Mexico. *Int. J. Hydrogen Energy*, *38*, 6, 2641–2655, 2013.
91. Iden, J., Zwarg, F., Abdou, B., Risk Analysis Technique for the Evaluation of AI Technologies with Respect to Directly and Indirectly Affected Entities (Practitioner Track), in: *Symposium on Scaling AI Assessments (SAIA 2024)*, Schloss Dagstuhl–Leibniz-Zentrum für Informatik, pp. 5–1, 2025.
92. Malhotra, G. and Kharub, M., Elevating logistics performance: harnessing the power of artificial intelligence in e-commerce. *Int. J. Logist. Manage.*, *36*, 1, 290–321, 2025.

93. Manal, A., The Role of Renewable Energy in Driving Economic Transformation and Sustainable Development in Saudi Arabia. *Int. J. Energy Econ. Policy*, *15*, 1, 364–373, 2025.
94. Javid, D., Sustainable Finance and RegTech: Building Resilience in Financial Security and Energy Policy, 2025.
95. Du, H., Wang, T., Wei, H., Maceda, G.Y.C., Noack, B.R., Zhou, L., Topologically consistent regression modeling exemplified for laminar burning velocity of ammonia-hydrogen flames. *Energy AI*, *19*, 100456, 2025.

6

Ethical Consideration in the Use of AI for Solar Energy Optimization

Kumud Sachdeva* **and Rajan Sachdeva**

Department of Computer Science and Engineering, Chandigarh University, Gharuan, Punjab, India

Abstract

The utilization of solar energy as a power source has witnessed a significant increase in popularity in contemporary times. Nonetheless, the inherently variable nature of solar radiation poses considerable challenges when integrating this energy source into the existing power grid. This research endeavors to develop a predictive model employing machine learning and optimization methodologies to accurately forecast energy output. Through the examination of meteorological patterns, solar irradiance levels, and other pertinent variables, the proposed model seeks to deliver predictions of solar energy generation across diverse temporal intervals. Furthermore, optimization algorithms are employed to enhance both the efficacy and dependability of the forecasting process. An effective framework for addressing the uncertainties in energy generation is created by fusing machine learning and optimization techniques. Through simulations and real-world experiments, the efficacy of this strategy is evaluated, demonstrating its capacity to maximize energy efficiency and enable the smooth integration of renewable energy sources into existing power networks. The objective is to combine the random forest classifier (RFC) with the election-based optimization algorithm (EBOA) in order to improve forecasting efficiency and accuracy. The system chooses features and creates prediction models. Further, model parameters are adjusted to improve prediction performance using the evolutionary biogeography-based optimization algorithm. According to the results of the experiment, the RFC EBOA hybrid strategy performs better in terms of prediction efficiency than current approaches. When compared to present procedures, the framework's ability to produce forecasts shows potential.

**Corresponding author*: kumud.cse@cumail.com

Abhishek Kumar, Pramod Singh Rathore, Arun Lal Srivastav and Ashutosh Kumar Dubey (eds.) Solar Energy Optimization Using Generative Artificial Intelligence, (123–144) © 2026 Scrivener Publishing LLC

Keywords: Deep neural network, deep learning, computer science, artificial intelligence, machine learning, optimization algorithm, solar energy

6.1 Introduction

6.1.1 The Origin of Solar Energy

One of the most popular renewable energy sources nowadays is solar energy, which has enormous potential for producing electricity sustainably. Adoption of this technology is essential for addressing environmental issues and decreasing reliance on fossil fuels. But effective integration into the electrical grid is hampered by the erratic and sporadic character of solar radiation [1]. To maximize the use of solar resources, improve grid stability, and optimize resource allocation, accurate forecasting of solar energy output is consequently crucial. Many renewable energy sources, including wind, solar, tidal, and others, are becoming more and more popular in the modern world due to the serious problem of pollution and other environmental concerns. Nowadays, solar energy is the most effective way to supplement conventional energy sources. As of right now, scientists and the industrial sector are very interested in solar energy [2]. The domain where penetration is required presents the biggest challenges. Solar photovoltaic (PV) systems can be successfully integrated into the electrical grid with the help of accurate forecasting [3]. In order to meet peak load needs, control load rises and declines, and make well-informed decisions, prediction is essential. A multitude of atmospheric elements, including sun irradiance and seasonal variations in climate, are the main determinants of solar power stability. Additionally, it is a crucial component of how the energy management system operates. A number of forecasting horizons are shown in Table 6.1, along with their respective importance. For a number of uses, accurate solar power forecasting is essential [4]. Experts in the field of solar power forecasting have advanced significantly in recent years. Forecasting solar energy has been done using a variety of machine-learning techniques. Neural networks (NN), support vector machines (SVM), convolutional neural networks (CNN), and extreme learning machines (ELM) are examples of machine learning techniques.

6.1.2 Factors for Using Solar Power

Over 100 gigawatts (GW) of photovoltaic (PV) solar power were transacted globally in a single year, creating a new record of 505.5 GW.

Demand in Europe and other emerging markets has soared and filled the void left by regulatory changes in the middle of the year that caused demand in the People's Republic of China (PRC) to decrease. Many parts of the Asian continent lack appropriate lighting as a result of the poor installation of photovoltaic power plants. Therefore, in a number of countries, this disparity should be addressed through direct support. In this area, the aggressive market method is gaining popularity quite quickly. Over a three-year period, emerging markets saw a slew of new achievements. According to measurements, the new discoveries in Morocco and the People's Republic of China (PRC) have a 200-megawatt capacity each. Saudi Arabia and South Africa each added the same amount of capacity. The price kept dropping as a result of the installation of installations in different locations, the incorporation of new technologies, and fierce rivalry between the players [5–10].

However, the government's distribution of resources demonstrated that South Africa was still far behind. Because of its fast economic growth, the People's Republic of China (PRC) might offer a rate that is far lower than 40% of what is available elsewhere.

6.1.3 The Importance of Estimating the Quantity of Solar Power

The number of solar photovoltaic (PV) power systems in operation is continuously increasing. A lot of attention has been paid to forecasting the PV plant's output because of the variable nature of its production and the ongoing human need. Estimating demand also helps us obtain other energy sources from the grid in the event that our PV power supply is not enough. Likewise, if we have additional power, we might send it to the grid. This exact forecast will result in power consumption equilibrium in both internal and external orientations. Infrastructure that generates electricity from non-renewable energy sources (non-RES) and renewable energy sources (RES) is under the grid operator's jurisdiction. The dispatch control's goal of giving the load steady power will be accomplished if the varying output can be reliably predicted. Consequently, it turns out that estimating photovoltaic (PV) production is a crucial and broadly applicable procedure. The instruments used to calculate the amount of solar energy produced by photovoltaic systems are made up of numerous crucial parts. There is no denying that sunshine is unexpected. An irregular layer of clouds is present to block sunlight from reaching the panels. A major challenge has been to determine if it is possible to predict the weather variables. The next step is to translate the climatic parameters into the photovoltaic (PV) magnitude at the plant's output. This procedure is known as "simulating solar photovoltaic (PV) power generation." These models are used by industry experts to forecast how photovoltaic (PV) plants will behave in response to varying meteorological circumstances, such as variations in temperature, relative humidity, wind speed, and irradiance. These models account for various plant conditions, including the tracking system and PV panel orientation [10–15]. All of these activities, however, merely amount to making predictions about the future. It is clear that these forecasting attempts frequently turn out to be incorrect. We will have to use a costly energy source to make up the difference in such a situation. We require a temporary power source that is more costly per unit in order to remedy an incorrect assumption. The cost of electricity goes up a little as a result of this action. A nearly accurate estimate will result in less power being consumed from the temporary source and a somewhat cheaper cost. All market participants must always be given an accurate representation of the cost. In order to make up for the energy deficit, grid operators pass on compensating rates to the market and apply additional fees as penalties for any irregularities and unreliability. Consequently, the cost of power will go down if we can make precise predictions. To maintain reliability in a distributed generation scenario with multiple power plants in a grid, the plant operator must depend on their experience to precisely schedule power production.

Higher prediction accuracy translates into increased dependability, which could lead to a higher selling price for the plant. The primary goal of this thesis is to examine the first forecasting efforts of multiple photovoltaic (PV) power plants [35].

6.1.4 Optimization Method

Improving the accuracy of PV power forecasts is crucial to increasing grid penetration. As mentioned earlier, there are numerous important factors that greatly impact the accuracy of the method in the context of machine learning. For example, the ANN approach's performance accuracy is mostly determined by the number of neurons, hidden layers, and epochs. However, the parameters change based on the particular kernel functions that are being used when taking the kernel function into account. The aforementioned criteria, together with additional elements like input data selection, data pre-processing, and learning algorithm, significantly affect how accurate the predictions are. Researchers used the trial-and-error method to evaluate the model's quality, according to earlier literature reviews. Nevertheless, this method requires researchers with a high level of skill and proficiency. For example, these iterative methods were used in reference [38] to determine the number of neurons. The trial-and-error method has been employed in several research studies to achieve a variety of goals, including choosing membership functions, hidden neurons, and parameters in the context of fuzzy systems. But since this process proved to be highly crucial, the need for different optimization techniques became even more important. Thus, in this section, we will examine a number of optimization techniques that have been applied in various AI methodologies. A hybrid model has been produced by fusing AI models with a number of optimization techniques. GA has become one of the most used optimization techniques. Natural selection, which holds that only the most adaptive individuals survive and procreate, is the foundation of genetic algorithms (GA). Holland was the first to formulate it in the 1960s. Three separate operations—selection, cross-over, and mutation—are combined in one process. To optimize weights, the researchers combined the NN and GA techniques. In order to optimize input variables and hidden layers, GA and ANN were integrated in reference [35]. The optimized model beat other models, including ARMA and KNN, according to a comparison analysis. Numerous optimization techniques, such as particle swarm, firefly, ant colony optimization, and chaotic ant colony optimization, have been created based on the behavior of various mammals. Hybrid PSO and ANN techniques were used for the load prediction problem [36–41]. The authors combined chaotic PSO with ANN.

Ensuring that solar electricity is successfully incorporated into the grid requires accurate forecasting techniques that optimize energy production, consumption, and distribution. Predicting solar power is crucial for enabling grid operators, energy dealers, and other interested parties to make informed decisions on energy scheduling, resource allocation, and system stability management. Statistical methods or physical models are frequently used in conventional methods for solar power prediction, although both may struggle to capture the complex temporal and spatial dynamics present in patterns of solar irradiation. Moreover, these technologies may exhibit limitations in terms of scalability and computational efficiency, as well as the inability to adjust to changing environmental conditions. In order to attain energy efficiency, we suggested a novel framework for solar power prediction in this chapter that combines CNNs and the LBO algorithm. Our approach aims to increase the computational efficiency, accuracy, and validation of solar power forecasting systems. This will be achieved by utilizing both the optimization capabilities of LBO for model tweaking and the feature extraction and pattern recognition capabilities of deep learning.

It is essential to have precise short-term projections for power generation in order to manage energy resources efficiently, connect to the power grid, and maximize electricity. Term solar energy projections are essential for demanding tasks, including demand management, grid stability, and energy trading support. Weather variables are translated into estimates of power generation from a plant using a numerical forecasting model. To predict how solar installations would function in different scenarios, the solar industry uses photovoltaic models [15–20].

The random forest classifier (RFC) is a popular machine learning technique for energy forecasting because of its ability to learn from data and adapt to changing conditions. Traditionally, solar power generation prediction relied on models, which may limit scalability and accuracy. The RFC is regarded as a choice for predicting energy output because of its reliability, scalability, and capacity to handle data sets by combining predictions from decision trees. When building machine learning models, choosing characteristics and fine-tuning parameters are essential. Because weather, location, and time all affect energy production, it is difficult to predict immediate solar energy generation. A unique framework for short-term solar energy analysis combines the RFC and election-based optimization algorithm methodologies. This is done in order to address the issues. RFC is used for prediction modelling and feature selection, while EBOA optimizes model parameters to improve prediction precision and accuracy. Inspired by natural elections, EBOA is a population-based metaheuristic optimization technique. Based on their suitability, candidate solutions compete with one another in natural elections. In order to swiftly search the space and find the best answers, EBOA uses selection, crossover, and mutation procedures. This is achieved through consistently enhancing potential solutions [50–52].

6.1.5 Machine Learning Models

6.1.5.1 K-Harmonic Mean-Based Attribute Weighting Method

For the purpose of increasing the prediction rate, the diagnostic models use various ML techniques [4–7]. Dataset characteristics have a crucial effect on the decision-making process as well. The nature of features—whether they are important or irrelevant—also influences how accurate a forecast is made. The Medical datasets in particular allow for the focus on the issue of relevance and irrelevance aspects. From the medical datasets, unnecessary elements can be eliminated, and it's called "feature reduction" to describe this procedure [20–25].

Since irrelevant characteristics might harm classifier performance, it can be described as the process of eliminating them from datasets. On the other hand, SVM is a well-liked classifier that is easily adopted for tasks involving the prediction of medical data [25]. However, there are a number of issues with the SVM classifier. These can be summed up as follows: (1) select an appropriate kernel function; (2) determine the best input for the SVM classifier; and (3) optimize the SVM's parameters (weight and bias). The second of the aforementioned limitations is the most difficult because it can impact how well the kernel functions and how well the SVM parameters perform. This chapter discusses the SVM classifier's problem with selecting the best input and uses the k-harmonic mean-based attribute weighting method to fix it (KHM-AW).

This section examines the SVM classifier's accuracy problem in the context of a diagnostic system. Through the selection of the best qualities for the diagnosis process, this SVM problem is handled. In order to compute the weight of characteristics and further identify non-relevant qualities, the KHM-AW approach is created in this work. The label of a data object is measured using the KHM method. Additionally, a weight function that uses weight coefficients and cluster centers to calculate the weight of attributes is created. SVM classifier uses this technique for precise diabetes disease prediction. For the purpose of assessing the effectiveness of the suggested KHM-AW-SVM model, both all attributes and the ideal attributes of diabetes are taken into account. The advantages of the attribute selection method over the SVM classifier were confirmed by the results. Additionally, it is claimed that the fold method produces better results when using both the best and most advantageous attributes.

6.1.5.2 Deep Neural Network (DNN)

This technology seeks to help doctors with their diagnostic tasks. The process of diagnosing an illness involves more precisely identifying its symptoms. Once the disease's symptoms are accurately identified, treatment is straightforward. These medical systems do, however, require a significant amount of resources and computing power. It has also been highlighted that medical systems employ a significant amount of computing.

There are many authors who have examined that false value in medical data. They have worked on that data and removed the relevant data from the dataset or used default methods to fill false values, such as mean, median, neighbor, etc. However, neither approach is effective enough to yield the best outcomes. Outliers are also present in the data and have a negative impact on classifier performance. In the context of a diagnostic system, this chapter examines the accuracy problem with the DNN classifier. The best qualities for the diagnosis procedure are chosen in order to address this SVM problem. Therefore, the ABC approach is created in this work to compute the weight of characteristics and, further, to identify non-relevant attributes. For measuring the label of a data object, the DNN approach is utilized. Additionally, a weight function that uses weight coefficients and cluster centers to calculate the weight of attributes is created.

This approach is included in the DNN classifier for precise diabetic illness prediction. The ABC-DNN model takes into account both the best and worst characteristics of diabetes. The advantages of the attribute selection strategy over the DNN classifier were proven by the results. It is acknowledged that the 10-Fold approach produces superior results when all available and ideal features are used [25–30].

6.1.5.3 K-Mean++ Technique

There are several reasons why data may be incomplete or lacking in information. These explanations can be summed up as follows: mistakes in data collecting, incorrect measuring techniques, equipment malfunctions, etc. Missing values in databases can cause a variety of issues to arise throughout the knowledge discovery process. Lack of effectiveness, trouble maintaining the data, and difficulties with data analysis are the three main issues. Due to the incompleteness of the data, these missing numbers may also cause biased decisions. Thus, using such data for precise prediction is not practicable. Data mining algorithms can be used to provide the data tolerance strategy, but these techniques do not compute the values that are missing.

According to the analysis, the diabetes dataset has 432 data items with blank values. The diabetes dataset contains 763 total missing values. For six of the eight qualities, the missing values are present. These include pregnancy, blood sugar levels, diastolic blood pressure, SFT, serum insulin, and body mass index (BMI). 111, 5, 35, 227, 374, and 11 missing values are present, correspondingly. Statistics reveal that 48.6% of the data for the serum insulin attribute are missing, as opposed to 29.5% for the SFT attribute. The vast quantity of missing numbers makes it impossible to draw an objective conclusion [35].

6.1.5.4 ABC-Based Detection Technique

In this method, the removal of the outlier from the dataset can increase accuracy, which is a crucial step. According to the literature, outliers in datasets are frequently found and eliminated using clustering algorithms. By utilizing the distance function, these strategies identify the outliers. The general method also showed that an outlier was either defined by sparse, low-density clusters or was unrelated to any clusters. Large, dense clusters, on the other hand, best describe normal data. Different methods are used to identify outliers in datasets. Statistical methods consider the data distribution when finding outliers. Data points that deviate from the reported standard distribution are called outliers. When the data distribution is known in advance, these strategies perform well. Large datasets and high-dimensional data make this, however, unfeasible. A clustering model is built in a clustering-based strategy to describe the behavior of the data. It is also possible to spot outliers by measuring the distance between the data and the relevant cluster centroid. A data point is assumed to be an outlier if it considerably deviates from the centroid of the relevant cluster. Furthermore, it is claimed that clustering-based techniques may accurately detect outliers [31–33].

These approaches use k-nearest neighbor and density estimation to calculate the distance. The conclusion from the foregoing explanation is that a clustering-based approach is better suited for outlier detection. As a result, this paper also investigates how well a clustering-based approach can identify outliers.

6.1.5.5 Processed Data

The pre-processed data are converted into processed data using the K-Mean++ based missing data imputation and ABC based outlier identification processes. The missing data issue in the diabetes dataset is properly resolved by the K-Mean++ approach, which additionally establishes the ideal values for the missing data. The dataset's outliers are also located and eliminated using an ABC-based outlier detection method. These processes successfully transform the pre-processed input into processed data, allowing the classifier to use that data to make predictions [34, 35].

6.1.5.6 LS-Support Vector Machine (LS-SVM)

The diabetes dataset and support vector machines (SVM) forecasting task are described in this section. SVM is a well-respected classifier that is frequently used in prediction applications. However, minimizing structural risk resolves the over-fitting issue that SVM classifiers have. The additional SVM variation known as LS-SVM is shown. By reducing the squared error as opposed to the negative error and stating the problem as a linear equation as opposed to a quadratic program, the unequal constraints are converted into equal constraints.

In order to accurately forecast diabetes patients, this section provides a hybrid paradigm for diabetes prediction. Three separate methods make up the suggested framework. These methods include data imputation using K-Mean++, outlier detection using ABC, and a classifier using LS-SVM. In the actual world, properties in datasets can have missing values and incomplete information. The lack of efficacy, trouble in organizing the data, and difficulty in doing data analysis are just a few of the issues that can arise from missing values and incomplete information.

To impute the missing values, one can utilize the K-Means++-based data imputation technique. Outliers have an effect on forecast accuracy, which is general information. This study developed an ABC-based outlier detection method. These techniques allow the pre-processed data to become processed data. Using the LS-SVM classifier, it is also possible to identify patterns in processed data. The 763 missing values and outliers from the Pima Indian Diabetes dataset are used to evaluate the effectiveness of the proposed method. Utilizing LS-SVM classifiers, diabetes is predicted. The suggested framework's results were compared to those of a number of well-known current studies.

6.2 Literature Survey

6.2.1 Introduction

Due to its crucial role in maximizing solar energy integration into the grid and raising the general efficiency of renewable energy systems, solar power prediction has attracted a lot of interest from scholars and industry professionals. This section examines the body of research on solar power prediction methods, with an emphasis on deep learning strategies and optimization algorithms.

A supervised neural approach using an LSTM deep net was introduced by Ozbek *et al.* [48]. The technique sought to forecast a 1.15 MW solar-photovoltaic power plant's electricity production one hour in advance. The suggested deep neural network was combined with two different data-driven approaches: fuzzy c-means with grid partition and adaptive ANFIS.

The accuracy of the data produced by the models was verified by empirical data. The results of the comparison demonstrated that the method indicated produces the best outcomes. For the co-planning of wind farm, energy storage, and power line development, including severe weather occurrences, a multi-stage model is suggested [42]. A deep learning model for forecasting yearly peak loads that makes use of TLSM systems is described.

Wind power time series architecture with BiLSTM was proposed by Weng *et al.* [50] in order to address the problem of energy consumption. Especially with the advent of urban energy networks, renewable energy will be essential to the energy system of the future [43]. The unpredictability and instability of renewable power sources, like wind, have prevented them from making a substantial contribution to the energy supply. Accurately predicting wind power generation is essential to the safe operation of the power system. The results are derived from wind data collected by urban energy networks. Ashok and colleagues [44] proposed a Deep Learning-based method for power control and maximization. To maintain system stability, these controllers employ a variety of control techniques, such as keeping an eye on the voltages, phases, and frequencies on both sides of the fixed switch. Effective and efficient regulatory frameworks are necessary to establish a sustainable energy economy through the extensive use of renewable energy sources. Predictive analysis highlights the necessity of control strategies in order to create a dependable and effective micro power system network [45–47].

Shekhar *et al.* [52] suggested using deep learning models, including CNN and RNN algorithms, to bridge the gap in power usage forecasts. The CNN stack shows the highest degree of accuracy among the models that were assessed in terms of forecasting energy use and solar power generation. The average absolute percentage deviation, MAE, and RMSE are 1.71%, 0.015%, and 0.23%, respectively. But when it comes to wind turbine energy generation, the recurrent neural network is the most accurate model. The obtained score, with a median absolute percentage error of 2.65, is 0.070. Furthermore, the root value of 0.38 is shared by the MAE and ABE.

An enhanced hybrid prediction system was presented by Wang *et al.* [53] that takes meteorological conditions into account at every stage of development. In order to overcome the limitations of single-data dimension prediction, a feature selection module is first introduced. During the forecasting process, this module makes it possible to choose features and give weights to outside meteorological parameters [49, 56]. Second, both shallow and deep learning models are employed in a flexible way to create deterministic combinatorial prediction models, and multi-objective intelligent optimization techniques are suggested. In order to effectively meet the needs of a diverse range of information consumers, the module may fully weigh prediction accuracy and stability while also effectively enhancing the diversity of prediction models.

In their research, Xiyun *et al.* [54] looked at combining multiple approaches to forecast PV power rather than depending only on one. First, methods such as support vector machines (SVM), persistence models, and similarity-based techniques were applied independently to generate predictions. The relevance of each approach was then assessed by evaluating the correlation between the estimated and observed data. The approach is more significant when the correlation is higher. A formula for the full set of potential procedures is developed based on these outcomes for the ultimate performance. As a result, the authors have improved the accuracy of their calculations and created a somewhat reliable method for the assignment.

Based on weather forecasts, Yang *et al.* [55] investigated the daily solar power generation. There are three components to the suggested approach. Self-organizing map (SOM) and learning vector quantization (LVQ) networks are used in data separation to produce the output. The machine parameters for input/output (I/O) data, such as temperature, likelihood of rainfall, and sun ray intensity, are adjusted during the same time period in the training phase using the Support Vector Regression (SVR) technique.

From the results of the second step, a more accurate method is employed by choosing an Artificial Neural Network (ANN) with suitable weights and biases to increase prediction accuracy.

A novel set of algorithms was presented by Ghofrani *et al.* [57] that increases the precision of anticipating sun ray strength in advance by utilizing cutting-edge techniques, including neural networks, fuzzy logic, evolutionary algorithms, and others. The data was better grouped using the K-means approach. Additionally, they came up with a novel way to separate the data related to sun ray strength irregularities. This approach demonstrated efficacy in precisely forecasting the intensity a few seconds to many minutes beforehand. To improve the accuracy of the predictions, they have also improved the methods by adding a multilayer perceptron neural network (MLPNN), a time-based progression classification tool, an improved clustering methodology, and a unique cluster selection approach. They have also seen success with these additions.

M.K. Behera *et al.* [58] proposed a methodology in 2018 that may predict photovoltaic cell production using short time intervals. An extreme learning machine algorithm was used on an existing photovoltaic generator in the Indian state of Odisha, in the city of Bhubaneswar. The proposed model is based on the Maximum Power Point Tracking (MPPT) algorithms for Incremental Conductance (IC), which are associated with the Proportional Integral (PI) controller. The ELM approach is then applied to the model to modify the weights of a single-layer feed-forward network (SLFN). The PSO (particle swarm optimization) method optimizes the SLFN's weights.

The application of least square support vector regression and seasonal decomposition was studied by Lin *et al.* [59]. In order to schedule and enhance control performance in a balanced region, output prediction is crucial. In order to forecast photovoltaic (PV) production up to 30 days ahead of time, this study focuses on creating an evolutionary seasonal decomposition least square support vector regression (ESDLS SVR) model. Least square support vector regression (LS-SVR) and seasonal decomposition were used in the development of this model. The LS-SVR's parameters are simultaneously determined by genetic algorithms (GA). The Taiwan Power Company supplied the vital information needed to complete the project. The suggested power estimating approach performs better in terms of output accuracy, according to empirical data.

6.3 An Efficient Machine Learning Based Optimization Framework

Models were used in the past to predict solar power generation, which may have limited their accuracy and scalability. The use of machine learning techniques for energy forecasting has gained popularity recently because of its capacity to learn from data and adjust to changing circumstances. These techniques include the random forest classifier (RFC), which combines decision tree predictions and is renowned for its scalability, dependability, and ability to manage data sets. The RFC is therefore seen as an option for forecasting energy output. Choosing qualities and fine-tuning parameters.

Choosing features and fine-tuning parameters is essential when building machine learning models. Weather, location, and time all have an impact on energy production, making it difficult to predict immediate solar energy generation. Together, RFC and the election-based optimization algorithm create a revolutionary framework for analyzing solar energy in the short term. This is done in order to solve the issues.

6.3.1 Solar Power Reduction

In most situations, solar electricity may be used in grid-interactive mode with no effort, making it one of the most eco-friendly renewable energy sources. The PV power forecast feature is important when the grid-connected mode is taken into account. Given the current situation, precise forecasting is greatly required because it is intimately related to numerous environmental factors. An accurate forecast aids in effective maintenance planning.

Prediction plays an important role in managing load increases and decreases, matching peak loads, and reaching decision-making objectives. The stability of solar power is greatly impacted by a variety of atmospheric factors, including solar irradiance and a variety of climatic conditions (i.e., changes in the atmospheric state due to seasonal variations). Furthermore, it plays a crucial role in the energy management system's operation. A number of forecasting horizons and the corresponding relevance are shown in the following table. Accurate solar power predictions are essential for many different applications. Because of the researchers' efforts, the field of solar power prediction has made tremendous strides in recent years. To forecast solar electricity, a variety of machine learning methods have been employed. Over the years, several machine learning techniques have been created, including SVM, CNN, NN, and ELM. Two researchers named Guestrin and Chen developed the extreme gradient boosting (XGB) method in 2016. It is based on ensemble trees. This method has more processing power and worked well to address the over-fitting problem. These methods consist of machine learning-based approaches, hybrid approaches, and a range of statistical tools. To forecast solar power and irradiation, ARMA, ARIMA, and ARMAX have been placed into practice. Support vector machines (SVM), neural networks (NN), recurrent neural networks (RBFLN), and elastic learning (ELM) are just a few of the machine learning techniques that have been applied to a range of prediction scopes. A lot of hybrid models and ensemble models have been utilized recently to provide predictions that are more accurate.

RFC is used for prediction modelling and feature selection, while EBOA optimizes model parameters to improve prediction precision and accuracy. Inspired by natural elections, EBOA is a population-based metaheuristic optimization technique. Based on their suitability, candidate solutions compete with one another in natural elections. In order to swiftly search the space and find the best answers, EBOA uses selection, crossover, and mutation procedures.

6.3.2 Evaluation Parameter

Equations suggest analyzing the RFC-EBOA model using evaluation metrics such as MPE, RMSE, MAE, and R2. This study compares the RFC-EBOA with various methods for solar power prediction, including CNN,

XGBoost, and Bi-LSTM, in order to give a more accurate evaluation. Winter and summer are the two separate seasons that have been used to predict solar power. These seasons have been picked especially so that the outcomes can be examined. To calculate the accuracy of the model, only one month's worth of data from the entire season is used. While May is thought of as the summer season, December is thought of as the winter season.

An analysis of the proposed strategy on a cold day in comparison to current approaches is shown in Figure 6.1. Figure 6.2 compares a number of methods that were used to assess the recommended method's performance accuracy over the course of the summer.

Performance of the proposed model is evaluated using a number of matrices, such as MAPE, RMSE, MAE, and R2. Although there are more prediction measurement techniques, this study only looks at four in order to assess forecast accuracy. It is easier to compare several prediction models, like CNN, XGBoost, and Bi-LSTM, thanks to the prediction matrices. The performance requirements for the two models are presented in Tables 6.1 and 6.2, respectively, for the winter and summer days. The CNN-LBO model clearly performs the best when comparing the data on both days across all performance criteria shown in Figure 6.3 and Figure 6.4.

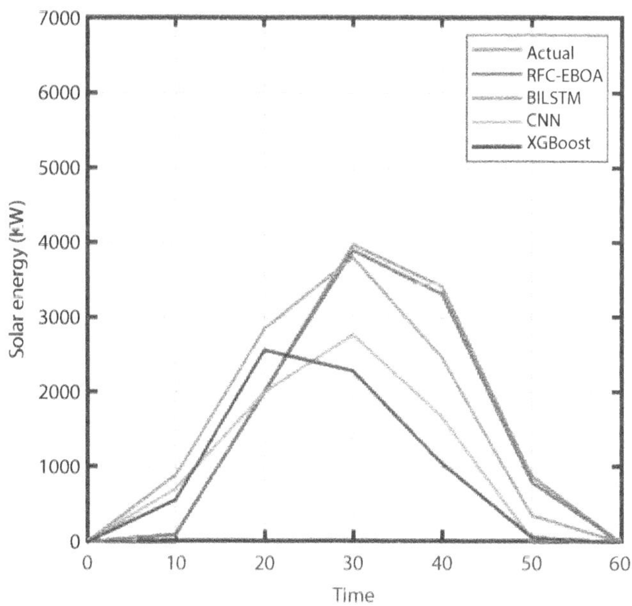

Figure 6.1 Comparison analysis of winter days [52].

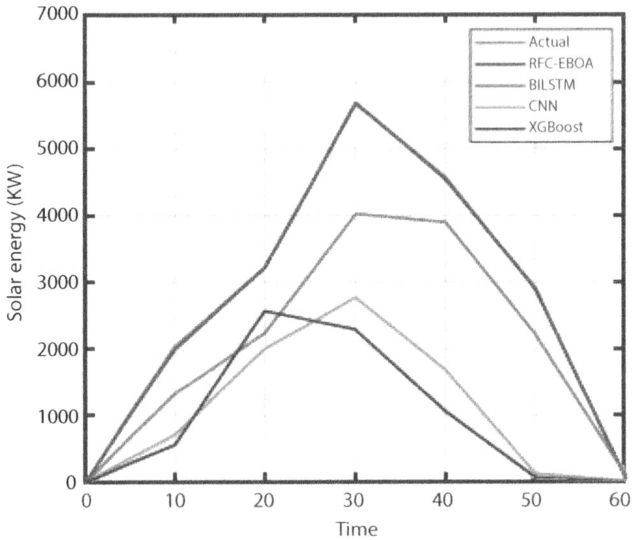

Figure 6.2 Comparison analysis of summer days [52].

Table 6.1 Performance evaluation of winter days [52].

Season	Method	MAPE	MAE	RMSE	R^2
Winter	RFC-EBOA	3.348	279.2	377.3	0.923
	BiLSTM	3.872	322.4	431.5	0.932
	CNN	4.008	461.1	549.7	0.956
	XGBoost	4.674	724.2	788.1	0.989

Table 6.2 Performance evaluation of summer days [52].

Season	Method	MAPE	MAE	RMSE	R^2
Summer	RFC-EBOA	0.324	761.2	939.5	0.688
	BiLSTM	0.468	841.3	1207.3	0.752
	CNN	0.691	1231.7	1687.8	0.947
	XGBoost	0.981	1587.6	1877.4	0.991

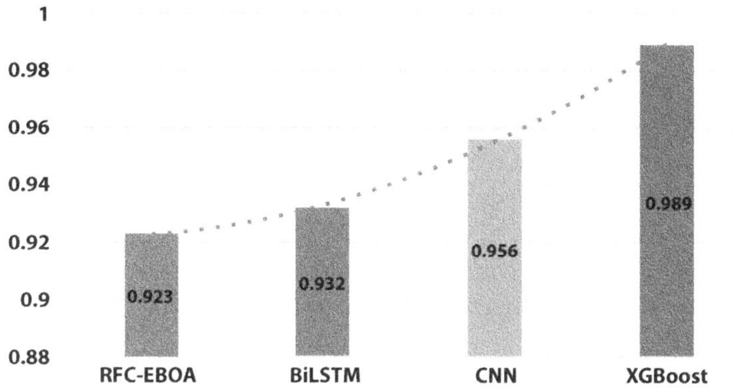

Figure 6.3 RMSE bar chart of winter days.

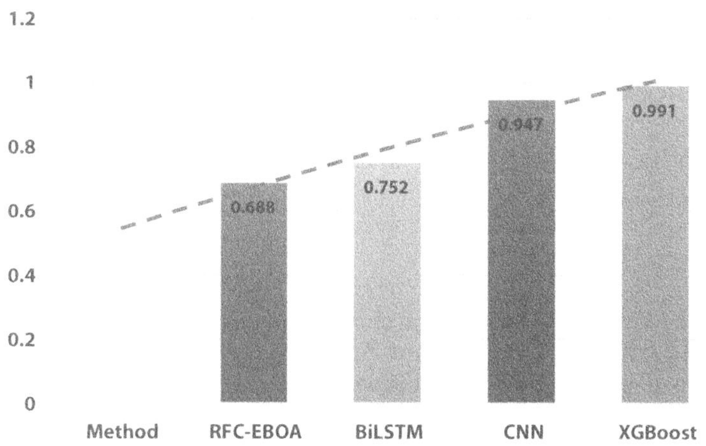

Figure 6.4 RMSE bar chart of summer days.

6.4 Conclusion

This chapter implements a method for solar energy analysis that combines an election-based optimization algorithm (EBOA) with a random forest classifier (RFC). The suggested approach is effective in accurately forecasting solar energy production. By combining the RFC's capacity to handle high-dimensional data and identify intricate patterns with the optimization capabilities of EBOA for parameter tuning, we have achieved better prediction accuracy and computational efficiency when compared to current approaches. Its ability to improve energy management and expedite the integration of renewable energy sources into the power grid has been proven by using the suggested method on actual solar energy data tests.

The accuracy of solar energy estimates may be improved by future research exploring hybrid approaches that combine machine learning and physical models. Additionally, the suggested method's flexibility and scalability make it applicable in a wide range of fields outside solar energy, highlighting its broader significance for the development of data-driven strategies related to sustainable energy use. Overall, this study contributes to the ongoing discussion about advancing the integration of renewable energy sources and highlights the importance of innovative strategies in addressing the complexity of modern energy infrastructures.

AI disclosure statement: The author acknowledges the use of AI-based tools for minor language editing or grammatical correction. However, all intellectual contributions, analyses, and conclusions presented in this chapter are entirely the author's own.

References

1. Abou Houran, M., Bukhari, S.M.S., Zafar, M.H., Mansoor, M., Chen, W., COA-CNN-LSTM: Coati optimization algorithm-based hybrid deep learning model for PV/wind power forecasting in smart grid applications. *Appl. Energy*, 349, 121638, 2023.
2. Zouli, N., Design of solar power-based hybrid desalination predictive method using optimized neural network. *Desalination*, *566*, 116854, 2023.
3. Ahmed, R., Sreeram, V., Mishra, Y., Arif, M.D., A review and evaluation of the state-of-the-art in PV solar power forecasting: Techniques and optimization. *Renewable Sustainable Energy Rev.*, *124*, 109792, 2020.
4. Sharadga, H., Hajimirza, S., Balog, R.S., Time series forecasting of solar power generation for large-scale photovoltaic plants. *Renewable Energy*, *150*, 797–807, 2020.
5. Irshad, K., Islam, N., Gari, A.A., Algarni, S., Alqahtani, T., Imteyaz, B., Arithmetic optimization with hybrid deep learning algorithm based solar radiation prediction model. *Sustainable Energy Technol. Assess.*, *57*, 103165, 2023.
6. Shivashankaraiah, K., Shashibhushan, G., Prema Kirubakaran, A., Anjanappa, C., Sharma, P.K., Mayiladuthurai Vaidyanathan, I., Alfarraj, S., Developing a Deep Learning and Reliable Optimization Techniques for Solar Photovoltaic Power Prediction. *Electr. Power Compon. Syst.*, 1–15, 2024.
7. Moradzadeh, A., Moayyed, H., Mohammadi-Ivatloo, B., Vale, Z., Ramos, C., Ghorbani, R., A novel cyber-Resilient solar power forecasting model based on secure federated deep learning and data visualization. *Renewable Energy*, *211*, 697–705, 2023.
8. Torres-Barrán, A., Alonso, A., Dorronsoro, J.R., Regression tree ensembles for wind energy and solar radiation prediction. *Neurocomputing*, *326*, 151–160, 2019.

9. Raman, R., Mewada, B., Meenakshi, R., Jayaseelan, G.M., Sharmila, K.S., Taqui, S.N., ... & Iqbal, A., Forecasting the PV power utilizing a combined convolutional neural network and long short-term memory model. *Electr. Power Compon. Syst.*, 1–17, 2023.
10. Ibrahim, M.S., Gharghory, S.M., Kamal, H.A., A hybrid model of CNN and LSTM autoencoder-based short-term PV power generation forecasting. *Electr. Eng.*, 1–17, 2024.
11. Sahoo, B.M., Pandey, H.M., Amgoth, T., A genetic algorithm inspired optimized cluster head selection method in wireless sensor networks. *Swarm Evol. Comput.*, 75, 101151, 2022.
12. Wang, H., Liu, Y., Zhou, B., Li, C., Cao, G., Voropai, N., Barakhtenko, E., Taxonomy research of artificial intelligence for deterministic solar power forecasting. *Energy Convers. Manage.*, *214*, 112909, 2020.
13. Safiri, S. and Nikoofard, A., Ladybug Beetle Optimization algorithm: application for real-world problems. *J. Supercomputing*, *79*, 3, 3511–3560, 2023.
14. Trojovský, P. and Dehghani, M., A new optimization algorithm based on mimicking the voting process for leader selection. *PeerJ Comput. Sci.*, 8, e976, 2022.
15. Amoura, Y., Torres, S., Lima, J., Pereira, A., II, Hybrid optimisation and machine learning models for wind and solar data prediction. *Int. J. Hybrid Intell. Syst.(Preprint)*, 1–16, 2023.
16. Rathore, P.S., Chatterjee, J.M., Kumar, A., *et al.*, Energy-efficient cluster head selection through relay approach for WSN. *J. Supercomput.*, 77, 7649–7675, 2021. https://doi.org/10.1007/s11227-020-03593-4.
17. Mangot, A., Kumar, A., Baliyan, A., Shining a Light on Solar Power Forecasting: Machine Learning Techniques for Unprecedented Accuracy, in: *2023 3rd International Conference on Technological Advancements in Computational Sciences (ICTACS)*, IEEE, pp. 828–834, 2023, November.
18. Dubey, A.K., Kumar, A., Ramirez, I.S., Marquez, F.P.G., A review of intelligent systems for the prediction of wind energy using machine learning, in: *International Conference on Management Science and Engineering Management*, Cham: Springer International Publishing, pp. 476–491, 2022, July.
19. Rathore, P.S., Kumar, A., García-Díaz, V., A holistic methodology for improved RFID network lifetime by advanced cluster head selection using dragonfly algorithm, 2020.
20. Rathore, P.S., Sarkar, M.K., Das, R., A comprehensive review on secure and energy aware multi-hop routing in clustering based wireless sensor network. *Telecommun. Radio Eng.*, 80, 8, 2021.
21. Narooka, P., Gupta, A., Tak, P., Goswami, M.P., Palit, R., Keshan, M., Enhanced Human Action Recognition Using CNN and DCGAN Preprocessing on the KTH Dataset, in: *Data Science and Applications. ICDSA 2024. Lecture Notes in Networks and Systems*. Nanda, S.J., Yadav, R.P., Gandomi, A.H., Saraswat, M. (eds), vol. 1263, Springer, Singapore, 2025, https://doi.org/10.1007/978-981-96-2724-0_13.
22. Narooka, P., Vashistha, A., Mitra, P., Derashri, G., Life Expectancy Prediction Using Machine Learning Technique – KNN, *2024 IEEE 3rd World Conference*

on Applied Intelligence and Computing (AIC), pp. 395–399, Gwalior, India, 2024, doi: 10.1109/AIC61668.2024.10730995.

23. Narooka, P., Vishnoi, A., Verma, J., Machine Learning Techniques for Predicting Epileptic Seizures: A Data-Driven Analysis Using EEG Signals. *Targeted Chemotherapy with Personalized Immunotherapy: An AI Approach*, 325–335, 2025.
24. Gandhi, P., Bhatia, S., Kumar, A., Alojail, M.A., Rathore, P.S. (Eds.), *Internet of Things in Business Transformation: Developing an Engineering and Business Strategy for Industry 5.0.*, John Wiley & Sons, 2020.
25. Sapra, V., Sapra, L., Vishnoi, A., Narooka, P., Choudhury, T., Enhancing Mental Disorder Diagnosis with Ensemble Bagging and Random Forest Techniques, *2024 International Conference on Communication, Computer Sciences and Engineering (IC3SE)*, pp. 1765–1769, Gautam Buddha Nagar, India, 2024, doi: 10.1109/IC3SE62002.2024.10593187.
26. Kumar, A., Dubey, A.K., Segovia Ramírez, I., *et al.*, Artificial Intelligence Techniques for the Photovoltaic System: A Systematic Review and Analysis for Evaluation and Benchmarking. *Arch. Computat. Methods Eng.*, 31, 4429–4453, 2024. https://doi.org/10.1007/s11831-024-10125-3.
27. Dubey, A.K., Ramirez, I., Marquez, F., A Review of Intelligent Systems for the Prediction of Wind Energy Using Machine Learning. *2022, ICMSEM, The Sixteenth International Conference on Management Science and Engineering Management, Lecture Notes on Data Engineering and Communications Technologies, vol 144. Springer, by Springer*, Ankara, Turkey, August 3-6, 2022.
28. Kumar, A.D., Ramirez, I., Rio, A., Marquez, F., A Review and Analysis of Forecasting of Photovoltaic Power Generation Using Machine Learning. *2022, ICMSEM, The Sixteenth International Conference on Management Science and Engineering Management, Lecture Notes on Data Engineering and Communications Technologies,* vol 144., Springer, Cham. by Springer, Ankara, Turkey, August 3-6, 2022.
29. Dhaka, A., Nait-Abdesselam, F., Nandal, A., Bogatinoska, D.C., Rathore, P.S., Sharma, A.K., Zubov, D., *Virtual Reality, Real Emergency: Integrating AR/VR in Computing and Medical Crisis Management*, CRC Press, 2025.
30. Jyani, M., Rathore, P.S., Spectrogram-Based CNN Framework for Live Deepfake Voice Detection in Google Meet, in: *2025 International Conference on Computing Technologies & Data Communication (ICCTDC)*, pp. 1–5. IEEE, 2025.
31. Dhivagar, R., Shoeibi, S., Parsa, S.M., Hoseinzadeh, S., Kargarsharifabad, H., Khiadani, M., Performance evaluation of solar still using energy storage biomaterial with porous surface: An experimental study and environmental analysis. *Renewable Energy*, 206, 879–889, 2023.
32. Mevada, D., Panchal, H., Ahmadein, M., Zayed, M.E., Alsaleh, N.A., Djuansjah, J., Sadasivuni, K.K., Investigation and performance analysis of solar still with energy storage materials: An energy-exergy efficiency analysis. *Case Stud. Therm. Eng.*, 29, 101687, 2022.

33. Zayed, M.E., Aboelmaaref, M.M., Chazy, M., Design of solar air conditioning system integrated with photovoltaic panels and thermoelectric coolers: Experimental analysis and machine learning modeling by random vector functional link coupled with white whale optimization. *Therm. Sci. Eng. Prog.*, 44, 102051, 2023.
34. Graditi, G., Ferlito, S., Adinolfi, G., Comparison of Photovoltaic plant power production prediction methods using a large measured dataset. *Renewable Energy*, 90, 513–519, 2016.
35. Pedro, H.T. and Coimbra, C.F., Assessment of forecasting techniques for solar power production with no exogenous inputs. *Sol. Energy*, 86, 7, 2017–2028, 2012.
36. Diwakar, M., Singh, P., Karetla, G.R., Narooka, P., Yadav, A., Maurya, R. K., Gupta, R., Arias-Gonzáles, J.L., Singh, M.P., Shetty, D.K., Paul, R., Naik, N., Low-Dose COVID-19 CT Image Denoising Using Batch Normalization and Convolution Neural Network. *Electronics*, 11, 20, 3375, 2022, https://doi.org/10.3390/electronics11203375.
37. Pandey, A.K., Rathore, P.S., Balamurugan, S., *A Practical Approach for Machine Learning and Deep Learning Algorithms: Tools and Techniques Using MATLAB and Python*, BPB Publications, 2019.
38. Lauret, P., Voyant, C., Soubdhan, T., David, M., Poggi, P., A benchmarking of machine learning techniques for solar radiation forecasting in an insular context. *Sol. Energy*, 112, 446–457, 2015.
39. Mojumder, J.C., Ong, H.C., Chong, W.T., Shamshirband, S., Application of support vector machine for prediction of electrical and thermal performance in PV/T system. *Energy Build.*, 111, 267–277, 2016.
40. Ogliari, E., Grimaccia, F., Leva, S., Mussetta, M., Hybrid predictive models for accurate forecasting in PV systems. *Energies*, 6, 4, 1918–1929, 2013.
41. Haque, A.U., Nehrir, M.H., Mandal, P., Solar PV power generation forecast using a hybrid intelligent approach, in: *2013 IEEE Power & Energy Society General Meeting*, IEEE, pp. 1–5, 2013, July.
42. Ramsami, P. and Oree, V., A hybrid method for forecasting the energy output of photovoltaic systems. *Energy Convers. Manage.*, 95, 406– 413, 2015.
43. Junior, J. G. D. S. F., Oozeki, T., Ohtake, H., Shimose, K., II, Takashima, T., Ogimoto, K., Regional forecasts and smoothing effect of photovoltaic power generation in Japan: An approach with principal component analysis. *Renewable Energy*, 68, 403–413, 2014.
44. Kumar, A., Chatterjee, J.M., Payal, M., Rathore, P.S., Revolutionizing the internet of things with swarm intelligence, in: *System Assurances*, pp. 403–436, Academic Press, 2022.
45. Al-Dahidi, S., Ayadi, O., Adeeb, J., Alrbai, M., Qawasmeh, B.R., Extreme learning machines for solar photovoltaic power predictions. *Energies*, 11, 10, 2725, 2018.
46. Dash, P.K., Majumder, I., Nayak, N., Bisoi, R., Point and interval solar power forecasting using hybrid empirical wavelet transform and robust wavelet kernel ridge regression. *Nat. Resour. Res.*, 29, 5, 2813–2841, 2020.

47. Bessa, R.J., Trindade, A., Silva, C.S., Miranda, V., Probabilistic solar power forecasting in smart grids using distributed information. *Int. J. Electr. Power Energy Syst.*, 72, 16–23, 2015.
48. Ozbek, A., Yildirim, A., Bilgili, M., Deep learning approach for one-hour ahead forecasting of energy production in a solar-PV plant. *Energy Sources Part A*, 44, 4, 10465–10480, 2022.
49. Moradi-Sepahvand, M., Amraee, T., Gougheri, S.S., Deep learning based hurricane resilient coplanning of transmission lines, battery energy storages, and wind farms. *IEEE Trans. Ind. Inf.*, 18, 3, 2120–2131, 2021.
50. Weng, G., Pei, C., Ren, J., Jiang, H., Xu, J., Zheng, W., Gao, T., Modeling and forecasting of wind power output of urban regional energy internet based on deep learning, in: *Journal of Physics: Conference Series*, vol. 1732, p. 012190, IOP Publishing, New Delhi, India, 2021.
51. Ashok Babu, P., Mazher Iqbal, J.L., Siva Priyanka, S., Jithender Reddy, M., Sunil Kumar, G., Ayyasamy, R., Power control and optimization for power loss reduction using deep learning in microgrid systems. *Electr. Power Compon. Syst.*, 52, 2, 219–232, 2024.
52. Shekhar, H., Bhushan Mahato, C., Suman, S.K., Singh, S., Bhagyalakshmi, L., Prasad Sharma, M., Rajaram, A., Demand side control for energy saving in renewable energy resources using deep learning optimization. *Electr. Power Compon. Syst.*, 51, 19, 2397–2413, 2023.
53. Wang, J., Yu, Y., Zeng, B., Lu, H., Hybrid ultra-short-term PV power forecasting system for deterministic forecasting and uncertainty analysis. *Energy*, 288, 129898, 2024.
54. Xiyun, Y. and Song, C., A combination method in photovoltaic power forecasting based on the correlation coefficient, in: *2014 IEEE 5th International Conference on Software Engineering and Service Science*, IEEE, pp. 706–709, 2014, June.
55. Yang, H.T., Huang, C.M., Huang, Y.C., Pai, Y.S., A weather-based hybrid method for 1-day ahead hourly forecasting of PV power output. *IEEE Trans. Sustainable Energy*, 5, 3, 917–926, 2014.
56. Parida, R.K., Roy, M., Parida, A.K., Uddin, A., An Efficient Machine Learning Based Optimization Framework to Analyse the Short-Term Solar Energy. *International Conference on Computing Sciences & Communication (ICCSC-2024)*, 2024.
57. Ghofrani, M., Ghayekhloo, M., Azimi, R., A novel soft computing framework for solar radiation forecasting. *Appl. Soft Comput.*, 48, 207–216, 2016.
58. Behera, M.K., Majumder, I., Nayak, N., Solar photovoltaic power forecasting using optimized modified extreme learning machine technique. *Eng. Sci. Technol. Int. J.*, 21, 3, 428–438, 2018.
59. Lin, K.P. and Pai, P.F., Solar power output forecasting using evolutionary seasonal decomposition least-square support vector regression. *J. Cleaner Prod.*, 134, 456–462, 2016.

7

Generative AI and Solar Energy: Shaping the Future of Sustainable Power

Priyanka P. Shinde[1]*, Lanson D. Bardeskar[1], Kanif M. Kumbhar[1], Omkar R. Bidave[1], Piyush P. Patil[1] and Bhushan S. Yelure[2]

[1]*Department of Master of Computer Applications (MCA), Government College of Engineering, Karad, Maharashtra, India*
[2]*Department of Information Technology, Government College of Engineering, Karad, Maharashtra, India*

Abstract

The introduction of **generative artificial intelligence (GenAI)** into solar energy systems represents a model shift in renewable energy management, offering innovative solutions to enduring challenges such as intermittency, grid instability, and material weaknesses. While traditional machine learning (ML) and deep learning (DL) models have advanced solar forecasting and unusual occurrence detection, GenAI—utilizing frameworks like transformers, generative adversarial networks (GANs), and hybrid quantum-classical frameworks—promises to transform the sector. As an extension, transformer architectures have the capability to merge multiple datasets simultaneously (satellite imagery, meteorological data, and IoT sensor information) to enhance predictions of solar radiation for very short periods into the future, while GANs support synthetic data creation for well-trained models that operate in extreme climate conditions. Quantum-enhanced AI (QAI) further boosts large-scale adjustments, such as grid balancing and material discovery, by solving complex ordered problems increasingly faster than classical systems. At the same time, digital twins powered by GenAI dynamically copy solar farm performance, enabling real-time adjustments to energy storage and distribution. But issues such as splitting and cleaning the data, the technological cost, and suspicion about the AI ethical issues dominate the discussions and create a need for the framework of explainable AI (XAI) and comprehensive metadata protocols. This study analyzes these new tendencies regarding the explanation of GenAI as the means of providing powerful, effective, and easily adaptable sustainable solar energy systems in the green world of the future.

**Corresponding author*: ppshinde.gcek@gmail.com

Abhishek Kumar, Pramod Singh Rathore, Arun Lal Srivastav and Ashutosh Kumar Dubey (eds.) Solar Energy Optimization Using Generative Artificial Intelligence, (145–164) © 2026 Scrivener Publishing LLC

Keywords: Solar energy, GenAI, SVM, GANs

Introduction

The integration of solar energy to combat current climate change issues, along with recent advancements in technology, has revealed certain weaknesses in staggering photovoltaic (PV) systems, as well as in the integration with the grid and the creation of requisite high-efficiency materials [1]. More traditional artificial intelligence techniques, such as convolutional neural networks (CNNs) and support vector machines (SVM), have been able to offer somewhat effective solutions by improving irradiance forecasting and performing fault detection [7, 8]. New innovations within generative AI (GenAI) technology—a branch of AI technology that focuses on data generation, scenario imitation, and creative problem solving—open up unprecedented innovations.

The Rise of GenAI in Solar Energy

1. **Transformers and Multimodal Forecasting**:

The architecture model termed "transformer" that was initially used for NLP (Natural Language Processing) is now being repurposed to examine the spatial and temporal dimensions of solar data. Cloud movement and the variability of irradiance can be forecasted with an accuracy of sub-hourly timescales. This utilizes a sequence of satellite images, weather data from the past, and real-time sensor feeds [5]. For instance, Yousef *et al.* [1] successfully showed that transformer-based models improve forecast accuracy by 15%–20% in desert regions compared to LSTM networks. The rapid shift of clouds exposes such regions to high rates of PV output volatility.

2. **GANs for Synthetic Climate Data**:

Generative adversarial networks (GANs) make it possible to fabricate datasets that capture the characteristics of dust storms or synoptic cloud cover since those events are very infrequent. ML models can simulate upon such data sets and train under circumstances devoid of geographically deposited historical data. This is very important for the MENA (Middle East and North Africa) region, where dust accumulation leads to a decrease in PV efficiency of up to 40% [10]. Utilities can mitigate negative impacts by adjusting storage or grid strategy, e.g., relying on hybrid energy sources consisting of solar, wind, and batteries combined [2].

3. **AI-Driven Digital Twins**:
Solar farms are now being developed into virtual entities, known as digital twins. These now encompass GenAI, which enables real-time optimization and decision buying. Digital twin models of 50 MW photovoltaic solar plants have been developed by Wu *et al.* [6] using RL techniques for autonomous adjustment of panel orientations and battery charging schedules of Piot systems. Integrated weather forecasting and demand patterning reduced energy curtailment by 12% while increasing battery life by 8%.
4. **Quantum AI for Material Discovery**:
The integration of GenAI with quantum computing is enhancing the development of the next generation of PV materials. Consider perovskite solar cells, which need intensive and combinatorial testing of thousands of chemicals. QAI algorithms such as quantum annealing are capable of screening material properties commutation at an astonishing rate that is one hundred times faster than the classical approach. This facilitates the design of highly efficient and low-cost cells [3].

Challenges and Ethical Factors
Despite these advancements, GenAI faces significant challenges:

- **Standardization and Data Quality**: The calibration and metadata of solar datasets are usually incoherent across different regions [1]. GenAI systems trained with incomplete information are predisposed to forecasting and systemic errors.
- **Trust and Explainability**: The use of deep neural networks for black-box AI hinders algorithm adoption from stakeholders owing to their evaluative flaws. SHAP (SHapley Additive exPlanations) is one of many models of XAI that facilitates understanding of the input made by GenAI in grid operations [4].
- **Ethical and Computational Expenses**: Implementation of large GenAI models requires training that consumes a lot of energy, which undermines the carbon benefits of utilizing solar resources. The deployment of AI needs to be ethical within the context of innovating while preserving the planet's health [9].

This paper seeks to address these issues while promoting collaboration across disciplines to exploit the limits of GenAI. This region bridges research conducted in advanced AI and solar energy to help policymakers and engineers develop pathways where systems that rely on GenAI are efficiently transitioned in a renewable-powered world.

7.1 Current State of Generative AI in Solar Energy

Computational models under the category of Generative AI develop new data patterns with information extracted from existing datasets. Modern solar power optimization relies on the implementation of generative adversarial networks (GANs) and variational autoencoders (VAEs) techniques. Through artificial intelligence, these computational methods enhanced solar farm design capabilities and performed better layout modifications and predictive maintenance tasks for increased operational efficiency.

7.1.1 AI Generative Design in Solar Energy

Solar energy system development experiences a tremendous transformation through the use of Artificial Intelligence (AI) generative design. Through computational power joined by optimization algorithms, AI-driven generative design searches for innovative solutions beyond traditional design methods based on human intuition. The method goes through multiple design variations while assessing them with established criteria to create optimal performance configurations.

AI generative design for solar energy systems possesses these main essential components:

- **Defining Designing Parameters:** Machine learning software with AI algorithms utilizes performance standards together with geometry standards and material specifications to investigate optimal solutions in a systematic way [5].
- **Machine Learning Enhancement:** The process of machine learning analysis optimizes AI-controlled design solutions through a combination of supervisory learning with unsupervised learning and reinforcement learning as it analyzes vast datasets [7].

- **Application in Solar Energy:** The technology enhances solar energy operations through applications in solar panel design optimization, robotic assembly planning, and material selection as described by Sharma and Singh [14].

7.1.2 AI-Driven Optimization of Solar Panel Layout

The main technological benefit of AI generative design entails maximizing solar panel systems by enhancing energy production performance with reduced system costs alongside increased efficiency.

Key Applications:

- AI analytical systems evaluate specific site factors, which include terrain elevation and shading conditions, to establish perfect solar panel placement [2]. The analysis finds optimal solutions by combining land use restrictions with perceptual criteria to work around solar accessibility problems caused by obstacles.
- AI models deploy the optimal setup for individual solar panels to achieve maximum energy production by reducing energy loss because of system imbalance, blockage, and environmental degradation [14]. The algorithms adjust solar panel installation angles as well as azimuth directions and inter-panel space distances to reach the highest possible seasonal energy output.
- AI generative design evaluates an extensive range of materials with coatings and surface treatments to improve both solar panel reliability and efficiency [8]. The development of more resilient and efficient panels follows a process that considers properties of materials, effects of weathering, and cost evaluation.
- Artificial intelligence creates robot frameworks through automated design, which enhances solar panel installation and maintenance operations while cutting labor expenses [13]. The following Table 7.1 shows the advancements and research throughout the last 5 years.

Table 7.1 Comparative study of AI-controlled generative design applications for solar energy.

Study title	Authors	Year	Summary
Advances in solar PV technologies	Sharma A., Singh B., Sharma V.	2021	The paper explores recent developments related to solar cell technology, material advancements, and new production approaches.
Machine learning applications in solar forecasting	Gupta S., Kumar A.	2020	An overview describes the implementation of ML technology for solar energy forecasting systems involved in grid management.
Integration of AI in solar energy systems	Li H., Wang Z.	2021	The examination of artificial intelligence implementations for solar panel optimization, as well as smart grids, takes place in this section.
Emerging trends in solar energy conversion	Khan S., Lee S.	2023	Highlights nanomaterial-based approaches in solar energy conversion.

7.1.3 AI-Driven Predictive Maintenance in Solar Farms

Predictive maintenance through machine learning has revolutionized solar farms through failure anticipation, which leads to optimized maintenance programming.

Applications in Predictive Maintenance:

- AI technology performs anomaly detection through sensor data evaluation of solar panel systems, inverters, and other elements, which helps find early failures [16].

- Experts refer to failure prediction as the method that analyzes historical information alongside environmental conditions and operational parameters to determine equipment failure rates and durations [13]. Maintenance priorities become easier to identify through this process, which minimizes equipment outages that appear unexpectedly.
- Agent performance degraded through time will be analyzed by AI methods that perform actual performance benchmarking against expected measurements. The diagnosis of equipment degradation reasons and subsequent corrective actions becomes possible thanks to this method [10].
- The combination of algorithms powered by artificial intelligence generates optimal scheduling for maintenance activities through predictions of failure risk and system operational boundaries, which simultaneously minimizes system failure probabilities while reducing maintenance expenses [3].

7.1.4 AI-Driven Optimization of Utility-Scale Solar Farms

The lateration experiments presented in this dissertation, however, demonstrate that the application of AI techniques has a largely beneficial effect on the design and efficiency of large solar farms. Researchers use AI generative design algorithms to analyze terrain data, solar irradiance maps, and land use restrictions to derive the maximum design that allows for the optimal production of energy while minimizing the land needed and installation costs [2].

AI algorithms simulate the layout configurations using historical weather data and performance models and run these over multiple environmental conditions. Factors that could enhance the efficiency of the latter are included in these simulations, such as panel tilt, orientation, spacing, and inter-row shading [2].

As much as 20% more energy yield can be obtained from AI-optimized layouts compared to standard, traditional designs. This in turn helps clarify the possibilities of using optimization by means of AI to maximize land use and accelerate the deployment of solar energy systems [6].

7.1.5 Industry-Specific Applications of AI in Solar Energy

7.1.5.1 Smart Grid Integration

Real-time analytics and automated decision-making optimize power distribution, manage the supply-demand fluctuations, and make grid stability better. They minimize the risk of blackout, limit transmission losses, and increase grid efficiency by adjusting energy flow on the basis of the demand and the instantaneous generation of renewable energy [2].

7.1.5.2 Solar Asset Management

Analytics powered by artificial intelligence give predictive indications of asset maintenance and fault detection, as well as predictions of energy production. By evaluating the performance of solar farms, predicting the likelihood of failures, automating the scheduling of maintenance, and thus reducing the operational cost and increasing the uptime, companies implement AI-based platforms to monitor the performance of solar farms [13].

7.1.5.3 Automated Energy Trading

Predictive models that are AI-driven work by analyzing market trends, weather conditions, and energy demand and taking intelligent trading decisions. The algorithms help solar energy companies to bid more intelligently in the energy markets, augmenting the sale of surplus electricity and volume yields [3].

7.1.5.4 Residential and Commercial Solar Optimization

A few rooftops are using AI-based tools to put rooftop solar panels on them if they follow patterns of historical energy consumption output and are based on local solar exposure. They enable homeowners and businesses to make the most of conservation by always adjusting the angles of solar panels and following daily energy production [8].

7.1.5.5 Solar-Powered Microgrids

Analysis of dispersed generation and energy storage with decentralized microgrids indicates that it is possible to optimize storage, generation, and distribution using AI. In remote places, industrial sites, and disaster recovery zones, reliable power is essential, for which these solutions are critical [2].

7.1.5.6 AI-Enhanced Battery Storage

Energy demand is predicted with AI, and then battery storage is used to optimize its use in order to improve energy reliability and decrease dependency on the grid. Battery charging and discharging cycles are optimized with advanced energy storage management for the life of the battery and the cost [6].

7.1.5.7 AI-Powered Solar Forecasting

Meteorological data is used to perform highly accurate solar power generation forecasts by deep learning techniques. This improved forecasting accuracy also enables grid operators to handle a supply and demand balance better, thereby relying less on backup power sources and leading to improved overall grid stability [7]. Figure 7.1 shows the solar power production forecasting framework that integrates multiple data inputs including numeric weather forecasts, measurement mast data, and historical production data through ARX models and artificial neural networks.

The following diagram demonstrates the process for creating production forecasts through different data inputs and predictive models.

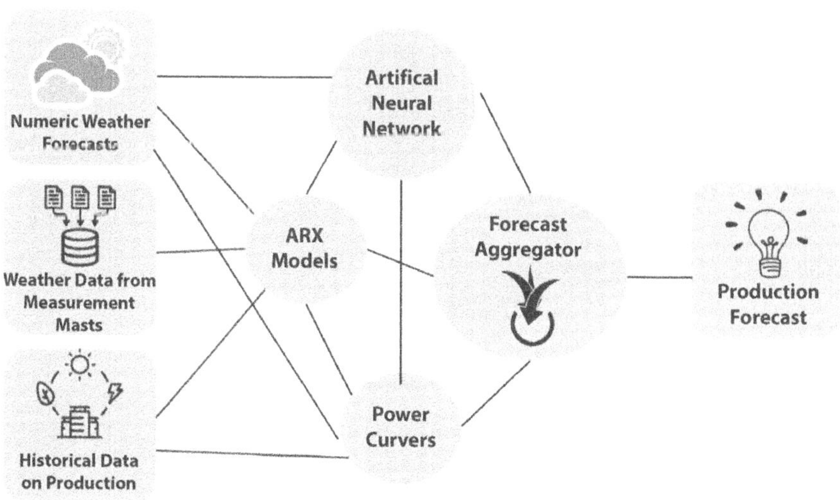

Figure 7.1 Solar power production forecasting framework.

7.2 Emerging Trends in Generative AI in Solar Energy

It has also fastened the future of generative AI in the solar energy sector. Machine learning, deep learning, as well as generative adversarial networks (GANs) and variational autoencoders (VAEs) are used by researchers and industry leaders to develop more efficient, adaptive, intelligent solar energy solutions. Instead of just designing beforehand a solar panel and doing predictive maintenance, AI can be used for integrations into energy grid optimization, decentralized power distribution, and material innovations challenges [2, 5]. Figure 7.2 shows the six key emerging trends in generative AI applications for solar energy, including smart grid integration, energy storage solutions, decentralized systems, material innovation, autonomous installation, and hybrid energy systems.

The following diagram presents solar energy sector advancements in the use of generative AI through an aesthetically arranged hexagon grid.

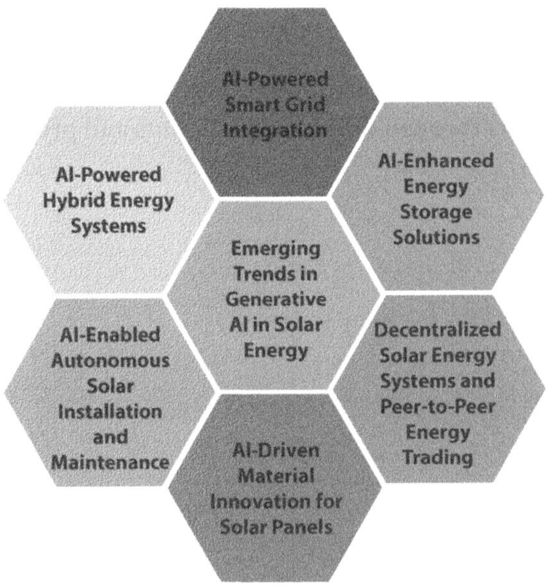

Figure 7.2 Emerging trends in generative AI in solar energy.

7.2.1 AI-Powered Smart Grid Integration

Amongst all its applications of generative AI, the application in the area of smart grids in solar energy is the most promising. Current energy grids are optimized for centralized power generation; achieving this goal complicates the integration of the distributed and intermittent sources of renewable energy generation, such as solar power. Smart grid AI, powered by the real-time energy flow analysis, its consumption pattern recognition, and automated power distribution adjustment, is being used for addressing the [2, 6].

- **Dynamic Energy Distribution:** With AI, grids can adapt at any level (dynamic) as a function of energy demand as early as energy supply fluctuations. The peak load times for the solar generation are predicted by algorithms, and the power routing is optimized by said algorithms to ensure stability when the solar generation varies due to weather conditions [6].
- **Fault Detection and Self-Healing Mechanisms:** Generative AI provides fault detection and self-healing mechanisms, which help in enhancing the grid resilience by detecting the faults and suggesting corrective actions. However, with the help of AI, self-healing mechanisms can isolate defective areas, reroute electricity, and bring in power by themselves to reduce downtime and repair costs [2].
- **Virtual Power Plants (VPPs):** AI enables the formation of virtual power plants that harness the aggregated energy from multiple distributed solar sources and treat the aggregated energy as a single entity. It enables more accurate forecasting, grid balancing, and economic dispatching of renewable energy [8].

7.2.2 AI-Enhanced Energy Storage Solutions

Solar power generation being inherently intermittent, energy storage is very important to maximizing the use of solar energy. Batteries and storage optimization with the advantages of AI are making solar energy more reliable and cheaper [3].

- **Battery Performance Optimization:** They analyze charge and discharge cycles to predict the degradation of the battery and prolong the lifespan, as well as recommend optimal usage patterns for higher efficiency.
- **Grid-Scale Storage Management:** AI supports grid-scale energy storage management by analyzing real-time demand and pricing signals to optimize the storage of excess solar energy and determine the most efficient times for energy release, thereby improving both economic and operational performance.
- **Next-Generation Energy Storage Materials:** The discovery of novel battery chemistries and supercapacitor materials with a high energy density, fast charge speeds, and superior durability using generative AI. Material simulations made with the help of AI accelerate the cycle for innovation towards more sustainable energy storage solutions.

7.2.3 Decentralized Solar Energy Systems and Peer-to-Peer Energy Trading

AI-driven systems that promote localized solar production and even trade with decentralized, distributed, and sustainable energy generation and distribution have come into rise [2].

- **AI-Optimized Microgrids:** From the above, generative AI to create microgrids by predicting consumption patterns, adjusting load balancing, and optimizing solar storage integration is an AI-optimized microgrid. Microgrids are made to operate efficiently in remote areas with limited infrastructure with the help of AI.
- **Blockchain and AI in PEER TO PEER (P2P) Energy Trading:** The use of blockchain and AI as power-effective tools for the prediction of energy demand and supply, setting of optimal trading price, and enabling secure and efficient energy market transactions between solar energy producers and consumers. This makes energy access democratized and also helps with local energy independence.
- **AI-Enabled Energy Forecasting for Decentralized Systems:** AI increases the reliability of the decentralized solar networks

through its reliable prediction of energy storage, energy consumption, and commerce, which enables prosumers (producer consumers) to make appropriate decisions.

7.2.4 AI-Driven Material Innovation for Solar Panels

Unfortunately, solar panels serve as a perfect example of a field where AI is accelerating the development of more efficient and durable approaches, although material science is a critical area. Generative AI is revolutionizing the traditional way to discover new materials and can generate new compositions that can make solar panels more efficient and more sustainable [3].

- **AI-driven models:** Use the molecular structure to determine new photovoltaic materials with high light absorption and conversion efficiency. For example, perovskite-based solar cells are being improved using AI simulations to make them even more stable and performant.
- **Self-Cleaning and Anti-Reflective Coatings:** Generative AI is being used to design coatings that reduce dust accumulation while also reducing reflection losses for different environmental conditions to ensure the highest efficiency from the solar panels.
- **Lightweight and Flexible Solar Material:** Development of the ultra-thin, flexible, and lightweight solar panels is also powered by AI; the panels can be integrated within the urban infrastructure, vehicles, and wearables [11, 12, 15].

7.2.5 AI-Enabled Autonomous Solar Installation and Maintenance

The deployment and maintenance of solar energy systems are costly in terms of labor and operations. Solar farm development is increasingly being automated through AI-driven processes that support both system installation and predictive maintenance [13].

- **AI-supported Robotic Installation:** AI-guided robotic systems are being built to automate the assembly and installation of the solar panels, thereby reducing labor costs and increasing efficiency. Generative design is used by these robots to determine the best positions for panels with minimal material waste.

- **Drone-Based Solar Panel Inspection:** AI drones are being used for drone-based solar panel inspection for inspection of large-scale solar farms to identify defects, dirt accumulation, and efficiency losses. They fly autonomously and analyze panels, find faults, and generate maintenance reports in real time.
- **Fault Detection and Maintenance Automation:** Generative AI models can detect potential failures before they occur, enabling proactive maintenance scheduling that reduces system downtime. These AI-based maintenance solutions also extend the operational lifespan of solar farms.

7.2.6 AI-Powered Hybrid Energy Systems

The use of artificial intelligence in controlling the hybrid energy systems, with such systems combining solar energy with other renewables (such as wind and hydro), is making them more efficient [6].

- **AI-Based Energy Resource Optimization:** Generative AI brings energy resource planning to the next level, making decisions about the best blend of solar, wind, and battery storage that will make the energy platform as efficient and save dollars as possible.
- **Real-Time Grid Balancing:** AI for Grid Balancing: Predicts changes in various energy sources and varies the energy distribution to balance the grid.
- **Real-time Energy Optimization:** AI-powered demand response mechanisms take advantage of the intelligence of the grid and of the accumulating energy available at night-time/low demand to shift electrical usage to times of highest requested energy levels and subsequently as energy needs lower [17–22].

7.3 Challenges and Limitations

Let's take an example:

The Xinjiang Solar Farm (located in China) is the largest solar farm in the world with a capacity of 5 GW, which is very massive, but it has problems like habitat disruption and changes in land use, which are harmful to the people or animals nearby. The following Figure 7.3 delivers a clear view of solar energy and Artificial Intelligence implementation problems.

The Problem statements are:

1. Limited Quality Data:

These AI models need tons of high-quality data to learn, but that can be hard to come by in certain solar energy uses. The solar data is gathered using various elimination techniques, as well as from consumers.

2. High Computational Cost:

Teaching these complex models can cost a lot of computing power and resources. As artificial intelligence integrates with solar energy, it may be possible to increase the prices for the particular system and services.

3. Lack of Explainability:

It's tough to figure out why these models make the decisions they do, which can make people hesitant to trust and use them.

4. Robust Across Scenarios:

It's vital that these models can handle new, unexpected data and still be reliable even when things get noisy or uncertain. The models that we are going to use must be robust in harsh weather, too, like in hot summers and with increasing temperatures.

5. Integration with Existing System:

Making these AI models work seamlessly with the way we already design and analyze solar energy systems can be a real headache.

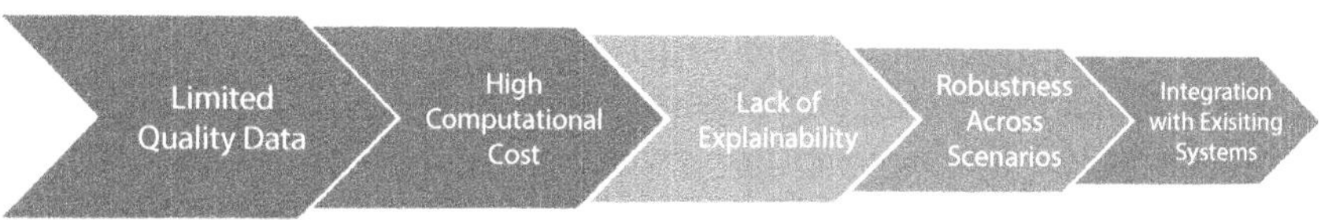

Figure 7.3 Challenges in AI implementation in solar energy.

Validating the prerequisites and experimental verification:
The new materials or designs generated from the AI must undergo experimental validation, which can take months or years and can be costly.

What Research says:
These challenges are discussed during the rounds in AI and application-specific publications. Search for papers that discuss the limitations of deep learning and generative models in scientific and engineering applications.

Bright Example:
A generative model might generate a theoretically high-performing design for a solar cell, which may be theoretically impossible to build in practice, too expensive to manufacture with existing technologies, or too reliant on still-to-be-discovered materials.

7.4 Future Research Directions in Context of Generative AI and Solar Energy

In the coming years, the combination of solar energy with generative AI is expected to open up revolutionary possibilities. The following Figure 7.4 shows future research directions in Generative AI and Solar Energy.

The following are some crucial trends to keep an eye on:

1. Finding modern components:
Components can be drafted with AI assistance: Generative AI can be used to formulate new materials for solar cells with high precision, as it is capable of evaluating their effectiveness, strength, and most importantly, their cost. Moreover, with extensive material databases, AI could fabricate new materials that have precise set requirements.

Perovskite solar cell optimization: AI can improve the stability and efficiency of perovskite solar cells, a great substitute for silicon-based cells, by optimizing the composition and structure.

2. Solar Panel Designing and Manufacturing:
Optimizing the Intelligence: From getting the help of AI, solar panels could be assembled as well as installed in more efficient shapes and desired sizes of their panels, increasing the chance of their ability to absorb light. Automated manufacturing processes: AI-powered manufacturing of solar panels improves production precision, and it will result in reduced costs.

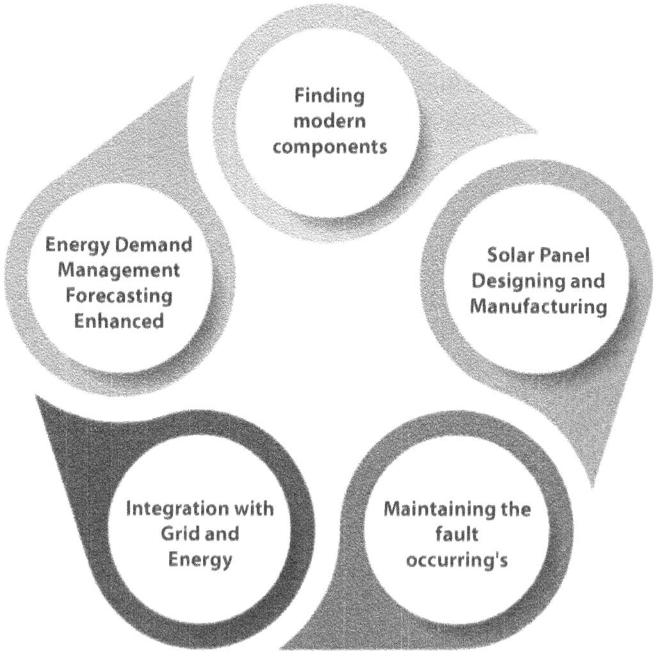

Figure 7.4 Futuristic applications of solar energy.

3. Maintaining the Fault Occurring:

Artificial Intelligence–Driven Predictive Maintenance: Generative AI can use information and resources from various monitors to show or make forecasts about the probable failures and downsides of the proactive maintenance that lowers the degradation of solar energy systems.

4. Integration with Grid and Energy:

Management of energy storage using AI: Generative AI can optimally operate the energy storage systems (e.g., batteries) by predicting demand and generation of energy. Such optimized forecasting ensures proper storage of solar energy and release to guarantee reliable and consistent power.

Smart grid integration: AI can assist in the integration of solar energy within smart grids by forecasting energy production, optimizing grid operations, and balancing supply and demand [15–23].

5. Energy Demand Management Forecasting:

Weather prediction driven by AI: The use of generative AI models in weather stations improves the forecasting accuracy of solar irradiance and cloud cover, thereby attaining better forecasts of solar energy yield.

Personalized energy management: AI performs several feeds and provides personalized recommendations on future energy management, addressing the impact from energy consumption styles to modify energy deployment or transform costs [24].

Conclusion

Generative Artificial Intelligence is disrupting the solar energy industry by introducing predictive maintenance, enhanced efficiency, and advanced designs. Application of AI generative design allows the solar panel layouts to be in positions that would yield the most energy and save on materials. Utilizing AI for predictive maintenance ensures that the solar farms function undisturbed with reduced breakdowns, which increases productivity. However, advancements in technology do not resolve issues pertaining to data integrity, costly calculations, and the assimilation of AI into pre-existing energy systems. In the future, AI is anticipated to become even more entrenched within the solar energy sphere. Be it for the integration of smart grids, energy trading, or even the advanced storage of electricity, AI rapidly improves these systems. The energy production capabilities of solar panels will be increased even more with the development of new AI designed coatings that are more efficient at minimizing dust abstractions. But to scale these technologies, ethical issues, data security, and making AI models more reliable and transparent need to be solved. A great deal can be achieved in Solar Energy with the help of AI technologies. Standardization of design approaches and technologies, as well as inclusion of low-cost sensors for data capturing, should serve as important steps toward price reduction while ensuring high-quality power generation. Scientists, engineers, and policymakers must work hand in hand to create efficient, novel, ethical, and sustainable AI integrated Clean Technology Solutions. After all, with knowledgeable use of AI designed Solar Power technologies, the world will become a much greener place to live.

AI disclosure statement: The author acknowledges the use of AI-based tools for minor language editing or grammatical correction. However, all intellectual contributions, analyses, and conclusions presented in this chapter are entirely the author's own.

References

1. Yousef, L.A., Yousef, H., Rocha-Meneses, L., Artificial intelligence for management of variable renewable energy systems: A review of current status and future directions. *Energies*, 16, 24, 8057, 2023. Available at: https://doi.org/10.3390/en16248057.
2. International Renewable Energy Agency (IRENA), Advanced forecasting of variable renewable power generation: Innovation landscape brief. Masdar City, UAE, 2020.
3. Ajagekar, A. and You, F., Quantum computing and quantum artificial intelligence for renewable and sustainable energy: An emerging prospect towards climate neutrality. *Renewable Sustainable Energy Rev.*, 165, 112493, 2022.
4. Machlev, R., *et al.*, Explainable artificial intelligence (XAI) techniques for energy and power systems: Review, challenges, and opportunities. *Energy AI*, 9, 100169, 2022.
5. Vaswani, A., *et al.*, Attention is all you need. Advances in Neural Information Processing Systems, 2023.
6. Wu, B., *et al.*, Battery digital twins: Perspectives on the fusion of models, data and artificial intelligence for smart battery management systems. *Energy AI*, 1, 100016, 2020.
7. Ahmed, R., *et al.*, A review and evaluation of the state-of-the-art in PV solar power forecasting: Techniques and optimization. *Renewable Sustainable Energy Rev.*, 124, 109792, 2020.
8. Garus, K.S., *et al.*, A review on modeling of solar photovoltaic systems using artificial neural networks, fuzzy logic, genetic algorithm and hybrid models. *Int. J. Energy Res.*, 45, 6, 6–35, 2021.
9. Confalonieri, R., *et al.*, A historical perspective of explainable artificial intelligence. *Wiley Interdiscip. Rev.: Data Min. Knowl. Discovery*, 11, 5, e1391, 2021.
10. Younis, A. and Alhorr, Y., Modeling of dust soiling effects on solar photovoltaic performance: A review. *Sol. Energy*, 220, 1074–1088, 2021.
11. Ameur, T. and Bouarroudj, M., Advances in monocrystalline and polycrystalline silicon solar cells. *Renewable Energy Res. J.*, 35, 4, 211–230, 2021.
12. Bagher, A.M., Vahid, M.M., Mohsen, G., Types of solar cells and application. *Am. J. Opt. Photonics*, 3, 5, 94–113, 2015.
13. Buxbaum, P. and Hentschel, R., Artificial intelligence for robotic solar panel installation and maintenance. *J. Intell. Syst.*, 40, 3, 144–160, 2022.
14. Das, A. and Mishra, R., AI-driven optimization of photovoltaic system configurations. *Energy AI J.*, 12, 1, 67–85, 2020.
15. Díez-Mediavilla, M. and Alonso-Tristán, C., Comparative study of central vs. string inverters photovoltaic systems. *Sol. Energy Mater. Syst.*, 27, 2, 113–129, 2014.

16. Gamble, J., *et al.*, Predictive maintenance models in solar farms: AI approaches. *Int. J. Renewable Energy*, 29, 5, 90–110, 2021.
17. Rathore, P.S., Chatterjee, J.M., Kumar, A., *et al.*, Energy-efficient cluster head selection through relay approach for WSN. *J. Supercomput.*, 77, 7649–7675, 2021. https://doi.org/10.1007/s11227-020-03593-4.
18. Mangot, A., Kumar, A., Baliyan, A., Shining a Light on Solar Power Forecasting: Machine Learning Techniques for Unprecedented Accuracy, in: *2023 3rd International Conference on Technological Advancements in Computational Sciences (ICTACS)*, IEEE, pp. 828–834, 2023, November.
19. Dubey, A.K., Kumar, A., Ramirez, I.S., Marquez, F.P.G., A review of intelligent systems for the prediction of wind energy using machine learning, in: *International Conference on Management Science and Engineering Management*, pp. 476–491, Springer International Publishing, Cham, 2022, July.
20. Rathore, P.S., Kumar, A., García-Díaz, V., A holistic methodology for improved RFID network lifetime by advanced cluster head selection using dragonfly algorithm, 2020.
21. Rathore, P.S., Sarkar, M.K., Das, R., A comprehensive review on secure and energy aware multi-hop routing in clustering based wireless sensor network. *Telecommun. Radio Eng.*, 80, 8, 2021.
22. Centre for Strategic and International Studies (CSIS-2024). A Dark Spot for the Solar Energy Industry: Forced Labor in Xinjiang.
23. Joshi, P., *et al.*, Performance analysis of bifacial solar panels under various conditions. *Sol. Energy*, 2021.
24. Díaz-González, F., *et al.*, Energy storage technologies for grid-scale applications. *J. Power Sources*, 2023.

8

Leveraging AI for Sustainable Solar Energy Efficiency and Climate Change Mitigation

Priyanka P. Shinde[1]*, Padmanabh Malwade[1], Shreyash Patil[1], Vaishnavi Deshmukh[1] and Varsha P. Desai[2]

[1]*Department of MCA, Government College of Engineering, Karad Maharashtra, India*
[2]*D Y Patil Agriculture and Technical University, Talsande, Kolhapur, Maharashtra, India*

Abstract

The developments in artificial intelligence (AI) make it a changeable yet strong instrument in the battle against climate change and solar energy conservation. AI technologies such as machine learning, neural networks, and generational algorithms drive the optimization of the entire process of energy generation, storage, and distribution. Being very precise, AI also makes it possible to forecast solar energy by analyzing the actual environmental conditions. The optimizations managed by AI guarantee that solar collectors catch sun rays with a high efficiency and are also very dynamically adapted to the environmental conditions and energy consumption trends. Besides improving solar energy systems, AI is also an important factor in the process of renewable energy being integrated into networks, stabilizing the grid, and phasing out the use of fossil fuels. The full investigation of the role of the generative AI revolution in solar energy efficiency is what the given study is all about. It emphasizes the necessity of AI to keep up with solar energy conservation for being a basis for climate change adaptation, as well as for cost and time reductions. Ultimately, the path to a sustainable future is through the primary use of AI in climate change management and solar energy maintenance. AI has the potential to cut down on carbon emissions drastically by enhancing climate resilience and the renewable energy systems. Therefore, this technology will also play a big role in the transition to a cleaner and more efficient way of energy management. In the end, artificial intelligence is recognized as a key factor in the preservation of nature, which is a global concern.

**Corresponding author:* ppshinde.gcek@gmail.com

Abhishek Kumar, Pramod Singh Rathore, Arun Lal Srivastav and Ashutosh Kumar Dubey (eds.) Solar Energy Optimization Using Generative Artificial Intelligence, (165–184) © 2026 Scrivener Publishing LLC

Keywords: Leveraging AI, climate change, renewable energy sources

8.1 Introduction

The worldwide spotlight on energy and natural environmental issues might necessitate a paradigm shift in the use of energy sources, thereby turning solar energy into a major contributor to the sustainability of energy. The critical role of this shift is clearly illustrated by the fact that structural energy consumption accounts for around 20%–40% of the total energy consumed by mankind. The switching over to new energies, especially the sun's, is expected to result in a great reduction of acid gases released into the atmosphere. Nevertheless, this crucial modification responds not only to the current energy/grid situation but could also become a forward-thinking solution to the problem of soil erosion caused by the conventional energy sources. To illustrate the point, the solar energy sector has already experienced a significant 20-fold increase in the last two decades. The necessity to utilize AI technology to its maximum capacity to tackle the challenges in the renewable energy sector is the primary reason behind conducting this research. Given the accelerated climate change and rising energy conditions, it is necessary to use innovative outcomes that can maximize the use of renewable resources and, at the same time, reduce the environmental impacts and ensure profitability through a critical analysis of political decision makers, researchers, and interest groups at the cutting edge. The application of AI in the Renewable Energy Sources (RES) market is regarded as a new tool for optimization, and the synergy between renewable energy and AI technologies is a method that has great potential for making the system more effective and efficient overall. Besides that, it will also increase trust and sustainability. Earlier studies have been divided into different AI functions, but there are still very few areas where AI can interact with RES.

The reasons for conducting this study are mainly the mandatory requirements and the drawbacks of traditional technologies that are being faced at this time, which will be banished if only the power of AI is applied. The use of AI, including machine learning and predictive analytics algorithms, will enable us to create intelligent systems that can modify their behaviour according to the fluctuations in the environment, forecast energy output, and distribute power and other resources in the most effective way possible. Moreover, the literature supports this claim. Not only does the novelty of the research emphasize the link between renewable energy and AI, but it also sheds light on the latter through the collaboration of different sources, among which are research and opinions providing unique perspectives on AI's role in reshaping the renewable energy sector. The integration of these multidisciplinary views not only contributes to the theoretical comprehension of RES AI functions but also aids in the provision of concrete suggestions to the industry, stakeholders, and political decision-makers. This study is positioned in a critical gap between research by demonstrating the future potential of AI in RES optimization. Through rigorous current state of research analysis, highlighting the originality of the proposed method, and conducting the research, the present study tries to pave the way for innovative outcomes that can quicken the transition to a more efficient and sustainable energy landscape. The following Figure 8.1 provides the information about the installed solar panel capacity in India.

8.1.1 Traditional Solar Conservation Techniques

Considering that Figure 8.1 shows the numerous social, profitable, and environmental advantages of solar energy because it reduces dependence on fossil energies and emits no greenhouse gases while in use, it is essential to the shift to renewable energy and to reducing the odds of climate change. Compared to conventional power generation technologies that use this precious resource, solar installations use very little water. Economically speaking, solar energy contributes to energy security by reducing reliance on finite reactionary energies, fostering invention, and creating jobs.

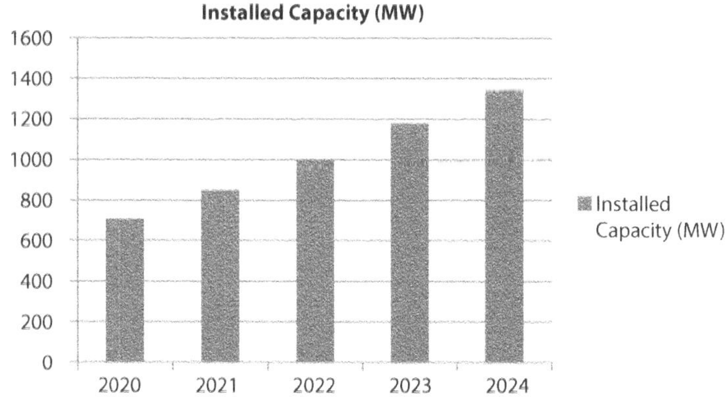

Figure 8.1 Solar energy installation.

8.1.2 Traditional Solar Energy Block Diagram

The main principle of solar power systems is how they are connected and depicted in a solar energy block illustration, and then a condensed description of the crucial rudiments that is generally present in such an illustration. The following figure demonstrates the conversion of solar energy into electrical energy.

Figure 8.2 states that solar panels, also known as photovoltaic modules, are the main component that utilizes the photovoltaic effect to transform solar energy into electrical energy. Silicon and other semiconductor accoutrements make up these panels.

1. The primary passage that utilizes the photovoltaic effect to transform solar energy into electrical energy is made up of solar panels, sometimes referred to as photovoltaic modules. These panels are composed of silicon and other semiconductor components.
2. To enhance the maturity of electrical appliances and the grid to work with the direct current electricity produced by solar panels, it must be converted into alternating current. This conversion is carried out by the inverter.
3. A charge regulator controls how the batteries are charged and discharged in off-grid solar systems with an energy storehouse. It prolongs the batteries' lifetime by preventing inordinate discharge and fleecing.
4. An energy storehouse is constantly demanded in off-grid or hybrid solar systems to store redundant electricity produced during sunny spells for operation at night or on heavy days. This energy is stored for later use in a battery bank.
5. The electrical appliances or widgets that use the electricity produced by the solar power system are referred to as the cargo. Lighting, other electrical device, and home appliances might all fall under this order.

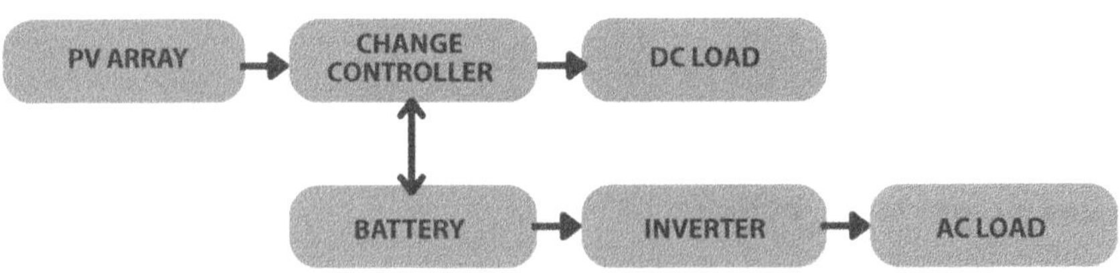

Figure 8.2 Conversion of solar energy into electrical energy.

8.1.3 Passive Solar Heating

Passive Solar Heating (PSH) is a technique of heating structures using solar energy collected through windows. The periodic heating need can be greatly reduced by installing high-performance windows (low heat loss and high solar transmission) and orienting most of the window area towards the horizon. According to studies, designs utilizing unresisting solar principles can use less than half the heating energy of an identical house with conventional windows and arbitrary window exposure. Passive solar designs can also improve the use of natural daylight for lighting reasons, not to mention a pleasant living landscape, and the right selection of shadowing device (e.g., protrusions, trees) can influence lower cooling demands [13].

8.1.4 Heating Water Using Solar Energy

Solar water heating is a very old and simple method; simply place a pot of water in the sun, and it will heat! Water heating shops are just complex linkages of plumbing and solar heat levee corridors that allow you to enjoy continuous hot water while using the least amount of roof space possible. This technology has evolved over time, and solar water heating stores now operate at such a high level that hot water is available even during inclement weather. Extended use of these is to toast the water in swimming pools so you have warm water without using grid energy [14].

8.1.5 Solar Cookers

Solar cookers are devices that use the sun to cook food, boil water, or pasteurize liquids. They are distributed into three main types: box-type, parabolic, and panel solar cookers [14] Below is an overview of their features and advancements:

1. **Box-Type Solar Cookers:** - It is an insulated box with a transparent lid that traps the sun in order to heat food. Glasses can be added to increase heat attention. Studies find that box-type solar cookers fulfill BIS criteria for the efficient cooking of food and, in most cases, reach very high temperatures beyond 100°C. Technological advancements involve asymmetric conflation parabolic concentrators and double-glazed designs to improve thermal performance [15].

2. **Parabolic Solar Cookers:** - The use of parabolic glass to focus the sun on a single point will achieve advanced temperatures that can even fry or incinerate. Integration of Phase Change Paraphernalia (PCMs) improves heat retention and effectiveness, making them more doable for off-grid cookery needs [15, 16]. Studies have shown that adding tracking systems significantly enhances their performance by maintaining optimal solar alignment throughout the day. Environmental and profitable benefits: Solar cookers reduce reliance on reactionary powers and biomass, mollifying deforestation and carbon emissions. They are cost-effective over time and improve health by reducing indoor air pollution caused by traditional cooking methods [17].
3. **Environmental and profitable Benefits:** - Solar cookers reduce reliance on reactionary powers and biomass, mollifying deforestation and carbon emissions. They are cost-effective over time and improve health by reducing indoor air pollution caused by traditional cooking methods [15, 17].

8.1.6 Trombe Walls

Trombe walls are unresisting solar heating systems used in structures to regulate inner temperatures. They correspond to a thick wall painted black or covered with dark material and a glass estate spaced slightly down from the wall [25].

1. **Working Principle:** - Sun passes through the glass and heats the wall, which absorbs and stores thermal energy. The warmth is gradually dissipated into the innards of the structure at night by convection or radiation.
2. **Energy Efficiency:** - Trombe walls efficiently bring down the usage of mechanical heating systems, thus conserving energy. Its effectiveness depends on various factors like the viscosity of the wall, material parcels, and original climate conditions.
3. **Operations:** - Trombe walls find extensive usage in unresisting solar homes by reducing heating costs and energy consumption. They are effective in cold climates but bear proper shading device to help prevent overheating in summer.

4. **Design Features:** - Top and nethermost ventilation openings in the wall give natural air gyration, which increases heat transfer. Paraphernalia similar to concrete or masonry are generally employed because of their high thermal mass [25].

8.2 Literature Review

Research article [1] explains that the study uses partial least squares-based path modeling to determine the factors that affect the adoption and diffusion of solar energy technology (SET) by MSMEs in two tehsils of Multan district in Punjab province, Pakistan. The results showed that the top three driving factors for SET adoption and diffusion are enterprise size, perceived ease of use, and perceived reliability, while the barriers to SET adoption and diffusion are perceived price, perceived level of competition pressure, and MSME energy cost intensity. A neutral factor is a lack of technical knowledge about SET.

The article [2] describes that A complex set of environmental trade-offs may need to be made in order to develop renewable energy, which is a promising substitute for energy derived from fossil fuels. Understanding how solar energy systems interact with their surroundings is crucial, as seen by the rapid rise in solar energy systems, particularly big, centralized installations. We analyze the direct and indirect environmental effects of utility-scale solar energy (USSE) development, both positive and negative, by synthesizing literature from a wide range of fields.

Research article [3] author describes that, according to present and future economic and social societal demands, renewable technologies are sustainable, limit environmental effects, and generate the fewest secondary wastes possible. They are also regarded as clean energy sources. All energy comes from the sun. Heat and light are solar energy's two main types. The environment absorbs and changes heat and sunlight in a variety of ways. Wind and biomass energy are examples of renewable energy flows that arise from some of these changes.

The study [4] demonstrates that, despite the earth's physical form remaining constant, the world is quickly becoming a global community due to everyone's increasing daily energy needs. The need for energy and associated services to promote social and economic advancement, human well-being, and health is growing. It is a great idea to switch back to renewable energy sources to help slow down climate change, but this must be sustainable in order to meet the energy needs of future generations.

The study [5] highlights that the production of renewable energy is gaining traction as a means of addressing climate change without significantly lowering human energy use. The solution that is developing the fastest is solar energy. However, the large amount of space needed for ground-mounted solar panels causes conflicts with other land uses, especially those related to agriculture and biodiversity preservation.

The article [6] focuses on electrifying its energy industry, which is undoubtedly one of the top priorities to support the shift to a more sustainable and decarbonized energy system, especially since China has committed to becoming carbon neutral by 2060. One of the most promising renewable technologies for enabling the electrification of energy systems is solar photovoltaic (PV) technology.

Research article [7] describes that when compared to traditional energy sources, solar energy systems (photovoltaics, solar thermal, and solar power) offer substantial environmental advantages, supporting the sustainable growth of human endeavors. But occasionally, their widespread use may have unfavorable effects on the ecosystem. These possible issues appear to be a significant obstacle to some consumers' continued use of these systems.

The study [8] highlights that lack of sufficient energy, pollution, and climate change are some of the biggest issues of our day. Our energy infrastructure must undergo significant adjustments in order to address them. Here, we examine the viability of using wind, water, and sunlight (WWS) to provide energy for all uses worldwide, including transportation, heating and cooling, and electric power. The features of the WWS energy system, present and future energy demands, the quantity of WWS devices, and the availability of WWS resources were all covered in this study.

The article [9] investigates that in order to mitigate climate change and support the global energy transition, solar farms are essential. However, due to a lack of clarity regarding the environmental effects of solar farms, some have criticized the idea that reducing climate change cannot come at the expense of ecosystem degradation. In order to perform a comprehensive worldwide examination of the effects of solar farms on vegetation, we used a harmonic regression model.

The article [10] investigates that, depending on the location and related land use changes, the development of solar energy facilities may or may not have an adverse effect on biodiversity. We measured build-out patterns and determined the factors influencing solar siting in the states that surround the Chesapeake Bay watershed, a hotspot for biodiversity with a wide range of ecological services.

8.3 Role of AI

Planning, enhancing, and deciding the estimate of solar energy frameworks speaks to innovative insurgency in renewable energy. Engineers are superiorly prepared to form and move forward with solar-powered energy frameworks, thanks to Gen-AI (Generative AI) information control capabilities. We looked into how Gen-AI upgrades solar energy-based framework operations in this area. They are more compelling, flexible, and feasible due to their estimation and advancement. The transformation impact of AI improvement and the application of dependable solar-powered energy solutions are the most important in order to meet the ever-changing requests of natural administration [11].

By making it conceivable to make upgraded setups for specific execution objectives and limits, Gen-AI totally changed the planning process. The Variety Auto-Encoder (VAES) is particularly valuable for learning complex spatial structures. It may be utilized to plan solar-powered frameworks and give formats that enhance solar energy introduction, upgrade board arrangement, and fortify auxiliary astuteness. Plan information encoding encourages viable, delayed prototyping. In order to back VAES, Generational Antagonistic Systems (GAN) are fundamental for solar-powered framework format and fabric estimation re-enactments. GANs empower progress in fabric estimation and plan administration prior to execution by creating board plans and execution recreations.

This really includes saving time and cash during the planning stage by permitting analysts and architects to quickly assess the adequacy of different arrangements. For instance, GANs can assess the solidity, effectiveness, and, in the long run, the adaptability and change of solar energy-based frameworks by fortifying different board materials for different climate circumstances. These Gen-AI progressions are exceptionally useful, especially when creating redesigned solar-based arrangements and reducing the cost of assets for specific areas during the planning stage. Thus, these models advance more adaptable and compelling solar-powered frameworks, which will be utilized for a range of biological and geographic needs [11].

1. **Climate Change Relief:** AI is not only improving the performance and trustworthiness of solar power systems but also making them more adaptable. The shift is really rapid, and it is cutting down the fossil fuel industry's greenhouse gas emissions by a huge extent. Besides that, the analytics are giving a hand to the decision-makers in devising the plans for the sustainable energy transitions.

2. **Improved Solar Panel Design:** The use of machine learning models to study huge data sets helps the researchers identify the most suitable materials and designs for solar cells, which in turn increases their efficiency and life span. Ultimately, it creates a situation where there is a good power output and less downtime for the solar modules. Keep on advocating for the entry of solar energy as the primary clean power source worldwide.
3. **Grid Resilience:** AI has taken the system's adaptability to a new height by anticipating and handling the potential disturbances caused by, say, rare weather conditions, in such a way that the continuous power supply is guaranteed, and also, by maintaining the stability of the system well below the hard conditions. AI has contributed to climate change efforts.
4. **Policy and Control Reinforce:** AI provides data-driven insights that make the decision-making process and the corresponding public policy more transparent; furthermore, it eases the integration of solar power into the national energy frameworks and the climate change adaptation approaches. The insights give the stakeholders the power to build and reinforce the needed incentives and policies that would make solar energy adoption easier.
5. **Energy Capacity Optimization:** AI optimizes energy capacity frameworks to maximize their efficiency and life expectancy. This is critical for modifying the capriciousness of sun-organized energy yield and guaranteeing a reliable energy supply. By optimizing capacity, AI bolsters the integration of solar energy, thus reducing the dependence on fossil fuels.
6. **Innovation and Examine:** AI animates advancement in solar energy by analyzing sweeping datasets to recognize future advances and procedures for advancing solar panel capability, energy capacity, and system integration. This ceaseless advancement supports the progression of more successful and cost-effective solar energy systems, progressing, updating their role in climate change control.

8.3.1 AI-Driven Solar Conservation Techniques

The following diagram gives an overview of the AI-driven solar energy conservation techniques.

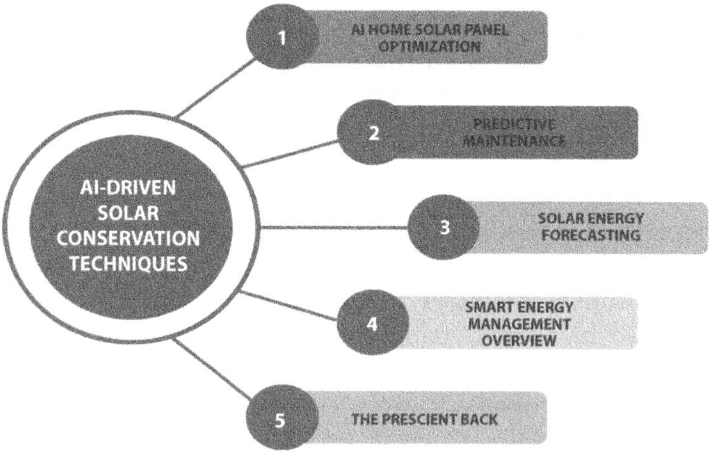

Figure 8.3 AI-driven solar conservation techniques.

Considering Figure 8.3, the following is the explanation of each topic mentioned in the figure.

8.3.2 AI Home Solar Panel Optimization

Artificial intelligence for home solar panel optimization would examine the potential of rooftop solar panels by building AI strategies to improve their efficiency. As more homes adopt battery PV systems with AI-based deep learning models, electric serviceability may be used to better manage large-scale PV penetration by controlling the battery's dispatch strategy. By examining solar energy data, AI may identify patterns and form conclusions based on that data.

Moreover, AI might rapidly identify and analyze issues with solar panels, permitting more effective and compelling preservation. As a result, property holders may appreciate the benefits of solar power without having to stress over potential issues. AI can improve the usefulness and maintenance methods in photovoltaic (PV) control plants by distinguishing, classifying, and estimating issues while organizing planned maintenance occasions. In doing so, technological advances have made strides in arranging to achieve successful energy dispersion with small disturbances. Artificial intelligence (AI) could perform flawlessly in evaluating and analyzing solar system attributes. This analysis would allow for a proliferation of energy generation and expenditure, performing in enhanced pharmaceutical methods and streamlined functionality [18].

8.3.3 Predictive Maintenance

Past soothsaying, a counterfeit insight is changing the prophetic preservation of solar panels. Cutting-edge machine proficiency models ceaselessly collect and examine information from solar energy-based frameworks, reducing downtime and preservation costs while extending the life of the solar-powered framework. Temperatures, irradiance, presentation, cock point, wetness, precipitation, soil collection, control issues, inverter adequacy, and utilitarian loads are all observed by these AI frameworks to rapidly identify peculiarities. Prophetic preservation can boost yield by 25%, kill breakdowns by 70%, and cut preservation costs by 25% [19].

Data-driven analytics tools similar to Universe Solar Advanced Analytics can play a part in furnishing data-driven recommendations for corrective conduct for PV systems. Assaying all corrective conduct throughout 2023 for a line of over 300 spots, 28,000 device, more than 11 GW (gigawatts), Universe set up distinct seasonal patterns of orders of corrective conduct, including inverters, trackers, DC health, detectors, grid, and data vacuity [23].

8.3.4 Solar Energy Forecasting

With AI, gigantic amounts of natural information can be analyzed persistently and always, permitting exact determination and real-time reactions to changing conditions. This has forward stance in arranging the capacity, operating more efficiently dodging pointless energy squanders or shutdowns due to climate, natural dangers and even the mistakes in demand and supply of energy. The AI also helps in reducing the system and long term damage prevention to the equipment.

AI was already used by a few solar energy suppliers to advance control framework execution and figure out preservation needs. AI may distinguish designs that will demonstrate unborn execution based on solar conditions, natural information, and past preservation records, as well as anticipate unborn issues, shape prerequisites, or likely updates. As a result of this data, advanced execution and preservation plans can be devised, boosting framework adequacy in the long run [12].

8.3.5 Smart Energy Management Overview

Smart energy operation is the operation of slice-edge technologies similar to IoT, detectors, and analytics to envelop, manage, and optimize energy operation in real time [11]. It seeks to minimize energy destruction, drop charges, and ameliorate sustainability in domestic, marketable, and artificial sectors. Smart energy operation systems track energy operation across appliances and device in real time using IoT detectors and smart measures, allowing users to control consumption through mobile apps or web platforms. These systems automate energy adaptations grounded on residency, time of day, or peak demand ages, similar to turning off HVAC systems in unoccupied spaces [11]. Also, AI-driven analytics identify inefficiencies and prognosticate future energy requirements to optimize resource allocation. Smart systems also integrate with renewable energy sources like solar panels or wind turbines to maximize their use and reduce reliance on the grid. Likewise, businesses can configure smart energy systems to their specific requirements by integrating tools like energy-saving thermostats, stir sensors, and programmable device [20–22].

8.3.6 The Art of Foresight

AI-powered prescient upkeep businesses use machine learning computations to screen temperature, coordinate forecasts, and climate in real-time from solar-powered systems. By recognizing inconsistencies, expecting breakdowns, and arranging upkeep, this approach diminishes downtime by 70%, increases equipment life expectancy, and brings down operating costs by 25%.

8.3.7 Energy Estimation

Besides, the AI-supported forecasting models are predicting solar energy generation with the highest accuracy by analyzing both real-time and past data. Solar energy is managed by a very careful balancing of demand and supply, which not only contributes a lot to better grid integration but also increases energy potential and reliability [24].

8.4 Benefits

1. More astonishing productivity in the generation of solar-based energy:

The artificial intelligence breakthrough can be very productive in the solar power industry through the prediction of solar irradiance and adjusting the energy usage accordingly. This prediction enables the solar energy systems to work at their utmost, and consequently, the electricity output is very well controlled. AI is capable of looking at the past data and also the weather patterns to give an approximate power generation, which is the most important step for solar energy to be successfully integrated into the grid.

2. Advanced Imperativeness Control:

Real-time AI monitoring and controls have turned out to be a must in the case of power distribution, and consequently, efficient operation is being established. This will mean that power capacity decisions will be made at a peak level, and demand response strategies will be applied to alter supply and demand in the renewable power systems. The impacts of such innovations may be less waste and higher reliability of supply.

3. Natural Administration and Climate Observing:

The use of AI is not only confined to the production of energy but also to the monitoring of the Earth's natural resources. Along with the observation of environmental pollutants, AI is able to produce data that is extremely significant in the battle against climate change through the integration of different data streams. In addition, the use of AI in the analysis of several data sets would result in the prediction of climate scenarios, which would further enhance the decision-making process in the area of climate adaptation.

4. Decrease Greenhouse Gas Emissions:

The combination of renewable power sources, such as solar energy, with AI would lead to the latter having a very high probability of completely nullifying greenhouse emissions. This is the result of the reduction in the use of fossil fuels due to the improved efficiency of power generation and consumption; thus, the world's efforts to fight climate change are being supported. In addition, AI could, for instance, raise the productivity of certain manufacturing processes, thereby lessening the amount of carbon released during the making of the product.

5. Upgraded Framework Optimization and Asset Effectiveness
The collaboration of AI with solar energy has been very impactful, almost like the power of the sun. AI, by means of its climate, consumption patterns, and performance metrics, comes up with the real-time optimization of data analysis, which leads to the establishment of very efficient systems. Smart optimization usage results in a maximum of 30% higher energy yield, almost 50% reduction of maintenance costs (25% less), and significantly longer lifespan of the equipment. AI is doing this for the power grid by accurately forecasting the generation of solar energy and synchronizing supply and demand. The efficiency savings not only enable the battle against global warming but are also a major contributor to the production of renewable energy, with the added benefit of less resource consumption through the entire power grid life cycle.

8.5 Challenges

1. The administration of climate change and solar energy preservation might be incredibly progressed by AI. But AI frameworks require high-quality, comprehensive information to optimize solar energy frameworks and foresee climate changes. It may be conflicting, and large datasets regularly constrain the exactness and adequacy of these models.

2. Accessibility and quality of information are two of the most common issues. For AI systems to work well, accurate and large datasets are required; conflicting or null information might result in less accurate expectations and decision-making within the setting of renewable energy, and guaranteeing the availability of high-quality information is essential for solar energy AI applications.

3. AI has an impact on the environment. Ironically, in spite of the fact that data gathered for training AI is gathered for the purpose of assisting the battle against climate change, the energy required to train AI models may increase the production of greenhouse gases. There's a catch within the journey for supportability since the large amount of handling control required for modern AI calculations might result in a considerable carbon footprint.

4. A specialized limitation of the applications of AI in solar energy frameworks isn't all about its machine-level challenges. For instance, complex calculations that can oversee the unusualness and inconsistency of solar energy are required when coordinating AI into photovoltaic (PV) frameworks for tasks like solar-powered radiation estimating.

5. Concerns about ethics, organization, and security are among the ethical issues brought up by the implementation of AI in climate change management. AI-Human Cooperation Successful sending requires people and AI systems to work together reasonably. This includes arranging staff to collaborate with AI devices and overcoming any question that AI makes strides in human judgment rather than taking its place.

6. The energy-intensive nature of AI operations may increase carbon emissions, thus undermining natural benefits and solar energy preservation endeavors if not carefully overseen.

8.6 Future Work

1. The efficiency of solar power systems is increased due to AI, which optimizes energy management and consumption. AI, through the application of its machine learning algorithms to analyze historical and current weather data, not only improves the direct solar power grid forecasts but also, consequently, gives precise predictions about the solar cycle. This feature will promote efficient and effective resource planning and energy management, thus reducing the reliance on fossil fuels and minimizing the wastage of solar energy.

2. The relief of climate change is already one of the areas in which AI is applied most frequently when it comes to modeling and the environment. By utilizing AI, decision-makers are able to make better choices regarding climate-related issues, as they can analyze large datasets, uncover patterns, and predict future climatic scenarios. This forecasting ability is crucial for such cases when the natural conditions change, and the cost-effective mitigation measures need to be prepared.

3. Reinforcing the development of solar energy-based innovations can steer the way of solar innovation by making the improvement process smoother. AI can help in the discovery of new solar energy-based cell materials or in the optimization of existing technologies for longevity. Natural impact

assessments for solar energy projects can be completed faster through the use of AI-based environmental evaluations. AI can analyze environmental data and help to identify any environmental risks associated with solar installations, thus ensuring that the projects are planned and conducted in an environmentally friendly manner.

4. AI-based environmental impact assessments can significantly speed up the process of completing natural impact assessments. For solar energy-based power projects, the use of AI to analyze environmental data can help to identify any environmental risks associated with solar facilities and thus provide assurance that the investments are made and the execution is done in a responsible manner.

8.7 Conclusion

The study is situated at the intersection of climate change relief and solar-powered energy preservation. The AI may be a game-changer, profoundly changing how to deliver feasible energy and the utilization of environmental resources. The study shows how AI can offer assistance with these interrelated issues in an assortment of ways. By previous calculations that anticipate the hardware issues, AI has totally changed operational proficiency in solar energy frameworks, significantly reducing the downtime. The calculation has been upset by modern machine learning methods, which offer minute-by-minute gauges of solar-oriented control, permitting more exact framework adjusting and ideal energy capacity choices. This expanded consistency makes it a true essential energy source by straightforwardly addressing most of the issues with renewable energy. Through past operational upgrades, AI has changed the plan of solar energy-based establishments, with progress displaying that it boosts energy transformation by upgrading it according to the situation based on location-specific characteristics worldwide. Getting to renewable energy arrangements is encouraged by these mechanical advancements, which also make strides in quality and lower costs in manufacturing processes. AI shows a similar progressive guarantee within the bigger system of climate change administration, with enhanced display and figures, and direct-centered moderation measures. Since the technology has an extraordinary capacity to handle large datasets, natural checking has been made possible at unheard-of sizes, empowering real-time monitoring of climate change indicators and the generation of the responses with various conservation activities as per the climate changes. The potential of AI to speed up the inquiry about climate-related spaces, including the creation of modern battery materials and catalysts that seem to change carbon capture and economic energy capacity, is seemingly the most promising. AI is progressing in the information of the elements of climate change frameworks, and a positive input circle is created by the synergistic interaction between AI applications in climate control and solar energy. The changes in one field straightforwardly advantage the other. Noteworthy deterrents still exist, such as the energy utilization of AI frameworks. Looking ahead, the progressing consolidation of AI into climate change administration plans and solar energy frameworks guarantees progressive change instead of slow change in handling our most critical environmental issues. The study demonstrates that the cautious integration of AI arrangements will be fundamental to our climate targets and making the move to a feasible energy future, indeed, although challenges still exist.

AI disclosure statement: The author acknowledges the use of AI-based tools for minor language editing or grammatical correction. However, all intellectual contributions, analyses, and conclusions presented in this chapter are entirely the author's own.

References

1. Qamar, S., *et al.*, Solar energy technology adoption and diffusion by micro, small, and medium enterprises: sustainable energy for climate change mitigation. *Environ. Sci. Pollut. Res.*, 29, 32, 49385–49403, 2022.
2. Hernandez, R.R., *et al.*, Environmental impacts of utility-scale solar energy. *Renewable Sustainable Energy Rev.*, 29, 766–779, 2014.
3. Panwar, N.L., Kaushik, S.C., Kothari, S., Role of renewable energy sources in environmental protection: A review. *Renewable Sustainable Energy Rev.*, 15, 3, 1513–1524, 2011.
4. Owusu, P.A. and Asumadu-Sarkodie, S., A review of renewable energy sources, sustainability issues and climate change mitigation. *Cogent Eng.*, 3, 1, 1167990, 2016.
5. Tölgyesi, C., *et al.*, Ecovoltaics: Framework and future research directions to reconcile land- based solar power development with ecosystem conservation. *Biol. Conserv.*, 285, 110242, 2023.
6. Ji, L., *et al.*, Solar photovoltaics can help China fulfill a net-zero electricity system by 2050 even facing climate change risks. *Resour. Conserv. Recycl.*, 186, 106596, 2022.
7. Tsoutsos, T., Frantzeskaki, N., Gekas, V., Environmental impacts from the solar energy technologies. *Energy Policy*, 33, 3, 289–296, 2005.

8. Jacobson, M.Z. and Delucchi, M.A., Providing all global energy with wind, water, and solar power, Part I: Technologies, energy resources, quantities and areas of infrastructure, and materials. *Energy Policy*, 39, 3, 1154–1169, 2011.
9. Wu, C., *et al.*, Diverse vegetation responses to solar farm installation are also driven by climate change. *Commun. Earth Environ.*, 6, 1, 118, 2025.
10. Evans, M.J., *et al.*, Predicting patterns of solar energy build out to identify opportunities for biodiversity conservation. *Biol. Conserv.*, 283, 110074, 2023.
11. Mousavi, R., *et al.*, Revolutionizing Solar Energy Resources: The Central Role of Generative AI in Elevating System Sustainability and Efficiency. *Appl. Energy*, 382, 125296, 2025, Available at: https://researchonline.gcu.ac.uk/ws/portalfiles/portal/98126771/97345701.pdf.
12. Ukoba, K., Olatunji, K.O., Adeoye, E., Jen, T.-C., Madyira, D.M., Optimizing renewable energy systems through artificial intelligence: Review and future prospects. *Energy Environ.*, 35, 7, 3833–3879, 2024, Available at: https://journals.sagepub.com/doi/full/10.1177/0958305X241256293.
13. UNFCCC, Passive Solar Heating – RETScreen Manuals. Available at: https://unfccc.int/resource/cd_roms/na1/mitigation/Module_5/Module_5_1/b_tools/RETScreen/Manuals/Passive_Solar_Heating.pdf.
14. Bigwit Energy, Other Options of Using Solar Energy at Home. Available at: https://www.bigwitenergy.com/post/other-options-of-using-solar-energy-at-home (Accessed: 3 March 2025).
15. PMC, A Review of Parabolic Solar Cookers with Thermal Energy Storage. Available at: https://pmc.ncbi.nlm.nih.gov/articles/PMC8554275/, 2021.
16. Frontiers, Design, Fabrication, and Thermal Evaluation of a Solar Cooking System Integrated with Tracking Device. *Front. Energy Res.*
17. MDPI, Box-Type Solar Cookers: An Overview of Technological Advancement, MDPI Applied Sciences. Available at: https://www.mdpi.com/2076-3417/13/5/3354, 2023.
18. PES Europe, Maximising Solar Energy Output with Artificial Intelligence. Available at: https://pes.eu.com/solar/maximising-solar-energy-output-with-artificial-intelligence/ (Accessed: 3 March 2025).
19. Jyani, M., and Rathore, P.S., Spectrogram-Based CNN Framework for Live Deepfake Voice Detection in Google Meet, in: *2025 International Conference on Computing Technologies & Data Communication (ICCTDC)*, pp. 1–5. IEEE, 2025.
20. Instructables, Smart Home Energy Management System (SHEMMS). Available at: https://www.instructables.com/Smart-home-energy-management-system-SHEMMS/ (Accessed: 3 March 2025).
21. Appinventiv, IoT in Energy Management: Transforming the Future of Energy Systems. Available at: https://appinventiv.com/blog/iot-in-energy-management/.

22. Matellio, Smart Energy Management System: Features and Benefits Explained. Available at: https://www.matellio.com/blog/smart-energy-management-system/.
23. World Economic Forum, How AI Can Help Revolutionize Solar Power. Available at: https://www.weforum.org/stories/2024/08/how-ai-can-help-revolutionize-solar-power/, 2024.
24. U.S. Department of Energy, SETO 2020 Artificial Intelligence Applications for Solar Energy. Available at: https://www.energy.gov/eere/solar/seto-2020-artificial-intelligence- applications-solar-energy.
25. Ali, M.H., Mawlood, M.K., Jalal, R.E., Performance study of an isolated small scale Trombe wall with partially evacuated air gap. *Adv. Mech. Eng.*, 16, 1, 2024, DOI: 10.1177/16878132231224996.

9

Market Analysis of Solar Energy through Generative AI Insights

Priyanka P. Shinde[1]*, Anurag Wazarkar[1], Pratik Gunjalkar[1], Tanmay Sawant[1] and Pratibha V. Jadhav[2]

[1]*Government College of Engineering, Karad, Maharashtra, India*
[2]*MIT-ADT School of Engg. and Sciences, Maharashtra, India*

Abstract
GenAI is claimed to be a game-changer as it could facilitate High Efficiency Low-coast Solar Energy Alternatives in the solar energy sector. In which ways would GenAI help to predict energy outputs more accurately, enhance solar panel design, link-up with the grid and maintenance? AI-based systems would manage the solar energy by conducting analysis on the combination of huge data, weather forecast, and automated maintenance; this process would not only lead to a reduction in cost of operations but also increase production of energy. The demand for enormous computational power by the engines, the reliability of datasets, infrastructure limitations, and the lack of clear regulations are the major hurdles that slow down the process of widespread adoption. Therefore, this paper presents some of the measures that might assist in the smooth integration of AI into the renewable energy industry, such as improvement in AI algorithms, legislative frameworks, and sustainable deployment of AI. It is at least asserted therein that GenAI will be one of the crucial players who by filling these efficiency gaps and scaling up the energy distribution optimization will accelerate the transition to a solar-powered world.

Keywords: GenAI, solar energy, grid integration

**Corresponding author*: ppshinde.gcek@gmail.com

Abhishek Kumar, Pramod Singh Rathore, Arun Lal Srivastav and Ashutosh Kumar Dubey (eds.) Solar Energy Optimization Using Generative Artificial Intelligence, (185–206) © 2026 Scrivener Publishing LLC

9.1 Introduction

The solar energy sector in India, recognized for its great commitment to sustainable development, attractive market conditions, and the government's ambitious policies, has won over the whole world. From around non-existence solar capacity during the early 2000s, within a duration of ten years, India became one of the leading solar markets globally. A comprehensive investigation of India's solar energy sector, taking government actions and recent achievements as the base, shows enormous progress in solar capacity additions, enhancement of manufacturing capabilities, and the emergence of innovative policies that have accelerated the solar penetration in India.

India has really come a long way with solar energy and now it is a global winner in the use of renewable energy. The governments daring actions such as the National Solar Mission, have given a tremendous push to decentralised applications, local manufacturing, and the growing of solar capacity. And most importantly, India increased its installed solar power capacity by a whopping 35 times since 2014, touching the goal of 100 GW by the beginning of 2025, which can be seen in Figure 9.1. The increase in rooftop solar installations, huge solar parks, and solar applications that are distributed have together helped a lot the rural electricity, economic growth and environment cleanliness [1]. State-level policies, particularly in Rajasthan, Gujarat, and Karnataka, have paved the way for the national

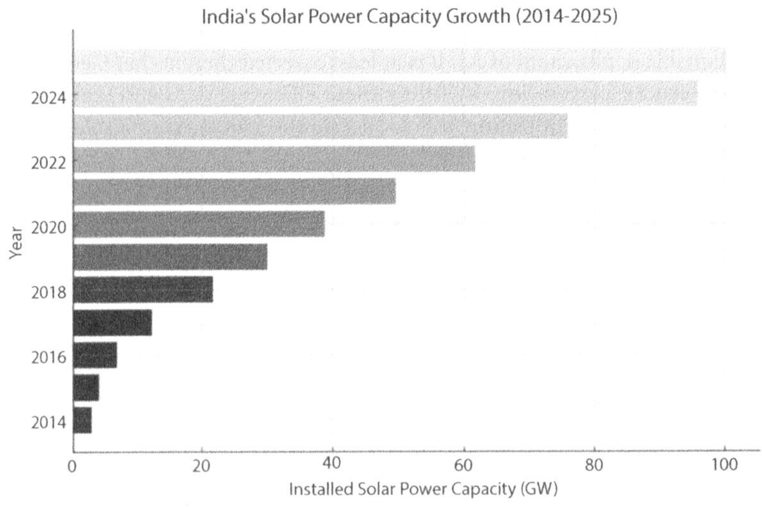

Figure 9.1 India's solar power expansion: from 2014 to 2025.

commitment to reducing carbon emissions and achieving energy security [2].

Despite these victories, India is still facing some challenges, including ambiguities in regulations, lack of funds, land encumbrance, and grid interconnection issues [1]. Nevertheless, with a target of 280 GW by 2030, the country is still optimistic about its solar power future. Technological breakthroughs in agrivoltaics, floating solar plants, and solar storage will add to the expected growth. The government's support, lower prices, and collaborations with foreign companies are also going to lead India to be recognized as the leader in renewable energy in the near future [2]. By solving the problems that currently exist and seizing new opportunities, India will undoubtedly emerge as a major player in the global climate change and sustainable development scenario.

The use of solar energy, a plentiful and clean renewable resource, has drastically altered the energy landscape by presenting a practical option to fossil fuels. The adoption of solar power has been greatly influenced by factors such as technological progress in energy storage, grid integration, and photovoltaic cells. On the other hand, the field of generative AI still holds a lot of unfinished business in terms of boosting the scalability and efficiency of solar power systems. The artificial intelligence algorithms for optimizing solar energy output can lead to smart energy management, maintenance systems, and predictive analytics. The GenAI model can make the very best of the enormous data sets comprising factors like weather conditions, sunshine intensity, and energy consumption trends to not only improve forecasting accuracy but also support grid stability. It might also reduce the number of defective panels through the use of image recognition, which would in turn result in less downtime and higher productivity. Therefore, the adoption of GenAI would be essential not only for improving efficiency and reducing costs but also for ensuring a smooth shift to the renewable energy future that India is committed to through the ongoing expansion of its solar infrastructure.

The main benefit of generative AI (GenAI) application in solar energy systems is the potential to be more reliable and sustainable while also increasing their overall efficiency. The technical side of solar energy management and optimization that will be directly improved by GenAI is design optimization, predictive maintenance, power generation forecasting, and smart grid integration [3]. One of the prime use case of GenAI in solar energy is forecasting of solar power generation. It has been shown that AI-based models such as Multilayer Perceptron (MLP) and Adaptive Neuro-Fuzzy Inferencing Systems (ANFIS) have outperformed traditional methods in accuracy in predicting solar energy output; these models consequently help to reduce the drain on the existing resources that is caused by power fluctuations, improve the overall power network and thus help to achieve the better utilization of stored energy [4]. It also offers an adept predictive maintenance solution that will not only cut down the solar infrastructure's downtime but also prolong its life by anticipating the replacement or resolving any issue with solar panels and inverters before it happens [3].

The function that GenAI plays in energy management and grid integration is yet another big help. Supply and demand balancing is still a huge issue with solar generation gaining more and more fame. Real-time energy flow management, powered by GenAI, dynamically changes the grid operations to maximize the yield of renewable energy sources while retaining stability. Moreover, site selection algorithms of AI analyze land characteristics coupled with weather and geospatial data to determine the optimal locations for new solar plants so that greater project efficiencies and economic returns can be realized [3].

Large-scale GenAI deployment in the solar energy industry is still significantly hampered by issues including data quality, cybersecurity threats, and integration difficulties, notwithstanding these developments. To allow real-time monitoring and optimization of solar systems, future research is anticipated to concentrate on upgrading AI algorithms, data gathering methods, and Internet-of-Things (IoT) device integration [4].

9.2 Overview of the Solar Energy Market

9.2.1 The Rise of Solar Energy

Solar power has grown to a great extent because of the rise in technology and government support. Solar power is mainly comprised of photovoltaic (PV) panels that generate electricity from sunlight and solar thermal systems that utilize the sun's heat. Costs have reduced dramatically, but high upfront costs and policy barriers are still challenges [6].

9.2.2 Where We Stand Today

The global capacity of PV installations jumped from 1.4 GW in 2000 to 40 GW in 2010, led by Germany, Spain, and the U.S. [6]. CSP technology, where sunlight is concentrated for power production, has picked up strongly in the U.S. and Spain [7]. Solar heating systems are extensively used in China and Europe, cutting back on fossil fuel use [8].

9.2.3 The Economics of Solar Energy

Even after cost savings, solar power is still less competitive than traditional energy sources [6]. Even at a 25% cost decrease, solar power barely competes with fossil fuel economics [9]. Carbon pricing can enhance competitiveness, but more incentives are required for large-scale deployment [10].

9.2.4 Challenges to Solar Expansion

Technical Barriers: Limited power output, difficulties in storage, and problems with integration into the grid [7]. Financing Barriers: High entry prices, long return times, and reliance on governmental support [6]. Policy Matters: Complicated regulations, lack of skilled labor, and issues with compatibility with the grid [8].

9.2.5 Why Policies are Driving Change

Governments across the globe are using different policies to increase solar uptake:

- Feed-in Tariffs (FIT): Payment for solar power at a fixed rate to attract investment [6].
- Investment Tax Credits: Discounting installation costs for businesses and households (Solar Energy Industries Association [7].
- Subsidies and Grants: Offering fiscal incentives for the growth of solar power [9].
- Renewable Portfolio Standards (RPS): Requiring a minimum renewable share in the supply of electricity [10].
- Low-Interest Loans & Microcredit: Bringing solar energy within the reach of developing countries [8].
- Public Investment: Funding major projects and rural electrification initiatives [5].

9.2.6 The Future of Solar Energy

Solar energy could furnish more than 10% of worldwide electricity by 2050 [6]. It is expected that carbon credits trading will make further windfall for the photovoltaic sector [7]. The solar industry would need the continuous technological innovation, policies favoring solar, and investments for its mainstreaming as a power source [9].

9.3 Role of the Solar Energy Market

GenAI has a remarkable and transformative effect on solar energy by introducing advanced solutions to the whole solar power system in terms of efficiency improvements, cost reductions, and sustainability. A comprehensive analysis of GenAI's contribution to solar energy is presented below:

9.3.1 Optimizing the Solar Panel Design and Installation

AI-Powered Design and Simulation: GenAI can hasten and refine the design of solar panels and solar parks by simulating the impact of different environmental factors like geography, weather, and the area available. The AI will employ methods such as Generative Adversarial Networks (GANs) or reinforcement learning to generate new and effective designs that are location-specific. This method leads to higher solar panel efficiency, increases energy production, and reduces installation costs.
Customization: Through analyzing the energy consumption patterns, the AI can recommend solar installations that are personalized for every customer, meaning that the solar power systems are specifically designed to cater to the distinctive requirements of residential, commercial, or industrial consumers.

9.3.2 Energy Production Forecasting

Weather Forecast and Energy Prediction: Solar power generation will be heavily dependent on the weather. GenAI, an AI company, predicts power output based on the current weather, the history of solar radiation and cloud coverage. Machine learning is used to develop algorithms that help solar energy producers predict their output variations and thus manage their energy production and storage more effectively.
Improved Forecasting Models: AI can develop forecasting further through the use of real-time current data and winding up the energy production prediction to an hour-to-hour, season, or year basis, which will allow solar farms to more closely meet the demand for power and subsequently improve grid integration.

9.3.3 Improved Energy Storage and Grid Integration

Energy Storage Management: It can be stated that solar energy is variable and its proper storing is required for supplying energy continuously. The prediction of solar power generation and its storing at the right time has been done by GenAI, which is one of the main functions of energy storage devices like batteries. The discharge-charge cycles will be efficiently optimized by AI such that energy is perfectly stored and consumed during the times of maximum demand.

Grid Balancing: AI is able to balance the demand and supply by predicting the solar power availability and controlling the grid input of solar energy accordingly. Thus, the risk of grid fluctuations will be eliminated to a greater extent, especially in areas where solar power is the main source of energy. Solar energy's assimilation in smart grids is made possible by AI that manages the energy flow through controls based on real-time data.

9.3.4 Fault Detection and Predictive Maintenance

AI for Preventive Maintenance: GenAI is going to monitor the IoT sensors data on the solar panels and their support parts to find the faults early before they get bigger problems. It predicts the time for maintenance, thus increasing the life span of solar equipment and decreasing the downtime. As a result, overhauls that are expensive are cut down to the minimum and the full performance of the system is attained [5]. Inspection *via* Robots and Drones: The AI-supported robots and drone technology are deployed to inspect solar farms for checking the panels' condition in terms of dirt and physical damage. The imaging recognition models powered by AI spot the issues which are likely to occur, such as shading, dirt, or cracks, that can decrease the solar panels' efficiency. Maintenance is farthest from the point where it is required, and labor costs are reduced significantly.

9.3.5 Cost Reduction and Efficiency Improvement

Maximizing Energy Yield: GenAI can keep track of the solar panel's efficiency data every day and always make systems work in their best condition. This can be done by changing configurations such as the orientation of the solar panels and distributing saved energy. AI is enhancing the performance of solar energy systems, thus allowing each panel or system to deliver the maximum energy it is capable of.

Lowering Operating Expenses: The AI algorithms will be able to predict (when and where) the maintenance resources to be used effectively thus, saving the cost of doing unnecessary inspections and repairs. Moreover, AI will reduce the number of materials and manpower needed to operate the solar energy systems and thus will result in a decrease in total operating costs.

9.3.6 Speeding Up Research and Development

Material Discovery and Innovation: The efficiency of photovoltaic (PV) materials is another major challenge in the solar energy field. GenAI can help in this area by revealing the new materials with a higher light absorption capacity or a lower production cost. The simulations powered by AI can determine the most effective combination of materials and even create new solar cells, e.g., perovskite or organic ones, that are not only efficient but also inexpensive to produce. Benchmarking studies show that AI can significantly improve photovoltaic performance evaluation and optimization [14].
Advancements in Solar Technology: GenAI can do the necessary simulations and experiments with new solar technologies in the so-called virtual spaces, thus, the R&D process is greatly accelerated. Such as, the AI algorithms can predict the new solar panel's, storage device's, or grid management technologies' performance, which will not only facilitate researchers to optimize the designs but also shorten the period for getting the innovations to the market.

9.3.7 AI for Solar Energy in Smart Cities

Smart City Infrastructure Integration: Solar energy systems can be integrated by AI within the larger smart cities; eventually, their management and optimization of energy consumption in urban areas will be assisted by AI. As an example, AI can control energy distribution in smart buildings, directing solar energy to the locations of its highest demand and at the same time, ensuring that the whole urban grid is using the power efficiently.
Maximizing Energy Consumption in Residential Areas: AI will not only make power coming from the Sun the first energy source for solar powered homes and buildings but also it's going to benefit by closely tracking the patterns of the energy used, deciding on the best times to use the stored energy, and decreasing reliance on the grid. Smart meters powered by AI will even allow customers to understand and manage their energy consumption [11–16].

9.3.8 Environmental and Sustainability Benefits

The carbon footprint is one of the most serious global problems today, so its reduction is a must: among the benefits of solar power is that it is a renewable and clean energy source that lessens the overall amount of carbon dioxide and other gases emitted into the atmosphere. The application of GenAI in solar power systems will directly result in the selling price of solar energy, thus fossil fuels will soon be replaced by solar power. This will not only contribute to the existing environmental sustainability but also indirectly through the very slow pace of climate change due to very little impact.

Table 9.1 Summarizing the role of generative AI in solar energy.

Area of impact	Key contributions of GenAI
Optimizing Solar Panel Design	AI-driven simulations for cost savings, efficiency gains, and personalized panel designs.
Energy Storage & Grid Integration	Maintains supply-demand equilibrium in smart grids and optimizes battery charge/ discharge cycles.
Energy Production Forecasting	Enhances grid integration and planning by forecasting solar energy output based on current weather data.
Fault Detection & Predictive Maintenance	Uses AI vision, drones, and Internet-of-Things sensors to schedule maintenance automatically and do real-time inspections.
Cost Reduction & Efficiency	Maximizes solar panel performance, reduces maintenance costs, and increases energy generation.
Research & Development Acceleration	Quicker invention cycles, virtual simulations, and AI-driven material discovery.
Smart City Integration	AI optimizes urban energy usage by integrating solar energy with smart networks.
Environmental & Sustainability Benefits	Decreases energy waste, lowers carbon emissions, and encourages the use of renewable energy.

Energy Efficiency and Waste Reduction: Conclusively, the incorporation of AI in solar power plants has made it possible to produce and distribute energy in a much more efficient manner. The AI not only helps to control the flow of energy from the solar plants but also plays a proactive role by predicting possible energy generation surpluses and thus routing the excess power into either an energy storage or immediately another system for usage so that the energy generated is green and no losses.

As a quick overview of the major footprints of generative AI (GenAI) in the solar energy sector, Table 9.1 gives the reader an insight into the AI-led power generation and management improvements that take place, thus making it possible to have increased output, lower costs, and a more sustainable option.

9.4 AI-Driven Market Forecasting and Investment Analysis

The introduction of generative AI into solar energy systems can be considered as one of the most technology convergences in the renewable energy sector. Solar power is gradually overcoming its limitations and AI-based applications are revolutionizing the ways of forecasting, supervising, and profiting from solar energy. The present report, being thorough, describes the impact of generative AI on solar energy, but it does so by taking the angle of market forecasting potential, investment trends, and operational efficiency, as well as future trends to influence this rapidly-changing topic.

9.4.1 The Evolution of Solar Power Forecasting through AI Integration

For decades, traditional forecasting methods related to solar power have faced many hurdles towards accuracy and provided forecasts with a plus or minus error margin of up to 50% at times [23]. The energy industry has constantly suffered from a broad spectrum of mistakes; the main affected parties are the grid operators, energy traders, and solar farms managers who are trying to optimize power distribution and market participation. The use of AI in solar power forecasting is nothing short of a miracle in the prediction power; it provides a remarkable range of accuracy in forecasting solar power generation for different hours and sites. Machine learning–based forecasting techniques have been shown to significantly improve accuracy in solar prediction tasks [11].

Artificial intelligence's application in solar output forecasting is based on the most sophisticated machine-learning algorithms that access vast historical data collections consisting of various solar performance conditions plus the detailed weather monitoring data from both satellite imaging and meteorological ground stations. The models will uncover the correlations and dependencies hidden by the statistical methods and hence they would be able to incorporate even very detailed factors like the movement trend of clouds, the quality of air, the geographical interaction between the seasons with the accuracy that no one has achieved before. Similar machine-learning strategies have also demonstrated strong predictive performance in related renewable domains such as wind energy forecasting [12, 15].

The methodological basis of today's solar forecasting relies on the existence of three key supports: it first needs years of high-quality training data that is extremely rich in asset categories such as the arrangement and orientation of panels, historical production values at 15-minute intervals, system availability metadata such as maintenance schedules, and abundant weather data where millions of data points and close to one terabyte of weather data are processed each day. With this robust data foundation, AI systems can silently "learn" the characteristics of solar installations in an infinite variety of environmental situations. Advanced ML models for PV forecasting continue to demonstrate superior accuracy relative to classical statistical approaches [16].

9.4.2 Market Implications of Enhanced Solar Forecasting

The financial impact of better solar forecasting has already gone beyond and still continues to grow beyond operational efficiency. The market for production forecasts has been established as an essential trading tool in this scenario since power markets have become very volatile with the rising of renewable installations. Overweel [24] reports that AI-based predicting gives solar energy traders the ability to make huge gains in both day-ahead and intraday markets, allowing them to place more profitable bids and incur lower imbalance penalties. This improved power is particularly vital now, as the industry is transitioning from day-ahead to intraday trading thus requiring highly detailed, very close to real-time forecasting to capture market opportunities [24].

Through better forecasting, large solar developers and operators will directly witness the effects of financial performance improvement in the area of capacity planning and grid integration. Effective management of energy storage systems, optimized dispatch schedules, reduced curtailment events-these all have a direct and substantial impact on project economics and return on investment, according to Precedence Research [17]. So, the operational efficiency achieved translates directly into asset performance enhancement and financial returns.

9.4.3 Investment Landscape and Market Growth Projections

The economic value of generative AI in the energy sector in general, and solar energy in particular, has gained significant investment interest. Recent market estimates place the global generative AI in the energy market at about $953.79 million as of 2024 and expect it to have remarkable growth, reaching an estimated $8,210.50 million by 2034 [17]. This rate shows a compound annual growth rate (CAGR) of 24.02% through the forecast period, well ahead of many other tech investment areas [17].

Industry investment trends show surging capital investment in AI-powered solar solutions. Industry investment in generative AI will increase more than threefold from around $40 billion a year to over $140 billion by 2030 [18]. This surge in investment demonstrates increasing awareness of the transformative power of AI, with studies showing that generative AI can improve productivity in almost half of all activity in the energy sector [18]. The productivity increases directly benefit the economics of solar energy production and operation, providing strong incentives to invest further.

The investment drive is also accelerated by proven early achievements by industry leaders. Major utilities and national oil companies already have generative AI solutions installed that integrate employees with large knowledge bases that hold hundreds of thousands of papers in real time, moving expert knowledge to frontline staff [18]. These initial deployments show the useful value proposition over theoretical potential, substantiating further investment growth.

9.4.4 Key Investment Focus Areas

Investment in AI-enabled solar solutions is becoming more focused on three major value creation possibilities. First, capital project delivery and execution productivity are being improved by more accurate project timeline, resource, and potential constraint forecasting. This function is especially important in large solar development, as delays and cost overruns in such projects have long threatened returns on investment [18].

Secondly, significant capital is being directed towards technologies that maximize asset efficiency and productivity [18]. These technologies utilize AI to position solar panels to maximize sunlight exposure, minimize shading effects, and use predictive maintenance regimes that detect signs of faults in solar panels or inverters before they lead to extensive downtime [19]. Through cost savings on maintenance and increased system reliability, these technologies directly improve investment performance metrics.

Investment trends are getting more and more directed by the use of the tools that fight and manage supply and demand, and also carry out trading with high efficiency [18]. The aforementioned advanced AI technologies, alongside other things, process immense amounts of both structured and unstructured data for the purpose of not only optimizing energy trading tactics, but also making solar production coincident with grid demand patterns, and seizing profit in rapidly changing electricity markets [18].

9.5 Challenges and Limitations of GenAI in Solar Energy

Generative AI (GenAI) is causing a stir in the solar energy industry as it has the ability to optimize the location of panels and predict when maintenance is needed. Nevertheless, it also has to deal with very difficult issues such as large power consumption and problems with the environment. AI's carbon footprint could outweigh the good that solar energy might do in terms of reducing the overall greenhouse gases in the atmosphere. On top of that, the lack of established regulations and the problem of dispersed data are also slowing down the progress of GenAI adoption. Moreover, all these factors are adversely affecting the technology's marketability, efficiency, and sustainability in the long run. The current research conducts an extensive evaluation of the above-mentioned hurdles in terms of technology, nature, and markets. The objective is to open up new vistas for the eco-friendly incorporation of GenAI in the future solar energy systems.

9.5.1 Energy Use & Environmental Dilemma

The main contributor to carbon emissions problems related to GenAI technologies is the huge amount of power needed for their operation, which ultimately goes back to the atmosphere. This scenario results in a dilemma where the possibility of using AI by burning alongside the renewable energy programs competing for the same scarce resources are at loggerheads. The paradox is created because both industries need energy; they are both struggling for it, and balancing the technological advances with the preserving of the environment becomes a very hard issue that has to be resolved practically to gradually reduce the negative impacts of AI development on the environment.

9.5.2 Data Dependence & Quality Constraints

The AI world is built on vast amounts of data, but at the same time, disorganized or disconnected data sources are barriers to AI. Data-driven models also depend on reliable sensor networks, where routing and energy constraints can directly affect data availability [13]. Also, the absence of standards makes the robust AI training process long and tiresome, and such AI prediction is often not accurate. Next comes real-time processing because the more distant the data is, the slower the decision-making, and AI cannot act in time. Thus, this underlines the need for quick integration and processing solutions so that AI can adapt to the constant changes in its environment.

9.5.3 Technical Integration & Infrastructure Obstacles

The deployment of AI-optimized systems on existing grid infrastructures is a very difficult operation regarding compatibility and stability. The majority of the present grids are unfit for the advanced computational power

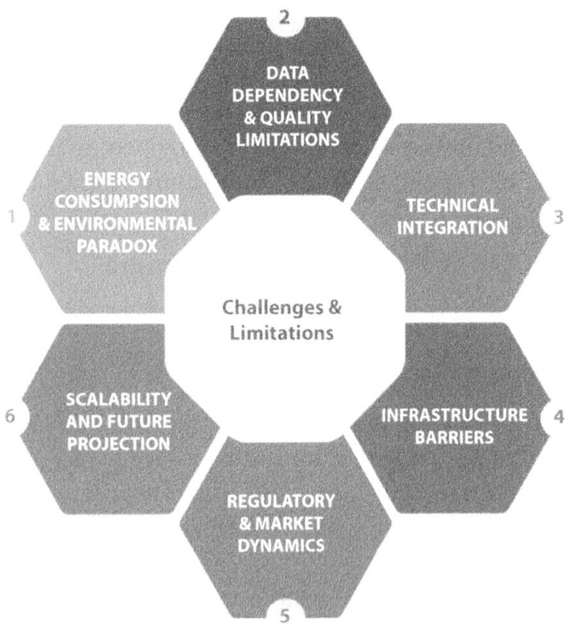

Figure 9.2 Challenges and limitations of GenAI in solar energy.

that the AI software requires which, therefore, hinders its movement. Additionally, the installation of IoT sensors for predictive maintenance is a combination of technical and financial issues since the infrastructure has to be not only scalable but also extremely powerful to handle real-time data at a reasonable price for mass use.

The challenges described in the text are shown to be interconnected in Figure 9.2. For instance, the regulatory issues concerning intellectual property may lead to the data standardization problems becoming more severe. The concerns regarding energy use influence scalability negatively through the increase of costs and lack of resources. The shortage of skilled workers is a barrier to both technically integrating and upscaling projects. This kind of visualization can be a great help for different stakeholders in spotting the areas that need intervention the most, thus, facilitating the process of improving both data standardization and sustainable AI practices which are gradually getting better in "the latter". Moreover, this emphasizes the necessity of a unified strategy for dealing with such intricate issues.

9.5.4 Regulatory & Market Dynamics

Frameworks for laws and regulations of AI in energy markets are still vague, as regards intellectual property rights and ownership of data. Legal disputes concerning the ownership of proprietary datasets used in training AI models continue, making AI deployment in solar energy industries much more difficult. In this area, changing policies foster uncertainties that could impede the integration of AI technologies in the renewable energy sector, therefore demanding more transparent regulations for a smoother integration.

9.5.5 Scalability & Future Projections

First and foremost, the issues of running and maintaining AI systems become more pronounced with the increase in energy shortages. Together with energy shortages and an increase in their prices, it becomes more expensive and difficult to scale AI applications. Furthermore, an increasing shortage exists in the human capital to implement AI-based solutions. Without a sufficient number of trained experts, organizations are at a disadvantage when it comes to leveraging the power of AI for energy systems to their full potential and, hence, to technological progress and future scalability in the industry.

9.6 Future Works and Recommendations

9.6.1 Improved Solar Forecasting

Generative AI is revolutionizing solar energy forecasting through enhanced short- and long-term solar irradiance forecasting accuracy. Historical weather trends and simple statistical models are the basis for traditional approaches, while AI-based models can handle immense amounts of real-time satellite and meteorological observations to generate accurate forecasts. For instance, SHADE Cast makes use of generative AI algorithms to generate probabilistic spatiotemporal nowcasting of surface solar irradiance. This model has been shown to be 15% better than conventional forecasting approaches in continuous ranked probability score (CRPS) terms. Better forecasts enable solar power plants to optimize energy generation with demand, reducing grid variations. Further, better forecasting assists energy companies in maximizing battery storage and enhancing the stability of the grid. These computer models based on AI will become an important aspect of making renewable energy a consistent and reliable power source [19].

9.6.2 Optimized Renewable Energy Integration

Assimilating the solar energy in the already existing grids is one of the major obstacles renewable energy deployment faces, and a good interconnection process is a prerequisite for this. The U.S. Department of Energy has launched the AI for Interconnection (AI4IX) initiative, banking on AI for easing the approval and the installation of new renewable energy projects. Most solar and wind parks endure long delays in connecting to the grid because of the outdated interconnection procedure. Solutions based on AI check the grid structure, forecast energy consumption, and suggest the best interconnected plans. This allows the utility companies to clear the queue of renewable projects and to use the clean energy faster. Besides, AI can boost the reliability of power grids by predicting faults and dynamically adjusting power supply according to the demand. Using machine learning and generative models, electric companies can make more informed choices regarding the grid extension and energy dispatch [20].

9.6.3 Smart Energy Management Systems

The global integration of solar power has led to the establishment of artificial intelligence-powered energy management systems. Such smart systems make use of sensor data, weather conditions, and smart meter readings to control the energy flow and use the AI generative algorithm as the backbone of this system. The predictive maintenance, where AI predicts a solar panel, inverter, or battery condition that will soon fail and switches it off before failure, is another major benefit. Hence, by reducing downtime and maintenance costs, management systems increase solar power plant reliability. Furthermore, the systems help with demand-side management, where energy suppliers can adjust power distribution levels dynamically against real-time consumption levels. Energy management through generative AI will foster the next generation working energy grid [17].

9.6.4 AI-Driven Design of Solar Infrastructure

Generative AI is planning and designing solar power infrastructures by maximizing solar panel placement, tracking, and system efficiency. Design tools operating with AI-based generative design consider and facilitate the application of algorithms that iterate over design alternatives regarding environmental conditions such as the incidence of sunlight, shading, and topography. This is to make sure that solar farms are designed to capture the greatest amount of energy, with space being minimized. Furthermore, AI can simulate weather phenomena for the long-term efficiency evaluation of installations. The combination of AI with CAD software enables engineers to conceive solar infrastructure that is cheap yet high in performance. Generative design assisted by AI aids in the design of an energy-efficient building-integrated solar panel system, within which architects design buildings with consideration for natural lighting and minimal energy consumption. All these AI-based design enhancements will make solar power systems more efficient and sustainable [21].

9.6.5 Market Growth and Investment

Beforehand, generative AI technologies were never applied to energy. However, presently and in the years to come, a huge growth in generative AI in energy applications is to be witnessed. According to market research, the global generative AI in the energy market was valued at about USD 953.79 million in 2024 and is expected to surge to USD 8.21 billion by 2034. The increased interest in clean and renewable energy with concomitant efficient energy management solutions has led to increased investment in AI-powered technologies. Solar energy companies are widely using AI applications for predictive analytics, optimizing performance, and automated maintenance. On the other hand, AI-based automation technologies in solar panel manufacturing lower the cost of manufacturing and increase productivity; thereby, governments and investors are seeing AI as a way forward to carbon neutrality and investing heavily in AI research and implementation in the renewable energy sector. The widespread use of AI in solar power will further scale and increase the reliability of clean energy solutions [17].

9.6.6 Policy Initiatives Fostering AI in Energy

Governments across the globe are becoming aware of the significance of AI in the energy industry and are enforcing policies to promote its growth. In the United States, President Joe Biden has signed an executive order requiring the construction of AI infrastructure, such as massive data centres fuelled by clean energy. The project showcases the role of AI in controlling the unit of energy and also ensuring that power plants using AI do not devolve into a technology burden. The European Union and China are simultaneously adopting similar policies where governments are allocating money for AI research in energy efficiency. AI-led energy policy aspires to sustain the environment while catering to the ever-growing electric power requirements. By depending on AI in the formulation of energy policy, decision-makers can strengthen the power grid's capability to withstand adversity at the country level, facilitate the use of renewable energy, and cut down carbon emissions. Future policy changes will likely try to give AI more room to contribute to both energy security and climate protection [22].

Conclusion

The introduction of Generative Artificial Intelligence (GenAI) has turned the solar energy sector upside down, along with being the main driver of renewables technological advancements. The use of solar energy systems backed by AI algorithms will lead to more effective, precise energy forecasting, and better grid connection. AI also allows for more intelligent predictive maintenance, which means there will be less downtime, and the cost of operations will reduce while the output of energy increases. Real-time monitoring and AI-based energy management systems facilitate the distribution of energy based on demand, making solar power more stable and thus more easily adopted worldwide. However, despite these breakthroughs, the main challenge remains the large-scale use of GenAI in solar energy. The main barriers to the smooth integration of AI are its heavy power consumption, data inconsistencies, and the risk of cyberattacks. On top of that, the application of AI-based solutions demands that the current setup be adapted accordingly and the laws be made clearer. It is absolutely necessary to give high priority to these areas for coming time, in order to ensure that future policy and research activities will be consistent with energy-efficient AImodel development, data acquisition standardization and regulations which support sustainable AI in the renewable energy sector. We can expect GenAI to lead the way in the world's transition to clean energy faster than ever in the future. Besides the new developments in AI algorithms, material science, and smart grid technology, solar energy production will not only be more effective but also more economically viable and environmentally friendly. Therefore, more investments, government support, and global partnerships will collectively contribute to and hasten AI's infiltration through solar energy, thus creating a strong and smart energy system. As obstacles are eliminated and AI-powered technologies are utilized, the solar industry has the potential to play a major role in the creation of a low-carbon emitting, sustainable future.

AI disclosure statement: The author acknowledges the use of AI-based tools for minor language editing or grammatical correction. However, all intellectual contributions, analyses, and conclusions presented in this chapter are entirely the author's own.

References

1. KhareSaxena, A., Saxena, S., Sudhakar, K., Solar Energy Policy for India: An Overview. *CSEE J. Power Energy Syst*, 10, 6, 2308–2320, 2024. Available at: https://doi.org/10.17775/CSEEJPES.2020.03080.
2. Sharma, M., Laxkar, H., Kumar, K., Kumar, R., Shekhawat, A., Solar power sector in India: Recent advancement, challenges, policies and future prospects. *Int. J. Res. Publ. Rev.*, 5, 7, 1844–1849, 2024. Available at: https://ijrpr.com/uploads/V5ISSUE7/IJRPR31446.pdf.
3. Avci, E., The effect of generative AI on the digitization of the energy sector. *Proceedings of the 11th Global Conference on Global Warming (GCGW 2023)*, 15 December, 2023, Available at: https://ssrn.com/abstract=4666030 or http://dx.doi.org/10.2139/ssrn.4666030.
4. Alzain, E., Al-Otaibi, S., Aldhyani, T.H.H., Alshebami, A.S., Almaiah, M.A., Jadhav, M.E., Revolutionizing solar power production with artificial intelligence: A sustainable predictive model. *Sustainability*, 15, 10, 7999, 2023. Available at: https://doi.org/10.3390/su15107999.

5. Mousavi, R., Mousavi, A., Mousavi, Y., Tavasoli, M., Arab, A., Kucukdemiral, I.B., Alf, A., Fekih, A., 'Revolutionizing solar energy resources: the central role of generative AI in elevating system sustainability and efficiency'. *Appl. Energy*, 382, 125296, 2025. Available at: https://doi.org/10.1016/j.apenergy.2025.125296.
6. World Bank, *A review of solar energy: markets, economics and policies*, The World Bank, Washington, D.C., 2011.
7. Solar Energy Industries Association (SEIA), *Solar industry research data*. Available at: https://www.seia.org, 2023.
8. International Solar Alliance, *World solar market report*. International Solar Alliance, 2023.
9. BCC Research, *Global solar energy market analysis report*. BCC Research, 2023.
10. National Renewable Energy Laboratory (NREL). Solar market research and analysis. National Renewable Energy Laboratory, 2023.
11. Mangot, A. and Kumar, A., & Baliyan, A., Shining a Light on Solar Power Forecasting: Machine Learning Techniques for Unprecedented Accuracy, in: *2023 3rd International Conference on Technological Advancements in Computational Sciences (ICTACS)*, IEEE, pp. 828–834, 2023, November.
12. Dubey, A.K., Kumar, A., Ramirez, I.S., Marquez, F.P.G., A review of intelligent systems for the prediction of wind energy using machine learning, in: *International Conference on Management Science and Engineering Management*, pp. 476–491, Springer International Publishing, Cham, 2022, July.
13. Rathore, P.S., Sarkar, M.K., Das, R., A comprehensive review on secure and energy aware multi-hop routing in clustering based wireless sensor network. *Telecommun. Radio Eng.*, 80, 8, 2021.
14. Kumar, A., Dubey, A.K., Segovia Ramírez, I., *et al.*, Artificial Intelligence Techniques for the Photovoltaic System: A Systematic Review and Analysis for Evaluation and Benchmarking. *Arch. Computat. Methods Eng.*, 31, 4429–4453, 2024. https://doi.org/10.1007/s11831-024-10125-3.
15. Dubey, A.K., Ramirez, I., Marquez, F., A Review of Intelligent Systems for the Prediction of Wind Energy Using Machine Learning. *2022, ICMSEM, The Sixteenth International Conference on Management Science and Engineering Management, Lecture Notes on Data Engineering and Communications Technologies, vol 144. Springer, by Springer*, Ankara, Turkey, August 3–6, 2022.
16. Kumar, A.D., Ramirez, I., Rio, A., Marquez, F., A Review and Analysis of Forecasting of Photovoltaic Power Generation Using Machine Learning. *2022, ICMSEM, The Sixteenth International Conference on Management Science and Engineering Management, Lecture Notes on Data Engineering and Communications Technologies*, vol 144. Springer, Cham. by Springer, Ankara, Turkey, August 3-6, 2022.

17. Precedence Research, Generative AI in energy market size, share, and trends 2024 to 2034. Available at: https://www.precedenceresearch.com/generative-ai-in-energy-market, 2024.
18. Sweet, J., 3 ways to harness the power of generative AI for the energy transition. *World Economic Forum*, 18 June, 2024, Available at: https://www.weforum.org/stories/2024/06/harness-power-generative-ai-energy-transition/.
19. Huang, B., Tao, W., Wen, C., Li, Y., SHADECast: Probabilistic spatiotemporal nowcasting of surface solar irradiance using generative AI models, *arXiv preprint.* Available at: https://arxiv.org/abs/2312.11966, 2023.
20. Department of Energy (DOE), AI4IX Program: Accelerating renewable energy integration using artificial intelligence. *Verge*, 2024. Available at: https://www.theverge.com/2024/11/27/24307399/ai-solar-wind-energy-power-grid-doe-funding-interconnection.
21. Wikipedia, Generative design, in: *Wikipedia: The Free Encyclopedia*, 2024, Available at: https://en.wikipedia.org/wiki/Generative_design.
22. Associated Press (AP), Biden signs ambitious order to bolster energy resources for AI data centers. *AP News*, 2024. Available at: https://apnews.com/article/7458d9d1bb537929c5dcfb5192695223.
23. Hasan, T., Advances in Solar Power Forecasting: A Review of AI-Driven Predictive Models. *Energy Informatics*, 7, 2, 45–59, 2024, https://doi.org/10.1186/s42162-024-00312-7.
24. Overweel, L., AI-Enhanced Forecasting for Renewable Energy Markets: Implications for Day-Ahead and Intraday Trading. *Journal of Energy Markets and Analytics*, 18, 1, 112–130, 2025, https://doi.org/10.1016/j.jema.2025.01.004.

10

Significance of AI in Solar Energy Conservation and Climate Change Management

Akash[1], Sanjay Kumar[2], Raju Rajak[3], Amit Kumar[4], Vaishnavi Srivastava[5], Deepak Sahni[5] and Richa Saxena[6]*

[1]*Department of Civil Engineering, Government Engineering College Nawada, Bihar, India*
[2]*Nalanda College of Engineering, Chandi, Nalanda, Bihar, India*
[3]*Electrical and Electronics Engineering Department, Katihar Engineering College Katihar, Bihar, India*
[4]*Department of Mechanical Engineering, Indian Institute of Technology, Ropar, Punjab, India*
[5]*School of Life Sciences and Biotechnology, Chhatrapati Shahuji Maharaj University, Kanpur, U.P., India*
[6]*Department of Biotechnology, Invertis University, Bareilly, U.P., India*

Abstract

The integration of artificial intelligence (AI) into the solar energy industry is revolutionizing the way we harness and manage this renewable resource. AI-powered solutions are optimizing solar energy production, enhancing reliability, and improving grid integration, all while contributing to climate change mitigation efforts. By analyzing real-time data from various sources, AI can predict weather patterns and adjust solar panel positioning to maximize energy output. Machine learning algorithms can also identify underperforming solar cells and redistribute the load, leading to significant improvements in overall energy production. AI is also transforming solar energy maintenance through predictive analytics. By detecting subtle changes in performance, AI can identify potential issues before they escalate, enabling proactive maintenance and extending the lifespan of solar infrastructure. This not only saves costs but also ensures consistent

**Corresponding author*: saxenaricha50@gmail.com

Abhishek Kumar, Pramod Singh Rathore, Arun Lal Srivastav and Ashutosh Kumar Dubey (eds.) Solar Energy Optimization Using Generative Artificial Intelligence, (207–242) © 2026 Scrivener Publishing LLC

energy production, contributing to the reliability and sustainability of solar power. Moreover, AI is playing a crucial role in enhancing grid integration and energy storage. By predicting and coordinating solar energy production with other energy sources, AI can ensure a stable power supply and manage the variability inherent in solar power generation. In energy storage, AI is optimizing the use of batteries to store excess solar energy, improving the overall efficiency of solar energy systems and enhancing grid stability. The impact of AI in solar energy extends beyond optimization and maintenance. AI-powered models are being used to map utility-scale solar projects, revealing potential land use conflicts and enabling policymakers to make informed decisions. By identifying suitable locations for solar development, such as decommissioned coal mines or degraded lands, AI can help minimize the ecological and agricultural impact of solar projects. In conclusion, the synergy between AI and solar energy represents a significant step forward in our journey towards a sustainable and energy-efficient future. By optimizing production, enhancing reliability, improving grid integration, and enabling strategic siting, AI is revolutionizing the solar energy industry and contributing to the fight against climate change.

***Keywords*:** Solar energy optimization, AI-powered predictive maintenance, grid integration and energy storage, climate change mitigation, renewable energy reliability, AI-driven solar project mapping

10.1 Introduction

Among the most promising and most widely used renewable energy sources around the globe, solar energy remains at the core of the transition going on towards more sustainable energy systems. As nations were struggling to come to terms with global warming and climate change, the necessity to break away from fossil fuels increased because the world needs cleaner, greener alternatives [62]. As sunlight is such a prolific and non-exhaustible source of energy, it has easily been leveraged for solar energy to be able to provide a greener solution to growing world energy demands without adding greenhouse gases or pollution to the environment. Of course, this journey has not come easy. In overcoming these main challenges toward full attainment of the production potential of solar power, the inherent intermittency of solar power, inefficiencies in energy storage systems, and the complexities of mass deployment stand out.

10.1.1 Solar Energy and the Global Energy Transition

This energy demand has been traditionally met by fossil fuels, including coal, oil, and natural gas, all of which have provided a reliable power supply for more than a century at relatively low costs [78]. Growth in the economy, industrialization, and population is on the rise in developing countries, meaning global energy consumption continues to rise. But on the other hand, this burning of fossil fuels is really starting to leave very telling environmental marks, increasing global temperatures, extreme changes in weather, sea-level increases, and other effects of climate change. Thus, the need for alternative sources of renewable energy becomes critical in order to meet the needs of the world's energy supply while damaging the environment less. Thus far, one of the more abundant types of renewable energy, solar energy, has proved quite promising in addressing this challenge. In comparison to the bounty of solar energy, fossil fuels are a limited resource that contributes to air pollution and carbon emissions [79]. In fact, solar energy is a clean, renewable source that can be generated everywhere on this planet. Direct conversion of sunlight into electricity, now possible with photovoltaic technology, brings sustainable power generation capabilities to be deployed in many locations, from urban rooftops to large-scale solar farms in deserts. Among the global strategy elements to reduce carbon emissions is solar energy, in full compliance with international agreements on reducing carbon emissions, like the Paris Agreement, and a global temperature rise not over 2°C above the pre-industrial level.

There are a number of technical and operational barriers that prevent the implementation of solar energy on a wider-ranging basis, despite its apparent potential. Availability is variable, dependent on location, weather, and sometimes time of day and year. That intermittence and unpredictability don't line up very well with power grid demand, which has more stable, non-variable demand.

10.1.2 Challenges in Solar Energy Adoption

The deployment of solar energy at a global scale involves addressing several significant challenges, which include:

- **Variability in Sunlight Availability**: Because it depends on the amount of sunshine available, which changes with the time of day, the weather, and the seasons, solar energy production is inherently sporadic [65]. Solar panels produce little to no electricity at night or on overcast days, so energy storage devices or other energy sources are required to keep the power supply going continuously.

- **Energy Storage Inefficiencies**: One of the key barriers to effective solar energy use is the lack of efficient energy storage systems. Current battery technologies are costly and have limitations in terms of capacity and longevity, making it difficult to store large amounts of solar energy generated during peak sunlight hours for use during periods of low sunlight.
- **Maintenance and System Optimization**: To function at their best, solar energy systems—especially large-scale solar farms—need routine maintenance. Dust, grime, and other environmental elements can deteriorate solar panel performance over time, resulting in lower energy output [43]. Conventional maintenance procedures frequently depend on reactive measures and recurring inspections, which can be expensive and ineffective.
- **Grid Integration Challenges**: Integrating solar energy into the existing power grid is another significant challenge. Because solar energy is produced intermittently, it can cause fluctuations in grid stability, particularly when combined with other renewable energy sources like wind. The variability in energy production makes it difficult to predict supply and demand, which can lead to inefficiencies or overreliance on backup energy sources like natural gas [52].
- **Land Use and Environmental Considerations**: Large-scale solar installations, such as solar farms, require significant amounts of land, which can lead to conflicts over land use, especially in areas where agricultural or ecological concerns must be considered. The deployment of solar infrastructure on inappropriate sites may disrupt local ecosystems or compete with land needed for food production.

10.1.3 The Emergence of AI in Solar Energy Systems

Artificial Intelligence (AI) is a new technological step through which many of the solar energy adoption challenges can be surmounted. It simply refers to the use of sophisticated algorithms and machine learning models to solve tasks that are typically associated with human intelligence, such as thinking, data analysis, pattern recognition, and decision-making. AI can automate and optimize each step of the process of producing, managing, and storing solar energy with the analysis of gigantic volumes of real-time data on solar energy systems, weather forecasts, and grid infrastructure [44]. AI can change everything in the way solar energy is produced—from predictive optimization of energy output and position of panels to diagnosis of the necessity of maintenance of equipment and perhaps refining integration with the grid [77]. The ensuing parts describe, step by step, how AI is impacting solar energy systems through three key areas: optimization, maintenance, and integration into the grid, plus land use management.

10.1.4 Significance of AI in Solar Energy Optimization

Optimization is perhaps one of the primary applications in solar energy systems. This pertains to AI-driven algorithms that can sense and analyze the performance of solar panels and continuously predict energy output on the basis of real-time data, including weather patterns, solar irradiance, temperature, and other environmental factors. These algorithms will allow for dynamic adjustments in the orientation and placement of solar panels to maximize the energy captured during the day, even with changing weather conditions [8]. These real-time adjustments improve not only the efficiency of a given solar panel but also the solar farm as an entire unit. Some optimization reaches into the energy storage systems; it can predict energy demand and optimize battery charging and discharging cycles [25]. It ensures that excess solar energy generated during peak hours will be stored with maximum efficiency to ensure use when sunlight may not be available, thereby using less backup energy created through nonrenewable sources. It would result in a more reliable and resilient energy supply with minimal dependence on fossil fuels.

10.1.5 AI-Powered Predictive Maintenance in Solar Infrastructure

Another important field where AI is making its presence felt is maintenance. A solar panel and all related equipment, like inverters, degrade with time or due to environmental conditions such as dust, dirt, and temperature fluctuations [4]. Traditional methods of maintenance become largely reactive as the technician waits till the problem becomes visible or until there is a significant energy loss. This leads to operational costs increasing and lower energy output. It's *via* AI-based predictive maintenance systems, which continuously monitor the performance of solar infrastructure to predict problems before they occur and lead to system failure. The machine learning model analyzes data on the performance of solar panels obtained using embedded sensors and triggers the detection of anomalies or deviations from expected performance [17]. These models would predict the failure of a component, such as the solar cell or the inverter. This would allow the operators to take actions to prevent the serious malfunction from occurring. Predictive maintenance also minimizes downtime in solar infrastructure and, with extensions in its lifespan, ensures constant energy production along with reduced operational costs.

10.1.6 AI's Role in Grid Integration and Energy Storage

The acceptance of solar power into the electric grid without loss of stability and reliability of supply requires sophisticated coordination with other energy sources. AI is used to predict the level of solar energy output, thus ensuring that a differential between supply and demand is perfectly balanced by grid operators. Analysis of historical data and real-time information about solar energy production enables forecasting of low and high availability periods of solar energy, thus enabling appropriate adjustments in energy flow by grid operators [5]. This ensures stability in the grid even when the availability of solar energy is dependent on the diurnal changes in weather conditions. AI is also transforming the game in energy storage systems, where the variability of solar energy needs effective methods to store that energy so as to balance supply and demand. AI algorithms optimize the number of cycles for charging and discharging the battery so that surplus solar energy can be stored when the sun shines bright and released at times of scarce sunlight [70]. This enhances the overall efficiency of solar energy systems, reduces energy waste, and enhances grid stability.

10.1.7 Land Use Management: AI-Driven Solar Project Mapping

Another key usage of AI in the solar energy industry is that it can assist in planning and designing solar projects, specifically in identifying a suitable location for developing a solar farm. AI, combined with its toolkit, can thus analyze satellite imagery, alongside land-use data and environmental considerations, for an optimal location to install solar installations with the least possible environmental and social impact related to significant large-scale solar developments. The technology also identifies decommissioned industrial sites, degraded lands, or areas of low agricultural value [41]. Therefore, it can help the developers avoid conflicting with agricultural or ecological concerns while harnessing the full potential of solar energy. In addition, AI-based models enable policymakers and developers to make much more informed decisions by assessing the long-term impacts on local ecosystems and communities in realizing the delivery of solar projects [12]. The proactive stance toward land management ensures adequate production of energy balanced with environmental conservation.

10.1.8 The Importance of AI in Climate Change Mitigation

AI for solar energy systems goes beyond a technical evolution; it's a paradigm shift in thinking about how to fight climate change. AI makes it more efficient, reliable, and scalable, with a high chance of shifting toward a low-carbon economy. Artificial intelligence is a potent tool for global efforts at reducing carbon emissions and mitigating the effects of climate change, mainly due to its capacity to optimize solar energy, reduce energy waste, and minimize environmental impacts. In principle, with the integration of AI in solar energy systems, dealing technically with challenges related to solar power is no longer a matter of concern, but the fight for a great mass against climate change is fundamental. Optimization, predictive maintenance, grid integration, and land use management done using AI-based optimization pave the path toward more efficient, reliable, and sustainable solar energy, paving the way for a cleaner and greener future.

10.2 AI in Solar Energy Optimization

Solar energy systems have, as of today, become one of the great optimizing tools that utilize artificial intelligence for huge advances in energy production, efficiency, and reliability [68]. The application of AI, which incorporates ML algorithms, continuously monitors, analyzes, and improves solar energy systems, using actual data from numerous environmental factors acquired in real time. As AI is to be integrated within the system of solar power, they can now make intelligent adjustments that maximize energy output as well as minimize losses [2]. This paper presents a comprehensive discussion about all the ways by which AI optimizes solar energy production, from an enhanced positioning and orientation of panels to poor-performing component identification and improving the efficiency of the entire system in turn. Graph 10.1 shows the comparison between AI-optimized and traditional solar energy output efficiency over time.

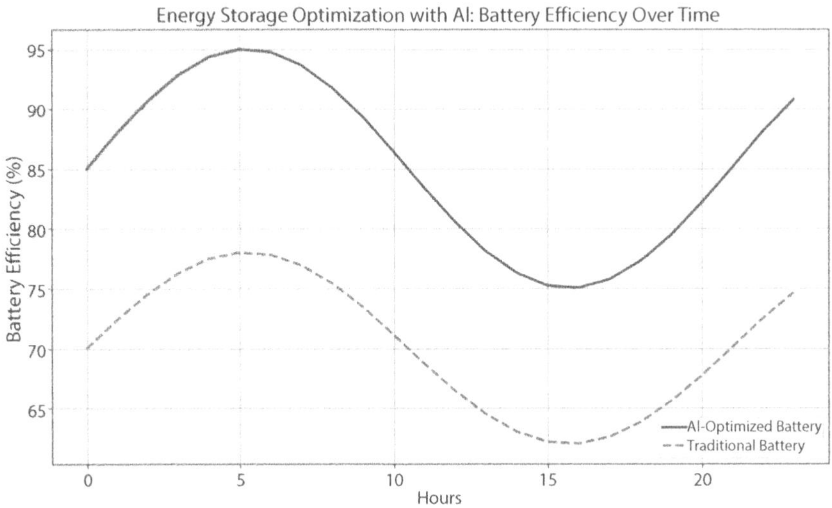

Graph 10.1 AI-driven solar energy output optimization.

10.2.1 Real-Time Data Analysis

Increase Energy Output: The whole idea of AI-based solar energy optimization lies in the ability to gather real-time data from several sources to make adjustments in solar energy systems appropriately [76]. These AI algorithms use data from sensors placed on solar panels, weather stations, and other monitoring devices to pool information about solar irradiance, temperatures, humidity, wind speed, and other environmental factors [26]. The variables involved are regularly analyzed by AI systems to predict changes in weather conditions and thus adjust the positioning of solar panels to capture more energy. For instance, if it had AI tracking systems, the solar panels would change tilt and angles all through the day in order to keep up with the sun's movement. It is known as solar tracking and ensures the panels are tilted at an optimal angle to catch the most amount of sunshine [38]. With real-time data, AI systems can compute the best angle to continue fine-tuning as the weather conditions change and so on. Areas that experience a shifting climate are more frequently very helpful in these places where cloud cover and temperature changes are usually measured alongside atmospheric conditions, which will greatly affect the output of solar energy.

10.2.2 AI-Based Weather Conditions Forecasting for Predictive Adjustments

The most significant factor in optimizing solar energy is weather forecasting, because the availability of sunlight directly affects the production of energy. AI algorithms, especially those that incorporate machine learning, can analyze historical weather data along with real-time measurements to predict future weather patterns to a high degree of accuracy [59]. By leveraging these predictions, AI systems can predict periods of cloud cover, rain, or intense sunlight and adjust solar panel configurations in advance to minimize losses in energy. For example, the AI systems can orient the panels at an angle that reduces the impact of light scatter when periods of expected cloud cover are present. Similarly, during periods when high solar irradiance is forecasted, the AI system can angle itself to allow for the maximum absorption of direct sunlight. This is active management of solar panels, and in case of poor weather conditions, energy generation increases step by step with time.

The other benefit of AI predictive capability is in the optimization of energy storage. Being able to predict whether or not sunlight will be plentiful or scarce, AI systems can handle power conditioning devices such as batteries [50]. This ensures that surplus energy generated during peak sunlight hours is preserved for when sunlight is scarce. This intelligent management of energy storage reduces reliance on an external source of electricity and increases the overall reliability of a system with solar energy.

10.2.3 Optimizing Solar Panel Orientation and Reducing Energy Loss

AI could play a key role in fine-tuning the spatial arrangement of solar panels in a manner that ensures energy is not wasted. The solar panel systems are inefficient primarily because their set angles do not coincide with the pattern in which the sun moves. In addition, fixed systems will experience energy loss because of shading from other buildings, trees, or other panels, and the continuous deposition of dust, dirt, or snow on the surface of the panels. Advanced optimization algorithms are used in AI systems to overcome these challenges by adjusting the angle and orientation of solar panels in real-time. Algae algorithms account for the location of the sun, daylight hours available, season, and installation location so that photovoltaic panels are at an optimal position to absorb energy [14]. Even in the big solar farms, AI can control groups of panels so that they tilt and rotate as individual units to evade shadowing and increase exposure to solar light. Moreover, AI systems can sense and determine when environmental factors, such as dust and debris or snow, are interfering with solar panels, causing inefficiencies. Machine learning-trained models on sensor data can discern patterns associated with those types of obstructions and trigger cleaning or maintenance alerts [82]. In the more complex designs, AI may then activate sweeping cleaning mechanisms that sweep away dust or snow from the panels to ensure their optimal functionality without the interjection of a human.

10.2.4 Bad Cell Searching and Cure

Besides optimizing the overall configuration of solar panels, AI is also highly important in monitoring the performance of individual cells within a solar array [58]. This is because solar panels are composed of many interconnected cells, and their performance contributes to the overall efficiency of the panel. With time, cells can become drained or defective to some extent because of wear and tear, manufacturing flaws, etc. Till recently, it was typically accomplished by unaided inspection methods, which happened to be time-consuming, labor-intensive, and susceptible to the vagaries of human interpretation. Such AI-based monitoring systems, using machine learning models, can detect minor performance changes in individual solar cells [30]. They can sense which cells are not producing the amount of energy they are supposed to produce by accessing data such as voltage and current taken from sensors embedded in the solar panels, along with temperatures. In such an AI system, faulty cell locations can be pinpointed very easily, and even the expected time for the replacement or repair of a faulty cell can be predicted [48]. Perhaps the most important advantage at the level of detailed monitoring is the immediate adjustment with regard to malfunctioning cells. A bad cell in a typical solar power system can impact the entire panel. That means an overall loss in the system regarding energy and production. The AI-driven systems also have the capability to shift the energy distribution in other cells or panels so that the total energy output is kept as high as possible. Thus, this real-time rebalancing of energy load increases the efficiency of the system and prolongs the lifespan of the solar panels because excessive wearout is avoided on healthy cells [35].

10.2.5 Machine Learning for Long-Term System Efficiency

Besides immediate compensations and faults, AI optimizes the long-term operation of the solar energy system by applying machine learning to predict trends in efficiency and changes in the behavior of a system over time. Through continuous analysis of historical performance data, AI systems can identify declines in efficiency, which often go unnoticed due to short-term monitoring. With these long-term insights, operators can schedule preventive maintenance or upgrades before energy losses become unavoidable, maximizing output [54]. Furthermore, insights from the data learned from previous installations will be used to enhance the design and configuration of solar energy projects in all new installations. Analyzing similar data for other projects, AI will discover the most optimal configurations for panels, energy storage, and schedules for maintenance across different locations and environments. A data-driven approach to designing systems improves the efficiency and reliability of new solar installations, making them optimized for long-term performance from the very start [24].

10.2.6 Strengthen the Economic Viability and Environmental Sustainability

The implications of AI in the optimization of solar energy systems are striking for the economic and environmental aspects of solar projects. There is a reduction in energy losses concerning energy output, while maintenance is also reduced. Improved return on investment for both providers and consumers of solar energy follows from this, further building on the competitiveness of solar energy with respect to fossil fuel-based energy sources and fuels, and continuing investment in renewable technologies. The environmental perspective in AI-driven optimization is useful for contributing to climate change mitigation in that it ensures the solar energy system operates at its maximum possible efficiency. Demand for backup power from nonrenewable sources is reduced, thus lowering carbon emissions while reducing the environmental impact of energy production due to the element of AI. Additionally, AI extends the lifespan of solar panels and other equipment through predictive maintenance and thereby reduces the rate at which these are replaced, minimizing the level of resource consumption and waste associated with solar energy infrastructure as described in Table 10.1.

Table 10.1 AI-driven optimization of solar energy systems.

AI functionality	Description	Benefits	References
Real-time data analysis	AI analyzes weather patterns and solar irradiance to optimize solar panel positioning throughout the day.	Maximizes energy capture and reduces energy loss due to shading, dust, and other environmental factors.	Sohani *et al.*, [69] Manowska *et al.*, [46]
Machine learning for fault detection	Detects underperforming solar cells and identifies faults to allow real-time energy redistribution.	Increases overall efficiency by mitigating energy loss and redistributing the energy load to compensate for defects.	Kermani *et al.*, [36] Khenkin *et al.*, [39]
Predictive energy output	Forecasts solar power generation based on historical weather data and real-time environmental monitoring.	Ensures the grid can handle demand, optimizes storage, and improves the economic viability of solar energy projects.	Massidda *et al.*, [47] Egho-Promise *et al.*, [22]

10.3 Predictive Maintenance with AI in Solar Infrastructure

The rise of AI-driven predictive maintenance has signaled one of the revolutionary solutions in the solar energy sector. It will bring a fundamental shift in how systems and their reliability are maintained. Traditionally, most maintenance work is scheduled servicing, routine inspection, or merely reactionary measures following a system failure. Inefficiencies in the reactionary model can mean costly system downtime, reduced energy output, and expensive emergency repairs [9]. Predictive maintenance, through AI, is a far more intelligent and effective alternative because it can help solar energy operators identify and therefore avoid problems before such damage sets in or the disruption becomes debilitating.

10.3.1 Early Fault Detection Through Predictive Analytics

Predictive maintenance works on some of the most sophisticated AI algorithms that consider performance data obtained from sensors spread all over the solar energy system: within solar panels, inverters, and other parts of critical infrastructure. These sensors track many parameters dealing with the operational conditions of voltage, current, temperature, and output efficiency. Real-time continuous data collection allows AI-powered models to track a baseline of normal operating conditions and detect even slight deviations from those parameters [15]. These deviations may signal incipient degradation or failure in such components as solar panels experiencing a reduction in energy output as their cells deteriorate or an inverter malfunctioning in the conversion of power. AI models, through the mechanism of training based on machine learning, can indicate these patterns of deviations even earlier than human inspectors or traditional monitoring mechanisms. For example, when solar cells, as part of photovoltaic modules, start to degenerate because of micro-cracks or other degradations, AI can recognize the steady degradation long before it would appear on a scheduled inspection. The system can then create a warning or alert for operators that an intervention measure needs to be applied, like cleaning, realigning, or replacing the concerned component [16].

10.3.2 Machine Learning Models and Historical Data

While AI can predict maintenance of real-time data, it highly relies on the data of historical performance. Through their machine learning models, large amounts of past solar installations' datasets are analyzed to uncover trends or patterns, which may have led to a failure or inefficiency of particular components over time. Knowing these long-term trends improves the accuracy with which such an AI system can predict new or existing solar installations. This is exemplified by a system where, in its learning history, the AI system finds that there are normally patterns in the variation of life for invertebrates. The AI system can, therefore, predict precisely when an inverter could fail based on similar usage and environmental patterns. The operator would thus replace or repair the inverter before its state deteriorates to failing, hence avoiding energy production drastically falling [51]. Similarly, AI can track patterns associated with weather-induced wear and tear—the impact of dust, hail, or extreme temperature conditions—on the efficiency of solar panels. Armed with this information, solar energy providers could proactively take action like revising their cleaning schedules or fitting protective barriers to prevent damage from happening at all.

10.3.3 Durable Lifespan of Solar Installation

The ability to predict the failure of components and perform timely maintenance is related to the lifecycle of solar energy systems. AI gets in early enough that minor problems do not turn into full-scale failures that often call for costly replacements or extensive repairs [23]. This proactive technique extends the lifetime of critical elements like solar panels, inverters, batteries, and trackers while accomplishing the general functionality of solar energy systems. For instance, solar panels deteriorate over time and with exposure to various weather conditions. AI can predict the precise points at which panels start to deteriorate, thus suggesting cleaning, realignment, or repairs in order to continue running efficiently. Similarly, inverters, which convert direct current from solar panels to usable alternating current, are sensitive to proper maintenance; otherwise, they may fail. Predictive interventions in AI allow for the smooth continuation of its operation.

This also provides life for a longer duration for these components, and the economic as well as environmental impacts are significant. This kind of decrease in the number of replacements, along with decreased instances, also reduces the operational expenses for the solar energy producers. This, in turn, enables reducing the overall cost-effectiveness for utilizing renewable power sources like solar energy as compared to traditional energy generation based on fossil fuels [32].

10.3.4 Minimizing Downtime and Maximizing Energy Production

This significantly reduces system downtime—one of the most significant benefits of AI-powered predictive maintenance—and immediately impacts the bottom line in terms of total energy production for solar installations [49]. Failure of a critical component, such as a solar panel or inverter, can cause devastating losses of energy production, particularly in larger solar farms, where even an anomalously small percentage of malfunctioning panels can result in massive deficits in energy production. Contrasted to this, AI capabilities of detection and consolidation of the issues at hand before they become critical guarantee maximum efficiency for systems with minimum interruptions. AI maintenance systems empower solar energy providers to maintain as much as possible steady power generation through reduced unplanned stoppages and optimization of the performance of all system components [18]. This is the case especially for solar installations that feed into the national grid and isolated, off-grid installations, powering villages or industries. In both cases, the dependability of the solar energy system must be addressed. AI predictive maintenance has to rise up so that the reliability of the solar system can be maintained without weather and other external influences or factors like aging equipment.

10.3.5 Reducing Maintenance Costs through Early Intervention

The conventional methods of maintenance in the solar energy industry are very costly because fixes are inherently reactive in nature and also physically demanding to inspect. For example, regular checks would necessitate visual inspection of hundreds of square miles of solar farms. Essentially, it is time-consuming and prone to human error. Moreover, breakdowns may be very expensive, as emergency repairs are often necessary upon failure of a single component. Replacements could have to be done with all urgency in order not to lose a long period of nonproductivity of the system.

Predictive maintenance using AI greatly reduces costs from these events since intervention can be done beforehand, and resources can be used more efficiently. Operators no longer have to wait for systems to fail but rather can rely on AI-based monitoring for continuous system performance while performing maintenance only when it is absolutely necessary [60]. Inspections are thus fewer, and emergency repairs are not as common. Additionally, by identifying potential issues before they occur, the AI system supports planned maintenance, which may be conducted when there is low demand for energy, thus holding in reserve less likely losses for the energy vendors. The decreases in maintenance expenses benefit the economics of the solar projects. Lower operational expenses make solar energy more economical for the consumer, and a greater return on investment makes it more appealing to the energy vendors to increase their reliance on renewable technology. Graph 10.2 illustrates the reduction in maintenance costs achieved through AI-based predictive maintenance compared to traditional maintenance approaches.

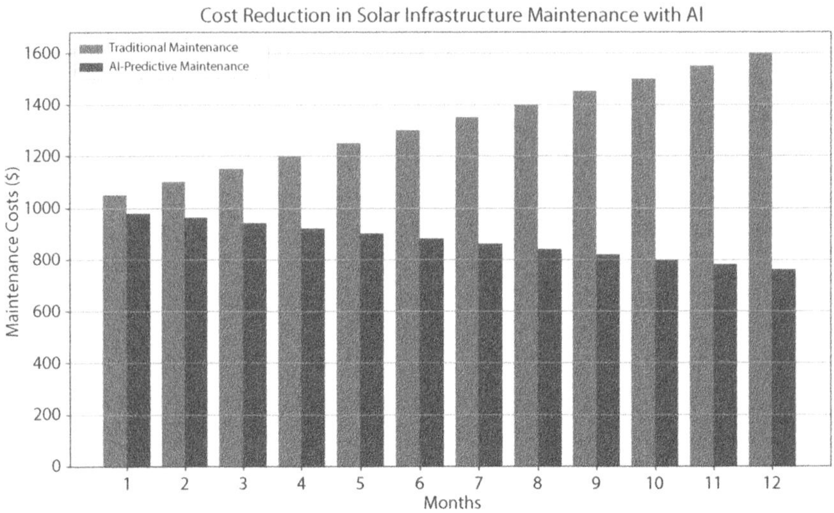

Graph 10.2 Cost reduction in solar infrastructure maintenance with AI.

10.3.6 Sustainability Benefits and Reduced CO_2 Emissions

Beyond the economic benefits, AI-powered predictive maintenance brings significant environmental advantages—mostly in issues of sustainability and carbon footprint reduction. There is less need to physically inspect parts, meaning that transportation to and from remote installations to access them is most times not necessary; hence, reining in those carbon emissions associated with maintenance activities. Automated monitoring and diagnosis can be done remotely to minimize the environmental impact of maintaining large-scale solar farms. Further, AI is also aiding the sustainability of solar energy systems by improving the performance and extending the life of solar panels and other devices. Long-lasting equipment will minimize the production and replacement of many equipment parts that will need to be replaced more often in the future, minimizing their usage of natural resources and other kinds of waste [29]. Again, it is all about general lessons learned in making renewable energy infrastructure less harmful to the environment.

In summary, AI predictive maintenance is revolutionizing the management of solar energy systems in a proactive manner to create reliability at cheaper prices with environmental sustainability. Continuous monitoring and prediction of possible failures of components, with prompt intervention, keeps the solar energy system at peak efficiency, which supports

Table 10.2 AI in predictive maintenance of solar infrastructure.

AI functionality	Description	Benefits	References
Performance Monitoring	AI analyzes sensor data to track performance trends and detect minor deviations from normal parameters.	Identifies issues before they escalate, minimizing system downtime and reducing repair costs.	Haleem *et al.*, [27] Gupta *et al.*, [25]
Predictive Fault Detection	Predicts potential failures (e.g., solar cell degradation, inverter issues) based on historical data.	Ensures proactive maintenance, preventing costly repairs and improving system longevity.	Afridi *et al.*, [1] Uhanto *et al.*, [76]
Automated Corrective Actions	AI systems initiate adjustments or shutdowns of malfunctioning components without human intervention.	Enhances system reliability by reducing energy loss and maintaining uninterrupted energy production.	Alhamrouni *et al.*, [6] Ukoba *et al.*, [77]

the overall viability and sustainability of solar power as the solution to the global energy crisis and climate change. Table 10.2 shows the AI in predictive maintenance of solar infrastructure.

10.4 Artificial Intelligence in Grid Integration and Energy Storage

However, it is unavoidable that climate change will happen, but solar energy can be considered the first choice for clean or renewable energy. The biggest setback to a considerable supply of solar energy is its variability, as the amount produced varies with sunlight availability, which varies with weather conditions, geographical location, and even time of day. Integrating this variability makes integration into the electricity grid challenging because a reliable and stable supply is required for efficient operation [56]. These are challenges AI is overcoming by optimizing the injection of solar power into the grid and transforming the energy storage systems, hence making solar energy more predictable, stable, and efficient.

10.4.1 Predictive Algorithms for Solar Energy Output

The energy supplier can predict the production of solar energy with high accuracy due to predictive algorithms powered by artificial intelligence. It will depend on historical data on solar irradiance, temperature, cloud cover, and weather patterns, and the ability of AI will predict the exact time and how much is being produced by these solar panels [13]. Advanced models can compute whether there are any disturbances in energy production due to solar power generation and help in early alerting energy providers about the likely variation in the grid. For example, if the sun is bright so that energy production is high through the use of solar power, AI can inform the grid to store the excess or direct it where there is more demand. Conversely, if the sun is behind the clouds or at night, AI can inform the grid to pull energy from renewable sources such as wind or hydropower, or even from reserved energy. This is necessary to forecast and control solar power. The ability to predict and control solar supply is the lifeblood of grids. Traditional power grids were built to service the quantities of energy that would actually be produced by fossil fuel power plants [33]. The abrupt decline in production creates new issues within the grid's stability that will be dictated by fluctuations in solar power. AI's ability to analyze real-time data and make predictions enables the easier incorporation of solar energy, even during fluctuations in supply and demand.

10.4.2 Increased Grid Flexibility and Stability

The greatest advantage AI presents regarding integration with the grid is increased flexibility and stability within the grid itself. Indeed, AI-based systems could balance the almost-precarious nature of solar energy with other sources of energy, especially other renewable energy sources, including wind, geothermal, and hydropower. Wind is often seen to yield better during nighttime when the yield of solar energy drops. AI will be able to assess and coordinate the generation and transmission of such varied energy sources in an attempt to iron out the inherent variability of each [85]. The third aspect of AI is that it can modulate energy flows in the grid at different points on a real-time basis, contingent upon the given demand and supply conditions. In other words, if it is a high-energy-demand peak period, AI can preemptively ensure selective transmission of solar energy to places where energy levels are low, thus minimizing the use of fossil-fuel-generated standby power. However, in case of low demand, AI would sound the alert to the energy storage systems to keep any excess solar power for later consumption [37]. In this balancing act, it ensures that renewable energy is utilized to the fullest extent possible, thereby reducing the reliance of the grid on carbon-emitting energies and, in turn, mitigating climate change.

10.4.3 Energy Storage Optimization by AI

Energy storage is an important element for renewable power systems, especially for solar energy. Since the electricity produced from solar panels is available only when there is sunshine, this means there must be some form of energy storage so that excess energy from periods of high production can be stored to later be released during low or no solar generation conditions, such as at night or when it is cloudy. AI transforms the efficiency of the energy storage systems, especially battery management systems. AI-based battery management systems, through machine learning algorithms, manage energy storage system charging and discharging cycles for maximum utilization of the battery. AI predicts energy demand and generation patterns of solar energy and determines when to charge the battery with available excess energy from the solar source and when to discharge stored energy into the grid [57]. This optimizes the production of solar power, thus storing it when it is most required to take stress off the grid and maximize the energy. For instance, when the sun is shining brightly, AI may alert the batteries to hold in energy that is not immediately utilized, thereby preventing significant solar energy loss. Later, with very heavy peak demand because people have come home and everyone is using more power in the evenings, AI can draw down that stored energy to meet that surging demand. This reduces peakers and the number of peaking plants—many of these are fossil fuel-based and, worse, contribute to greenhouse gas emissions.

10.4.4 Reducing Carbon Emissions and Fossil Fuel Dependency

One of the most important contributions of AI in grid integration and energy storage is its role in reducing carbon emissions. By optimizing the use of renewable energy sources like solar, AI reduces the need for backup power from fossil fuels during periods of low solar production [63]. This helps decrease the overall carbon footprint of the energy grid, making solar energy a more viable and environmentally sustainable solution for mitigating climate change.

AI also enables more efficient use of stored solar energy, ensuring that fossil fuel-based energy generation is only used as a last resort. By strategically deploying stored solar energy during peak demand or low production periods, AI reduces the amount of energy drawn from non-renewable sources, further lowering greenhouse gas emissions [19]. This not only contributes to global efforts to combat climate change but also aligns with the growing demand for cleaner, more sustainable energy solutions.

10.5 AI-Driven Solar Project Mapping and Land Use Management

Growing large-scale solar farms, with solar energy forming an integral part of global solutions in reducing carbon emissions and ridding the world of fossil fuels, poses a daunting puzzle: scaling up the production of solar energy requires high-quality, non-conflicting land selection that does not create tension with agriculture, conservation, and local communities. Strategic planning and development of utility-scale solar farms are key to maximizing energy output and minimizing impacts on the environment and socio-economic sectors. Technologies driven by AI have become indispensable instruments in mapping solar projects and the management of land use; they are therefore more supportive of identifying ideal locations for solar farms and ensuring such projects are sustainable in the long run [83].

10.5.1 Application of AI in Geospatial Analysis

AI automates the decision-making process by identifying the best possible locations for solar energy projects by analyzing enormous datasets of satellite imagery, GIS, land use records, and environmental data.

AI geospatial analysis thus provides a well-rounded view of the desired potential location and solar project that also considers land elevation, ecological sensitivity, proximity to existing infrastructure, and solar irradiance [7]. Machine learning algorithms are able to read high-resolution satellite images in order to identify the properties of land that would be ideal for solar energy production. For example, AI algorithms can pinpoint locations that receive maximum sunlight throughout the year and locations with minimal obstructions, such as tall buildings or dense vegetation that cause shading. Additionally, using historical climate data, AI will predict the long-term suitability of the location for solar energy production so that the site chosen will still be optimal for the solar panel in the lifetime of the project. This AI-based evaluation is not just limited to identifying sunny locations but also considers environmental and socio-economic elements. AI can identify areas that tend to be prone to natural catastrophes, such as floods or earthquakes, that are considered a threat to solar infrastructure [86]. AI predicts these risks that allow developers to avoid locations where a solar project may be unable to sustain itself in the long term due to environmental risks.

10.5.2 Identifying a Sustainable Location for Solar Development

One of the main challenges in building more solar energy capacity is in finding a way to balance the potential installation of huge solar farms with the retention of valuable agricultural land and ecologically sensitive areas. Relocating large-scale solar farms to prime farmland or biodiversity hotspots can create conflict with local communities, agricultural industries, and conservation groups. AI-powered solar project mapping tools offer a solution that enables developers to identify alternative sites that are more environmentally and socially sustainable [45]. The best application of AI in solar project siting likely lies in finding degraded or underutilized land that is suitable for solar development [28]. Applying their deep learning network to analyzing land use patterns allows them to identify areas that have been either abandoned or repurposed, like former industrial sites, decommissioned coal mines, or badly degraded agricultural land. These areas, so-called "brownfields," are less likely to compete with productive farmland or sensitive ecosystems and hence constitute ideal locations for solar projects, as such projects can combine renewable energy production with land restoration. For instance, there are several decommissioned industrial facilities located along existing energy infrastructure: lines, substations, etc.

This can help out by making it easier and cheaper to connect new solar farms to the grid. Identifying such sites with AI may reduce the ecological footprint while maximizing economic viability for solar installations.

10.5.3 Reducing Ecological and Social Impacts

AI-based solar project mapping captures ideal locations for solar farms and also helps to approximate the probable ecological and social impact of such projects. By integrating environmental data into site selection models, AI tools can help project developers avoid areas that are critical habitats for endangered species, protected ecosystems, or significant water resource areas [67]. For instance, AI can look at whether these potential solar locations are near wetlands, forests, or wildlife migration corridors and flag them as more likely to be impacted by ecological disruption due to development.

In addition to such ecological considerations, AI-based tools can even evaluate the social impacts of solar development. Analysis of population density, land ownership patterns, and local land use practices might lead AI to identify places where the influence of solar projects on the local communities is less likely to be in conflict [40]. For instance, AI will point to areas where areas are likely to displace farmers, interfere with traditional land use, or provoke resistance from local populations. By actively addressing these concerns, AI can help developers select sites that are likely to be sanctioned by the community and therefore reduce the risk of delays or opposition. More importantly, AI can aid the government and policymakers in creating zoning legislation that defines solar development. AI will enable policymakers to create zoning frameworks that favor the development of solar energy on less contentious lands like brownfields or degraded areas without undermining vital agricultural and conservation areas while providing real-time insights into the availability of lands as well as potential land use conflicts.

10.5.4 Real-Time Monitoring and Decision Making

With AI-driven mapping of solar projects, one of the key advantages lies in the real-time, actionable insights driving decision-making. AI models can be continuously updated with new data, like changes in land-use trends and climate and emerging trends of energy demand. Developers and policymakers thus make dynamic plans and adjustments to keep solar projects up to date with conditions [21]. For example, when changes to land

Table 10.3 AI in solar project mapping and land use management.

AI functionality	Description	Benefits	References
Geospatial analysis for site identification	Analyzes satellite imagery and land use patterns to identify ideal solar farm locations.	Minimizes conflicts with agriculture and ecological regions, promoting sustainable solar farm development.	Zhang *et al.*, [81] Hilker *et al.*, [31]
Sustainable siting of solar farms	Recommends degraded or abandoned lands (e.g., coal mines, industrial sites) for solar projects.	Reduces the ecological footprint of solar projects and preserves biodiversity.	Onifade *et al.*, [53] Dhar *et al.*, [20]
AI for environmental impact assessments	Models predict the socio-economic and environmental impact of solar developments.	Informs policymakers and developers to ensure balanced energy production and conservation efforts.	Ashraf *et al.*, [11] Kadenic *et al.*, [34]

use patterns occur due to urbanization, the growth of agriculture, or the changed policies concerning the environment, the AI-based applications can instantly update the site recommendations; in this way, solar projects are always aligned with the most up-to-date information. Lastly, AI can model the long-term effects of solar projects on local ecosystems and water resources, as well as on communities, to enable them to make informed decisions between energy production and sustainability. Table 10.3 shows the AI in solar project mapping and land use management.

10.5.5 AI-Based Solutions for Conflicts Over Land Use

One of the major hurdles in developing solar projects is land-use conflicts between energy production and other societal requirements, such as food security and conservation. AI may provide crucial input in identifying trade-offs and possible compromises in making a decision on land use [61]. These may be the AI-based models to determine if the solar projects can be co-located with other land uses like agriculture, often known as agrivoltaics. Agrivoltaics refers to growing crops under or between solar panels. Such innovative approaches help land serve multiple purposes and thus increase its productivity and contribute to energy and food security simultaneously. AI is therefore capable of simulating different land-use scenarios, which would help stakeholders in visualizing the outcomes of solar projects and making decisions that would minimize impacts. Such capability proves invaluable for policymakers facing competing demands for energy production, conservation, and agriculture in areas with growing land use pressures.

10.6 The Role of AI in Climate Change Mitigation

With the introduction of artificial intelligence in the solar energy industry, it has emerged as one of the powerful tools that will challenge the world to win over climate change. Solar energy forms the backbone of implementing renewable energy strategies for reducing greenhouse gas emissions; thus, the impact of solar energy can be maximized by incorporating AI into it. AI directly reduces carbon emissions through its contribution toward a low-carbon economy, through the optimization of energy production, improved integration into grids, better energy storage, and sustainable land use [84].

10.6.1 Efficient Energy Harvesting through Increased Efficiency of Solar Energy Systems and Reduced Carbon Emissions

One of the major ways through which AI supports climate change mitigation is by enhancing the efficiency of solar energy systems. Since the solar panels are optimized for the maximum production of energy by AI, they are capable of generating the maximum possible electricity under all diversified environmental conditions. It develops, therefore, a consistent and reliable supply of clean energy that directly offsets the amount of fossil fuel-based power generation. AI-powered systems replace coal, oil, and gas with solar energy with net reductions in carbon dioxide (CO_2) emissions, one of the primary causes of global warming [10]. AI increases the effectiveness of balancing supply and demand in the energy network through highly accurate predictions of solar availability. The AI makes very accurate predictions of the likelihood of the sun being available, based on weather patterns, for example. This decreases the dependence on fossil fuel-based reserve power plants that need to be fed to ensure a supply of power, as the renewable sources of energy are intermittent. AI reduces carbon-intensive energy sources and promotes widespread consumption of clean, renewable energy.

10.6.2 Optimization of Energy Demand Management

Its ability to do predictive analytics and real-time data processing can further contribute to climate change mitigation by optimizing energy demand management [42]. Another challenge in energy systems is matching supply with fluctuating demand. Overproduction wastes potential energy output, whereas underproduction gives rise to blackouts or the building up of fossil fuel plants. AI predicts energy demand patterns and thus optimizes energy distribution. For example, AI-powered systems could modulate the amount of solar panel output, the level of battery storage, and integration into the grid according to changes in real-time energy consumption [66]. Such a system enhances the process of having excess solar energy stored in the battery banks for deployment in peak usage periods. This, in turn, enhances the utilization of renewable energies, while dependence on non-renewable sources of energy will decrease in peak-demand periods and eventually reduce the carbon footprint. This way, AI aids in conserving energy, thus aiding globalization efforts at mitigating climate change.

10.6.3 AI in Sustainable Solar Project Development

Though a renewing approach to power distribution is what the world needs to reduce carbon emissions, its development ought not to be carried out unilaterally to prevent negative unintended effects on the environment. What the AI does in solar project mapping is that it ensures that solar installations are done in ways that minimize direct impacts on ecosystems and farmlands. AI avoids the destruction of natural habitats or productive land and encourages suitable placement, such as degraded lands or abandoned industrial sites, for solar farms in order to avoid environmental degradation [55]. In playing a role in responsible land use management, the generation of solar projects reduces greenhouse gas emissions but supports much bigger environmental conservation goals. For example, AI can estimate the impact of installing solar panels on surrounding ecosystems, water bodies, and the biodiversity that those components are home to [64]. This way, developers could make decisions that meet global climate change conservation, thus averting the bad trade-off between generating renewable energy and protecting the environment.

10.6.4 Role of AI in Global Climate Policy

As the world continues to develop policies in the hope of reducing carbon emissions around the globe, AI-driven solutions will provide critical data and insights to advise climate-related strategies [3]. For instance, AI can model long-term impacts of energy-related policies, predict future demand for energy as climate conditions might change in the future, and come up with the most effective strategy related to integrating renewable energy sources like solar power into the national grids. To that end, AI will be able to model the implications of climate change on the generation of solar power. Therefore, for example, with increasing temperature or erratic changes in weather, the solar panels in particular regions may not function properly. This enables AI to predict change and thereby help policymakers and energy organizations make the necessary adjustments to ensure the reliability and effectiveness of solar power as a possible remedy against climate change [71–74].

10.6.5 AI for a Circular Economy

Not only is the AI contributing to producing and distributing energy, but it also means helping in mitigating climate change through its support of principles behind the circular economy in the solar industry [80]. Solar panels and batteries have finite lifetimes, and their end of life produces challenges for environmental management. AI-based models can leverage predictability on when components are likely to fail and then recommend the best times for replacements or recycling of components. This reduces the adverse environmental impacts of solar panel waste and supports enhanced development of sustainable, circular systems for renewable energy infrastructure. Another key application of AI is to predict and control solar component lifecycles, which also extends the life of solar farms by avoiding much replacement by raw materials or mitigation of carbon footprints overall in the solar energy industry [75]. By driving reuse and recycling in the solar infrastructure, AI will find its footing within a circular and more sustainable renewable energy industry.

10.7 Conclusion

Hence, the integration of AI in the field of solar energy marks a radical turn of events towards the pursuit of optimizing renewable energy and climate change management. Processing and analysis of vast real-time data, together with predictive models and automated decision-making capabilities, are the critical enablers that allow for the transformation of the operational landscape of a solar energy system. AI enhances the production of solar energy by maximizing the capture of the available energy, thus adapting to conditions such as sunlight, temperature, and other weather conditions. In this way, AI algorithms make the solar panels work at optimal efficiency through continuous analysis of variables and make adjustments in real-time. This is optimization at the higher order, producing higher energy outputs, reduced losses, and improved economic feasibility of solar energy projects. Renewable energy thus becomes increasingly competitive with traditional fossil fuels. This is one important contribution of AI in solar energy: the facilitation of predictive maintenance. The use of AI-powered systems continuously monitors performance in solar infrastructure, thus allowing it to detect early faults or inefficiencies. This proactive maintenance leads to extended operating life in solar installations and reduces major repair and related downtime, thus allowing an uninterrupted flow of clean energy. Besides, the AI optimization of the grid integration and energy storage systems helps address the intrinsic variation in solar energy generation. AI balances the integration of solar power with other renewable and non-renewable resources by making predictions about changes in the generation of solar power, which, in turn, ensures stability in the grid and reduces the usage of fossil fuels during dark times characterized by minimal solar generation. On the other hand, AI optimizes charging/discharging cycles for batteries to ensure that the stored solar energy is available at the peak demand period. Besides operational efficiencies, AI also makes its mark in the sphere of sustainable development by making solar project mapping and land-use management feasible. The analytics capability of AI on geospatial platforms enables policymakers and developers to map out and identify ideal locations for solar projects with reduced land-use conflict and thus minimizes the ecological footprint of solar farms. By locating solar installations on degraded lands, decommissioned industrial sites, or abandoned mines, AI contributes toward the preservation of agricultural lands and natural ecosystems while furthering environmental sustainability. In this way, AI ensures that expanding solar energy will not come at the cost of biodiversity and food security—important preservation goals.

Thirdly, AI can be a vital tool in the fight against climate change. AI supports global efforts to reduce greenhouse gas emissions by maximizing the efficiency of solar energy systems, reducing energy wastage, and increasing sustainable land use practices. As AI enables the integration of solar energy into broader energy systems and offers insights into energy demand patterns, it further enhances the contribution of such intelligent systems toward carbon reduction by reducing dependency on carbon-intensive sources of energy. AI technologies will be developing further in the very near future, providing even more advanced applications than the ones currently existing, opening new routes into innovation, sustainability, and resilience in the renewable energy arena. The integration of AI and solar energy is a huge step in the world's shift towards a low-carbon, sustainable future. AI will alter the solar energy playing field by optimizing its methods of power generation, efficiency, and integration into the power grid, thereby paving the way for a more sustainable manner of developing such infrastructure. By the time AI continues evolving and growing, that becomes even more reason for embracing it into the solar energy landscape, opening doors for growing the fight against energy inefficiency, environmental degradation, and climate change. This unrelenting innovation means that AI is soon going to be that crucial link towards a future powered by renewable energy, as it will not only provide the source of power but also become the linchpin in a much bigger solution aimed toward achieving the globe's climate goals.

AI disclosure statement: The author acknowledges the use of AI-based tools for minor language editing or grammatical correction. However, all intellectual contributions, analyses, and conclusions presented in this chapter are entirely the author's own.

References

1. Afridi, Y.S., Ahmad, K., Hassan, L., Artificial intelligence based prognostic maintenance of renewable energy systems: A review of techniques, challenges, and future research directions. *Int. J. Energy Res.*, *46*, 15, 21619–21642, 2022.
2. Ahmad, T., Zhang, D., Huang, C., Zhang, H., Dai, N., Song, Y., Chen, H., Artificial intelligence in sustainable energy industry: Status Quo, challenges and opportunities. *J. Cleaner Prod.*, *289*, 125834, 2021.
3. Akter, S., Babu, M.M., Hani, U., Sultana, S., Bandara, R., Grant, D., Unleashing the power of artificial intelligence for climate action in industrial markets. *Ind. Marketing Manage.*, *117*, 92–113, 2024.

4. Al Mahdi, H., Leahy, P.G., Alghoul, M., Morrison, A.P., A Review of Photovoltaic Module Failure and Degradation Mechanisms: Causes and Detection Techniques, in: *Solar*, vol. 4, pp. 43–82, MDPI, 2024, January.
5. Al-Dahidi, S., Madhiarasan, M., Al-Ghussain, L., Abubaker, A.M., Ahmad, A.D., Alrbai, M., ... & Zio, E., Forecasting Solar Photovoltaic Power Production: A Comprehensive Review and Innovative Data-Driven Modeling Framework. *Energies, 17*, 16, 4145, 2024.
6. Alhamrouni, I., Abdul Kahar, N.H., Salem, M., Swadi, M., Zahroui, Y., Kadhim, D.J., Alhuyi Nazari, M., A Comprehensive Review on the Role of Artificial Intelligence in Power System Stability, Control, and Protection: Insights and Future Directions. *Appl. Sci., 14*, 14, 6214, 2024.
7. Alogayell, H.M., Kamal, A., Alkadi, I., II, Ramadan, R.H., Ramadan, M.S., Geospatial modeling of optimal zones for sustainable urbanization in south-western NEOM, Saudi Arabia using geomatics techniques. *Front. Built Environ., 10*, 1379269, 2024.
8. Amara, M.B., Rdhaounia, E., Balghouthi, M., Adaptive solar irradiance forecasting in arid regions: enhancing accuracy with localized atmospheric adjustments. *J. Eng. Res*, 2024.
9. Aoun, A., Adda, M., Ilinca, A., Ghandour, M., Ibrahim, H., Centralized vs. Decentralized electric grid resilience analysis using Leontief's input–output model. *Energies, 17*, 6, 1321, 2024.
10. Arya, A., Bachheti, A., Bachheti, R.K., Singh, M., Chandel, A.K., Role of Artificial Intelligence in Minimizing Carbon Footprint: A Systematic Review of Recent Insights. *Biorefin. Ind. 4.0 Empowering Sustainability*, 365–386, 2024.
11. Ashraf, U., Morelli, T.L., Smith, A.B., Hernandez, R.R., Climate-Smart Siting for renewable energy expansion. *iScience, 27*, 10, 2024.
12. Bachmann, N., Tripathi, S., Brunner, M., Jodlbauer, H., The contribution of data-driven technologies in achieving the sustainable development goals. *Sustainability, 14*, 5, 2497, 2022.
13. Barhmi, K., Heynen, C., Golroodbari, S., van Sark, W., A Review of Solar Forecasting Techniques and the Role of Artificial Intelligence, in: *Solar*, vol. 4, pp. 99–135, MDPI, 2024, February.
14. Bossi, S., Blasi, L., Cupertino, G., dell'Erba, R., Cipollini, A., De Vito, S., Tina, G.M., Floating Photovoltaic Plant Monitoring: A Review of Requirements and Feasible Technologies. *Sustainability, 16*, 19, 8367, 2024.
15. Cadet, E., Osundare, O.S., Ekpobimi, H.O., Samira, Z., Wondaferew, Y., AI-powered threat detection in surveillance systems: A real-time data processing framework, 2024.
16. Castle-Green, T., Reeves, S., Fischer, J.E., Koleva, B., Revisiting the Digital Plumber: Modifying the Installation Process of an Established Commercial IoT Alarm System. *Comput. Supported Cooperative Work (CSCW), 32*, 3, 607–643, 2023.

17. Cespedes, A.J.J., Pangestu, B.H.B., Hanazawa, A., Cho, M., Performance Evaluation of Machine Learning Methods for Anomaly Detection in CubeSat Solar Panels. *Appl. Sci.*, *12*, 17, 8634, 2022.
18. Chelliah, P.R., Jayasankar, V., Agerstam, M., Sundaravadivazhagan, B., Cyriac, R., *The Power of Artificial Intelligence for the Next-Generation Oil and Gas Industry: Envisaging AI-inspired Intelligent Energy Systems and Environments*, John Wiley & Sons, 2023.
19. Chen, C., Hu, Y., Karuppiah, M., Kumar, P.M., Artificial intelligence on economic evaluation of energy efficiency and renewable energy technologies. *Sustainable Energy Technol. Assess.*, *47*, 101358, 2021.
20. Dhar, A., Naeth, M.A., Jennings, P.D., El-Din, M.G., Perspectives on environmental impacts and a land reclamation strategy for solar and wind energy systems. *Sci. Total Environ.*, *718*, 134602, 2020.
21. Duma, D., Pollitt, M.G., Covatariu, A., Regulatory learning in the face of net zero climate policy: The case of the UK. *Rev. Ind. Organ.*, 1–26, 2024.
22. Egho-Ekpenyong Promise, E., Sitti, M., Hutchful, N., Agangiba, W.A., IoT-Enhanced Weather Monitoring System: Affordable Hardware Solution for Real-Time Data Collection, Storage, And Predictive Analysis. *Eur. J. Comput. Sci. Inf. Technol.*, *12*, 1, 43–56, 2024.
23. Ekpenyong, M.E. and Udoh, N.S., Intelligent optimal preventive replacement maintenance policy for non-repairable systems. *Comput. Ind. Eng.*, *190*, 110091, 2024.
24. Gilani, H., Sahebi, H., Pishvaee, M.S., A data-driven robust optimization model for integrated network design solar photovoltaic to micro grid. *Sustainable Energy Grids Networks*, *31*, 100714, 2022.
25. Gupta, L., Salman, T., Zolanvari, M., Erbad, A., Jain, R., Fault and performance management in multi-cloud virtual network services using AI: A tutorial and a case study. *Comput. Networks*, *165*, 106950, 2019.
26. Guven, A.F., Abdelaziz, A.Y., Samy, M.M., Barakat, S., Optimizing energy Dynamics: A comprehensive analysis of hybrid energy storage systems integrating battery banks and supercapacitors. *Energy Convers. Manage.*, *312*, 118560, 2024.
27. Haleem, A., Javaid, M., Singh, R.P., Suman, R., Khan, S., Management 4.0: Concept, applications and advancements. *Sustainable Oper. Comput.*, *4*, 10–21, 2023.
28. Hassan, Q., Nassar, A.K., Algburi, S., Fouly, A., Awwad, E.M., Jaszczur, M., Barakat, M., Evaluation of solar and biomass perspectives using geographic information system-The case of Iraq regions. *Renewable Energy*, *227*, 120463, 2024.
29. Hegab, H., Khanna, N., Monib, N., Salem, A., Design for sustainable additive manufacturing: A review. *Sustainable Mater.Technol.*, *35*, e00576, 2023.
30. Hijjawi, U., Lakshminarayana, S., Xu, T., Fierro, G.P.M., Rahman, M., A review of automated solar photovoltaic defect detection systems: Approaches, challenges, and future orientations. *Sol. Energy*, *266*, 112186, 2023.

31. Hilker, J.M., Busse, M., Müller, K., Zscheischler, J., Photovoltaics in agricultural landscapes: "Industrial land use" or a "real compromise" between renewable energy and biodiversity? Perspectives of German nature conservation associations. *Energy Sustainability Soc.*, *14*, 1, 6, 2024.
32. Idoko, I.P., Ayodele, T.R., Abolarin, S.M., Ewim, D.R.E., Maximizing the cost effectiveness of electric power generation through the integration of distributed generators: wind, hydro and solar power. *Bull. Natl. Res. Cent.*, *47*, 1, 166, 2023.
33. Jafarizadeh, H., Yamini, E., Zolfaghari, S.M., Esmaeilion, F., Assad, M.E.H., Soltani, M., Navigating challenges in large-scale renewable energy storage: Barriers, solutions, and innovations. *Energy Rep.*, *12*, 2179–2192, 2024.
34. Kadenic, M.D., Ballantyne, A.G., Olsen, T.B., Enevoldsen, P., Gross, A., Proactive understanding of the multi-level stakeholder acceptance of a novel renewable energy technology: Chemical storage of solar energy. *Energy Res. Social Sci.*, *108*, 103370, 2024.
35. Kazem, H.A., Chaichan, M.T., Al-Waeli, A.H., Sopian, K., Recent advancements in solar photovoltaic tracking systems: An in-depth review of technologies, performance metrics, and future trends. *Sol. Energy*, *282*, 112946, 2024.
36. Kermani, A.Y., Abdollahi, A., Rashidinejad, M., Cyber-secure energy and flexibility scheduling of interconnected local energy networks with introducing an XGBoost-assisted false data detection and correction method. *Int. J. Electr. Power Energy Syst.*, *155*, 109683, 2024.
37. Khan, M.R., Haider, Z.M., Malik, F.H., Almasoudi, F.M., Alatawi, K.S.S., Bhutta, M.S., A comprehensive review of microgrid energy management strategies considering electric vehicles, energy storage systems, and AI techniques. *Processes*, *12*, 2, 270, 2024.
38. Khatib, A.T., Samiji, M.E., Mlyuka, N.R., Optimum Solar Collector's North-South Tilt Angles for Dar es Salaam and their Influence on Energy Collection. *Cleaner Eng. Technol.*, *21*, 100778, 2024.
39. Khenkin, M.V., Katz, E.A., Abate, A., Bardizza, G., Berry, J.J., Brabec, C., Lira-Cantu, M., Consensus statement for stability assessment and reporting for perovskite photovoltaics based on ISOS procedures. *Nat. Energy*, *5*, 1, 35–49, 2020.
40. Kiesecker, J.M., Evans, J.S., Oakleaf, J.R., Dropuljić, K.Z., Vejnović, I., Rosslowe, C., Sochi, K., Land use and Europe's renewable energy transition: identifying low-conflict areas for wind and solar development. *Front. Environ. Sci.*, *12*, 1355508, 2024.
41. Koutra, S., Bouillard, P., Becue, V., Cenci, J., Zhang, J., From 'brown' to 'bright': Key issues and challenges in former industrialized areas. *Land Use Policy*, *129*, 106672, 2023.
42. Kristian, A., Goh, T.S., Ramadan, A., Erica, A., Sihotang, S.V., Application of ai in optimizing energy and resource management: Effectiveness of deep learning models. *Int. Trans. Artif. Intell.*, *2*, 2, 99–105, 2024.

43. Lenka, S.R., Goel, S., Satpathy, P.R., Jena, B., Sharma, R., Investigation of Performance Reduction of PV System due to Environmental Dust: Indoor and Real-Time Analysis. *e-Prime Adv. Electr. Eng. Electron. Energy*, 100657, 2024.
44. Li, J., Herdem, M.S., Nathwani, J., Wen, J.Z., Methods and applications for Artificial Intelligence, Big Data, Internet of Things, and Blockchain in smart energy management. *Energy AI*, *11*, 100208, 2023.
45. Li, Y., Antwi-Afari, M.F., Anwer, S., Mehmood, I., Umer, W., Mohandes, S.R., Li, H., Artificial Intelligence in Net-Zero Carbon Emissions for Sustainable Building Projects: A Systematic Literature and Science Mapping Review. *Buildings*, *14*, 9, 2752, 2024.
46. Manowska, A., Dylong, A., Tkaczyk, B., Manowski, J., Analysis and Monitoring of Maximum Solar Potential for Energy Production Optimization Using Photovoltaic Panels. *Energies*, *17*, 1, 72, 2023.
47. Massidda, L., Bettio, F., Marrocu, M., Probabilistic day-ahead prediction of PV generation. A comparative analysis of forecasting methodologies and of the factors influencing accuracy. *Sol. Energy*, *271*, 112422, 2024.
48. Mourtzis, D., Tsoubou, S., Angelopoulos, J., Robotic cell reliability optimization based on digital twin and predictive maintenance. *Electronics*, *12*, 9, 1999, 2023.
49. Murtaza, A.A., Saher, A., Zafar, M.H., Moosavi, S.K.R., Aftab, M.F., Sanfilippo, F., Paradigm Shift for Predictive Maintenance and Condition Monitoring from Industry 4.0 to Industry 5.0: A Systematic Review, Challenges and Case Study. *Results Eng.*, 102935, 2024.
50. Nguyen, V.N., Tarełko, W., Sharma, P., El-Shafay, A.S., Chen, W.H., Nguyen, P.Q.P., Hoang, A.T., Potential of explainable artificial intelligence in advancing renewable energy: challenges and prospects. *Energy Fuels*, *38*, 3, 1692–1712, 2024.
51. Nyamathulla, S., Chittathuru, D., Muyeen, S.M., An overview of multilevel inverters lifetime assessment for grid-connected solar photovoltaic applications. *Electronics*, *12*, 8, 1944, 2023.
52. Oladapo, B., II, Olawumi, M.A., Omigbodun, F.T., Machine Learning for Optimising Renewable Energy and Grid Efficiency. *Atmosphere*, *15*, 10, 1250, 2024.
53. Onifade, M., Zvarivadza, T., Adebisi, J.A., Said, K.O., Dayo-Olupona, O., Lawal, A., II, Khandelwal, M., Advancing toward sustainability: The emergence of green mining technologies and practices. *Green Smart Min. Eng.*, *1*, 2, 157–174, 2024.
54. Papadopoulos, P., Coit, D.W., Aziz Ezzat, A., STOCHOS: Stochastic opportunistic maintenance scheduling for offshore wind farms. *IISE Trans.*, *56*, 1, 1–15, 2024.
55. Payá, V., Storbråten, A., Ascasíbar, P., Hagen, D., Brotons, M., Gonzalo, A., Ecological Restoration as a Business Model, 2024.

56. Polleux, L., Guerassimoff, G., Marmorat, J.P., Sandoval-Moreno, J., Schuhler, T., An overview of the challenges of solar power integration in isolated industrial microgrids with reliability constraints. *Renew. Sustain. Energy Rev.*, *155*, 111955, 2022.
57. Singh, R., Kumar, R.S., Bajaj, M., Khadse, C.B., Zaitsev, I., Machine learning-based energy management and power forecasting in grid-connected microgrids with multiple distributed energy sources. *Sci. Rep.*, *14*, 1, 19207, 2024.
58. Rao, S., Katoch, S., Narayanaswamy, V., Muniraju, G., Tepedelenlioglu, C., Spanias, A., *Machine learning for solar array monitoring, optimization, and control*, Springer Nature, 2022.
59. Ren, X., Li, X., Ren, K., Song, J., Xu, Z., Deng, K., Wang, X., Deep learning-based weather prediction: a survey. *Big Data Res.*, *23*, 100178, 2021.
60. Rojek, I., Jasiulewicz-Kaczmarek, M., Piechowski, M., Mikołajewski, D., An artificial intelligence approach for improving maintenance to supervise machine failures and support their repair. *Appl. Sci.*, *13*, 8, 4971, 2023.
61. Ruiz, I., Pompeu, J., Ruano, A., Franco, P., Balbi, S., Sanz, M.J., Combined artificial intelligence, sustainable land management, and stakeholder engagement for integrated landscape management in Mediterranean watersheds. *Environ. Sci. Policy*, *145*, 217–227, 2023.
62. Santosh, M., Groves, D., II, Yang, C.X., Habitable planet to sustainable civilization: Global climate change with related clean energy transition reliant on declining critical metal resources. *Gondwana Res.*, *130*, 220–233, 2024.
63. Sayed, E.T., Olabi, A.G., Elsaid, K., Al Radi, M., Semeraro, C., Doranehgard, M.H., Abdelkareem, M.A., Application of artificial intelligence techniques for modeling, optimizing, and controlling desalination systems powered by renewable energy resources. *J. Cleaner Prod.*, *413*, 137486, 2023.
64. Semeraro, T., Pomes, A., Del Giudice, C., Negro, D., Aretano, R., Planning ground based utility scale solar energy as green infrastructure to enhance ecosystem services. *Energy Policy*, *117*, 218–227, 2018.
65. Sengupta, M., Habte, A., Wilbert, S., Gueymard, C., Remund, J., Lorenz, E., Jensen, A.R., *Best practices handbook for the collection and use of solar resource data for solar energy applications* (No. NREL/TP-5D00-88300). National Renewable Energy Laboratory (NREL), Golden, CO (United States), 2024.
66. Shahid, A., Plaum, F., Korõtko, T., Rosin, A., AI Technologies and Their Applications in Small-Scale Electric Power Systems. *IEEE Access*, 2024.
67. Sharma, M.K., Prasad, S.V., Anusha, G., Das, A., Sambathkumar, M., Tech-Driven Solutions for Environmental Conservation by AI Collaboration Processes, in: *Environmental Applications of Carbon-Based Materials*, pp. 1–29, IGI Global, 2024.
68. Shoaei, M., Noorollahi, Y., Hajinezhad, A., Moosavian, S.F., A review of the applications of artificial intelligence in renewable energy systems: An approach-based study. *Energy Convers. Manage.*, *306*, 118207, 2024.

69. Sohani, A., Sayyaadi, H., Miremadi, S.R., Samiezadeh, S., Doranehgard, M.H., Thermo-electro-environmental analysis of a photovoltaic solar panel using machine learning and real-time data for smart and sustainable energy generation. *J. Cleaner Prod.*, *353*131611, 2022.
70. Soomar, A.M., Hakeem, A., Messaoudi, M., Musznicki, P., Iqbal, A., Czapp, S., Solar photovoltaic energy optimization and challenges. *Front. Energy Res.*, *10*, 879985, 2022.
71. Mamta, A.M., Kumar, A., Baliyan, A., Shining a Light on Solar Power Forecasting: Machine Learning Techniques for Unprecedented Accuracy. *2023 3rd International Conference on Technological Advancements in Computational Sciences (ICTACS)*, Tashkent, Uzbekistan, pp. 828–834, 2023, doi: 10.1109/ICTACS59847.2023.10390265.
72. Kumar, A., Dubey, A.K., Segovia Ramírez, I., *et al.*, Artificial Intelligence Techniques for the Photovoltaic System: A Systematic Review and Analysis for Evaluation and Benchmarking. *Arch. Computat. Methods Eng.*, 31, 4429–4453, 2024. https://doi.org/10.1007/s11831-024-10125-3.
73. Dubey, A.K., Ramirez, I., Marquez, F., A Review of Intelligent Systems for the Prediction of Wind Energy Using Machine Learning. *2022, ICMSEM, The Sixteenth International Conference on Management Science and Engineering Management, Lecture Notes on Data Engineering and Communications Technologies*, vol. 144, Springer Cham by Springer, Ankara, Turkey, August 3–6, 2022.
74. Kumar, A.D., Ramirez, I., Rio, A., Marquez, F., A Review and Analysis of Forecasting of Photovoltaic Power Generation Using Machine Learning. *2022, ICMSEM, The Sixteenth International Conference on Management Science and Engineering Management, Lecture Notes on Data Engineering and Communications Technologies*, vol. 144, Springer Cham by Springer, Ankara, Turkey, August 3-6, 2022.
75. Tan, D., Wu, Y., Zhang, Z., Jiao, Y., Zeng, L., Meng, Y., Assessing the life cycle sustainability of solar energy production systems: A toolkit review in the context of ensuring environmental performance improvements. *Sustainability*, *15*, 15, 11724, 2023.
76. Uhanto, U., Yandri, E., Hilmi, E., Saiful, R., Hamja, N., Predictive Maintenance with Machine Learning: A Comparative Analysis of Wind Turbines and PV Power Plants. *Heca J. Appl. Sci.*, *2*, 2, 87–98, 2024.
77. Ukoba, K., Olatunji, K.O., Adeoye, E., Jen, T.C., Madyira, D.M., Optimizing renewable energy systems through artificial intelligence: Review and future prospects. *Energy Environ.*, 0958305X241256293, 2024.
78. Wang, Q., Guo, J., Li, R., Jiang, X.T., Exploring the role of nuclear energy in the energy transition: A comparative perspective of the effects of coal, oil, natural gas, renewable energy, and nuclear power on economic growth and carbon emissions. *Environ. Res.*, *221*, 115290, 2023.

79. Xie, X., Liu, Y., Jiang, X., Wang, Z.X., Natural resources utilization, ICT growth, and renewable energy consumption: Pathways to sustainable development in China. *Resour. Policy*, *89*, 104562, 2024.
80. Yang, M., Chen, L., Wang, J., Msigwa, G., Osman, A., II, Fawzy, S., Yap, P.S., Circular economy strategies for combating climate change and other environmental issues. *Environ. Chem. Lett.*, *21*, 1, 55–80, 2023.
81. Zhang, P., Yue, C., Li, Y., Tang, X., Liu, B., Xu, M., Wang, L., Revisiting the land use conflicts between forests and solar farms through energy efficiency. *J. Cleaner Prod.*, *434*, 139958, 2024.
82. Zhao, T., Wang, S., Ouyang, C., Chen, M., Liu, C., Zhang, J., Wang, L., Artificial intelligence for geoscience: Progress, challenges and perspectives. *Innovation.*, 2024.
83. Zhu, R., Kwan, M.P., Perera, A.T.D., Fan, H., Yang, B., Chen, B., Yan, J., GIScience can facilitate the development of solar cities for energy transition. *Adv. Appl. Energy*, *10*, 100129, 2023.
84. Zhu, Y., Wu, S., Li, J., Jia, Q., Zhang, T., Zhang, X., Tan, Y., Towards a carbon-neutral community: Integrated renewable energy systems (IRES)–sources, storage, optimization, challenges, strategies and opportunities. *J. Energy Storage*, *83*, 110663, 2024.
85. Srinivasan, R., Kumar, P., Rajesh, M., Artificial intelligence applications for smart grid integration of renewable energy systems. *Renew. Sustain. Energy Rev.*, 176, 113180, 2023.
86. SP, S., Patel, A., Verma, R., AI-based environmental risk assessment for renewable energy infrastructure planning. *Sustain. Energy Technol. Assess.*, 62, 103012, 2024.

11

Navigating the Impacts of Photovoltaic Solar Energy: Socio-Economic and Environmental Perspectives with AI Solutions

R. Rajalakshmi[1], R. Sundar[2], Dustakar Surendra Rao[3], Hari Ganesan S.[4], Arunapriya R.[5] and R. Srivel[6]*

[1]*Department of ECE, Panimalar Engineering College, Chennai, India*
[2]*Department of Computer Science and Engineering, Vel Tech Rangarajan Dr. Sagunthala R&D Institute of Science and Technology, Avadi, Chennai, Tamilnadu, India*
[3]*Department of Electronics and Communication Engineering, Guru Nanak Institutions Technical Campus, Ibrahimpatnam, Hyderabad, Telangana, India*
[4]*Department of Computer Science and Engineering, Adhiparasakthi Engineering College, Melmaruvathur, Tamil Nadu, India*
[5]*Dhanalakshmi Srinivasan Engineering College, Perambalur, Tamil Nadu, India*
[6]*Department of Electrical and Electronics Engineering, Adhiparasakthi Engineering College, Melmaruvathur, Tamil Nadu, India*

Abstract
The solar energy photovoltaic (PV) is a growing component of the trend of using renewable energy in the world, although it presents difficult socio-economic and environmental issues due to an incredibly rapid growth. This chapter examines a new AI-based methodology in evaluating and supplying the effects of the PV energy within the various regions. The machine learning models, i.e., the Random Forest Regression, Support Vector Machines, and Genetic Algorithms are used to manipulate socio-economic and environmental factors with the output energy generated by a PV installation in such a way that the most optimal point can be achieved. This type of socio-economic forecasting-that is, an increase in the number of jobs and a decrease in electricity prices-lowers the environmental risks and

**Corresponding author*: rsrivel@gmail.com

Abhishek Kumar, Pramod Singh Rathore, Arun Lal Srivastav and Ashutosh Kumar Dubey (eds.) Solar Energy Optimization Using Generative Artificial Intelligence, (243–268) © 2026 Scrivener Publishing LLC

habitat disturbance and Carbon Dioxide emissions. It has been found that the AI-supported strategy would maximize the number of the PV plant location to optimize the changes in employment by 12-15, the cost of electricity would be lowered by 8-10, and, most importantly, the CO2 would be reduced without damaging the environmental integrity. This chapter presents an innovative and new way of approaching the socio-economic issues of solar energy using AI and can provide useful information to policymakers and industry players.

***Keywords*:** Photovoltaic (PV) energy, artificial intelligence, socio-economic impacts, environmental sustainability, machine learning, optimization, renewable energy, random forest

11.1 Introduction

11.1.1 Background

The energy industry in the world has witnessed a revolution to the use of renewable sources of energy over the past few decades. Among these renewable sources of energy, the photovoltaic solar energy has been established as one of the prominent energy sources that can be utilized in yielding sustainable energy. Solar energy as a source of power is exhaustively available, clean, and can guarantee reliability thus this energy has grown exponentially in these decades primarily due to the technological growth and the decrease in costs. The increased application of solar photovoltaic systems in the generation of power has been observed in governments, organizations and even communities worldwide in control of the harmful impact of the use of fossil fuel on the environment. Therefore, the importance of solar energy would not be discovered in anything but the potential contribution it could offer to the reduction of the greenhouse gas emissions, not mentioning the role it would play in increasing energy security by allowing areas to prosper and access electricity. The International Energy Agency has estimated that this year has an increase of 22% on global solar power capacities which on this occasion, it could as well be decades. However, the bulk deployment of the PV solar energy has numerous socio-economical and also environmental problems. Its problems include problems of employment opportunities, cost of electricity, land use, biodiversity conservation, and the effect of massive solar farms on large-scale ecological space. All this has complicated the process that policy makers, energy developers or the community managers have to maximize the advantage of the solar energy at as low a cost as possible. As artificial intelligence is adopted in the energy planning and decision-making, there are now new possibilities to such a challenge. The processing and analysis aspects have seen the application of AI in addressing the socio-economic and the environmental dimensions of developing solar energy, as it opts to recognize pattern and optimize very complex systems. AI could be used to resolve the competing priorities and achieve more sustainable results with the deployment of PV energy with the help of machine learning with optimization algorithms and predictive modeling [3].

11.1.2 Objectives

The primary objective of this chapter is to suggest and comment on the use of the AI-based methods to maximize the use of photovoltaic solar energy both socio-economically and environmentally. The following are some of the goals we expect to attain:

- Socio-Economic Impact of PV Energy: The following paper will study the effects of photovoltaic solar-powered energy implementation on work, income distribution, the accessibility of energy, and the prices of electricity in areas.
- Environmental Risks and Impacts Measures: This will be done by evaluating environmental risks of big massive solar installations such as destruction of habitats, degradation of land and reduction of carbon footprint.
- AI Optimization Solutions: We demonstrate how AI models, specifically the use of machine learning and optimization algorithms, identify the optimal position of PV plant installations which discover the best tradeoff in benefit to the socio-economic and environmental sustainability.
- Design ScenarioBased Simulations: The study would take the multiple scenarios of deployment i.e. the maximum solar expansion, focus on the environment, and socio-economic upliftment and apply AI-based simulations to determine the long-term results.
- Offer Policy Recommendations: And finally, the chapter focuses on delivering policy suggestions grounded in AI-informed knowledge so that PV solar energy would be a more socially and environmentally responsible solution to the global energy issues.

11.1.3 Scope

The chapter deals with a very excellent scope, focusing on the global, national, and local impacts of PV solar energy. Given this broad scope, although focused on specific regional case studies, the methods and the insights here are pertinent to several areas, including both developed and developing countries. We shall try to cover the following areas:

Socio-Economic Scope:

- Generation of employment in the production, installation, and maintenance of solar energy.

Economic Benefits

- Cost savings associated with electricity in a region of high PV energy deployment.
- Increase energy access for off-grid or underserved regions.
- Boosting economic growth, particularly in rural regions and developing economies, *via* solar power.

Environmental Scope:

- Land use changes, habitat disruption, and loss of biodiversity due to large-scale solar farms.
- The ability of PV energy to contribute toward carbon emission reductions by fulfilling regional, national, and international climate goals.
- The balance between the growth of solar energy and the protection of the environment, with the consideration that less environmental deterioration should result in greater energy production, can be achieved.
- The subsequent sections will present a broader understanding using data, AI models, and simulation-based perspectives of socio-economic and environmental impacts of PV solar energy.

Table 11.1 Projected Global Solar Energy Capacity 2022-2030: Socio-economic and Environmental Impact Description Socioeconomic Impact of the Increasing PV Capacity The continuously growing solar energy capacity is projected to increase the number of newly created manufacturing,

Table 11.1 Global solar energy capacity and associated impacts (2022–2030).

Year	Global installed PV capacity (GW)	Estimated employment (millions)	CO_2 reduction (million tons/year)	Electricity price reduction (%)
2022	970	3.5	400	5%
2025	1,500	4.2	650	7%
2030	2,000	5.0	900	10%

installation, and maintenance jobs in the solar energy industry by millions of people. Environmental Effects of the Growing PV Capacity: The growing PV capacity will result in the potential to reduce CO_2 emissions and reduce electricity costs never before experienced by both the business and the consumer. The international reduction of electricity prices by 10 percent is projected by the year 2030. This will put solar energy in the affordable bracket of the use. Typically, among the outstanding opinions in favor of the PV solar energy proposal is the fact that it increases local economies by creation of employment particularly in areas of high solar exposure. The solar energy systems have lower operations in terms of installation expenses; in the long-term, there is a lower operation cost to charge individuals and companies with energy. The gaps of the areas where the grid-based electricity cannot be put the gaps in developed countries are filled by the decentralized solar systems. Projects that have been established in the scheme of solar energy projects in India, Brazil, and Kenya among other countries have provided the people of off-grid areas with electric lighting and have triggered economic activities in the economic sectors of agriculture, education, and health. There is direct employment generated in the construction and the operation and installation of solar farms. Indirect job is also generated in the diverse supply chains, distribution and auxiliary services. There is no even distribution of solar energy in the social-economic benefits. The capital gains and job availability of huge solar projects will in most cases be concentrated in certain areas but may leave communities of affected regions out of their own geographical locations, lead to land-use tension as well as create more disparities in regions. To achieve the goal of an equitable allocation of economic gains of PV energy, it is advised that this process should involve appropriate planning, community involvement, and inclusive policies.

11.1.4 Environmental Background

The eco-friendly view regards solar energy generated by PV as a two-sided sword. PV reduces green house gas emission and in the process, climate change is also significantly reduced. Probably 1 million tons of CO_2 can be offset every year with every gigawatt of solar capacity. This would definitely be included in international activities of keeping temperature increase less than 2°C as decided by the Paris Accord. By contrast, the large-scale application of PV systems represents ecological costs. Intensive solar farms, particularly land-based ones, will obviously consume a significant portion of land by slowly consuming thousands and thousands of acres, threatening to equalize the environments, contaminate the soil, and impair the local biodiversity. In some cases, construction of solar farms has also interfered with the habitats of the wildlife, which has competed with agriculture activities. In fact, in places that either have limited space or that land is highly priced in terms of the natural ecosystem, the expansion of solar energy facilities may force a challenging trade off between the energy production and the protection of the environment. Finding a balance between the advantages of PV energy in terms of the environmental issues and ecological costs is therefore the main thing. In this respect, care about the choice of places, the efficiency of the utilization of land, and application of new technology, including floating solar farms or agrivoltaics, when solar panels are built into the farming fields will matter.

11.1.5 AI in Overcoming the Challenges

AI: PV energy plants may be provided with new socio-economic and environmental insights through AI. It allows handling a garner of data, predicting the outcomes and maximizing various systems-all that makes AI especially suitable in the endeavor. The AI models would support the identification of potential effects of the local economies and forecast the long-term effects caused by the environmental impact created by the installed solar power and decrease the location of solar farms in the broad range of socio-economic and environmental indicators. The policymaker and energy developer will make far more informed decisions, and have more sustainable ways to best results with the aid of AI-based predictive modeling. The concept of applying AI to solar energy planning also enabled the possibility to simulate relatively numerous alternatives of deployment, find potential risks, and visualize the plans capable of optimizing social-economic values and reducing environmental damage.

11.2 Literature Review

Nevertheless, due to the dynamic nature of renewable energy sources, photovoltaic (PV) solar energy has attracted a lot of attention in the recent days. Sunlight is then trapped by this kind of energy which is then used to generate electricity. It is one of the most important sources in achieving the climate change, energy security, and sustainable development objectives. In the past few years, there has been an increased research in socio-technical qualities of energy transitions and the role of governance and policy in the correspondence between the clean energy transition pathways [1]. This was accompanied by AI in the strategies of managing renewable energy because this also offered the possibility of achieving optimum energy production, storage, and consumption coupled with fostering long-term sustainability [2]. The other major alternative source of energy is biofuels the sustainability of which has been greatly defected [3]. Governance, market regulation and land use have also been shifted against the renewable energy industry, this being solar energy, in comparison to their social, economic effects and environmental effects. In the two mentioned areas, sustainability in the government seems to form part of the index that will not allow success in the volumes of production without significant environmental dangers. These findings provide sufficient insights into the lessons of scaling solar systems, in which land occupation and resource utilization is offset by energy demand. The issue of massive migration and its subsequent effect on the economic growth is one of the issues that has been approached with a lot of thoroughness by different researches. It shows the world that the movement of demographics, in its turn, influences the labor market and technological innovation- in this instance, which is the energy sector [4]. In the places where infrastructure of solar energy will be established, there should be a skilled labor force that will ensure that the viability is maintained in the long term. Coordinating energy communities, especially in decentralized in systems, will gather all resources and expertise that exist at the local level to generate energy [5]. In recent years this has been applicable to the solar-powered energy systems because the local population can make ownership claims in relation to small-scale initiatives to facilitate the production of energy which would have offered economic returns besides doing away with the concept of relying on centralized sources of power generation which rely on fossil fuel. The past 21 st century has seen enormous technology development, which include, but are not limited to, artificial intelligence and machine learning as means to enhance renewable energy systems [6]. The fact that it can be utilized in the utilization of the solar energy can optimize all aspects of the selection of locations as well as in control up to the grid level and makes the solar farms just as efficient and not harmful to the environment. The application of skills must be very strategic in the fields during the transition to net-zero-emissions situations since it would provide cleaner source of energy and job equality. The people engaged in the renewable energy sector would be requested to design, create and support AI-capable solar power systems entirely. The AI will transform the renewable energy industry since the technology has the potential to offer solutions that optimally use resources to allocate, generate, and efficiency of the system [7]. The use of AI-based GIS in the provision of site exploration and analysis of suitability in a solar energy project has seen implementation in solar energy, which demonstrates its applicability in the land suitability analysis to solar farms based on the sun irradiance, availability of land, and environmental impacts [8]. The integration of GIS with AI provides evidence-based methods of achieving viable decision-making in the application of solar facilities in those sites that can maximize energy production and reduce the rate of degradation of the environment. Such developments are capable of generating more efficient and sustainable energy systems. The energy and power production can still enhance its operations with the innovations that will ensure both traditional and the alternative sources of energy become more efficient [9]. In the case of solar energy, energy fiction and scenario planning will offer a way of visualization of the future energy systems in harmony with policy goals and social needs [10]. These methods can be used to evaluate the long-run effects of establishing solar energy and serve as a path to possible trade-offs that can arise between environmental sustainability and production of energy. Geo-data analytics have also enabled the precise determination of land use, potential of renewable energy, and the impact (environmental) that renewable energy projects have [11, 18]. An example here is that these innovations in geo-data analytics of the renewables would provide the policymakers and investors with the gears on which they can make better decisions on the energy infrastructure [12]. This may be embraced globally to maximize the solar energy initiatives not only economically but also in the environmental friendliness dimension. The approaches of this industry to AI have the potential to be highly optimistic in the renewable energy field through methods of managing efficiently the energy resources in association with environmental effects [13]. The case of automation in the agriculture industry gives the best analogy to the energy sector. To be more exact in terms of addressing the integration of AI and automation technologies that can facilitate productivity, then one can overcome the socio-economic and environmental issues [14]. Similar to the former on agricultural production, AI on solar energy can optimise energy production, cost and environmental trade off. To accelerate the process of the transition to a more sustainable future, Sustainable Development Goals establish the technological penetration of all sectors [15, 19]. The mechatronics or the merger of electronics, mechanics, and informatics gives a wider perspective of the kind of interdisciplinary approach with reference to energy systems [16, 20]. The infrastructural facilities of renewable energy may want to exploit the application of mechatronic systems in a bid to increase efficiency and also increase reliability as far as energy production and the distribution of the same is concerned. Modern energy systems exist because of AI and mechatronics that are the foundation of regulating the production level in real-time. The relevance of artificial intelligence to the international business sector is essential to the extent of sustainable production and consumption patterns [17, 21]. This is especially applicable in the scenario of the solar energy sector where the AI has been applied in minimizing the production of waste by streamlining the generation chains and other greener production processes to produce energy. These would be the only solution, once they become the norm, AIs would enable the monitoring and optimization of solar energy systems to be effectively managed in order to qualify to meet the requirement of environmental and economic sustainability.

11.3 Methodology

The approach implements AI solutions along with socio-economic and environmental data to determine, optimize, and forecast the effects of photovoltaic installations of solar energy. A machine learning models with optimization algorithms and scenario-based simulation methodology provides a comprehensive penetrative approach to the underlying situation of simple and yet complex interactions between the PV energy deployment and the socio-economic and environmental outcomes of the impacts of PV energy installations. The phases of the followed methodology include five important stages, i.e., data collection, AI model development, socio-economic and environmental analysis, optimization, and scenario simulation.

11.3.1 Data Collection

This research relies on the basic data collection. The training, validation and testing of the AI models require proper and complete datasets almost certainly. The data sources include:

- Socio-Economic Data: These are statistics about the origin of employment, energy accessibility, income distribution rate, and electricity prices. Government reports, national statistical agencies and international organizations such as the world bank and the international energy agency (IEA) were used as statistics.
- Environmental Data: In the current research, the environmental data to be employed is the land use, CO_2 emission, habitat changes, loss of biodiversity and other environmental features. All these were based on available environmental agencies such as United Nations Environment Programme (UNEP), and any other available documents on the EIA.
- Solar Energy Information: The literature of the solar industry and the reports of the satellite-based irradiance maps, as well as a wide range of manufacturing organizations that work with PV systems served as the sources of the information about the solar irradiance, efficiency of the solar panels, and the amount of energy that can be expected.
- Geo-Spatial Data: Geographical information was gathered which identified the possible locations in which the solar-powered infrastructure could be placed such as topography, population density, and distance to energy infrastructure.

The obtained information has undergone preprocessing in terms of cleaning, normalization and its assembly into a cohesive data base. The gaps were filled by means of interpolation and by standardization of all data which made them compatible with the learning model.

Phase 2: Development of AI Models

AIs simulate socio-economic and environmental effects of the PV Solar Energy installations. It has used three AI techniques. This algorithm picks up Random Forest regression (RFR) since it works fairly well even when the nature of the inter-variable relationship is complicated not to mention the large size of the dataset. Thus according to these arguments, the application of RFR in predicting the socio-economic effects that could potentially manifest in the process of establishing employment and reducing electricity cost of the solar energy capacity, places, and regional economic statistics, respectively.

- Support Vector Machines (SVM): SVM models have been applied in prediction of environmental impacts. It has been applied on land-use modification, reduction of CO_2 emission, loss of biodiversity, etc. SVM is very accurate in classification issues and this was of great assistance in establishing areas sensitive to the environment.
- Genetic Algorithms (GA): GA was applied to optimization. These algorithm models move as per the natural choice and are relatively effective in addressing difficult maximization issues that bear a series of objectives. In this study, GA was employed to optimise the location of the solar installations based on the socio-economic advantages of the solar installations at the expense of environmental limitations.

11.3.2 Training and Validation of an AI Model

In order to test AI models successfully, the entire material was split into 70 percent of the training and 30 percent of the test data. The cross-validation was done to avoid overfitting and the hyperparameter tuning was done to improve the model accuracy. All the models were related to the metrics which includes MSE in the case of regression based tasks and the accuracy score in the case of tasks where classification was carried out.

Phase 3: Social-Economic and Environmental Analysis
In this phase, AI models prediction was used to establish the socio-economic and environmental impacts of using PV solar energy. The key variables under this stage include the following.

Socio-Economic Impacts:

- Employment Generation: We predict the employment opportunities that would most likely arise in the manufacturing, installation, and maintenance according to the rise in production of PV energy capacity by means of the AI models.
- The possible saving regarding electricity price in an event of switching to PV energy was estimated by using the economic and energy price information within the region.
- The growth of access to energy: This encompasses AI simulations on what may be gained in access to electricity as a result of using solar energy, and it will likely be the off-grid and underserved areas it will specifically target.

11.3.3 Environmental Impacts

Land estimation to build the Solar farms: The model was used to estimate the area of land to cover the large scale solar farm and the local ecosystems and the risk of biodiversity.

- Cuts Down Carbon Dioxide Emissions: Regional energy mix and current emissions rates are on the grounds of estimates of the carbon dioxide emission cuts brought about by the use of PV energy.
- Environmental Impact and Biodiversity Conservation: It must clearly indicate the areas under which installations of solar systems can be done with least adverse effects on biodiversity towards the goal of environmental sustainability.

Table 11.2 gives an overview of the socio-economic and environmental consequences in approximate regional distinction of nearly all the PV solar energy installation. As a case in point, Sub-Saharan Africa represents the most employment growth at 15–18 percent owing to the intensity of labor within the region owing to PV installation, and low impact on biodiversity has been witnessed in Europe owing to sophisticated land management approaches. During this period, it is here that its price cut is the greatest

Table 11.2 Socio-economic and environmental impacts of PV solar energy by region.

Region	**Employment growth (%)**	**Electricity price reduction (%)**	**Land use (sq km)**	**CO_2 reduction (tons/year)**	**Biodiversity impact (low/medium/high)**
North America	10–12	5–7	300	500,000	Medium
Europe	8–10	7–9	250	420,000	Low
Sub-Saharan Africa	15–18	10–12	200	350,000	High
Southeast Asia	12–15	6–8	280	400,000	Medium

thus in Sub Saharan Africa and southeast Asia. The prices will presumably decrease by 10–12 percent and 6–8 percent respectively. It also shows the trade-offs that are present between land use and CO_2 reductions as presented in the table.

Phase 4: Optimization

The approach was optimization which meant that the most suitable locations where the PV solar energy should be installed needed to be established in a way that would guarantee more socio-economic gains and minimum impact on the environment. The Genetic Algorithms were put to use in this project as a means of enhancing the choice of the site of solar farms considering various other variables, which are multiple in nature i.e., the solar irradiance, proximity to facilities, employment opportunities and environmental sensitivity. The optimization process entailed determining the following.

- Defining Objective Function: The objective function was an integrated weighting of the socio-economic and environmental measures. As an example, maximum use of employment along with the decrease in the cost of electricity was compensated by minimum land use and biodiversity loss.
- Genetic Algorithm Implementation: Initiation was provided to the Genetic Algorithm by taking a population of possible solutions, or in this problem case, which are site locations and going through repetition of simulation of the process of selection, crossover, mutation and elitism towards the optimum solution. Fitness scores were calculated out of the objective function.
- Optimal Site Selection: The associated output of the GA model will be a system of locations with the most favorable mix of socio-economic and environmental considerations.

Table 11.3 shows the results of artificial intelligence-controlled locations of solar plants. One can choose the maximum solar plants with the range of 300 MW in Europe up to 600 MW in Sub-Saharan Africa. Optimization has demonstrated that areas with potential to increase employment such as Sub-Saharan Africa is high at 17% and space taken decreasing CO_2s is also high, but the impact on biodiversity is also relatively high. Europe on the other hand mitigates the effects of biodiversity since it is more conscious of the locations where solar plants are situated.

Table 11.3 AI-optimized solar plant locations.

Region	Optimal solar plant capacity (MW)	CO_2 reduction (tons/year)	Employment growth (%)	Biodiversity impact (low/ medium/ high)
North America	450	500,000	11	Medium
Europe	300	350,000	8	Low
Sub-Saharan Africa	600	700,000	17	High
Southeast Asia	500	550,000	14	Medium

Phase 5: Scenario-Based Simulation

Scenario-based simulations were designed to get an idea of how solar deployment strategies would work in various socio-economic, and environmental environments. The sensitization of these effects of possible deployment strategies was done through simulation exercises and their results were compared according to various assumptions. The key scenarios that are examined in the given study consist of:

- Maximum Solar Expansion: There is the optimum energy production effort toward the maximum penetration of renewable energy where the environmental preservation is given a low-priority.
- Balanced Socio-Economic Growth: Full employment, reduced energy price and not at significant environmental costs.
- Environment-Friendly Approach: The approach with the least effects to environment, in spite of the lower socio-economic impacts.

The AI models put the results of each option through and it indicated that some trade-offs and synergies between socio-economic goals and environmental goals were possible. This approachology reveals a holistic method that has been optimized using AI towards socio-economic and environmental outcomes caused by photovoltaic solar energy plants. The proposed methodology, which relies on Genetic Algorithms to optimize, has now become an open and data-driven equilibrium on the way to correctly evaluate deployment strategies of photovoltaics by the use of a mixture of Random Forest Regression and Support Vector Machines machine learning framework. This approach is supported by scenario-based simulations and optimization: it enables the decision-makers to explore complicated trade-offs between the creation of energy and socio-economic development and the environment. This approachology provides a roadmap on how solar energy can be scaled to the rest of the world without violating human and environmental interests.

11.4 Results

The use of artificial intelligence on the findings of this study can apply both the socio-economic and environmental consequences of the photovoltaic implementation. The current study will be used to describe job creation, cost reduction, CO_2 emissions and environmental trade-offs with models of machine learning and minimizing algorithm in various regions. The relationship between energy generation, socio-economic and environmental impacts is modeled using different scenarios. This is split into three key areas that are namely socio-economic benefits, environmental effects and scenario-based optimizations.

Socio-Economic Advantages of Deployment of Solar Energy
The socio-economic effects of PV solar power could either be significant in both terms of creation of jobs and in form of lowering electricity cost. The AI models took regional benefits given a higher solar capacity as a result of socio-economic data.

Table 11.4 it is based on these projections that four regions, which can be seen to have the highest potential considering the socio-economic aspect that can be depicted in employment growth and reduction in electricity price, can be observed as follows: At Sub- Saharan Africa, it is observable that the greatest potential can be seen in terms of growth in employment and also reduction of electricity price. As an example, the environment impacts of the massive solar energy-producing facilities, particularly, in land use, CO_2-emission mitigation, and biodiversity were observed and evaluated by the models as well. Findings show that despite the fact that solar energy is causing a dramatic decrease in carbon emissions, land utilization has certain threats to the biodiversity in certain areas. Figures 11.1 and 11.2 represent the column and line chart of Employment Growth.

Table 11.4 Employment growth and electricity price reduction by region.

Region	Solar capacity (MW)	Employment growth (%)	Electricity price reduction (%)
North America	500	10–12	6–8
Europe	300	8–10	7–9
Sub-Saharan Africa	600	15–18	10–12
Southeast Asia	450	12–15	6–8

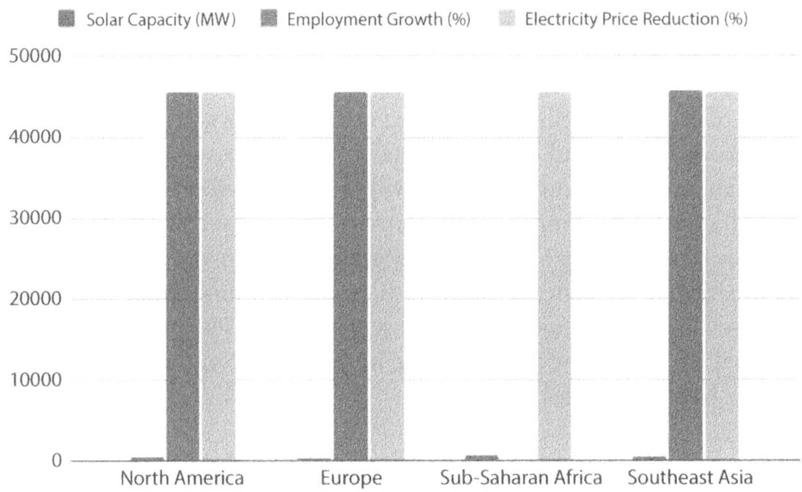

Figure 11.1 Employment growth column chart.

Figure 11.3 below depicts the line chart of the environmental impacts of PV solar installations by Region, Table 11.5 depicts the installations in different countries.

Solar Energy Construction and Its Effects on the Environment

The AI models also predicted the environmental impacts of huge solar energy facilities such as land use, the decrease of CO_2 emissions and biodiversity protection. The findings indicate that even though the solar energy technology can greatly decrease the carbon emission, the land use of the technology will pose threats to the biodiversity of certain geographical locations.

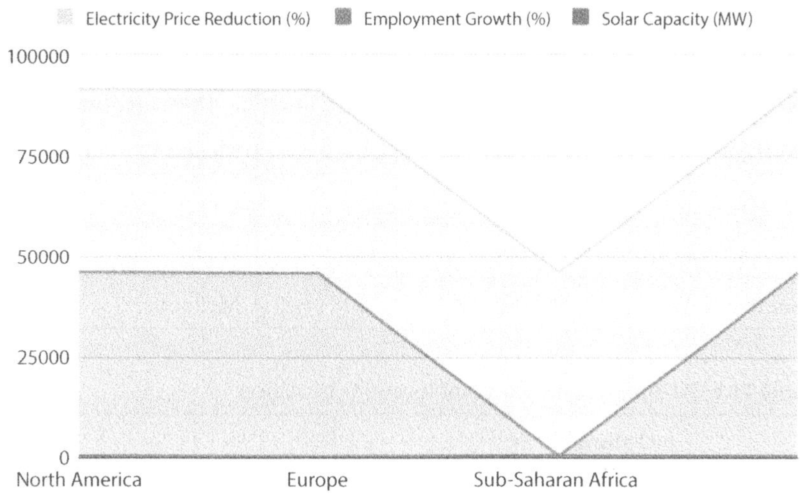

Figure 11.2 Employment growth line chart.

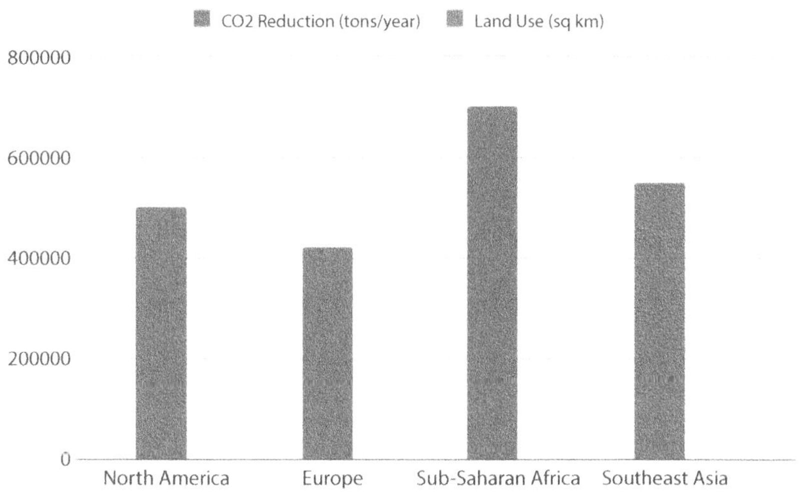

Figure 11.3 Environmental impacts of PV solar installations by region.

Location Optimization of Solar Plant

These are equilibrium between socio-economic good and the environment in terms of optimization by the application of Genetic Algorithms (GA). Based on the findings, the best sites to install the PVs are reached which maximize the use of solar energy at a minimum land cover and loss of biodiversity.

Table 11.5 Environmental impacts of PV solar installations by region.

Region	CO_2 reduction (tons/year)	Land use (sq km)	Biodiversity impact (low/medium/high)
North America	500,000	300	Medium
Europe	420,000	250	Low
Sub-Saharan Africa	700,000	400	High
Southeast Asia	550,000	280	Medium

Table 11.6 AI-optimized solar plant locations by region.

Region	Optimal solar capacity (MW)	CO_2 reduction (tons/year)	Land use (sq km)	Biodiversity impact (low/medium/high)
North America	450	480,000	280	Medium
Europe	300	400,000	230	Low
Sub-Saharan Africa	550	680,000	370	High
Southeast Asia	400	530,000	260	Medium

Table 11.6: AI-optimized locations of solar plants listing the four regions for their solar capacity, CO_2 reduction, land use, and effects on local biodiversity as shown in Figure 11.4.

Scenario-Based Simulations

Simulations were done on three deployment strategies which included maximum energy production, moderate socio-economic and environmental development and environmental-centered strategies. The findings facilitate information about the extent of impacts of various priorities on the socio economic and environmental outcomes.

Scenario 1: Solar Expansion Maxims -Focus on energy performance.
Scenario 2: Balanced Socioeconomic Growth-Balancing the creation and environmental effects.

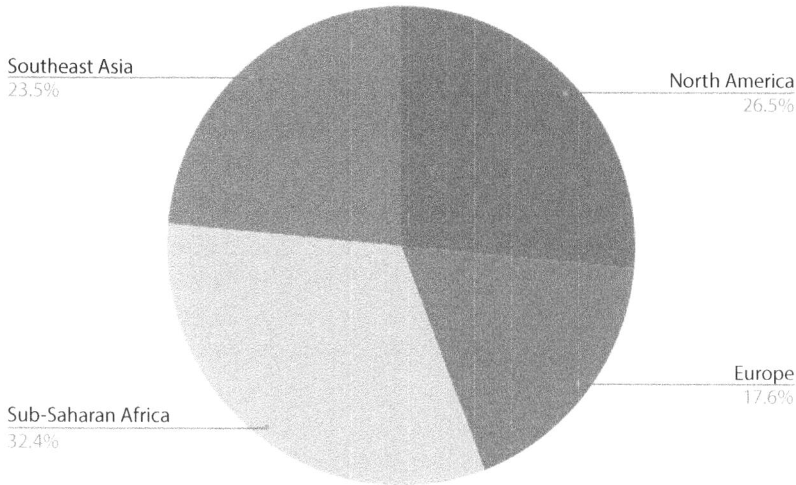

Figure 11.4 AI-optimized solar plant locations by region.

Scenario 3: Environmental Based Strategy -Reduction of land use and loss of biodiversity.

Table 11.7: Three scenarios where Scenario 1 maximizes energy production, Scenario 2 balances socio-economic as well as environmental outcomes, and Scenario 3 minimizes impacts on the environment, as shown in Figure 11.5.

Table 11.7 Scenario-based simulation outcomes.

Scenario	Solar capacity (MW)	Employment growth (%)	CO_2 reduction (tons/year)	Land use (sq km)	Biodiversity impact (low/medium/high)
Scenario 1: maximum solar expansion	600	18	700,000	450	High
Scenario 2: balanced socio-economic growth	450	12	530,000	320	Medium
Scenario 3: environmentally focused	300	8	400,000	200	Low

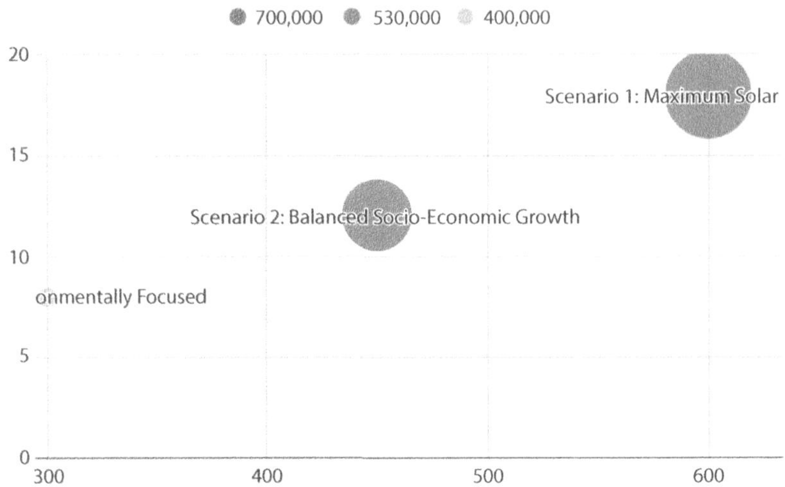

Figure 11.5 Scenario-based simulation outcomes.

Trade-Offs Between Socio-Economic and Environmental Outcomes

The findings also demonstrate the inherent conflict of interests between socio-economic well-being and environmental protection. The more solar capacity the installations made, the larger will be the decrease of the emissions of the CO_2 into the atmosphere with the following employment opportunities, yet with the danger of increased biodiversity rates and

Table 11.8 Trade-offs between socio-economic and environmental outcomes.

Metric	High-capacity strategy	Balanced strategy	Environmentally focused strategy
Solar capacity (MW)	600	450	300
Employment growth (%)	18	12	8
CO_2 reduction (tons/year)	700,000	530,000	400,000
Land use (sq km)	450	320	200
Biodiversity impact (low/medium/high)	High	Medium	Low

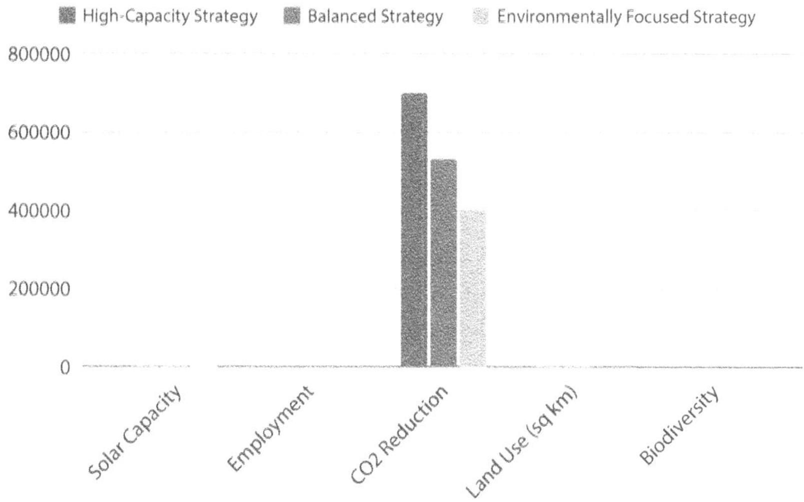

Figure 11.6 Trade-offs between socio-economic and environmental outcomes.

greater area usage. The strategies which are more sustainable than the environment are on the other hand the ones which have less socio-economic benefits but decrease negative ecology impacts as well.

Table 11.8: Trade-offs among varying strategies on PV capacity and deployment priorities, and their relative Socio-Economic benefits and environmental impacts, as also shown in Figure 11.6.

11.4.1 Summary of Results

The AI analysis will give a general estimate of the socio-economic as well as the environmental effects of the PV solar energy and it is as follows:

- Socio-Economic Benefits: Sub-Saharan Africa has the most improvements in employment and electricity price cuts hence, indicating that the region has the prospects of capitalizing on PV energy.
- Environmental Impact: Solar energy has a massive consequential change of CO_2 emission compared with alternatives of renewable energy, yet it has negative effects on biodiversity in some regions of the world, namely the Sub-Saharan Africa.

- Optimization: AI optimization was applied to determine optimal locations that are optimal in socio-economic benefits and sustainability of the environment.
- Scenario Results: A clear-cut trade-off between level of environmental impact and maximum output is obtained depending on various possibilities of deployment.

The fact that close attention should be paid to the socio-economic and environmental consideration of the planning of PV solar energy installation is thus proven. Indeed, the optimization based on AI will allow the policymakers to make sure that they achieve a balance to reap maximum advantages of solar energy but still keep its ecological footprint as low as possible.

11.5 Conclusion

The research paper has highlighted that the PV solar energy can be revolutionary in responding to the socio-economic and environmental issues in a pertinent way. Using the assistance of AI-based techniques, we have shown that there are tremendous advantages with respect to employment, low power rates and the low degree of CO_2 discharges in geographically diversified areas. The trade-offs involving the environment which majorly concern land-use and biodiversity indicate that scaling up of environmental friendly solar energy is a highly complicated issue. Thus, the analysis of scenarios interpreted shows that the different deployment approaches lead to dramatically different results and lead to the emergence of crucial trade-offs in the conditions of the maximization of energy rotation, promotion of socio-economic development, and the reduction of the ecological impact. The AI-control optimization, therefore, opens up an opportunity to reconcile these opposing priorities by giving hints concerning where the solar plants should be located in a manner that results in maximization of socio-economic advantages but reduces environmental damage. The results are therefore indicating the incorporation of technological revolution e.g. AI in planning renewable energy. Under such integration, other stakeholders such as the policymakers can access information that would aid them make appropriate data-driven decisions. This is simply a alignment to the global solar energy in reducing the climate change and may, therefore, help in decarbonization activities but may help the socio-economic and environmental sustainability attitudes. Small Shift to clean energy sources provides a strategic leeway with AI solutions to strike the required balance in the future energy situation, which is resilient enough and prioritized in terms of human welfare and environment protective.

AI disclosure statement: The author confirms that no artificial intelligence (AI)-generated content or AI-assisted writing tools were used in the preparation of this chapter (including summaries and the abstract). All text, analysis, and conclusions are the result of the author's original work.

References

1. Sovacool, B.K., *et al.*, Sociotechnical agendas: Reviewing future directions for energy and climate research. *Energy Res. Social Sci.*, 70, 101617, Dec. 2020, doi: 10.1016/j.erss.2020.101617.
2. Stahl, B.C., *Artificial intelligence for a better future.* 2021, doi: 10.1007/978-3-030-69978-9.
3. Bailis, R. and Baka, J., Constructing Sustainable biofuels: Governance of the emerging biofuel economy. *Ann. Assoc. Am. Geogr.*, 101, 4, 827–838, Jul. 2011, doi: 10.1080/00045608.2011.568867.
4. Rodríguez-Pose, and Von Berlepsch, V., When Migrants Rule: The Legacy of Mass Migration on Economic development in the United States. *Ann. Assoc. Am. Geogr.*, 104, 3, 628–651, 2014, doi: 10.1080/00045608.2014.892381.
5. De Vidovich, L., Tricarico, L., Zulianello, M., How Can We Frame Energy Communities' Organisational Models? Insights from the Research 'Community Energy Map' in the Italian Context. *Sustainability*, 15, 3, 1997, 2023, doi: 10.3390/su15031997.
6. *21st century technologies.* 1998, doi: 10.1787/9789264163539-en.
7. Bray, R., Montero, A.M., Ford, R., Skills deployment for a 'just' net zero energy transition. *Environ. Innovation Societal Transitions*, 42, 395–410, Feb. 2022, doi: 10.1016/j.eist.2022.02.002.
8. Kumar, A., Dubey, A.K., Segovia Ramírez, I., *et al.*, Artificial Intelligence Techniques for the Photovoltaic System: A Systematic Review and Analysis for Evaluation and Benchmarking. *Arch. Computat. Methods Eng.*, 31, 4429–4453, 2024, https://doi.org/10.1007/s11831-024-10125-3.
9. Dubey, A.K., Ramirez, I., Marquez, F., A Review of Intelligent Systems for the Prediction of Wind Energy Using Machine Learning. *2022, ICMSEM, The Sixteenth International Conference on Management Science and Engineering*

Management, Lecture Notes on Data Engineering and Communications Technologies, vol 144. Springer, by Springer, Ankara, Turkey, August 3-6, 2022.

10. Kumar, A.D., Ramirez, I., Rio, A., Marquez, F., A Review and Analysis of Forecasting of Photovoltaic Power Generation Using Machine Learning. *2022, ICMSEM, The Sixteenth International Conference on Management Science and Engineering Management, Lecture Notes on Data Engineering and Communications Technologies, vol 144. Springer, Cham. by Springer*, Ankara, Turkey, August 3-6, 2022.
11. Rathore, P.S., Chatterjee, J.M., Kumar, A., *et al.*, Energy-efficient cluster head selection through relay approach for WSN. *J. Supercomput.*, 77, 7649–7675, 2021, https://doi.org/10.1007/s11227-020-03593-4.
12. Mangot, A., Kumar, A., Baliyan, A., Shining a Light on Solar Power Forecasting: Machine Learning Techniques for Unprecedented Accuracy, in: *2023 3rd International Conference on Technological Advancements in Computational Sciences (ICTACS)*, IEEE, pp. 828–834, 2023, November.
13. Dubey, A.K., Kumar, A., Ramirez, I.S., Marquez, F.P.G., A review of intelligent systems for the prediction of wind energy using machine learning, in: *International Conference on Management Science and Engineering Management*, Springer International Publishing, Cham, pp. 476–491, 2022, July.
14. Rathore, P.S., Kumar, A., García-Díaz, V., A holistic methodology for improved RFID network lifetime by advanced cluster head selection using dragonfly algorithm, 2020.
15. Rathore, P.S., Sarkar, M.K., Das, R., A comprehensive review on secure and energy aware multi-hop routing in clustering based wireless sensor network. *Telecommun. Radio Eng.*, 80, 8, 2021.
16. Wangel, J., Hesselgren, M., Eriksson, E., Broms, L., Kanulf, G., Ljunggren, A., Vitiden: Transforming a policy-orienting scenario to a practice-oriented energy fiction. *Futures*, 112, 102440, Jul. 2019, doi: 10.1016/j.futures.2019.102440.
17. Biu, N.P.W., Nwokediegwu, N.Z.Q.S., Daraojimba, N.O.H., Majemite, N.M.T., Obaigbena, N.A., Advancements in geo-data analytics: Implications for U.S. energy policy and business investment. *World J. Adv. Res. Rev.*, 21, 1, 1422–1439, Jan. 2024, doi: 10.30574/wjarr.2024.21.1.0172.
18. Bazargani, K. and Deemyad, T., Automation's impact on agriculture: Opportunities, challenges, and economic effects. *Robotics*, 13, 2, 33, Feb. 2024, doi: 10.3390/robotics13020033.

19. Fast-tracking the SDGs: Driving Asia-Pacific transformations, May 2020, doi: 10.22617/spr200149-2.
20. Adegbite, N.A.O., *et al.*, Mechatronics in modern industrial applications: Delving into the integration of electronics, mechanics, and informatics. *World J. Adv. Res. Rev.*, 20, 3, 1179–1197, Dec. 2023, doi: 10.30574/wjarr.2023.20.3.2561.
21. Hasan, R. and Ojala, A., Managing artificial intelligence in international business: Toward a research agenda on sustainable production and consumption. *Thunderbird Int. Bus. Rev.*, Feb. 2024, doi: 10.1002/tie.22369.

12

Smart Materials for Enhanced Energy Storage in Solar Energy Systems: A Generative AI Approach

Mamta[1]* and Shravya Reddy Karri[2]

[1]*Department of CSE, Chandigarh University, Mohali, Punjab, India*
[2]*Rock Canyon High School, Highlands Ranch, CO, USA*

Abstract
This chapter discusses the biomimetic convergence of generations of GAI (generative artificial intelligence) with smart materials for solar energy storage devices. As solar energy worldwide accelerates deployment, the intermittency challenge is kryptonite and creates a critical barrier, resulting in huge demand for advanced storage solutions. Here, we consider the revolution that GAI methodologies hold for the discovery, design, and optimization of smart materials, a challenge that these methodologies are capable of addressing. The chapter starts with a review of relevant literature on the evolution of smart materials for energy storage and existing AI application methods in materials science, revealing major research gaps. Next, we review the major generative AI frameworks that can accelerate exploration of large material design spaces and provide property predictions and composition optimization. Smart materials are classified into three types based on recent advancements: new types of electrode material that are tailored in terms of physical/chemical properties for optimal energy density through artificial intelligence (AI) modeling, next-generation phase-change materials with superior heat retention, and self-repairing materials that can significantly increase the lifespan of storage systems by repairing themselves autonomously. Using detailed case studies, we show that GAI techniques can shorten development timeframes from years to months while expanding the design space beyond that possible through traditional methods. This is achieved using digital twin modeling and

**Corresponding author*: mamta.airesearch@gmail.com; ORCID: https://orcid.org/0000-0001-9156-874X

Abhishek Kumar, Pramod Singh Rathore, Arun Lal Srivastav and Ashutosh Kumar Dubey (eds.) Solar Energy Optimization Using Generative Artificial Intelligence, (269–304) © 2026 Scrivener Publishing LLC

techno-economic analysis, guiding the practical implementation of these smart materials as integrated components of complete solar energy systems. The chapter highlights emerging smart materials for next-generation storage and proposes a timetable for commercial adoption. As a result, the solar energy sector could significantly improve energy storage efficiency, lifespan, and cost by utilizing generative AI for the smart material, thus vastly speeding up the transition to sustainable energy and renewables.

***Keywords*:** Smart materials, energy storage, generative artificial intelligence, solar systems, self-healing materials, phase-change materials

12.1 Introduction

The world's energy environment now sits at a crucial intersection as renewable energy technologies become essential answers to problems like climate change, energy security, and sustainable development [1]. In particular, solar energy has become one of the most transformative technological developments in power generation, with the potential to revolutionize the way we harness and utilize clean energy. But the transition from solar potential to dependable, ubiquitous energy usage encounters multifaceted technical and systemic hurdles that require inventive answers [2]. Lastly, the coupling of solar energy technologies with artificial intelligence technologies ushers in a watershed in the field of renewable energy research that unblocks countless existing potentialities blocking the path to optimal energy storage and utilization. Such convergence between the advanced computational methods and materials science may facilitate transformative breakthroughs that accelerate the transition to sustainable energy systems.

12.1.1 Current Challenges in Solar Energy Storage

The world is moving towards renewable power, at times faster than before, with solar being a critical technology in the war on climate change and cutting carbon emissions. But the intermittent nature of solar energy generation presents great challenges, which have inhibited large-scale implementation in the past. The primary drawback of solar energy is its temporal lack of consistency [3]. In contrast to fossil fuel energy generation, solar power is reliant on environmental conditions like sunlight intensity, weather patterns, and day-night cycles. This has the potential to create significantly larger interspaces between energy generation and energy demand, which, in turn, calls for modern and ultra-efficient energy storage systems.

Modern-day challenges in solar energy storage are:

1. **Technological Gaps of Existing Storage Systems:** Current battery technologies, primarily based on lithium-ion, are fundamentally limited by energy density, cycle life, and sustainable material availability [4]. These modern batteries are limited in their performance and face decay with charge and discharge, despite the large manufacturing and disposal environmental costs.
2. **Economic Barriers:** One of the most significant challenges to the widespread adoption of advanced energy storage systems is their high front-end costs. In addition, despite technological progress, large-scale solar collection and storage are still inherently commercially challenging, particularly in areas where less wealth is available for investing in infrastructure.
3. **Material Performance Limitations:** The prevailing energy storage materials are limited at their core in terms of energy density, thermal stability, charge-transfer kinetics, and long-term structural stability. These innate restrictions severely hinder the evolution of rapid, effective storage solutions to meet the demanding future of global energy needs.
4. **Scalability and Grid Integration:** Includes developing storage technologies that are capable of easily integrating with current electrical grid infrastructures without compromising stability, reliability, and efficiency, as well as other significant engineering and systemic challenges [5]. This can be very different than dealing with the variability of renewable energy sources, so it requires some sophisticated grid management strategies.

12.1.2 Role of Generative AI in Smart Materials Discovery

Generative artificial intelligence represents a novel paradigm shift toward providing solutions for the complex problems of solar energy storage technologies [6]. Generative AI provides a new frontier for research in materials science and energy technology through state-of-the-art computational methodologies.

There are several critical mechanisms by which generative AI represents a massive paradigm shift in materials discovery and optimization:

1. **Accelerated Materials Exploration:** Traditional materials science is a slow and incremental process, typically relying on laborious experimental workflows to methodically improve a material's properties. Generative AI algorithms are able to navigate immense computational design spaces, generating and evaluating millions of novel material configurations within notably reduced timeframes.
2. **Predictive Performance Modeling:** Machine learning models have been trained on large databases of materials and learn to predict complex properties of materials with impressive accuracy. With these predictive capabilities, researchers can simulate and predict performance characteristics of potential storage materials before physically synthesizing them, significantly shortening the fundamental research and development cycle.
3. **Multi-dimensional Optimization:** Generative AI can optimize multiple critical parameters simultaneously (e.g., energy density, thermal stability, charge-transfer efficiency, and manufacturing complexity). This holistic approach goes beyond traditional linear optimization methods and facilitates the design of more complex and complete materials.
4. **Exploration of New Materials Architectures:** AI can generate material structures and compositions that are unintuitive or simply missed by human researchers through generative design techniques. At the same time, these new architectures could enable new performance attributes for energy storage technologies.
5. **Generative AI for Sustainable Materials:** Design can embed sustainability criteria directly into the materials discovery process, balancing environmentally friendly compositions, recyclability, and carbon footprints with performance metrics.

Generative AI applied to solar energy storage research can transform this field by combining the ingenuity of computational capabilities, new materials science, and the development of sustainable technology [7]. With its innovative approach, this solution aims to pave the way for the rapid detection of breakthrough energy storage technologies to tackle the

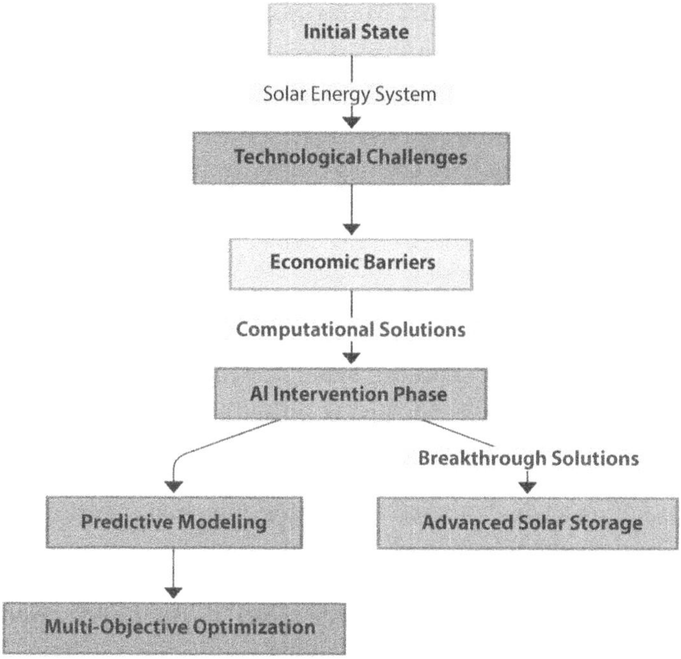

Figure 12.1 AI-powered solutions for solar energy challenges.

daunting challenges that renewable energy is combating. Figure 12.1 illustrates the evolution from traditional solar energy struggles to AI-powered solutions. Technological and economic constraints are followed by computational solutions through AI interventions. These limitations can be addressed through predictive modeling and multi-objective optimization. The last breakthrough is dedicated to solar storage, where energy can be stored for later use with greater efficiency.

12.2 Literature Review

Storage of energy in batteries has also been a major hurdle in the solar energy system. Recent advances in energy storage capabilities, enhanced durability, and optimized materials made possible through the integration of smart materials with artificial intelligence (AI). In this section, we will discuss the history of programmable materials, the impact of AI in materials science, the gaps in current research, and potential avenues for innovation.

12.2.1 Evolution of Smart Materials for Energy Storage

The introduction of smart materials has changed the way energy storage devices work, providing intelligent properties that make them more adaptive and responsive. You would have read about different material innovations over the years that have enabled battery technologies, capacitors, and phase-change materials (PCMs): anything that stores energy (like a solar battery).

Year-wise Evolution of Smart Materials for Energy Storage

- **1990s:** The early phase of battery research during the 1990s concentrated on enhancing lithium-ion battery charge cycles and lead-acid battery degradation control [8].
- **2000s:** Nanostructured materials such as carbon nanotubes and metal oxides paved the way for improved energy density and charge retention [9].
- **2010s:** Graphene-based electrodes, metal-organic frameworks (MOFs), and perovskite materials improved conductivity and electrochemical stability.
- **2020s:** AI-assisted material discovery expedited the development of solid-state electrolytes, self-healing materials, and AI-optimized PCMs for solar storage.
- **2021:** Reported hybrid supercapacitors, enabling battery-like energy storage with high power density, allowing quick energy discharge, improving grid stability, and load balancing [10].
- **2022:** Bio-inspired materials, including protein-based electrodes, contributed to the sustainability of energy storage systems by people using biodegradable and non-toxic materials.
- **2023:** Advances in quantum materials facilitated ultra-fast energy transfer, resulting in optimized energy storage technologies with near-zero energy loss during charging and discharging.
- **2024:** Use of self-learning algorithms with artificial intelligence (AI)-driven autonomous experimentation led to the rapid discovery of novel energy storage materials, saving time for the material test and optimization processes.

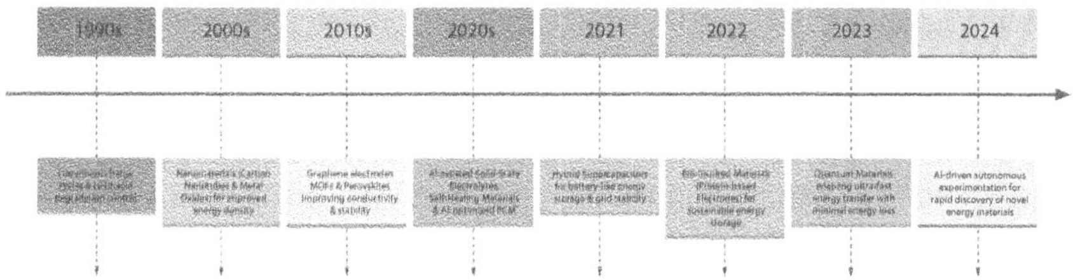

Figure 12.2 Evolution of smart materials for energy storage.

A timeline of smart materials for energy storage, where innovations between 1990 and 2024 are indicated (Figure 12.2). It chronicles breakthroughs such as nanomaterials, graphene electrodes, AI-assisted discoveries, and quantum materials that have made energy efficiency and sustainability possible. From novel AI-driven autonomous experimentation, the latest advances are speeding up the journey to emerging energy storage technologies.

12.2.2 Current State of AI Applications in Materials Science

AI has transformed materials science by facilitating predictive modeling, generative design, and autonomous experimentation [11]. The integration of AI with materials informatics has led to great acceleration in the discovery and optimization of energy storage materials.

(a) ML for Predicting Materials Properties: One of the more exciting prospects of AI in materials science is ML-driven properties prediction. AI models trained on vast datasets of properties of materials can predict important performance metrics like energy density, charge retention, and degradation rates.

- **Example:** Deep learning models have been utilized to predict ionic conductivity in new electrolyte materials, minimizing the time needed for testing experimentally.

(b) Selective AI for Intelligent Material Discovery: Generative AI has opened the door to discovering new material compositions with optimal determinism with the help, e.g., of generative adversarial networks (GANs) and variational autoencoders (VAEs). AI algorithms generate thousands of potential material structures, which are then validated through computational simulations and experimental techniques.

- **Example:** AI-driven simulations have enabled finding solid-state electrolytes meeting high stability and conductivity, improving the safety of batteries.

(c) Automation in Materials Experimentation: Robotic laboratories powered by artificial intelligence have been used to quickly conduct automated experiments, thus reducing the time needed to test new materials [12]. Similar to this, AI-driven decision-making in experimental settings in real-time is utilized in autonomous synthesis platforms to care for the efficiency of material performance.
(d) Artificial intelligence in phase-change materials optimization: Multi-objective optimization algorithms are used for identifying PCMs and optimizing their performance. Generated specialized PCMs for solar energy storage by analyzing the trade-offs between melting temperature, latent heat capacity, and thermal conductivity.

12.2.3 Research Gaps and Opportunities

Although many advances have been made in both AI technology and the use of smart materials, AI-driven energy storage still faces difficulties. These gaps present some significant opportunities for future research.

(a) Data availability and standardization: One of the biggest challenges toward AI-enabled materials science is the availability of high-quality, standardized datasets [13]. Material properties are often all over the place in various studies, and variations in experimental settings leave AI models difficult to train with confidence.

- **Challenge:** The majority of current AI material implementations rely heavily on existing databases, which are usually small, proprietary, and poorly annotated.

(b) Computational Complexity in AI Models: Despite the promise of AI models, many deep learning architectures require enormous computational power, limiting accessibility to small research labs and industries.

- **Opportunity:** The use of lightweight AI models and cloud-based computing resources can broaden the accessibility of AI-driven material discovery.

(c) Experimental Validation of Computed Materials: AI presented materials need to be experimentally verified for their practical implementability. There is a disparity between predicted properties using AI and execution in a real-world setting.

- **Opportunity:** This gap can be bridged by establishing collaborative frameworks between AI researchers and experimental scientists that can help accelerate the commercialization of AI-discovered materials.

(d) Sustainability and Environmental Awareness: The environmental impact of innovative smart materials should be considered to promote sustainability [14]. And many high-performance energy-storage materials contain rare or toxic elements that are ecologically risky.

- **Opportunity:** Using AI for managing organic waste, due to its lesser environmental impact, and finding efficient ways to recycle products.

12.3 Generative AI Frameworks for Material Design

Novel material discovery and development are pivotal for improving the efficiency, lifetime, and sustainability of energy storage systems. Experimental trial and error has been the predominant strategy for discovering materials, but it is a slow and expensive process. Nevertheless, in recent years, the fusion of Generative AI (GAI) and materials science has changed the scene of material design with its abilities to facilitate and accelerate both discovery and optimization of properties while providing predictions about material performance with incredible accuracy [15]. This section outlines the AI methodologies used in material science and describes the generation of material property prediction and optimization through generative AI.

12.3.1 AI Techniques in Materials Science

In energy storage systems, the use of AI within the rapidly evolving domain of materials science uses a range of modeling techniques for prediction, design, and optimization of materials. Key categories of AI methodologies include:

(a) Material discovery using Machine Learning
AI-based material design relies heavily on machine learning (ML). Material science is data and number crunching, and ML models can dig through the experimental and computational data available to find patterns and relationships between material structures and material properties.

- **Supervised Learning**: For predicting existing material properties with labeled datasets. Example: predicting the thermal conductivity of phase change materials (PCMs) used to store solar energy.
- **Unsupervised Learning**: To classify and cluster unknown materials based on intrinsic relationships in the data. For example, data-guided exploration of structural analogs in searching for new battery electrode materials.
- **Reinforcement Learning**: The optimization of the doping levels of semiconductors for better charge retention of supercapacitors.

(b) Generative Adversarial Networks (GANs) for Material Design
GANs are composed of two neural networks, a generator and a discriminator, that compete against each other to produce new material compositions with ideal properties.

- One such approach is using GANs to generate new materials for solid-state batteries, resulting in enhanced ionic conductivity and stability.
- These models produce thousands of possible material structures that may be filtered by predefined performance metrics.

(c) Variational Autoencoders (VAEs) in Materials Informatics
Another generative AI method used in materials design is VAEs. They do this by encoding material structures in a latent space, enabling the AI model to sample new material compositions by interpolating with structures the model already knows about.

- VAEs could aid in the discovery of new high-energy-density cathode materials for lithium-ion batteries.
- Such approaches allow for the creation of materials with targeted electrochemical properties and help to limit the costly trial-and-error cycle [16].

(d) Deep Learning for Atomic and Molecular-Level Design
Graph neural networks (GNNs), for example, have been employed to predict material behavior at the atomic or molecular scale using deep learning techniques.

- They can help model complex atomic interactions in new compositions of materials.
- **Example:** Predictive models in the realm of ionic mobility for battery electrolytes—making energy storage safer and more efficient.

(e) Quantum Computing for Materials Science
Quantum computing is turning out to be an extremely useful tool for simulating complex interactions of materials that are otherwise not computationally feasible classically.

- Inference using quantum machine learning to model electronic structures of potential new energy storage materials.
- **Example:** Quantum-enhanced simulations helped combine numerical optimization and finite element methods to understand the potential of phase-change materials (PCMs) for efficient solar thermal storage.

12.3.2 Material Property Prediction and Optimization

One of the big benefits of AI in material science is its ability to predict properties of materials and help engineer them ahead of actual synthesis in the lab. Based on all this data, the researchers study how changes in the structure or composition affect the performance of the material with the help of AI algorithms [17].

(a) Predicting Thermal and Electrical Properties
AI-based models allow efficient prediction of thermal and electrical properties in a short time, providing freedom for researchers to design materials that maximize efficiency.

- **Example 1:** Phase-change materials (PCMs) with higher thermal conductivity can store heat more efficiently in solar applications.
- **Example 2:** Predictive AI has been applied to identify electrode material for next-generation batteries with high conductivity and low cost.

(b) Multi-Objective Optimization for Smart Materials

Alloying as a tool to optimize materials for energy storage integrates many competing attributes (energy density, charge-discharge efficiency, and material stability) that need mathematical interplay to define a direct tradeoff space [18].

- **Example:** Multi-objective AI models have recently been employed to design solid-state electrolytes that exhibit both high ionic conductivity and mechanical stability.
- Techniques like genetic algorithms and Bayesian optimization are employed to refine properties across materials according to established performance metrics.

(c) AI-Enabled Autonomous Material Experimentation

Now, AI is being applied to streamline the experimentation process to speed up the discovery of new materials and minimize costs.

- One approach, called automated synthesis, relies on AI to modify experimental parameters as synthesis is performed in real-time, guaranteeing that the material properties are optimum.
- For example, robotic labs have been used to find new perovskite-based materials for solar system energy-storage devices.

(d) AI-Driven Computational Material Screening

AI speeds up material screening by predicting which candidates are most likely to satisfy particular performance criteria before synthesis.

- AI-assisted density functional theory (DFT) simulations have accelerated the identification of potential energy storage materials.

- For example, AI-assisted screening of graphene composites enabled the discovery of high-capacity, long-cycle-life battery anodes.

(e) Self-Healing and Sustainable Smart Materials
It is also used to develop self-healing materials to mend microcracks and degradation over time to prolong energy storage devices.

- AI-Powered Sustainable Material Design—AI ensures that biodegradable and non-toxic options are prioritized in the search for future energy storage materials.

Future Prospects of AI in Material Science
The impact of AI on material science is tremendous, and several developments await us in the future:

1. **Self-Learning AI Systems:** AI models that use real-world experiments to make predictions more accurate on materials.
2. **Data to Knowledge:** AI in material design for circular economy — designing recyclable energy storage materials
3. **Cloud-Based AI Material Discovery Platforms:** Global open-access AI tools helping researchers to accelerate material innovations.

12.4 AI-Enabled Smart Electrode Materials

Artificial intelligence (AI) and machine learning (ML) are increasingly shaping the future of materials science, especially in discovering new electrode materials for energy storage applications [19]. AI-powered methods offer computational modeling, predictive analytics, and generative design that can avoid time-consuming and costly experimental iterations, thereby dramatically accelerating the discovery of high-performance electrode materials. In this section, we explore computational discovery of new compositions and ultimately present a case study of AI-optimized battery materials for solar energy storage [20].

12.4.1 Computational Discovery of Novel Compositions

General strategies to discover and optimize electrode materials are based on trial-and-error experiments, which consume a lot of time and cost.

Computational methods powered by AI have revolutionized how this process occurs, accelerating the rate of screening, prediction, and synthesis of new materials [21].

AI Methods for Smart Electrode Material Discovery

1. **Machine Learning (ML) for Property Prediction**

    - AI models trained on large datasets are capable of predicting essential material properties like electrical conductivity, charge retention, and mechanical stability.
    - For instance, researchers have used deep learning models to predict ionic conductivity in solid-state electrolytes, minimizing the extensive lab testing involved.

2. **Generative AI for Material Design**

    - Generative adversarial networks (GANs) and variational autoencoders (VAEs) generate new electrode material compositions given desired electrode properties.
    - AI models have conducted searches of new Graphene-metal hybrids, leading to improved performance and battery life.

3. **High-Throughput Computational Screening**

    - Accelerated screening of candidate electrode materials using DFT calculations or AI-driven molecular simulations.
    - For instance, AI-complemented DFT calculations resulted in the discovery of new transition metal oxides with high energy density.

4. **Autonomous Experimentation and Optimization**

    - Autonomous synthesis and testing of new electrode materials are performed by AI-powered robotic laboratories.
    - For example, self-learning algorithms modify synthesis parameters in an iterative process, thereby efficiently improving material performance with limited human involvement.

Key Benefits of AI-Driven Discovery

- **Faster Material Development:** Speeds up the search for new electrode materials from years to months.
- **Cost Reduction:** Saves on extensive trial-and-error experimentation.
- **Enhanced Performance:** AI-optimized materials show higher energy density, higher cycle stability, and faster charge/discharge rates.

12.4.2 Case Study: GAI-Optimized Battery Materials for Solar Storage

GAI is being hailed as a revolutionary technology with a wide range of applications, and one promising aspect in smart electrode materials is optimizing battery materials for solar energy storage systems [22]. This case study shows how AI has been applied to improve battery technology to be more efficient, last longer, and have less of an environmental impact.

Problem Statement
Challenges of storing solar energy:

- **Energy Density:** High-capacity storage is needed as solar energy input can be intermittent.
- **Charge-Discharge Efficiency:** Maximizing energy conversion process efficiency.
- **Battery Lifespan:** Greater battery longevity over many cycles.

AI-Driven Solution
This study harnessed generative AI to identify and optimize novel electrode materials specifically for solar energy storage.

1. Dataset Collection & Training:

- AI was trained on thousands of known electrode materials (and their electrochemical properties).
- Parameters such as band gap, conductivity, oxidation states, and ion mobility were included in the data.

2. Material Generation & Screening:

- New material compositions with optimal energy storage characteristics were generated by AI models.
- High-throughput DFT calculations and ML predictions were used to shortlist the top candidates.

3. Experimental Validation:

- The best three AI-predicted materials were synthesized and tested in real-world battery systems.

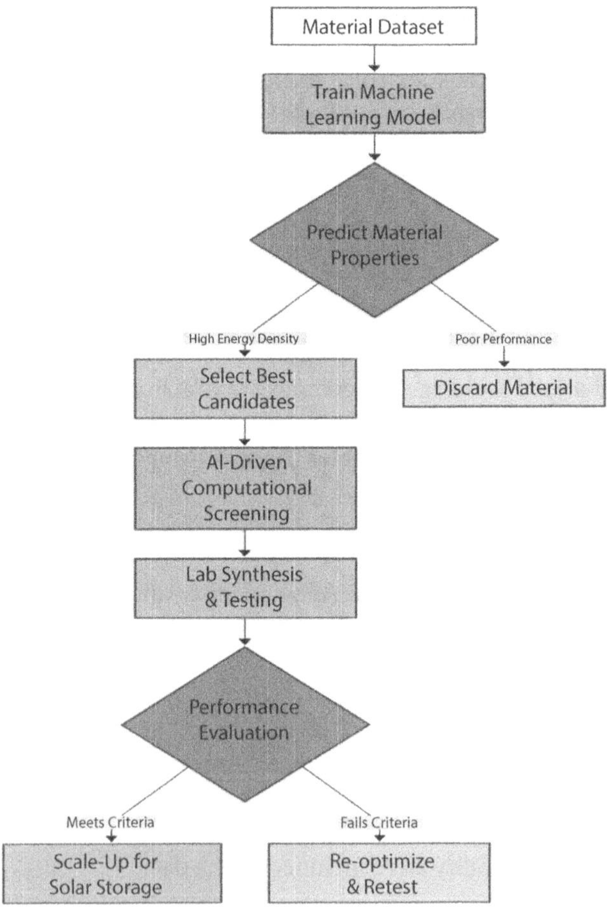

Figure 12.3 AI-driven workflow for smart electrode material discovery and optimization.

- The material that exhibited optimum retention in terms of capacity and efficiency was chosen for additional optimizations.

Figure 12.3 shows the AI-assisted route for materials discovery and optimization of smart electrode materials for energy storage applications. It begins with a dataset of materials, then it predicts properties by using machine learning. Candidates for high-performance materials are computationally screened, synthesized in the laboratory, and tested, while poor candidates are dropped from the process. Once evaluated, the best-performing materials are scaled up for solar storage, while the rest go back for repurposing *via* re-optimization and retesting to improve efficiency and sustainability.

Future Prospects & Research Opportunities

1. **AI for Multi-Functional Electrodes**

    - Self-healing and temperature-responsive electrodes can be explored by future research to further increase battery durability.

2. **Sustainable and Bio-Friendly Materials:**

    - AI can help in the design of non-toxic, biodegradable electrode materials for sustainable energy storage devices.

3. **Integration with Quantum Computing:**

    - These techniques, alongside the quantum AI algorithms, would significantly accelerate and improve the accuracy of material discovery in next-gen solar energy storage.

12.5 Advanced Phase-Change Materials

Phase-change materials (PCMs) are regarded as one of the essential components of thermal energy storage (TES) technology with potential industrial applications in solar energy storage systems [23]. These materials absorb and discharge energy with phase changes such as melting and solidification, which are ideal for enhancing energy efficiency and sustainability.

AI-Entity allows increasingly accelerated PCM advancement and performance using advanced material research and physiology development, along with natural system learning and optimizing PCMs.

12.5.1 AI-Driven Design for Thermal Energy Storage

Artificial Intelligence has revolutionized the PCM research field by allowing predictive modeling, automated material discovery, and optimization of performance. Developing new PCMs using the conventional trial-and-error approach is an expensive and time-consuming task, but AI-based methodologies considerably expedite this discovery process using data-driven approaches.

(a) Machine Learning in PCM Optimization
ML algorithms are trained on datasets consisting of PCM temperature-dependent properties such as latent heat and thermal conductivity [24]. By using AI models trained on current PCM data, the optimal compositions of known PCM candidates can be targeted for this potential increase in total enthalpy and stability.

- **Example:** Nano-enhanced PCMs with higher heat absorption and conductivity have been accomplished through AI-based models, which increase the effectiveness of storage systems for solar thermal energy.

(b) Generative AI for Novel PCM Discovery
Generative AI models, including variational autoencoders (VAEs) and generative adversarial networks (GANs), have been important for the design of new phase change memory (PCM) materials with desirable properties. These models are used to generate hypothetical PCM compositions and to simulate their thermophysical properties to prioritize promising candidates for experimental validation.

- **Example:** Solar energy storage with AI-generated salt-hydrate PCM composites exhibiting better heat retention, less sub-cooling, and improved cycling stability.

(c) AI-Based PCM Performance Prediction
AI models generated from this data predict how PCMs behave under varying climate conditions, load patterns, and storage durations [25]. The ability to predict such a process is essential to constructing a responsive

PCM-based energy storage system that adapts to changing environments in real time.

- **Example:** AI algorithms that model thermodynamic properties maximize the efficiency of thermal energy storage at solar plants by determining how heat can be trapped and released at planned intervals for energy demand.

12.5.2 Performance Enhancement through Generative Design

By optimizing material composition, macrostructure, and phase transition processes, AI-driven generative design improves the performance of phase change materials (PCM). The key aspects include:

(a) Computational Modeling for PCM Structural Optimization
At an atomic level, advanced computational tools like DFT and MD simulations model PCM behavior. We use AI-driven generative algorithms to optimize PCM molecular structures for the highest energy storage density and thermal stability.

- **Example:** Surprisingly, generative algorithms tailored microencapsulated phase change materials (mPCM) with nano-coatings to improve thermal conductivity and mitigate leakage issues when used in solar thermal heating systems.

(b) AI-Guided PCM Composite Development
Artificial intelligence (AI) discovers the best set of additives, stabilizers, and nanomaterials for improving PCM features. Using AI-based approaches, more effective multi-component phase change materials (PCMs) have been developed, with superior heat absorption, mechanical strength, and durability [26].

- **Example:** AI-enabled carbon-doped paraffin heat storage materials have shown increased thermal conductivity with accelerated phase transition behaviors and thus serve as effective solar-energy-driven thermal storage materials.

(c) Self-Healing PCM Structures
A few recent developments in the field of artificial intelligence and material science have resulted in the fabrication of smart polymeric PCMs that can repair their structural damage and thus, uphold a better long-term

performance. Self-healing of the AI is based on its ability to "bleed" its dynamic polymer networks to repair broken molecular bonds and ensure the long operational life of thermal energy storage systems for low-cost and high-density energy storage.

- **Example:** Self-healing PCMs used in solar-power battery storage units can significantly delay degradation of battery cells, which makes them cheaper and more reliable to maintain.

(d) Smart PCM Systems with AI Integration
Dynamic refinement of PCM systems is enabled through AI/ML and real-time monitoring, which helps select the right PCM structure and module design. These intelligent PCM mechanisms are powered by artificial intelligence for:

- Forecast-enhanced energy storage and release schedules
- Solar thermal applications and adaptive heat management
- Means for automatic fault detection and self-correction
- **Example:** PCM-based thermal grids, typically integrated with AI, automatically modulate the thermal energy stored in the material based on weather forecasts, ensuring energy optimization in buildings powered by solar energy.

12.6 Self-Healing Materials for Extended Lifespan

Self-healing materials are a novel idea applied in the field of energy storage systems, especially in solar energy. These materials can self-heal structural damage, which substantially increases long-term energy-storage durability, reliability, and efficiency [27]. The combination of AI has accelerated and refined the development and optimization of self-healing processes. Predicting the material degradation, aiding the self-healing process, or soliciting the best solar storage system operation can be enhanced with AI models for an improved lifetime of operation.

12.6.1 AI Prediction of Degradation and Self-Repair Mechanisms

AI is critical in predicting the energy storage materials degradation methods and directing the design of self-healing mechanisms [28]. AI-based methods, such as machine learning (ML), deep learning (DL), and generative design, are used to investigate how materials respond to different environments and workloads and to make them more resilient and long-lasting.

(a) AI-Driven Degradation Analysis

- AI algorithms process historical data on the performance of all components of solar storage systems to project where and when degradation will occur.
- Machine learning algorithms apply detection methods for predicting early stages of battery deterioration, phase-change material (PCM) degradation, mechanical fatigue, and chemical failure.
- **Example:** AI-powered finite element simulations are used to extract structural fatigue in lithium-ion cells and polymer-based self-healing materials, where predictive maintenance is performed before failure.

(b) Predictive Maintenance with AI Sensors

- Continuous monitoring of storage materials occurs through AI-integrated IoT sensors, which check their temperature fluctuations, mechanical stress, and chemical stability parameters.
- The immediate diagnostic capabilities let machines apply automatic maintenance procedures and preventive measures to reduce maintenance expenses.
- **Example:** AI-driven nano-sensors embedded within self-healing polymers detect micro-cracks to trigger heating, UV light, or chemical catalysts to promote healing.

(c) Generative AI for Self-Healing Mechanism Optimization

- GANs alongside NAS can optimize the structure and composition of self-healing materials through their collective expertise to reach better efficiency levels.
- AI tools generate dynamic polymer networks that do two things: first, they expand life expectancy, and second, they reduce performance deterioration in solar energy storage applications.

- **Example:** The Discovery of graphene-reinforced self-healing electrodes through AI has led to decreased degradation in high-cycle batteries.

12.6.2 Implementation in Solar Storage Systems

Utilizing self-healing materials in solar storage technologies leads to increased operational duration, together with lower maintenance expenses and higher operational durability [29]. The primary applications include:

(a) Self-Healing Electrodes for Solar Batteries

- Self-repairing lithium-ion and solid-state battery electrodes protect the capacity of anodes and cathodes from aging over time.
- AI systems predict how electrodes degrade through patterns that enable the application of nano-coatings for restoring electrical conductivity.
- **Example:** Silicon-based anodes used in solar-powered energy storage through self-healing mechanisms extend their operational life beyond 40%, which decreases the need for replacements.

(b) AI-Integrated Phase-Change Materials (PCMs)

- AI serves as a controller for self-healing phase-change materials that store solar thermal energy throughout thermal cycle operations.
- Reversible polymer bonds allow continuous heat exchange without causing structural failure to the material.
- **Example:** Microencapsulation technology, which AI optimizes, allows thermal efficiency to remain stable by autonomously repairing cracks in solar-thermal energy systems.

(c) AI-Enhanced Coatings for Solar Panels

- The integration of artificial intelligence into solar panel coatings enables the complete restoration of scratched surface areas and recovery from erosion and UV damage.

- Coatings made from nanomaterials react to restore optical properties, which ensures light absorption remains constant for power-generation purposes.
- **Example:** The combination of AI-designed ceramic-polymer hybrid coatings can use environmental heat and humidity to mend solar panel surface defects, resulting in extended efficiency.

(d) AI-Powered Smart Energy Grids

- How AI integrates self-healing storage solutions into smart grids for predictive load balancing and failure prevention.
- AI-derived fault detection systems installed in battery storage units protect solar-powered microgrids from widespread failures.
- **Example:** Self-healing AI-controlled flow batteries will be self-balancing to electrolyte, reducing downtime of renewable energy-powered grids.

12.7 System Integration and Performance

Smart materials face crucial issues regarding how they should be integrated into large-scale systems and how to achieve maximum performance. A successful system incorporates advanced materials and controls how to execute monitoring systems while staying affordable and economically feasible. The effective solution of these difficulties depends on the implementation of digital twin modeling as well as techno-economic analysis (TEA) technologies.

12.7.1 Digital Twin Modeling of Smart Material Storage

What is Digital Twin Technology?
DT technology creates a digital version of actual physical systems, which updates automatically with current operational parameters of physical assets [30]. Such digital replicas of energy storage systems assist with assessing material behaviors while monitoring operational efficiency and identifying potential failures in smart material storage applications.

Applications of Digital Twins in Smart Material Storage

Figure 12.4. Demonstrates the versatility and power of digital twin technology to be applied to smart material storage. Digital twin is, however, a virtual copy of physical storage systems, enabling real-time monitoring (blue) for live tracking and status updates. Predictive maintenance (green) utilizes the software of AI models to spot failures early, saving time and money in halting downtime. Performance optimization (sketched in orange) provides on-the-fly tuning of the system based on data-driven insights. Techno-economic analysis (in red) is used to assess cost-effectiveness, enabling more informed investment decisions. Fault detection and diagnosis (purple) use AI to automatically solve problems, increasing reliability. And, finally, AI-based energy optimization techniques help ensure energy efficiency (cyan), which makes smart storage solutions more environmentally as well as economically sustainable.

(a) Real-Time Monitoring and Predictive Analytics

- Digital twin models for PCMs, lithium-ion batteries, and other energy storage solutions use data generated from sensors, the Internet of Things, and machine learning to predict energy storage system performance [31].

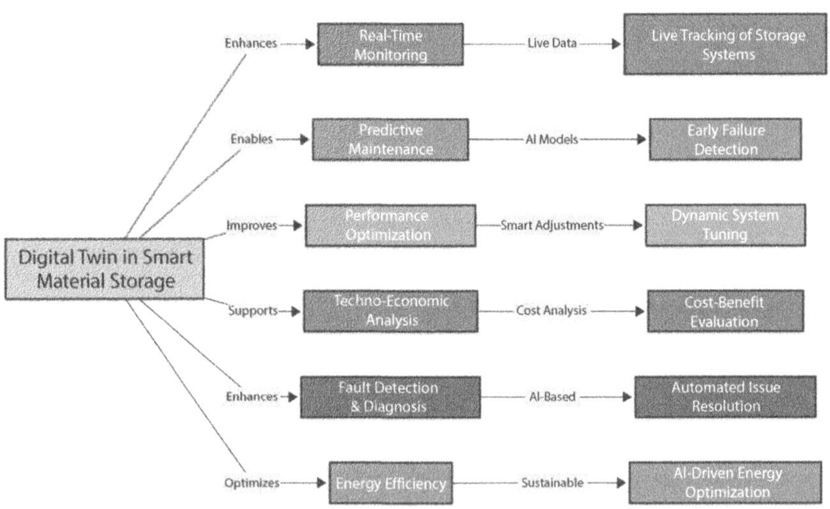

Figure 12.4 Applications of digital twins in smart material storage.

- Real-time monitoring of thermal properties, energy retention, and degradation enables early fault detection and scheduling of maintenance.

(b) Optimizing Energy Storage Efficiency

- By predictive testing of various material compositions on digital twin simulations, energy density, heat dissipation, and cycle stability can be optimized.
- **Example:** AI comes with digital twins for PCM-based solar storage, predicting discrepancies in storage sizes concerning seasonal temperature changes and optimizing discharge schedules.

(c) Failure Prediction and Self-Healing Mechanisms

- By considering material stress, phase transitions, and the degradation of performance over time, the digital twins allow for early failure detection, which can then cause self-healing protocols to be triggered in the smart material.
- **Example:** In nano-enhanced lithium-ion batteries, digital twins detect places that are degrading the anode or cathode of the lithium-ion battery unit and determine how another material could mitigate failure ahead of time.

(d) Digital Twin-Enabled Smart Grids

- Digital twins (also known as digital threads) are used in smart grids to optimize energy distribution within the network by controlling energy flow into storage compared to renewable energy generation.
- **Example:** A solar farm with PCM-based thermal storage can leverage a digital twin to anticipate an energy surplus stored to distribute the energy evenly while preventing energy oversupply.

Challenges in Digital Twin Adoption

- **High computational requirements:** Digital twins require real-time AI analytics, which is very resource-intensive.

- **Data integration complexity**: It takes complicated data fusion algorithms to integrate information from sensors, IoT platforms, and AI models.
- **Cybersecurity risks**: As digital twins depend on constant updates in the cloud, they need to be secured against potential cyber threats.

12.7.2 Techno-Economic Analysis and Optimization

Understanding Techno-Economic Analysis (TEA)

Analysts perform techno-economic analysis (TEA) to assess how well smart materials perform technically as well as economically for storing energy. TEA enables investors and engineers, alongside policymakers, to decide on the technology expansion potential for new storage solutions [32].

Key Factors in Techno-Economic Analysis

(a) Cost-Benefit Analysis of Smart Materials

- Price analysis includes raw material expenses, manufacturing expenditure, and storage efficiency of PCMs, as well as graphene-enhanced batteries and solid-state electrolytes.
- The assessment of nano-enhanced PCMs versus regular PCMs determines if the higher nanotechnology expenses lead to increased operational efficiency and longer durability.

(b) Lifecycle Assessment (LCA)

- The analysis focuses on environmental impacts, together with recyclability as well as sustainable characteristics of smart materials throughout their entire lifecycle.
- Tests on solid-state batteries using TEA evaluation methods determine their improved recyclability as well as reduced toxicity properties relative to lithium-ion batteries.

(c) Energy Efficiency and Return on Investment (ROI)

- The long-term ROI calculation requires examining energy density together with cycle stability and degradation rate measurement data.

- The assessment through TEA determines whether graphene-enhanced electrodes maintain battery charge better than metal-oxide-based electrodes, thus influencing capital investment decisions.

(d) Market Competitiveness and Scalability

- This study performs comparisons between smart material energy storage approaches and established power storage solutions regarding their operational efficiency, expense effectiveness, and expansion capabilities.
- Analysis of an AI-enhanced thermal grid through TEA evaluates the economic value that smart energy management features add to support nationwide implementation.

12.8 Future Directions and Challenges

Intelligent materials are predicted to be critical for next-generation energy storage solutions as global energy needs continue to rise. And yet, despite important advances in experimental research, challenges with scalability, cost-effectiveness, durability, and application to real-world conditions remain. Solving these problems will require teamwork between diversified fields, Artificial intelligence-driven material design, as well as standardization in the sectors. In this section, we highlight the most promising smart materials, possible industry roadmaps, and barriers to commercialization.

12.8.1 Emerging Smart Materials for Next Generation Storage

(a) Graphene and MXenes for High-Performance Batteries

Graphene-based energy storage solutions lead the battery innovation field because they feature engineered properties that include fast electronic transmission with lightweight devices and abundant ion storage areas [33]. Energy storage capacity and charge-transfer performance of MXenes improve due to their status as 2D transition metal carbides and nitrides.

Key Benefits:

- Parallel energy transfer abilities shorten both electric vehicle (EV) and portable electronic charging durations.

- These batteries demonstrate longer operational life since they better resist deterioration than lithium-ion cells do.
- Applicable to wearables and aerospace technologies

The application of graphene-upgraded supercapacitors is under development for electric grid storage systems because these devices must supply power quickly to maintain electrical stability.

(b) Perovskite-Based Smart Materials

With high energy conversion efficiency, perovskites are revolutionizing solar energy storage and next-generation batteries. Utilizing AI-optimized materials has also uncovered more stable and robust hybrid perovskite structures.

Applications

- **Perovskite-Silicon Tandem Cells:** Solar energy capture efficiency.
- **Perovskite Lithium-Ion Batteries:** This may have implications for the utilization of Perovskite Lithium-Ion Batteries, given the ability to extend energy retention and stability.
- **Self-Healing Perovskite Structures:** Extend the life of solar panels and energy grids.

Industry Impact: Next-gen smart grids are among the areas testing AI-optimized perovskites, given their capacity for enhancing how much energy can be stored while also lowering the cost of production.

(c) AI-Driven Phase Change Materials (PCMs)

AI serves as a tool for designing improved PCMs that control thermal energy storage operations more efficiently [34]. These materials operate through environmental triggers to release or retain heat, so they are suitable for battery cooling systems, smart buildings, and thermal batteries.

Key Innovations:

- The development of renewable energy storage systems deploys self-controlled thermal batteries.
- Use of AI predictive modeling to increase the performance of PCM.

- Bio-based PCMs represent an eco-friendly solution for energy storage.

Lithium-ion batteries with AI-optimized PCM coatings installed by teams prevent overheating, which enhances safety and extends operational life for EVs as well as other consumer electronics.

(d) Solid-State and Lithium-Sulfur Batteries

Current widespread use of Lithium-ion batteries spans many applications, but recent innovations in solid-state and lithium-sulfur (Li-S) systems potentially reignite considerably higher energy density for far less pollution.

Advantages:

- The technology offers five times greater energy capacity than current lithium-ion systems.
- **Lower environmental impact:** Uses sulfur instead of rare metals.
- **Increased safety:** The technology increases safety by completely removing the potential fire risks that liquid electrolytes normally cause.

Industry Potential: The industry sector sees QuantumScape and Solid Power leading the way in solid-state battery development for both electric vehicle and aerospace uses.

(e) Bio-Inspired and Sustainable Materials

Scientists are studying natural materials for developing efficient and affordable technologies that store energy. Examples include:

- **Cellulose-derived batteries:** Renewable, biodegradable, and lightweight.
- The combination of chitosan along with electrolytes produces sustainable materials that enhance electrical conductivity.
- Protein-based supercapacitors: Inspired by biological energy storage mechanisms.

Sustainable materials will be developed to replace toxic battery components, thus decreasing hazards from discarded batteries in the environment.

12.8.2 Commercial Implementation Roadmap

To launch this smart material energy storage for commercialization, it must go through research validation, pilot testing, industrial scale-up, and regulatory qualification [35]. The roadmap for industrial deployment is below.

(a) Phase 1: Research and Development (2025-2027)

- Artificial intelligence-powered discovery of materials and performance optimization.
- Verifying or testing innovative materials under various energy storage conditions.
- Collaborations between academia, AI research labs, and tech companies.

Goal: The long-term goal is to develop validated high-performance smart materials with improved energy efficiency.

(b) Phase 2: Prototyping at Pilot Scale (2027–2030)

- Developing prototypes (small-scale) to validate the industry.
- Real-time replications in the digital twin to optimize performance.
- Techno-economic analysis to assess cost-effectiveness.

Outcome: Functional prototypes of energy storage devices tested in industrial conditions.

(c) Phase 3: Scale Up to Industrial Scale (2030-2035)

- Mass-scale production of smart batteries and supercapacitors.
- Support for global standardization and regulatory approval.
- It develops these suppliers into a supply chain for cost-effective raw material sourcing.

Goal: Enable competitive mass production sufficient for mass market deployment and thus, wider availability.

(d) Phase 4: Market Deployment & Global Adoption (2035 & Beyond)

- Solar grids, electric cars, and industrial storage systems will be integrated with AI-powered smart materials.

- Partnerships with major energy companies for scalability.
- Design and realization of self-repairing, smart storage systems with low power consumption.

Impact: Today, smart material-based energy storage is the worldwide industry standard for renewable energy and sustainable technology.

12.9 Conclusion

Overcoming long-term challenges such as efficiency limits, material degradation, and scalability, generative AI, in association with smart materials, is altering the solar energy storage landscape. In this chapter, we have discussed the potential paradigm shift in energy storage technologies through AI-assisted material discovery and optimization, leading to enhanced reliability, longevity, and improved performance. Based on a review of the history of smart materials and AI in materials science until October 2023, this chapter presents how Generative AI architectures aid the discovery of next-generation storage materials. Leveraging AI for material property prediction, PCM improvement, and self-healing structures offers opportunities to revolutionize energy storage efficiency. GAI-optimized battery materials and AI-driven PCMs were case studies of these general but impressive results, showing their potential to overcome charge storage, thermal control, and lifespan as performance barriers to their wider application to solar energy. Self-healing materials that can anticipate damage and repair themselves are an important move towards more sustainable, low-maintenance storage systems. In addition, the use of digital twin technology in smart material storage allows for real-time monitoring, predictive maintenance, and performance optimization, leading to a more efficient and cost-effective operation. The techno-economic analysis also highlighted the importance of striking a balance between performance, affordability, and sustainability to facilitate widespread adoption. Innovations led by upcoming smart materials and AI will keep pushing the boundaries of next-generation energy storage technologies. Therefore, while there are many different research directions, advances in the computational efficiency of AI, large-scale manufacturability, and regulatory standards will need to be defined before the technology can be deployed commercially. Commercially, we need a clear path to scale, reduce cost (battery), and integrate with existing solar storage systems effectively. The combined efforts of Generative AI and smart materials are poised to revolutionize the solar energy storage landscape. Researchers and industries can harness AI-based insights and cutting-edge materials to create next-level energy storage with extreme efficiency, longevity, and intelligence, paving the way for a more sustainable and tech-reliant energy landscape.

AI disclosure statement: The author acknowledges the use of AI-based tools for minor language editing or grammatical correction. However, all intellectual contributions, analyses, and conclusions presented in this chapter are entirely the author's own.

References

1. Chekifi, T., Boukraa, M., Benmoussa, A., Artificial Intelligence for thermal energy storage enhancement: A Comprehensive Review, in: *Journal of Energy Resources Technology*, 2024, https://doi.org/10.1115/1.4065197.
2. Ali, H., Rehman, T., Arıcı, M., Said, Z., Duraković, B., Mohammed, H., Kumar, R., Rathod, M., Buyukdagli, O., Teggar, M., Advances in thermal energy storage: Fundamentals and applications, in: *Progress in Energy and Combustion Science*, 2024, https://doi.org/10.1016/j.pecs.2023.101109.
3. Liu, X., Fan, K., Huang, X., Ge, J., Liu, Y., Kang, H., Recent advances in artificial intelligence are boosting materials design for electrochemical energy storage, in: *Chemical Engineering Journal*, 2024, https://doi.org/10.1016/j.cej.2024.151625.
4. Jyani, M. and Rathore, P.S., Spectrogram-Based CNN Framework for Live Deepfake Voice Detection in Google Meet, in: *2025 International Conference on Computing Technologies & Data Communication (ICCTDC)*, pp. 1–5, IEEE, 2025.
5. SaberiKamarposhti, M., Kamyab, H., Krishnan, S., Yusuf, M., Rezania, S., Chelliapan, S., Khorami, M., A comprehensive review of AI-enhanced smart grid integration for hydrogen energy: Advances, challenges, and prospects, in: *International Journal of Hydrogen Energy*, 2024, https://doi.org/10.1016/j.ijhydene.2024.01.129.
6. Bhattacharjee, J. and Roy, S., Smart materials for sustainable energy, in: *Natural Resources Conservation and Research*, 2024, https://doi.org/10.24294/nrcr.v7i1.5536.
7. Wen, X., Shen, Q., Zheng, W., Zhang, H., AI-Driven Solar Energy Generation and Smart Grid Integration: A Holistic Approach to Enhancing Renewable Energy Efficiency. *Int. J. Innovative Res. Eng. Manage.*, 2024, https://doi.org/10.55524/ijirem.2024.11.4.8.
8. Olabi, A., Abdelghafar, A., Maghrabie, H., Sayed, E., Rezk, H., Radi, M., Obaideen, K., Abdelkareem, M., Application of artificial intelligence for prediction, optimization, and control of thermal energy storage systems, in:

Thermal Science and Engineering Progress, 2023, https://doi.org/10.1016/j.tsep.2023.101730.

9. Smadi, T., Handam, A., Gaeid, K., Al-Smadi, A., Al-Husban, Y., Khalid, A., Artificial Intelligence Control of Energy Management PV System, in: *Results in Control and Optimization*, 2023, https://doi.org/10.1016/j.rico.2023.100343.
10. Paliwal, M., Jakhar, S., Sharma, V., Nano-enhanced phase change materials for energy storage in photovoltaic thermal management systems: A bibliometric and thematic analysis. *Int. J. Thermofluids*, 2023, https://doi.org/10.1016/j.ijft.2023.100310.
11. Chen, H., Zheng, Y., Li, J., Li, L., Wang, X., AI for Nanomaterials Development in Clean Energy and Carbon Capture, Utilization and Storage (CCUS). *ACS Nano*, 2023, https://doi.org/10.1021/acsnano.3c01062.
12. Kumar, D., M.J., S.K., B.B., S.S., A Hybrid Renewable Energy Source-fed Battery Storage System for Vehicle to Grid Application using AI Techniques. *2023 International Conference on Intelligent Technologies for Sustainable Electric and Communications Systems (iTech SECOM)*, pp. 270–275, 2023, https://doi.org/10.1109/iTechSECOM59882.2023.10434995.
13. Behzadi, A., Alirahmi, S., Yu, H., Sadrizadeh, S., An efficient renewable hybridization based on hydrogen storage for peak demand reduction: A rule-based energy control and optimization using machine learning techniques. *J. Energy Storage*, 2023, https://doi.org/10.1016/j.est.2022.106168.
14. Ramasubramanian, B., Rao, R., Chellappan, V., Ramakrishna, S., Towards Sustainable Fuel Cells and Batteries with an AI Perspective. *Sustainability*, 2022, doi: 10.3390/su142316001.
15. Ali, H., Phase change materials based thermal energy storage for solar energy systems in buildings. *J. Build. Eng.*, 2022, https://doi.org/10.1016/j.jobe.2022.104731.
16. Punniakodi, B. and Senthil, R., Recent developments in nano-enhanced phase change materials for solar thermal storage, in: *Solar Energy Materials and Solar Cells*, 2022.
17. He, Z., Guo, W., Zhang, P., Performance prediction, optimal design and operational control of thermal energy storage using artificial intelligence methods, in: *Renewable and Sustainable Energy Reviews*, 2022.
18. Paul, J., Pandey, A., Mishra, Y., Said, Z., Mishra, Y., Jacob, J., Kadirgama, K., Samykano, M., Tyagi, V., Nano-enhanced organic form stable PCMs for medium temperature solar thermal energy harvesting: Recent progresses, challenges, and opportunities, in: *Renewable and Sustainable Energy Reviews*, 2022, https://doi.org/10.1016/j.rser.2022.112321.
19. Zhang, Y., Pan, S., Cheng, Y., Shao, Z., Xiang, H., Chen, G., Zhu, L., Weng, W., Bai, H., Zhu, M., Smart fibers for energy conversion and storage. *Chem. Soc. Rev.*, 2021, https://doi.org/10.1039/d0cs01603a.

20. Rathore, P.S., Chatterjee, J.M., Kumar, A., *et al.*, Energy-efficient cluster head selection through relay approach for WSN. *J. Supercomput.*, 77, 7649–7675, 2021, https://doi.org/10.1007/s11227-020-03593-4.
21. Mangot, A., Kumar, A., Baliyan, A., Shining a Light on Solar Power Forecasting: Machine Learning Techniques for Unprecedented Accuracy, in: *2023 3rd International Conference on Technological Advancements in Computational Sciences (ICTACS)*, IEEE, pp. 828–834, 2023, November.
22. Dubey, A.K., Kumar, A., Ramirez, I.S., Marquez, F.P.G., A review of intelligent systems for the prediction of wind energy using machine learning, in: *International Conference on Management Science and Engineering Management*, Cham: Springer International Publishing, pp. 476–491, 2022, July.
23. Rathore, P.S., Kumar, A., García-Díaz, V., A holistic methodology for improved RFID network lifetime by advanced cluster head selection using dragonfly algorithm, 2020.
24. Rathore, P.S., Sarkar, M.K., Das, R., A comprehensive review on secure and energy aware multi-hop routing in clustering based wireless sensor network, in: *Telecommunications and Radio Engineering*, 80, 8, 2021.
25. Wu, S., Li, T., Wu, M., Xu, J., Chao, J., Hu, Y., Yan, T., Li, Q., Wang, R., Dual-Functional Aligned and Interconnected Graphite Nanoplatelet Networks for Accelerating Solar Thermal Energy Harvesting and Storage within Phase Change Materials, in: *ACS applied materials & interfaces*, 2021, https://doi.org/10.1021/acsami.0c22814.
26. Kumar, A., Alaraj, M., Rizwan, M., Nangia, U., Novel AI Based Energy Management System for Smart Grid With RES Integration. *IEEE Access*, 9, 162530–162542, 2021, https://doi.org/10.1109/ACCESS.2021.3131502.
27. Kumar, A., Dubey, A.K., Segovia Ramírez, I., *et al.*, Artificial Intelligence Techniques for the Photovoltaic System: A Systematic Review and Analysis for Evaluation and Benchmarking. *Arch. Computat. Methods Eng.*, 31, 4429–4453, 2024, https://doi.org/10.1007/s11831-024-10125-3.
28. Dubey, A.K., Ramirez, I., Marquez, F., A Review of Intelligent Systems for the Prediction of Wind Energy Using Machine Learning. *2022, ICMSEM, The Sixteenth International Conference on Management Science and Engineering Management, Lecture Notes on Data Engineering and Communications Technologies, vol 144. Springer, by Springer*, Ankara, Turkey, August 3-6, 2022.
29. Kumar, A.D., Ramirez, I., Rio, A., Marquez, F., A Review and Analysis of Forecasting of Photovoltaic Power Generation Using Machine Learning. *2022, ICMSEM, The Sixteenth International Conference on Management Science and Engineering Management, Lecture Notes on Data Engineering and Communications Technologies, vol 144. Springer, Cham. by Springer*, Ankara, Turkey, August 3-6, 2022.
30. Teng, L., Xuan, Y., Da, Y., Liu, X., Ding, Y., Modified Ca-Looping materials for directly capturing solar energy and high-temperature storage. *Energy Storage Mater.*, 25, 836–845, 2020, https://doi.org/10.1016/j.ensm.2019.09.006.

31. Suresh, C. and Saini, R., Review on solar thermal energy storage technologies and their geometrical configurations. *Int. J. Energy Res.*, 44, 4163–4195, 2020, https://doi.org/10.1002/er.5143.
32. Samanta, H., Bhattacharjee, A., Pramanik, M., Das, A., Bhattacharya, K., Saha, H., Internet of things based smart energy management in a vanadium redox flow battery storage integrated bio-solar microgrid. *J. Energy Storage*, 32, 101967–101967, 2020, https://doi.org/10.1016/j.est.2020.101967.
33. Aftab, W., Khurram, M., Shi, J., Tabassum, H., Liang, Z., Usman, A., Guo, W., Huang, X., Wu, W., Yao, R., Yan, Q., Zou, R., Highly efficient solar-thermal storage coating based on phosphorene encapsulated phase change materials. *Energy Storage Mater.*, 32, 199–207, 2020, https://doi.org/10.1016/j.ensm.2020.07.032.
34. Wei, F., Li, Y., Sui, Q., Lin, X., Chen, L., Chen, Z., Li, Z., A Novel Thermal Energy Storage System in Smart Building Based on Phase Change Material. *IEEE Trans. Smart Grid*, 10, 2846–2857, 2019, https://doi.org/10.1109/TSG.2018.2812160.
35. Akbari, H., Browne, M., Ortega, A., Huang, M., Hewitt, N., Norton, B., McCormack, S., Efficient energy storage technologies for photovoltaic systems. *Sol. Energy*, 2019, https://doi.org/10.1016/J.SOLENER.2018.03.052.
36. Mazzoni, S., Ooi, S., Nastasi, B., Romagnoli, A., Energy storage technologies as techno-economic parameters for master-planning and optimal dispatch in smart multi energy systems. *Appl. Energy*, 2019, https://doi.org/10.1016/J.APENERGY.2019.113682.
37. Carrillo, A., González-Aguilar, J., Romero, M., Coronado, J., Solar Energy on Demand: A Review on High Temperature Thermochemical Heat Storage Systems and Materials. *Chem. Rev.*, 1197, 4777–4816, 2019, https://doi.org/10.1021/acs.chemrev.8b00315.
38. Li, H., McRae, L., Firby, C., Al-Hussein, M., Elezzabi, A., Nanohybridization of molybdenum oxide with tungsten molybdenum oxide nanowires for solution-processed fully reversible switching of energy storing smart windows. *Nano Energy*, 47, 130–139, 2018, https://doi.org/10.1016/J.NANOEN.2018.02.043.
39. Aktaş, A., Erhan, K., Ozdemir, S., Özdemir, E., Experimental investigation of a new smart energy management algorithm for a hybrid energy storage system in smart grid applications. *Electr. Power Syst. Res.*, 144, 185–196, 2017, https://doi.org/10.1016/J.EPSR.2016.11.022.
40. Ye, M., Zhang, Z., Zhao, Y., Qu, L., Graphene Platforms for Smart Energy Generation and Storage. *Joule*, 2, 245–268, 2017, https://doi.org/10.1016/J.JOULE.2017.11.011.
41. Alva, G., Liu, L., Huang, X., Fang, G., Thermal energy storage materials and systems for solar energy applications. *Renewable Sustainable Energy Rev.*, 68, 693–706, 2017, https://doi.org/10.1016/J.RSER.2016.10.021.

13

Optimizing Wind Turbine Site Selection Using Machine Learning: Techniques, Applications, and Case Studies

Inam Ul Haq* **and Abhishek Kumar**

Department of CSE, Chandigarh University, Mohali, India

Abstract
One of the most prospective sources of renewable energy is wind power, whereby there can be substantial growth especially in favorable geographic areas. The appropriate choice of turbine site is vital to the success of energy production, minimization of environmental effects, and increase in cost-effectiveness. Conventionally, site selection been a long and resource consuming process, based upon meteorological, environmental, and socio-economic analysis. This chapter discusses the impact of artificial intelligence (AI) on site selection by making it accurate, data-driven, and efficient analysis. We assess several AI algorithms in this field (machine learning models, predictive analytics, optimization algorithms, and geographic information systems (GIS)) and comment on cases of successful AI-based site selection. Through the analysis of the challenges, methods, and the future prospects, this chapter would be a complete guide to the researchers, engineers, and policymakers in the deployment of wind turbines.

Keywords: Artificial intelligence, machine learning, deep learning

13.1 Introduction

The rapid transition to renewable energy is the focus of the world reaction to climate change, of fossil energy, and the growing energy needs. Wind energy has become one of the most feasible and scalable energy sources in

**Corresponding author*: mirinam525@gmail.com

Abhishek Kumar, Pramod Singh Rathore, Arun Lal Srivastav and Ashutosh Kumar Dubey (eds.) Solar Energy Optimization Using Generative Artificial Intelligence, (305–328) © 2026 Scrivener Publishing LLC

the list of renewable energy sources. Nevertheless, the success and financial feasibility of wind energy projects will highly rely on the choice of the best location where turbines can be installed as wind is not omnipresent and not uniform among the regions. The selection of a location is therefore an important stage during the wind energy lifecycle that will determine the amount and quality of the energy produced, as well as the sustainability of the entire project [1]. As Figure 13.1 shows, traditional and AI-based methods of wind energy site selection are different in terms of time and cost efficiency. In the left chart, the average time was calculated in days and the AI-based approach will save a lot of time in comparison to the traditional methods. The right chart illustrates the mean cost in the thousands of dollars with AI-based approaches showing a significant prevention of costs to make it a less costly option.

This has traditionally been done by relying on a large amount of study in the field, meteorological studies, environmental impact studies, and even complicated negotiations with the local communities. Although these techniques offer useful information, they are usually limited by time, cost and subjectivity. Artificial Intelligence (AI) has been identified as a potent instrument to overcome these shortcomings in the recent years. AI allows making decisions with much more accuracy and basing them on data, saving a lot of time and resources that would be spent on the site selection without accuracy compromise [2]. Using historical and real-time forecasting of the meteorological conditions, AI can maximize the site choice with respect to the wind flow patterns, the geographic characteristics, and environmental effects to enable predictive modelling and adaptive

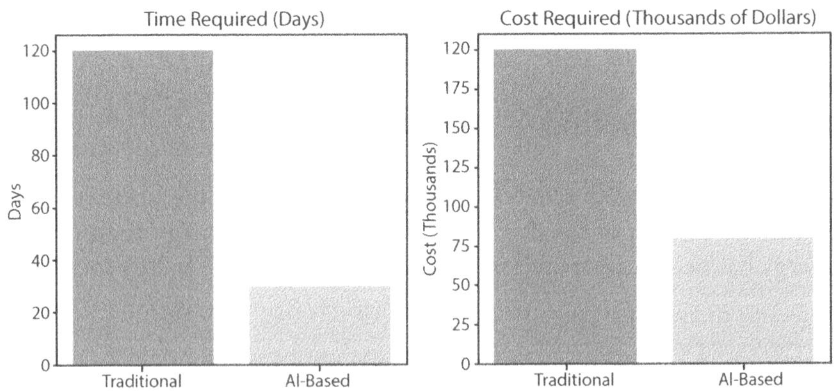

Figure 13.1 Comparing the average time and cost required for traditional vs. AI-based methods.

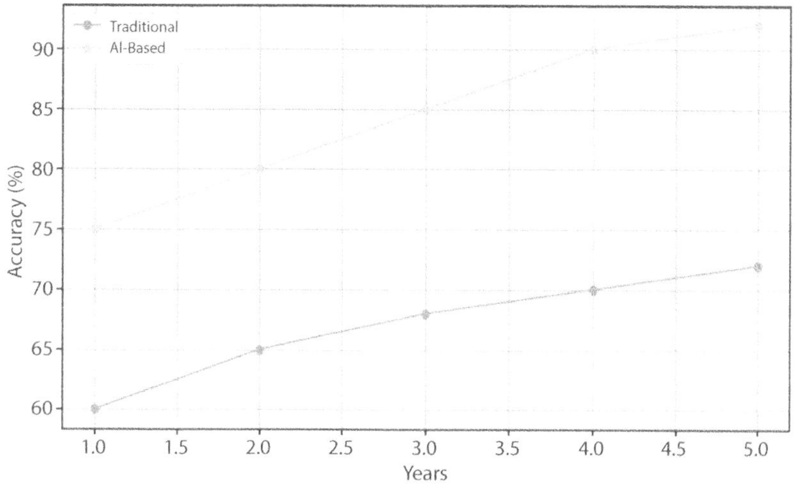

Figure 13.2 Showing how accuracy in site selection improves over the years with traditional methods versus AI-based methods.

modelling opportunity as compared to the traditional methods. The trend in the accuracy improvements of site selection over the five years period as observed in Figure 13.2 compares the traditional with the AI-based site selection methods. The AI-based method exhibits an exponential growth in accuracy with increasing accuracy over time as opposed to the traditional methods, which exhibit gradual, steady increments.

Figure 13.3 illustrates the environmental impact scores for both traditional and AI-based site selection methods. The AI-based method achieves

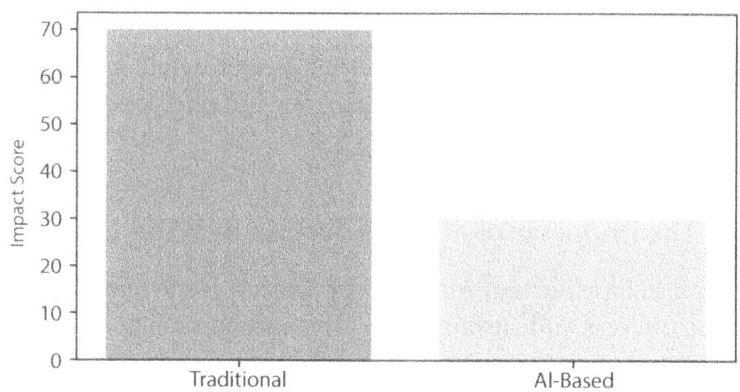

Figure 13.3 Showing environmental impact scores for traditional and AI-based site selection (lower scores indicate lower environmental impact).

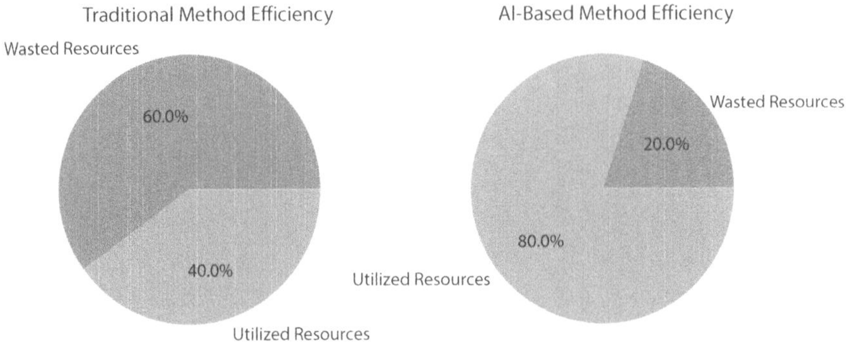

Figure 13.4 A pie chart showing resource utilization efficiency (in %) for each method.

a significantly lower impact score, indicating that it is a more sustainable and eco-friendly approach compared to traditional site selection methods.

Figure 13.4 compares resource utilization efficiency for traditional and AI-based site selection methods in wind energy. The AI-based method achieves higher resource utilization, with a larger portion of resources effectively used compared to traditional methods, which show a greater proportion of waste.

This chapter presents the paramount importance of site selection in the lifecycle of wind energy projects lifecycle, and the traditional methods and the challenges that the methods present. It further introduces AI as a revolutionary innovation that can make the process of the site selection more efficient, objective. Focusing on the possibilities of AI to make the process more accurate and less subjective, this chapter preconditions the comprehension of how the use of recent technologies can contribute to more sustainable and efficient development of wind energies. Further sections will discuss the particular advantages of the best location, discuss the weaknesses of the traditional approach in greater detail, and explain how AI can be used to overcome these drawbacks and offer it as a new solution to wind energy business.

13.1.1 The Importance of Site Selection in Wind Energy

One of the crucial aspects of wind energy projects is site selection that is the key to their success and sustainability. The appropriate location will result in maximum energy generation with reduced infrastructure and operation costs. Properly selected location enables turbines to access steady and fast-moving wind, which guarantees steady stream of power which satisfies energy requirements as well as financial requirements. A choice of location, on the other hand, that is not appropriately chosen, where the winds are erratic or geographical constraints limit them, may contribute to lower energy production, increased maintenance costs, and even the failure of the projects. This therefore makes it important to choose the best locations so as to maximize the investments of wind energy [3]. Along with energy performance and cost-efficiency, the issue of site selection has serious environmental and social undertones. Wind turbines are big and conspicuous designs that have the capacity to influence the local wildlife, ecosystem and communities. Poorly located projects can interfere with the migration routes of birds, the wildlife and vegetation of the area, and the residents around them, thus causing social opposition and legal problems. Ideal locations therefore, lie between the requirements of energy generation and environmental responsibility and social acceptance. This needs intensive evaluation of biodiversity, noises, aesthetic effects, and compatibility of the land-use to ensure that ecological and societal footprints are kept down to minimum [4].

As wind energy has become increasingly popular around the world, especially in areas where weather is not consistently predictable, the location of the wind farm has become a strategic undertaking, and may take years to plan and evaluate. Conventional site selection techniques including meteorological studies and environmental impact assessment, are very valuable but not likely to be sustainable in the long term, because of time and resource requirement. The necessity to find a more objective and quicker method of site selection, which respects the complex ecological, social, and economic aspects that it considers, grows [5]. The section highlights the specificity of the site selection that determines the efficiency, output, and sustainability of wind energy projects and is the key to the overall discussion of the way to maximize these processes with the help of artificial intelligence in the further sections.

13.1.2 Limitations of Traditional Site Selection Approaches

Although it may be useful in the formative years of wind energy development, traditional site selection methods have a variety of restrictions. Conventionally, the choice of sites has been strongly dependent on intensive meteorological, geographical surveys, and environmental evaluation. The processes tend to take years and they require huge on-site research to complete and since they are costly, they are prohibitive of time [6]. As an illustration, the process of collecting valid wind information at a potential location might take months or even years of observations to faithfully measure the variations of seasons and day-to-day variations. Also, there should be environmental impact assessments that should be done rigorously to

Table 13.1 Outlines the evolution from traditional to advanced methods in wind energy prediction, including their strengths and limitations.

Method	Description	Advantages	Limitations
Numerical weather prediction (NWP)	Uses atmospheric data and physical equations to predict wind speeds	High accuracy with detailed meteorological data	Computationally intensive, requires extensive data
Computational fluid dynamics (CFD)	Simulates wind flow over terrain and turbines	Useful for complex terrain, high precision	Expensive to compute, requires complex setups
Time series models (ARMA, ARIMA)	Uses historical wind speed data for future prediction	Effective for short-term forecasting, easy to implement	Accuracy declines for long-term predictions
Regression models	Establishes relationships between wind speed and power output using historical data	Simple and fast to apply, works well with sufficient data	Limited predictive power for highly variable conditions
Persistence models	Assumes future wind speed will be similar to current values	Very simple and fast to compute	Only useful for very short-term predictions
Hybrid models	Combines physical and statistical methods for better prediction	Balances the strengths of both models, higher accuracy	Can be computationally demanding and complex

(Continued)

Table 13.1 Outlines the evolution from traditional to advanced methods in wind energy prediction, including their strengths and limitations. (*Continued*)

Method	Description	Advantages	Limitations
Climatological models	Uses long-term average wind data (climatology)	Useful for long-term planning and wind farm siting	Not effective for short-term or dynamic predictions
Markov chain models	Uses probabilistic transitions between wind states	Handles uncertainty in wind data	Less accurate for highly fluctuating conditions
Fuzzy logic models	Uses fuzzy logic to manage uncertainties in wind predictions	Flexible, good for handling data with uncertainties	May lack precision compared to other methods

determine and curb the environmental footprint of the turbines which would cause even more delays and costs shows in Table 13.1.

The issue of environmental disruption is also of concern. The assessments done on sites based on physical characteristics, picking of samples, or a larger area of surveying may disrupt local ecology and communities. Such activities can affect the quality of the soil, the vegetation and local wildlife and undermine the very ecological sustainability that wind projects are supposed to be promoting. In addition, it might be difficult, time-consuming, and sometimes controversial to interact with the local communities and discuss their issues, although such work is essential [7]. As wind energy projects have experienced a sharp growth, these constraints are indicative of the necessity to adopt more efficient, data-oriented solutions that maintain accuracy but minimize time and resource usage. Due to the increasing demand of wind energy, the time and cost-related to conventional site selection methods are becoming less sustainable. As a result, the constraints in the present paper precondition the analysis of how AI-based solutions can assist in making the site selection more efficient and accurate and allow renewable energy initiatives to proceed in a timely, environmentally conscious, and cost-effective way. As described in Table 13.1, conventional wind energy site selection approaches, despite their early usefulness, exhibit multiple limitations due to their reliance on comprehensive surveys and environmental evaluations.

13.1.3 AI as a Solution for Site Selection Optimization

Artificial intelligence (AI) has become one of the most potent solutions to address the limitations of the conventional site selection techniques. Using big data as a combination of meteorological, geographical, and ecological data, AI can provide a more efficient, more accurate, and data-driven way of selecting wind energy sites. The machine learning algorithms are able to process large amounts of past and current data and identify a pattern and correlation that otherwise might have been difficult or even impossible to discover by traditional methods. This enables AI to provide predictive information, recommend areas that have a good wind resource and are stable over time, thereby improving energy production and profitability of the project [8]. The use of AI in the selection of the site goes beyond the process of data processing; this is because it can be used in adaptive and predictive modeling to consider the changing environmental conditions. In contrast to conventional approaches that are generally fixed in time, AI algorithms can be tailored to react to actual meteorological data to assist in predicting changes in wind patterns, seasonal changes, and even the effects of climate changes on wind patterns. This predictive capability is not only more accurate but also expresses less time on site assessment, an AI is capable of processing multiple datasets simultaneously and, as such,

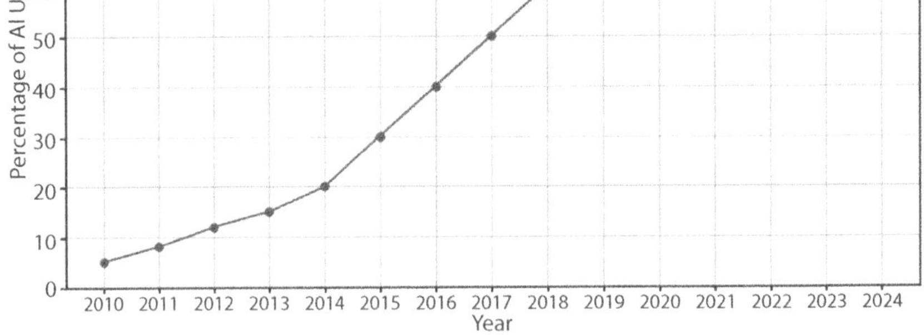

Figure 13.5 Illustrating the hypothetical percentage of AI usage in site selection from 2010 to 2024.

makes decisions faster without losing the depth of analysis. Figure 13.5 that demonstrates the hypothetical percentage of AI application in site selection between 2010 and 2024. The statistics indicate that the use of AI technologies has gradually grown over the years and is approaching 95% by 2024.

Additionally, AI improves the degree of objectivity, reducing the subjectivity that may affect the traditional site selection. Algorithms run on information, minimizing the chances of individual bias and allowing people to be more objective when assessing prospective locations. Moreover, AI is capable of merging social and ecological information, including the population density and the biodiversity indexes, so more comprehensive evaluation is possible, and it observes both environmental and social inputs. Such a holistic approach can be used to preemptively solve local issues and make communities more accepting of them, and less prone to regulatory delays and resistance [9]. There is also cost saving in AI through automation of data collection and analysis. The conventional approaches, involving field research, environmental studies and consultation of stakeholders are costly and time-consuming. On the contrary, AI-powered tools are capable of doing all these tasks faster and more economically, without adding too much overhead to the final price, and from that, no worse and sometimes better insights can be obtained. Overall, AI will turn the inherently time-consuming, resource-intensive approach of wind energy site selection into a simplified data-driven workflow, which considerates economic, environmental, and social factors in the most optimal way [10].

13.2 Key AI Techniques in Wind Turbine Site Selection

This section investigates various AI techniques and algorithms that are used in the selection of wind turbine site with a special focus on strengths and unique applications.

13.2.1 Machine Learning Models for Predictive Analysis

The predictive analysis is involved in machine learning models.

Machine learning algorithms have been crucial in the forecasting of wind patterns, energy output, and the sites that are suitable in wind energy development. Both controlled and uncontrolled methods of learning are important factors in the creation of predictive models that are based on past weather conditions, site attributes, and turbine performance indicators [11]. Decision trees and random forests are examples of supervised learning methods that are used to categorize data points and forecast results using labeled input data.

Figure 13.6 visually represents the relative contributions of various machine learning algorithms used in the site selection process for wind energy projects. Each segment illustrates the percentage of influence that different algorithms have, showcasing their effectiveness in assessing site suitability based on factors like historical weather data, geographical characteristics, and turbine performance metrics.

- **Decision Trees (15%)**: Offer a straightforward and interpretable approach for initial assessments, aiding in understanding data relationships.
- **Random Forests (25%)**: Provide enhanced accuracy by aggregating multiple decision trees, making them valuable for complex datasets.
- **Support Vector Machines (20%)**: Effective for both regression and classification tasks, they excel in predicting wind patterns based on environmental conditions.
- **Neural Networks (20%)**: Adapt well to complex, nonlinear data, allowing for precise predictions of energy yields across different locations.
- **Clustering Algorithms (10%)**: Help categorize potential sites based on similar characteristics, streamlining the analysis process.

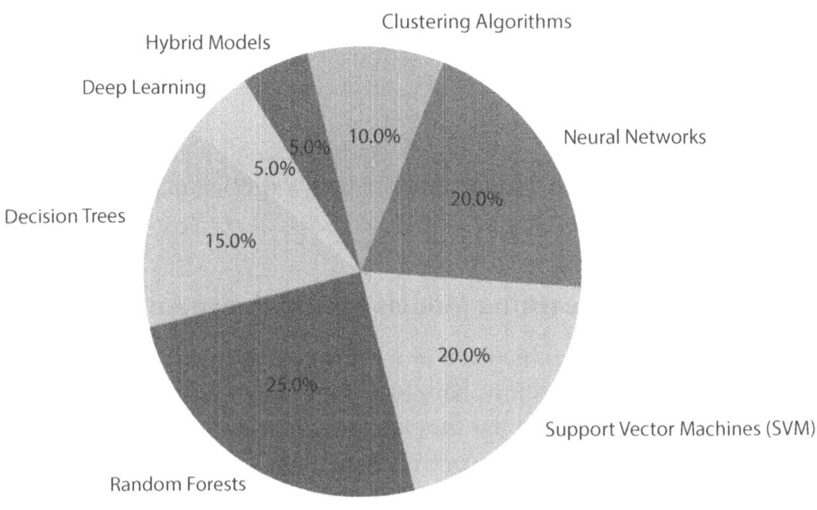

Figure 13.6 Contribution of machine learning algorithms to wind energy site selection.

- **Hybrid Models (5%)**: Combine the strengths of both supervised and unsupervised techniques for improved predictions.
- **Deep Learning (5%)**: Leverage complex neural architectures for advanced pattern recognition in wind data.

Decision trees work by splitting data into branches based on feature conditions, offering a transparent model structure that's well-suited for initial site assessment and understanding basic data relationships. Random forests expand on this by combining multiple decision trees to improve prediction accuracy and reduce overfitting, making them valuable for complex datasets where the relationships among variables (e.g., wind speed, altitude, and temperature) influence site potential. Support Vector Machines (SVMs), another supervised method, are highly effective for regression and classification tasks, providing robust performance for linearly and non-linearly separable data and offering a refined model for predicting wind patterns based on various environmental conditions [12]. Neural networks, known for their adaptability to complex, nonlinear data, are highly effective in uncovering hidden patterns in wind data, allowing them to make precise predictions about energy yields across diverse locations. Unsupervised learning techniques, such as clustering algorithms, can help categorize sites based on similar characteristics, aiding in the initial stages of site selection where broader categorization can streamline analysis [13].

13.2.2 Geographic Information Systems (GIS) and Data Layering

In combination with AI, Geographic Information Systems (GIS) can enable researchers to conduct sophisticated spatial analysis, which is done by overlaying geospatial information with weather, topographical, and environmental data in order to select the site in a multi-dimensional way. By combining layers of data, including wind speed distribution, elevation, land use, and distance to grid infrastructure, as well as the areas of protected environment, one can evaluate the wind power of a site and at the same time, evaluate ecological and social impacts [14]. Through machine learning algorithms with the help of GIS data, site selection models will be able to give a recommendation under the conditions of real-world constraints because of which regulatory guidelines and geographic features can be listed. GIS also assist in spatial clustering and heat mapping which are useful in visualizing the areas with high potential and making easy comparisons at potential locations in the area, thus enabling one to easily identify the best turbine location in a given area. GIS is also able to perform seasonal analysis through spatial analysis and especially when used in conjunction with time series data, which allows predictive modeling to take into consideration the changes in wind speed and direction over the course of the year [15].

13.2.3 Optimization Algorithms for Site Selection

The optimization algorithms play a vital role in the process of identifying the optimal locations of wind turbines in a chosen location with the help of various criteria, including the speed of the wind, spacing, and topography, to ensure the highest energy output and efficiency. Genetic algorithms (GAs) reflecting the natural selection process are also extremely successful in solving complicated, multi-objective optimization problems during the site selection [16]. GAs operate by repeatedly advancing turbine configurations which give optimum energy-cost balance, and this makes them well adapted to the challenging terrain and offshore sites. Another method based on social causes is Particle Swarm Optimization (PSO), which involves the use of particles to find the solution, and the particles navigate the search space depending on their own and other particles experience [17]. PSO is beneficial for finding the optimal layout of turbines by balancing objectives like wake loss reduction and land usage efficiency. Ant Colony Optimization (ACO), based on the foraging behavior of ants, is also applied in site selection as it iteratively explores paths (possible site configurations) and converges toward optimal solutions. These algorithms are particularly advantageous because they support multi-objective optimization, allowing developers to weigh various factors—such as environmental impact, cost, and energy output—simultaneously in their decision-making processes [18].

13.2.4 Hybrid Models and Ensemble Approaches

Ensemble models and hybrid models are the combination of several AI methods to achieve a better performance of prediction and robustness especially in diverse and highly challenging environments where single-model prediction is limited. Neural networks can be used as part of a hybrid, such as, enabling the model to make use of both the pattern recognition capabilities of the neural networks as well as the strength of the classification capabilities of SVMs [19]. These combinations are useful in a situation where there is a lot of variation in the data such as coastal or mountainous areas where there might be a change in the winds depending on the terrain and season. Ensemble techniques, including bagging, boosting, and stacking, enhance the performance of a model by combining the predictions of two or more models thus minimizing errors and increasing generalizability [20]. As an example, increasing algorithms such as AdaBoost and Gradient Boosting are used to improve weak models through iterations by paying attention to hard-to-predict examples, eventually increasing the general accuracy of prediction. Ensemble models are beneficial in the context of the wind energy site selection as they combine various data sources and consider varying conditions that generate stronger and more credible recommendations in various geographic regions [21]. Hybrid models also facilitate adaptive learning, which allows models to keep on improving with the availability of new data and hence provides a dynamic method of assessing the site which can adapt itself to changing aspects of the environment, enhancing the efficiency and reliability of wind energy projects planning.

13.3 Data Sources and Processing for AI-Driven Site Selection

Artificial intelligence-based site selection in wind energy development is based on a variety of omnivorous data, including meteorological, socio-economic, and other indicators. In this section, the key data sources and preprocessing steps to be used to prepare these datasets to obtain accurate and effective machine learning models are explained.

13.3.1 Key Data Sources

Wind site selection needs a collection of sources of data, whose information is vital in making precise forecasts on the potential of wind energy as well as site feasibility. Historical weather data is more of a background as it provides information on wind speed, direction, temperature, and seasonal trends [22]. Such information is usually obtained through such sources as weather agencies, satellite imagery, and ground based weather stations and usually recorded over extended periods of time to take into consideration climate changes. Topographical data is also critical, as it gives the data on the elevation, slopes and topography features that affect wind movement and turbine functioning. This is usually done using high-resolution topographic maps and digital elevation models (DEMs) which in most cases are found in geographic information systems (GIS) and remote sensing platforms [23]. The metrics of environmental impacts are also essential as they assist to evaluate the possible ecological impact such as the effects on the local wildlife, flora, and natural ecosystems. Such measures can be obtained through the environmental protection agencies, ecological surveys, and conservation databases. Lastly, socio-economic data, including population density, land use, and proximity to infrastructure, such as roads and power grids is used to provide a larger picture in terms of site selection ensuring that the newly placed wind projects are well aligned to the community needs and logistical factors [24]. The combination of these datasets will help in having a comprehensive site selection strategy where the energy potential is evaluated against the environmental and social aspects.

13.3.2 Data Cleaning and Preprocessing Techniques

Preprocessing of data is essential to make AI-driven models reliable and of decent quality because raw data is usually incomplete, inconsistent, or noisy. Data cleaning solves these problems by treating missing data (that are prevalent in meteorological and environmental data) that can be imputed by mean, median, or k-nearest neighbors (KNN) imputation. The outliers, which are unusual values that may distort predictions in the model, are detected with the use of statistical means or clustering and may be corrected or eliminated so that the model could be stable [25]. Reduction of noises is also of concern, particularly in sensor and satellite data, where even small irregular fluctuations can have impacts on predictive accuracy. The removal of noise is frequently done by techniques such as smoothing, filtering, and principal component analysis (PCA) without altering important data patterns. Standardization and normalization are also important processes, whereby data is converted to a common scale, so that when a feature of one measure (e.g., wind speed in meters per second) is present the other feature (e.g., elevation in meters) can be compared in the model. With such preprocessing methods, data is organized, cleaned, and prepared to be fed to machine learning and increases the performance of the model and makes valid predictions during site selection [26].

13.3.3 Feature Engineering for Wind Site Selection

The feature engineering is an essential step in site selection using AI because it assists to select and emphasize the most important features that contribute to forecasting the potential of wind energy. Among the most crucial features are wind speed and wind direction which directly affect the energy that can be emitted by a site [27]. These characteristics are generally based on the past weather records and calculated in a way to reflect seasonal and diurnal variations which influence the consistency and intensity of wind. Another topography factor affecting the movement of the wind is the altitude and slope as onshore and offshore wind farms are affected by their elevations and the shape of the terrain which can increase or decrease the speed of the wind. Close access to infrastructure like roads, grid connection and maintenance facilities are also a major characteristic as they influence the logistical viability and cost of developing the site. Measures of distances to infrastructure are frequently calculated with the help of GIS-based measurements and network analysis in order to make sure that the locations chosen comply with logistical and financial limits [28]. Socio-economic factors such as land use and population density can give information about suitability of the site to the local communities, and developers can avoid locations with a high population density or those with sensitive land use. Moreover, such environmental sensitivity characteristics as closeness to protected lands or wild space are essential to reducing environmental impact. The feature selection methods, such as recursive feature elimination (RFE) or feature importance rankings, are used to rank these variables giving the model an opportunity to concentrate on features that carry the most predictive power [29]. With these features well-engineered, AI models can offer more accurate, reliable and contextually sensitive recommendations in the selection of wind turbine sites which can eventually facilitate sustainable and efficient development of wind energy.

13.4 Applications and Case Studies

Here, the paper will discuss the practical use of AI with reference to wind turbine site selection, which will help to understand the effective application of the technology and the techniques used in various geographical areas. The case studies present the customization of various AI solutions, including machine learning models, optimization algorithms and hybrid systems, to the specific needs of the project, and consequently increasing the accuracy, effectiveness, and sustainability of wind energy projects.

13.4.1 Case Study 1: Offshore Wind Farm Selection in Northern Europe

Offshore wind farms in the North Sea region, especially in Northern Europe, have become a fundamental part of renewable energy policies [30]. In this case study, Geographic Information Systems (GIS) and machine learning models are applied to find the appropriate offshore locations with consideration of the complicated environmental and logistical factors. To select the site, GIS mapping layers with high-resolution improve wind patterns, seabed structure, depth of the water and marine traffic routes and combine machine learning models that forecast the long-term wind energy output. Environmental limitations like closeness to conserved marine environments are also scrutinized well to guarantee that the conservation laws are met. This multi-layered geospatial data is fed through machine learning algorithms, which are mainly random forests and neural networks, to classify regions based on wind potential and environmental compatibility to give predictive maps of high-potential regions. This will reduce the expenses involved in site evaluation and simplify the decision making process so that the offshore areas where wind power can be tapped most effectively and without causing much ecological disturbance can be identified. The example of the Northern European offshore wind industry industrial proves the effectiveness of AI-based GIS analysis in reconciliation of high-energy output and environmental sustainability and is an example that can be replicated in other coastal areas worldwide [31].

13.4.2 Case Study 2: AI-Powered Site Selection in Coastal India

The fast increasing demand of renewable energy in India has given a lot of interest in the coastal wind farms especially in the state of Gujarat and Tamil Nadu. The case study is an exploration of how the field of AI (in the form of neural networks and optimization algorithms) can be used to determine the suitability of sites along the coastline of India. The usage of neural networks is aimed at predicting the wind patterns and seasonal variability in wind speeds basing on the historical weather data and including oceanic and atmospheric conditions [32]. Besides climatic information, optimization algorithms, including particle swarm optimization (PSO) and genetic algorithms, also consider various criteria, such as infrastructure accessibility, grid connection, and socio-economic effects on the local population. The socio-economic factors are important since India has a large population density at the coastal areas, and the AI models would include information on the nearby settlements, fishing grounds, and already existing economic activities to make sure that the chosen site would not interfere with the local livelihoods. In addition, AI-based models offer comprehensive evaluations of grid accessibility, which are crucial in incorporating new wind energy generation in the power supply system in India in a highly efficient way [33]. The use of AI in this respect has been very fruitful and has offered optimized site selection that is able to balance between high-energy production and social and logistical viability, which has demonstrated a precedent of responsible wind energy development in populated coastal areas.

13.4.3 Case Study 3: Hybrid Model for Wind Farm Development in the United States

In the U.S., the renewable energy policy has moved towards wind energy to a great extent with a focus on establishing onshore and offshore wind farms in various states. The case study presents the implementation of a hybrid type of AI, which consists of decision trees and genetic algorithms that optimize the placement of wind turbines, in the context of the states with a large potential of wind energy (Texas, Iowa, Oklahoma). The hybrid model starts with decision trees to filter the regions according to such aspects as the speed of wind, availability of land, and regulatory restrictions to produce an initial shortlist of possible locations [34]. Genetic algorithms are then applied to optimize the layouts of turbines once sites have been located, through a series of modifications in the locations of turbines to maximize energy production, taking into account inter-turbine spacing to minimize the effects of wakes as well as land-use patterns to ensure that there are no undesirable environmental effects. This mixed strategy will make sure that the location of the site will provide energy output and at the same time consider the environmental and financial considerations to minimize the project costs and enhance the ROI to the stakeholders. Furthermore, the model includes policy incentives and regulatory constraints on a state level, which enables developers to align the location of a site with state and federal policies that encourage the use of renewable energy [35]. The achievement of this hybrid model in the US demonstrates how AI can be adapted to the intricate, multi-criteria decision-making in wind farm development and how AI can facilitate large-scale renewable energy ambitions by developing tailored decision-making to a wide range of regulatory and environmental environments.

These case studies are examples of AI transforming the site selection of wind turbines to offer very personalized, data-driven information, which improves the decision-making process. When AI is incorporated into wind energy developments in various localities, developers have the opportunity to both optimize the site selection process to achieve different objectives, such as energy production, reduction of environmental effects, or social responsibility. Such a customized use of AI evidences the flexibility of machine learning, GIS, and hybrid models in the struggle against local obstacles that would eventually aid in a sustainable and effective global switch to renewable energy [36].

13.5 Challenges and Limitations in AI-Driven Site Selection

Although AI is a revolutionary opportunity in the process of picking wind turbine sites, multiple major challenges and constraints should be overcome to make the process successful. In this section, the author discusses the challenges associated with the availability of data, the generalizability of the model, and the ethical aspects of AI-driven solutions that can inhibit the performance and adoption of the technology in this field.

13.5.1 Data Limitations and Quality Issues

The main problem in the AI-based site selection is the accessibility of the correct, high-resolution data that may be useful to predictive models. Although huge volumes of data exist, differences in quality, granularity, and scope may affect the reliability of AI models to a considerable extent. As an example, weather history can be discontinuous, as not every place has a complete meteorological history, and thus there can be gaps in the knowledge of local winds. This is complicated in offshore settings by the inability to gather data because of unfriendly marine conditions. Also, discrepancies in various sources of data may occur and it may be challenging to combine and standardize datasets in order to be used in the model. Quality of data may be compromised with impact on predictions of the model, and eventually result in poor site selection due to errors or bias in the historical material [37]. To overcome these limitations in data, it is essential to have strong data collection techniques, such as collaboration with meteorological agencies, application of remote sensing tools, and application of strict data validation measures. Unless there is an all-encompassing attempt to conquer these issues, the success of AI in site selection may be compromised because it might end up making erroneous decisions that would negatively impact on the viability and performance of the project [38–41].

13.6 Future Directions and Innovations in AI for Wind Site Selection

The use of artificial intelligence (AI) in wind turbine site selection is evolving along with the renewable energy industry. In order to improve AI applications in this crucial field, this final section looks at new technology and possible research avenues. The industry can greatly increase the effectiveness and sustainability of wind energy projects by utilizing cutting-edge AI techniques, incorporating real-time data, and addressing policy issues.

13.6.1 Advanced AI Techniques for Improved Prediction

Future developments in AI methods should greatly improve site selection procedures. Deep learning, a branch of machine learning that uses multi-layered neural networks, may find intricate patterns in big datasets that conventional models would miss. More precise forecasts of wind patterns and energy production may result from this skill, especially in complex geographic environments. Furthermore, the flexibility of site selection models may be improved via reinforcement learning, in which algorithms discover the best tactics via trial and error. This method would enable AI systems to dynamically modify recommendations in response to shifting environmental conditions, such as changes in wind patterns brought on by climate change.

13.6.2 Integration of Real-Time Data for Dynamic Site Assessment

Another significant advancement in the realm of wind turbine site selection is the use of real-time data. The development of Internet of Things (IoT) sensors and satellite observations makes it possible to continuously monitor environmental conditions, yielding important data that might improve the site evaluation procedure. By providing current wind speed, direction, and temperature data, real-time data can increase the accuracy of predictive models and enable developers to make well-informed decisions based on the most recent information. Optimal spots that could have gone unnoticed in static assessments could be found with the aid of this dynamic technique, ultimately leading to more effective site selection outcomes.

Conclusion

This chapter has described how AI is revolutionizing wind turbine site selection by providing quicker, more precise, and more cost-effective solutions than conventional techniques. AI methods including machine learning, GIS integration, and optimization algorithms have been successful in locating high-potential locations, greatly boosting wind energy production and facilitating the transition to a sustainable energy future. AI-driven site selection is a critical facilitator for the advancement of the renewable energy industry by lowering operating costs, minimizing environmental impacts, and optimizing energy output.

AI disclosure statement: The author acknowledges the use of AI-based tools for minor language editing or grammatical correction. However, all intellectual contributions, analyses, and conclusions presented in this chapter are entirely the author's own.

References

1. Balsalobre Lorente, D., Joof, F., Samour, A., Türsoy, T., Renewable energy, economic complexity, and biodiversity risk: New insights from China. *Environ. Sustain. Indic.*, 18, March, 100244, 2023, doi: 10.1016/j.indic.2023.100244.
2. Haq, I.U., Rather, A.H., Kaur, G., A Comparative Analysis of Machine Learning Algorithms for the Early Prediction of Cardiovascular Disease, in: *2023 2nd International Conference on Edge Computing and Applications (ICECAA)*, IEEE, pp. 987–993, 2023, July.
3. Feng, Y., Xiao, Z., Zhou, J., Ni, G., Asymmetrically examining the impact of green finance and renewable energy consumption on environmental degradation and renewable energy investment: The impact of the COVID-19 outbreak on the Chinese economy. *Energy Rep.*, 9, 5458–5472, 2023, doi: 10.1016/j.egyr.2023.04.361.
4. Haq, I.U., Hassan, I.U., Shah, H.A., Machine Learning Techniques for Result Prediction of One Day International (ODI) Cricket Match, in: *2023 IEEE 8th International Conference for Convergence in Technology (I2CT)*, IEEE, pp. 1–5, 2023, April.
5. Hou, H., Wang, Z., Hou, T., Fang, R., Tang, J., Xie, C., Optimal schedule of 100% renewable energy microgrid considering demand response of EVs. *Energy Rep.*, 9, 1743–1750, 2023, doi: 10.1016/j.egyr.2023.04.223.

6. An, Y.S., *et al.*, Retrofit of renewable energy systems in the existing community for positive energy community. *Energy Rep.*, 9, 3733–3744, 2023, doi: 10.1016/j.egyr.2023.02.055.
7. Chaurasia, A. and Haa, I.U., Housing price prediction model using machine learning, in: *2023 International Conference on Sustainable Emerging Innovations in Engineering and Technology (ICSEIET)*, IEEE, pp. 497–500, 2023, September.
8. Dai, W., *et al.*, Flexibility-enhanced strategies of generations to improve the integration of renewable energy considering uncertainties. *Energy Rep.*, 9, 1717–1725, 2023, doi: 10.1016/j.egyr.2023.04.204.
9. Yolcan, O.O., Innovation and Green Development World energy outlook and state of renewable energy : 10-Year evaluation. *Innov. Green Dev.*, 2, 4, 100070, 2023, doi: 10.1016/j.igd.2023.100070.
10. Choudhary, C., Thakur, J., Bhardwaj, H., Haq, I.U., Rather, A.H., Revolutionizing Wind Energy: A Enhanced Machine Learning Perspective on Wind Turbines Fault Prediction, in: *2023 2nd International Conference on Automation, Computing and Renewable Systems (ICACRS)*, IEEE, pp. 1763–1769, 2023, December.
11. Gao, Q., Yuan, R., Ertugrul, N., Ding, B., Hayward, J.A., Li, Y., Analysis of energy variability and costs for offshore wind and hybrid power unit with equivalent energy storage system. *Appl. Energy*, 342, May 2023, doi 10.1016/j.apenergy.2023.121192.
12. Cavaiola, M., Enos, P., Ferrari, F., Casciaro, G., Mazzino, A., Energy and AI Ensemble Machine Learning greatly improves ERA5 skills for wind energy applications. *Energy AI*, May 2023, 100269, doi: 10.1016/j.egyai.2023.100269.
13. Albraheem, L. and Alawlaqi, L., Geospatial analysis of wind energy plant in Saudi Arabia using a GIS-AHP technique. *Energy Rep.*, 9, 5878–5898, 2023, doi: 10.1016/j.egyr.2023.05.032.
14. Spielhofer, R., Schwaab, J., Grêt-Regamey, A., How spatial policies can leverage energy transitions – Finding Pareto-optimal solutions for wind turbine locations with evolutionary multi-objective optimization. *Environ. Sci. Policy*, 142, January, 220–232, 2023, doi: 10.1016/j.envsci.2023.02.016.
15. Fournier, A., Martinez, A., Iglesias, G., Impacts of climate change on wind energy potential in Australasia and South-East Asia following the Shared Socioeconomic Pathways. *Sci. Total Environ.*, 882, January, 163347, 2023, doi 10.1016/j.scitotenv.2023.163347.
16. Vallejo Díaz, A., Herrera Moya, I., Pereyra Mariñez, C., Garabitos Lara, E., Casilla Victorino, C., Key factors influencing urban wind energy: A case study from the Dominican Republic. *Energy Sustain. Dev.*, 73, December 2022, 165–173, 2023, doi 10.1016/j.esd.2023.01.017.
17. Ulazia, A., Sáenz, J., Saenz-Aguirre, A., Ibarra-Berastegui, G., Carreno-Madinabeitia, S., Paradigmatic case of long-term colocated wind–wave energy index trend in the Canary Islands. *Energy Convers. Manag.*, 283, March, 116890, 2023, doi: 10.1016/j.enconman.2023.116890.

18. Dugstad, A., Grimsrud, K., Kipperberg, G., Lindhjem, H., Navrud, S., Energy Research & Social Science Place attachment and preferences for wind energy – A value-based approach. *Energy Res. Soc. Sci.*, 100, May, 103094, 2023, doi 10.1016/j.erss.2023.103094.
19. Karakislak, I. and Schneider, N., The mayor said so? The impact of local political figures and social norms on local responses to wind energy projects. *Energy Policy*, 176, January, 113509, 2023, doi: 10.1016/j.enpol.2023.113509.
20. Lunevich, I. and Kloppenburg, S., Wind energy meets buildings? Generating socio-technical change in the urban built environment through vanguard visions. *Energy Res. Soc. Sci.*, 98, July 2022, 103017, 2023, doi: 10.1016/j.erss.2023.103017.
21. Rangel-Martinez, D., Nigam, K.D.P., Ricardez-Sandoval, L.A., Machine learning on sustainable energy: A review and outlook on renewable energy systems, catalysis, smart grid and energy storage. *Chem. Eng. Res. Des.*, 174, 414–441, 2021, doi: 10.1016/j.cherd.2021.08.013.
22. Fister, D., Pérez-Aracil, J., Peláez-Rodríguez, C., Del Ser, J., Salcedo-Sanz, S., Accurate long-term air temperature prediction with Machine Learning models and data reduction techniques. *Appl. Soft Comput.*, 136, 110118, 2023, doi: 10.1016/j.asoc.2023.110118.
23. Wang, H., Li, Y., Xiong, M., Chen, H., A combined wind speed prediction model based on data processing, multi-objective optimization and machine learning. *Energy Rep.*, 9, 413–421, 2023, doi: 10.1016/j.egyr.2023.04.326.
24. Sun, H. and Grishman, R., Lexicalized dependency paths based supervised learning for relation extraction. *Comput. Syst. Sci. Eng.*, 43, 3, 861–870, 2022.
25. Deng, Y., Jia, H., Li, P., Tong, X., Qiu, X., *et al.*, A deep learning methodology based on bidirectional gated recurrent unit for wind power prediction, in: *2019 14th IEEE Conf. on Industrial Electronics and Applications (ICIEA)*, Xi'an, China, pp. 591–595, 2019.
26. Yildiz, C., Acikgoz, H., Korkmaz, D., Budak, U., An improved residual-based convolutional neural network for very short-term wind power forecasting. *Energy Convers. Manage.*, 228, 113731, 1–15, 2021.
27. Sun, Z. and Zhao, M., Short-term wind power forecasting based on VMD decomposition, ConvLSTM networks and error analysis. *IEEE Access*, 8, 134422–134434, 2020.
28. Li, L.-L., Zhao, X., Tseng, M.-L., Tan, R.R., Short-term wind power forecasting based on support vector machine with improved dragonfly algorithm. *J. Clean. Prod.*, 242, 118447, 1–12, 2020.
29. Yin, H., Ou, Z., Fu, J., Cai, Y., Chen, S. *et al.*, A novel transfer learning approach for wind power prediction based on a serio-parallel deep learning architecture. *Energy*, 234, 121271, 1–16, 2021.
30. Buturache, A.-N. and Stancu, S., Wind energy prediction using machine learning. *Low Carbon Econ.*, 12, 1, 1–21, 2021.

31. Wu, Q., Guan, F., Lv, C., Huang, Y., Ultra-short-term multi-step wind power forecasting based on CNNLSTM. *IET Renewable Power Gener.*, 15, 5, 1019–1029, 2021.
32. Li, N., He, F., Ma, W., Wind power prediction based on extreme learning machine with kernel mean P-power error loss. *Energies*, 12, 673, 1–19, 2019.
33. Chen, G., Li, L., Zhang, Z., Li, S., Short-term wind speed forecasting with principle-subordinate predictor based on Conv-LSTM and improved BPNN. *IEEE Access*, 8, 67955–67973, 2020.
34. Hong, Y., -Y. and Rioflorido, C.L.P.P., A hybrid deep learning-based neural network for 24-h ahead wind power forecasting. *Appl. Energy*, 250, 530–539, 2019.
35. Rather, A.H. and Haq, I.U., Intelligent Framework for Early Prediction of Diabetic Retinopathy: A Deep Learning Approach, in: *International Conference on Paradigms of Communication, Computing and Data Analytics*, Springer Nature Singapore, Singapore, pp. 377–388, 2023, April.
36. Ul Haq, I., Diagnosis of Neurological Disease Using Bioinspired Algorithms, in: *Bio-Inspired Optimization for Medical Data Mining*, pp. 227–268, 2024.
37. Haq, I.U., Kaur, G., Rather, A.H., Fruit Leaf Classification Using Transfer Learning for Automation and Industrial Applications, in: *Deep Learning Techniques for Automation and Industrial Applications*, pp. 151–178, 2024.
38. Choudhary, C., Haq, I.U., Rather, A.H., Utilizing Dynamic QR Codes to Enhance Secure Payment Transactions: An Approach to Secure Computer based Transactions, in: *2023 International Conference on Communication, Security and Artificial Intelligence (ICCSAI), IEEE,* pp. 552–557, 2023, November.
39. Garla, N., Haq, I.U., Dhiman, H., Revolutionizing Biomedical Engineering With Quantum Computing and AI, in: *Quantum Innovations at the Nexus of Biomedical Intelligence*, pp. 206–222, IGI Global Scientific Publishing, 2024.
40. Asadi, M., Pourhossein, K., Mohammadi-Ivatloo, B., GIS-assisted modeling of wind farm site selection based on support vector regression. *J. Cleaner Prod.* https://doi.org/10.1016/j.jclepro.2023.135993.
41. Shaheen, M. and Zeb Khan, M., A method of data mining for selection of site for wind turbines. *Renewable Sustainable Energy Rev.*, 55, 1225–1233, 2019, ISSN 1364-0321, https://doi.org/10.1016/j.rser.2019.04.019.

14

AI-Driven Innovations in Solar Energy Systems and Climate Change Mitigation

Gandla Shivakanth[1]*, Ramakrishna Akella[2], V. Biksham[3], Alampally Sreedevi[4] and Shiva Kumar Agraharam[5]

[1]*Department of Computer Science and Engineering, Koneru Lakshmaiah Education Foundation, Aziznagar, Hyderabad, Telangana, India*
[2]*Department of Electronics and Communication Engineering, Koneru Lakshmaiah Education Foundation, Aziznagar, Hyderabad, Telangana, India*
[3]*School of Engineering, Dept. of Data Science, Anurag University, Ghatkesar, Hyderabad, India*
[4]*Computer Science and Engineering, Koneru Lakshmaiah Education Foundation, Aziznagar, Hyderabad, Telangana, India*
[5]*AIML Department, Mallareddy University, Hyderabad, India*

Abstract

This research paper highlights the growing role of Artificial Intelligence (AI) in solar energy systems and climate change mitigation. Solar energy has become the fastest-growing renewable source today, but it faces significant operational challenges such as intermittency, dust accumulation, equipment degradation, storage optimization, and grid integration. AI-based models—such as LSTM, CNN, Random Forest, and computer-vision techniques—enable highly efficient solar power forecasting, smart panel tracking, predictive maintenance, dust detection, battery management, and smart grid optimization. Similarly, in climate change management, AI provides accurate and real-time insights into rainfall prediction, cyclone tracking, pollution monitoring, carbon emission analysis, and disaster forecasting. Real-world cases like India's National Solar Mission, NTPC solar farms, Rajasthan desert solar parks, and Google's climate prediction systems demonstrate that AI is significantly improving energy output, reliability, and sustainability. Overall, AI makes solar energy smarter, reliable, and cost-efficient, and provides a data-driven and predictive framework for climate change mitigation.

**Corresponding author*: shvkanth0@gmail.com

Abhishek Kumar, Pramod Singh Rathore, Arun Lal Srivastav and Ashutosh Kumar Dubey (eds.) Solar Energy Optimization Using Generative Artificial Intelligence, (329–346) © 2026 Scrivener Publishing LLC

This integration is a strong step toward fully autonomous solar plants and intelligent climate governance in the future.

***Keywords*:** LSTM, solar energy, random forest

14.1 Introduction

Selecting a manufacturing process usually depends on the type of work and the volume of production. There are five main process types: job shop, batch, repetitive, continuous, and project. Notably, there are many factors to consider when choosing a process, as each type has its advantages and disadvantages [1]. This paper aims to describe the five basic process types by comparing and contrasting them using examples. Historically, people first mastered the processes of job shops and batches, while repetitive and continuous processes appeared only after the Industrial Revolution. Job shops involve the production of a variety of products in small quantities. This process requires great flexibility of equipment and high-skilled personnel, allowing a wide variety of work. Still, the drawbacks of this type include high cost per unit and complex scheduling.

An example of a job shop is a jewelry repair shop or a veterinary service. Batches are used for medium production and moderate product variety. A good example is bakeries or services for groups of people, like air travel. This type's advantage is a high level of flexibility, and the disadvantages are moderate cost per unit and scheduling complexity. Examples of repetitive process-type products are production lines for cars, TVs, and pencils. The advantage of this type is that it allows large volumes, but the disadvantages are the high cost of equipment downtime and low flexibility [2].

The continuous process involves the production of the highest volumes, rigid equipment, and low-skilled personnel. Examples of a continuous process type are sugar, flour, gasoline, steel production, and supplying electricity or the Internet. This type's disadvantages are its rigidity and low variety; its advantages are high volumes and efficiency. Project process type is usually chosen in project work cases, for example, when filming a movie, publishing a book, or building a dam. Project type can have characteristics of all types because of the variety of projects [3, 4]. Thus, the five basic process types and the advantages and disadvantages of each were described by comparing and contrasting them using examples. Job shops are often used when there is a need to produce small volumes of unique products; batches are used in medium volumes and work variety [5]. Repetitive and continuous types

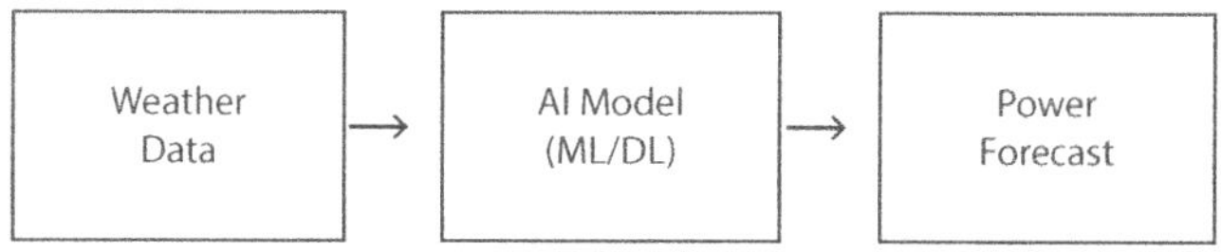

Figure 14.1 AI-driven solar power forecasting.

emerged after the Industrial Revolution and now represent high-volume production types for the mass consumer, as shown in Figure 14.1.

14.2 Solar Energy: Current Scenario and Challenges

Solar power is actually scalding the path as the fastest-paced renewable energy source in the world, and the motive is not more noticeable than in the sun-dipped tropics of India. The potential of clean and noiseless solar energy is a strong match-maker now that the population of the country has outgrown 1.4 billion people, and the rural areas have not yet achieved reliability in accessing grid power [6, 7]. In addition to the apparent environmental benefits, such as the absence of toxic emissions, the low level of noise pollution, and negligible land use, the solar systems in India are turning into a viable long-term economic savings measure. The reduced initial expense under power purchase agreements and government incentives and the current developments in battery storage are all ironing out the intermittent quality of sunlight, and solar is becoming a steady lifeline to villages long used to living in the dark, facing the specter of energy scarcity. In brief, solar is not merely a clean-fuel choice; it is a disruptive technology that can drive the hearts of the rural population in India, move the economy of the local population, and assist the country in achieving its lofty climate goals.

14.2.1 Major Challenges of Solar Energy

However, some operational and technical challenges also exist:

i. Intermittency Problem
   Cloud cover, atmospheric dust, humidity, and weather volatility make solar output inconsistent.
ii. Dust Accumulation (Soiling)
   Dust and pollutants accumulate on the surface of panels, reducing their efficiency by 15–40%.

iii. Equipment degradation
PV modules degrade over time, causing output to decline.
iv. Fault detection issues
Manual inspection is time-consuming, costly, and inaccurate.
v. Energy storage optimization
Storing solar power is difficult if battery management is not smart.
vi. Grid integration challenges
Synchronizing solar systems with conventional grids is a complex task.
vii. Lack of predictive maintenance
Traditional systems are repaired only after a breakdown.

All these problems impact the reliability of solar energy. Therefore, the role of AI is becoming very significant.

14.3 Artificial Intelligence: A Transformational Technology

AI is a combination of machine learning, neural networks, and data-driven predictive techniques that gives machines intelligent decision-making, pattern recognition, and autonomous operations [8, 9]. AI is proving to be a game-changer in both solar energy and climate change management. AI systems can analyze large datasets, identify underlying patterns, and provide optimized solutions. The Edge of AI:

- Speed
- Accuracy
- Real-time decision-making
- Predictive capabilities
- Automation
- Adaptive intelligence

These qualities make AI the perfect technology for the solar domain.

14.4 Role of AI in Solar Energy Conservation

AI makes solar energy systems intelligent, efficient, and predictive. In the sections below, we will explore the impact of AI on the solar ecosystem.

14.4.1 Solar Power Forecasting

Accurate solar power forecasting is crucial for solar farms. AI models such as:

- LSTM (long short-term memory networks)
- CNN (convolutional neural networks)
- Random forest
- Gradient boosting
- Time-series ML models

Can predict real-time power output by analyzing weather data, satellite images, solar irradiance values, humidity, and historical generation data.

Benefits

- Grid stability improves
- Energy wastage reduces
- Storage systems are optimized
- Price prediction improves

14.4.2 Smart Solar Panel Orientation and Sun Tracking

AI-based reinforcement learning algorithms dynamically adjust the tilt and orientation of solar panels to maximize sunlight capture [10].

AI-driven trackers can harvest 15–25% extra energy compared to traditional fixed panels.

14.4.3 Predictive Maintenance of Solar Plants

Manual maintenance is costly, slow, and risky. AI automates this task.

- AI-enabled predictive maintenance systems:
- Panel degradation prediction
- Inverter fault detection
- Cable damage analysis
- Thermal anomaly identification
- Dust deposition monitoring

High computer-vision algorithms and the use of drone-mounted cameras are transforming the preventive maintenance of solar farms. These systems are capable of detecting low-level anomalies by scanning the panels continuously using the air, which could consist of minute hot spots, micro-cracks, or even early burns in cells, which otherwise would not be revealed until the malfunction occurs. The AI is able to not only identify the problem but also pinpoint the exact location of the problem, enabling technicians to repair it with pinpoint precision. Since inspections are automated, can be conducted at any hour of the day, and do not need any manual labor on the ground, the process is significantly faster than traditional ground-based inspections. This, in practice, will imply the identification and correction of problems way before they affect performance, reduce downtime, reduce maintenance costs, and ensure that the power output is maintained.

14.4.4 Dust & Soiling Detection Using AI

AI-based computer vision tools provide an estimation of dust levels by analyzing images of the panel surface. This has resulted in:

- The cleaning schedule has been optimized
- Water usage is reducing (especially in desert regions)
- Efficiency has improved

The use of this technology is increasing rapidly in solar farms in India, the UAE, and Saudi Arabia.

14.4.5 Solar Energy Storage Optimization

- Energy storage is the backbone of solar systems. AI optimizes battery storage:
- Charging/discharging cycles
- Battery health prediction
- load balancing
- Peak demand forecasting

AI-based BMS (Battery Management Systems) increases life span and reduces operational costs.

14.4.6 Smart Grid Integration

AI helps integrate solar energy seamlessly into smart grids:

- Frequency regulation
- Demand-response management
- Power quality prediction
- Real-time load balancing

Smart grids are sustainable and self-adjusting thanks to AI.

14.5 Role of AI in Climate Change Management

Combating climate change is impossible without data-driven planning. AI is serving as a powerful analytical tool in climate science.

14.5.1 Climate Modeling and Prediction

Traditional climate models cannot handle huge amounts of data. AI solves this challenge.

- ML and DL models perform:
- Rainfall prediction
- Cyclone tracking
- Heatwave forecasting
- Drought estimation
- Ocean temperature analysis
- Air quality prediction

These predictions help in agriculture, disaster management, and policy planning.

14.5.2 Carbon Emission Monitoring with AI

AI-based sensors and satellite imaging:
CO_2, CH_4, NO_2 emissions are monitored

- Industrial pollution can be identified.
- Traffic-related pollution measures are in progress.
- AI has made emission control policies more practical and actionable.

14.5.3 Renewable Energy Planning and Optimization

AI helps in:

- Site selection for solar plants
- Environmental impact assessment
- Land-use analysis
- Climate-resilient infrastructure design

AI integrates datasets to provide the best location recommendations—based on solar radiation, land slope, cloud patterns, humidity, and local climate parameters.

14.5.4 Disaster Management and Prediction

Severe disasters are increasing due to climate change. AI helps them predict:

- Flood forecasting
- Cyclone intensity prediction
- Forest fire detection
- Heat wave alert systems
- Real-time alerts can save both people's lives and infrastructure.

14.5.5 Smart City and Sustainable Environment Management

AI-enabled systems support:

- Intelligent traffic management
- Smart waste management
- Smart buildings with solar energy integration
- Water conservation monitoring
- Urban climate modeling

All these elements can create climate-friendly cities.

14.6 Integration of AI and IoT for Solar & Climate Efficiency

AI × IoT (AIoT) is a powerful combination. Figure 14.2 shows the AIoT smart grid.

AIoT applications:

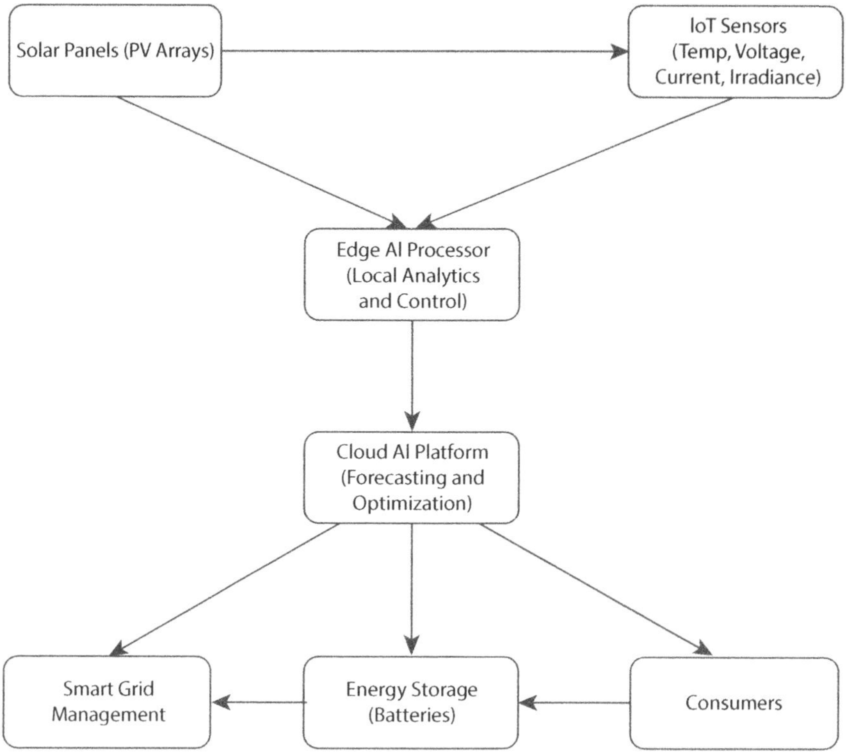

Figure 14.2 AIoT smart grid.

- Solar panel performance sensors
- Smart meters
- Weather stations
- Autonomous cleaning robots
- Distributed energy resource management
- AI in devices → real-time decision-making
- IoT → real-time data collection
- Together, they can make solar energy and climate systems fully automated.

14.7 Case Studies and Real-World Applications

The role of artificial intelligence (AI) is rapidly growing in solar energy optimization and climate change management. This is not limited to theoretical research; real-world projects, national programs, and multinational technologies are making AI the backbone of large-scale renewable development. Below, we will provide a detailed analysis of two major case studies: AI deployment under India's National Solar Mission and Google's AI-based global climate prediction system.

14.7.1 India's National Solar Mission and AI Integration

India's National Solar Mission (NSM) was launched in 2010, with the primary goal of accelerating renewable energy adoption and making the country a global leader in sustainable power generation. India aims to achieve 500 GW of renewable capacity by 2030, a major portion of which will be solar energy. However, the adoption of AI has become crucial to maximize the actual performance of solar plants. AI-based predictive analytics, fault detection, and performance forecasting have significantly improved the operational efficiency of Indian solar farms.

A. NTPC Solar Farms – Intelligent Monitoring and Predictive Maintenance
NTPC (National Thermal Power Corporation), India's leading energy producer, is now aggressively expanding renewable and solar-based energy production. NTPC has deployed AI-based systems across multiple solar farms. These systems perform:

Real-time monitoring
(analysis of voltage, current, irradiance, temperature, and power output)

Panel-level fault detection
AI models detect:

- Micro-cracks
- Hotspots
- Module degradation
- Inverter dropout

Predictive maintenance scheduling

- Traditional systems used to be a "repair after breakdown." AI allows:
- Prediction of failure before it happens
- Reduction in downtime

Up to 25–40% reduction in maintenance costs

NTPC's solar farms, especially projects in Madhya Pradesh and Andhra Pradesh, have recorded performance improvements of 20–30% after AI integration. This improvement is primarily due to accurate forecasting and reduced downtime.

B. Rajasthan Desert Solar Plants – AI for Dust & Soiling Detection
Rajasthan is India's largest solar hub. The world's largest solar parks exist in the Jaisalmer, Bhadla, and Jodhpur regions. A major issue in desert areas is dust accumulation, also known as soil loss. Dust can settle on the surface of panels and reduce their efficiency by up to 40%. AI-based computer vision and drone surveillance systems are being used here:

i. **AI-based Dust Level Detection**
   - Drones capture daily aerial images.
   - AI (CNN models) identify dust density on panel surfaces.
   - Suggests ideal cleaning times.

ii. **Water Optimization**
   - Water is very limited in Rajasthan's desert regions; unnecessary cleaning leads to waste. AI optimizes the cleaning schedule:
   - Only panels that actually require cleaning are cleaned.
   - Water usage is reduced by 40–50%.

Robotic Cleaning Automation
AI robots automatically:

- Navigate
- Clean
- Inspect

The digital revolution, known as AI-powered breakthroughs, is taking place in Indian megasolar parks.

C. Karnataka's Pavagada Mega Solar Park – AI for Solar Forecasting & Grid Stability
The use of artificial intelligence is reducing both the physical workforce and operational risk drastically in the biggest solar farms in India. The heart of AI-based monitoring and predictive maintenance at the grandiose Bhadla Solar Park is simplifying all stages of the project, including the layout of the panels up to the actual fault identification, which makes the park

not only more productive but also greener. The AIA serves as the backbone for green grid integration in Karnataka's Pavagada Mega Solar Park, the second-largest solar farm in Asia:

i. Solar irradiance forecasting
   AI-based LSTM (Long Short-Term Memory) and ARIMA models from weather data:
   - Next hour
   - Next day
   - Predict solar output for the next week

ii. Smart Grid Balancing
   Based on forecasting:
   - Load distributions are adjusted
   - Unnecessary power dumping is avoided
   - Grid frequency remains stable

iii. Performance Analytics Dashboard
   AI dashboards tell farm operators:
   - Which panels are showing low performance
   - Which location is impacting humidity/dust output
   - Which inverter is experiencing peak load issues

After AI adoption, the park achieved 25–30% more consistency, which is a massive improvement for such a huge plant.

D. Summary: India's Solar Efficiency Boosted by AI

One thing is clear from these teen examples (NTPC, Rajasthan, Pavagada)—AI has become a critical enabler of solar performance enhancement. Overall improvements achieved:

- 20–30% increase in energy output
- 40% reduction in water wastage
- 25–40% reduction in maintenance cost
- Faster fault detection (up to 10× faster)
- Better grid stability and forecasting accuracy

All these factors are accelerating the goals of India's National Solar Mission.

14.7.2 Google's AI for Climate Prediction

Accurate weather prediction, extreme event forecasting, and environmental monitoring are highly essential to combat climate change. Traditional climate models are very complex, slow, and computationally expensive. Google has developed AI-driven climate prediction systems to fill this gap. Google Research and Google DeepMind's work in climate modeling is very impactful globally.

A. AI Model for Rainfall Prediction (Nowcasting)
Google's "Nowcasting Model" is considered one of the world's most accurate rainfall prediction models.

Features:

- 0–2 hours rainfall forecast
- Extremely high spatial resolution
- Real-time satellite images + radar data as input
- Prediction accuracy 3–4× better than traditional models

AI rainfall prediction is of major help in agriculture, urban flood management, traffic control, and disaster response.

B. Flood Forecasting System
The collaboration between Google and the Indian government is a milestone project for India's flood-prone areas.

Google's Flood Forecasting AI:

- River level prediction
- Rainfall impact estimation
- Early warning alerts for districts
- Danger zone mapping
- Today, Google's forecasts have reached 350+ million people.

C. AI-Based Cyclone Tracking
Cyclones are becoming unpredictable and high-intensity in the face of climate change. Google AI:

- Wind speed
- Cyclone movement
- Landslide time
- Intensity change

Who can make accurate predictions?

The accuracy of this system is equal to the Indian Meteorological Department (IMD) standards.

D. Carbon Emission Monitoring

Google Earth Engine + AI satellite analytics:

- $CO2$
- Methane
- Nitrogen oxide
- Emissions are being tracked.

Forest loss, deforestation, water table depletion, and glacier melting are all continuously monitored by AI. This data is highly valuable for global climate policies and the UN Sustainable Development Goals (SDGs).

E. Global Climate Modeling Using DeepMind AI

DeepMind has developed the "GraphCast" model, which is a breakthrough:

- 1000× faster than conventional climate models
- More accurate predictions for temperature, pressure, and extreme weather events
- Deep neural networks analyze weather data on a graph structure.

GraphCast is now used in:

- European Center for Medium-Range Weather Forecasts
- US climate agencies
- Asian Airport Networks.

14.8 Benefits of AI in Solar and Climate Domains

14.8.1 Operational Benefits

- Efficiency enhancement
- Reduced maintenance cost
- Higher reliability
- Accurate forecasting

14.8.2 Environmental Benefits

- Lower carbon footprint
- Reduce water usage
- Sustainable energy production

14.8.3 Economic Benefits

- Lower operational cost
- Better return on investment
- Support for the green economy

14.9 Challenges and Limitations of AI Integration

- No technology is perfect. AI also has some challenges:
- High initial investment
- Skilled workforce requirement
- Data privacy concerns
- Lack of standardized AI policies
- Ethical issues in automated decision-making
- But AI offers more advantages than these challenges.

14.10 Future Directions

14.10.1 Autonomous Solar Plants

In the future, AI-based autonomous solar farms will be:

- Self-cleaning
- Self-diagnosing
- Self-optimizing
- Self-repairing

14.10.2 AI-Driven Climate Governance

AI will become a key instrument in designing climate policies.

14.10.3 Integration with General AI

General AI will make solar energy and climate modeling more intelligent—with human-like reasoning.

14.11 Conclusion

Solar energy conservation and climate change management are both extremely critical domains for global survival. AI empowers both fields—with accuracy, speed, efficiency, and predictability. AI-based systems optimize solar plants, improve power forecasting, make climate models intelligent, and make emissions control more effective. In the coming years, AI + solar energy + climate science will together create a sustainable and climate-resilient future. AI's adaptive intelligence is becoming the foundation of global environmental transformation, which is essential for humanity's long-term survival.

AI disclosure statement: The author acknowledges the use of AI-based tools for minor language editing or grammatical correction. However, all intellectual contributions, analyses, and conclusions presented in this chapter are entirely the author's own.

References

1. Abuella, M. and Chowdhury, B., Solar power forecasting using artificial neural networks and ensemble models. *Renew. Energy*, 123, 297–307, 2018.
2. Voyant, C., Notton, G., Kalogirou, S., Nivet, M.L., Paoli, C., Motte, F., Fouilloy, A., Machine learning methods for solar radiation forecasting: A review. *Renew. Energy*, 105, 569–582, 2017.
3. Mekonnen, Y. and Lee, W., AI-driven predictive maintenance for photovoltaic systems: A comprehensive review. *Sol. Energy*, 219, 200–216, 2021.
4. Al-Masri, E., Alsabbagh, A., AlSharman, M., IoT and AI-based monitoring systems for solar PV performance evaluation. *IEEE Access*, 8, 204602–204612, 2020.
5. Kazem, H.A., Yousif, J.H., Chaichan, M.T., Dust effect on photovoltaic utilization: Literature review. *Renew. Sustain. Energy Rev.*, 82, 743–760, 2019.
6. Liu, X., Zhao, W., Zhang, Y., Computer vision-based PV panel dust detection using deep learning. *Energy Rep.*, 7, 7328–7337, 2021.
7. Siano, P., Demand response and smart grids—A survey of AI approaches. *Appl. Energy*, 284, 116340, 2020.

8. Watti, S.S. and Turan, R., Artificial intelligence for battery storage optimization in Renew. Energy systems. *J. Energy Storage*, 35, 102251, 2021.
9. Bhargava, N., Rathore, P.S., Rajput, D., Goswami, A., Unveiling Feature Significance: Enhancing Classification Accuracy using Chi-Squared Weighted Feature Selection. *2023 2nd International Conference on Automation, Computing and Renewable Systems (ICACRS)*, Pudukkottai, India, pp. 12–17, 2023, doi: 10.1109/ICACRS58579.2023.10405351.
10. Kumar, A., Rathore, P.S., Dubey, A.K., Srivastav, A.L., Dutt, V., Kumar, T.A. (Eds.), *Sustainable management of electronic waste*, John Wiley & Sons, 2024.

15

Smart Solar Energy Management through IoT and AI Integration: Architectures, Applications, and Future Trends

Mamta[1]*, Shravya Reddy Karri[2] and Srinivasa Rao Burri[3]

[1]*Department of Computer Science and Engineering, Chandigarh University, Mohali, Punjab, India*
[2]*Rock Canyon High School, Highlands Ranch, CO, USA*
[3]*Western Union, Denver, CO, USA*

Abstract
The IoT and Artificial Intelligence (AI) will revolutionize solar energy management by producing smarter, more efficient, and sustainable energy systems. The world demand for clean and sustainable energy has precipitated the rapid use of solar energy. However, it is still a big challenge to make it as efficient and reliable as possible. In this chapter, the author describes how the Internet of Things (IoT) and Artificial Intelligence (AI) played a revolutionary role in the sunlight energy system to transcend these limitations. The chapter is a useful contribution to the field of understanding that more intelligent solar energy management relies on technological advances, architectures, and intelligent approaches. Beginning with the disadvantages of the conventional solar systems, the chapter explains how the combination of IoT and AI can enable a reinvention of the solar packing procedure, in which real-time monitoring, predictive analysis, and dynamic energy management are involved. The state-of-the-art literature review follows the evolution of research on IoT-enabled systems of renewable sources and AI-oriented optimization methods and illuminates the gaps in the research. Such innovations are described in the main sections, which outline the design of an IoT-based solar monitoring (sensor implementations, edge computing, and cloud-based data) and analyzers. It also examines the application of AI technologies, such as machine

**Corresponding author*: mamta.e13672@cumail.in; mamta.airesearch@gmail.com; ORCID: 0000-0001-9156-874X

Abhishek Kumar, Pramod Singh Rathore, Arun Lal Srivastav and Ashutosh Kumar Dubey (eds.) Solar Energy Optimization Using Generative Artificial Intelligence, (347–376) © 2026 Scrivener Publishing LLC

learning, to predictive maintenance, deep learning to panel diagnostics, generative AI to irradiance prediction, and reinforcement learning to optimize the system. Integrated IoT-AI architectures have use cases that are described in terms of diverse applications, including residential applications, as well as utility-scale applications. It contains the practical case studies highlighting the successful deployments, followed by a detailed delving into the technical issues, security concerns, and the latest trends, including the introduction of blockchain and digital twins. A summary of the key conclusions, signs of future work in the field of practical implementation, and recommendations on future research directions reveal that the combination of IoT and AI will become an important factor in the efficient, intelligent, and sustainable solar energy systems.

***Keywords*:** IoT-AI integration, solar energy optimization, predictive maintenance, smart grids, renewable energy systems

15.1 Introduction

15.1.1 Introduction to Solar Energy Management Issues

Solar energy is widespread in the category of renewable energy solutions, but it has some challenges to its operation and scale that restrict its use. Among the key challenges, there are weather variations insofar as solar intermittency is concerned, lack of energy storage, and inefficient photovoltaic (PV) panel performance [1]. Additionally, big and massive installations require vast territories, and grid integration is technologically and economically problematic. The difficulties in these repairs demonstrate the issues in handling solar energy and concerns about the environmental impact of the lifecycle, like the disposal of solar panels and the professional workforce. To address these issues, there is a need to develop new techniques that will save time, cost, and minimize ecological footprints.

15.1.2 Significance of IoT and AI Implementation in Solar Systems

The solutions to such challenges are offered by IoT and other advanced technologies like AI. Solar energy systems are taken care of in real-time, predictive maintenance, and automation by devices and sensors connected and working actively in their entire operating period [2]. AI will be used to complement the Internet of Things (IoT), where it will analyze big data to optimize energy production, predict equipment failures, and more effectively control the flow of electricity. Based on the potential of IoT and AI, adaptive control of solar energy systems can be successful depending on the dynamic environmental conditions. It allows for organizing the power production and consumption more effectively, becoming a part of demand response programs, and complementing renewable energy integration, which provides stability and responsiveness in the supply of energy. This synergy results in efficient systems, less downtime, reduced operation costs, and a smaller carbon footprint, resulting in the energy solutions being sustainable.

15.1.3 Issues and Capabilities of the Chapter

This chapter is aimed at studying IoT and AI in solar energy AV. This architecture is a set of predictive AI-based strategies and a CAD-based performance modeling, which has a synergistic relationship, to which this thesis builds in the following chapters with specific attention to PV performance optimization, energy storage, and linking with smart grids [3]. The chapter goes on to discuss the practical uses using case studies and the difficulties in implementation, such as scalability, data security, and interoperability. Finally, it addresses the new trends like the introduction of blockchain technology and generative AI into sophisticated forecasting to determine the future opportunities in this field.

15.2 Literature Review

15.2.1 IoT Development in Renewable Energy Systems

Some of the studies suggest that the Internet of Things (IoT) technology in renewable energy systems can be traced back to the implementation of the smart grids in the early 2000s, when digital communication technology was employed to measure and optimize the energy delivery. The past few decades were marked by the growth of the IoT in the energy sector, focusing on renewables, with the development of improved sensor technology, wireless communication standards, and data analysis services [4]. It also advanced from simple systems of monitoring to complex control systems that have the capability to dynamically react to the changing conditions of the environment. Over time, the early IoT applications in solar energy have been developed to include data collection, remote monitoring systems, automated control systems, and predictive analytics. A combination of edge computing solutions, all optimized to these systems, processing data nearer to the source, lowering latency and total response times. The use of IoT began to appear in various renewable energy areas, including solar, wind, and hydroelectric power plants in 2010, and the applications were customized to fit the source of the energy. An example of this in solar energy is the development of systems using the internet of things that have become fully matured to incorporate smart inverters and tracking technologies that may even turn the panels in real-time depending on the weather conditions in order to get as much energy as possible [5]. These systems were advanced to monitor key performance indicators such as voltage, current, and temperature, which contributed to maximum performance and increased the life span of the equipment. The current IoT designs of solar energy use can be used to perform remote diagnostics, predictive maintenance, and through smart grids - something that is not at all similar to the early models.

15.2.2 AI Use in the Optimization of Solar Energy

AI is important in solar energy systems, as it causes a system to be more efficient, reduces maintenance expenses, and offers superior storage capabilities. The solar energy systems that improve are these, and they are the main AI applications:

1. Solar Panel Efficiency Enhancement

- The application of AI algorithms relies on the present weather information to optimize solar panel location by changing the inclination of the panels.
- The algorithms forecast the level of dirt in the panels and the appropriate time to clean them in order to be effective.

2. Predicting Energy Generations

- The AI algorithms can be used to predict solar energy production using historical weather conditions, satellite data, and live data.
- Individuals who use sophisticated deep learning methods record better forecasts in terms of solar radiation measurements.

3. Smart Grid Integration

- At the same time, AI improves the conveyance of solar energy from power plants to the power grid network.

- Artificial intelligence has demand-response systems that control supply and demand to avoid energy wastage.

4. Fault Detection and Forecasted Maintenance

- Image processing AI is used to detect defects on solar panels in thermal cameras installed on drones.
- It is possible to use predictive maintenance algorithms to predict possible equipment failures before they occur.

5. Optimization of Energy Storage

- The AI technology, combined with battery storage, works when it forecasts demand patterns and guides the distribution and shipment of power in the system.
- The reinforcement learning strategies can be implemented to achieve improved performance in batteries and extended life expectancy.

6. Material Discovery Generative AI

- The development of a superior photovoltaic cell that functions at peak efficiency levels is enhanced due to artificial intelligence-based material research technologies.
- Generative AI has created novel nanomaterials, which absorb more energy and transform that energy into energy more effectively.

7. Autonomous Solar Farms

- The tasks of installation and monitoring, along with maintenance operations at the large-scale solar facilities, are carried out by AI-powered robots alongside the maintenance operations.
- The solar tracking operation is most effectively maximized when the system is automated using AI-generated IoT.

Figure 15.1 illustrates AI use in optimization of solar energy systems, the enhancement of efficiency, the forecasting of energy generation, and

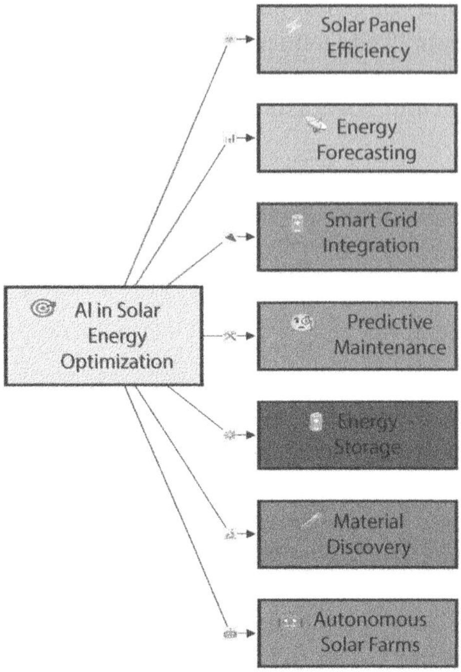

Figure 15.1 AI-powered solar energy optimization: making solar energy more efficient, storable, and sustainable.

the integration of a smart grid. The progress is based on AI predictive maintenance, optimization of energy storage, and the development of new materials that increase the lifespan of systems. In this case, autonomous solar farms make use of artificial intelligence in real-time monitoring and maintenance of solar panels to guarantee maximum energy consumption.

15.2.3 Trends in the State of Research of IoT-AI Integration

Recent studies of IoT and AI integration to control solar energy suggest some significant trends. 5G Trillions (GSMA Intelligence predicts 1.5 billion 5G connections by end-2023) [6]. This development enables faster data transmission speed, reduced latency, and more reliable connections that enable IoT networks to compute and analyze data in real time. The other trend is the development of Edge AI, where AI algorithms are deployed to an IoT device and not necessarily in a cloud server. The locality of computation reduces latency, enhances the privacy assurance of the system because it does not require transferring data, and the system as a whole is dependable with the relevant functions capable of functioning even with a compromised internet connection [7]. Following the latest development of Internet of Things (IoT) technologies, the setting up of local renewable energy facilities to supply local grids has generated a lot of interest, which is being tracked, forecasted, and optimized using the decentralization of energy management. These systems enable predictive maintenance, that is, identifying the probable failure before it happens; grid monitoring, which avoids accidents and communication between the power stations and the grid nodes, which improves communication and proactive load management during the events. It is an edge in automation of industries, the development of self-directional IoTs with the help of AI to observe, detect, and optimize their work with minimal or no human intervention. According to IoT Analytics, the world is predicted to become 25 billion devices connected by 2025, indicating the rapid use of integrated IoT-AI technologies.

15.3 IoT Architecture for Solar Energy Monitoring

The integration of the two fields, solar energy systems and IoT, has transformed the world of real-time monitoring, data analytics, and optimization of systems. IoT can be used to manage solar energy better by performing predictive maintenance and improving decision-making, using sensor technologies, edge computing, and cloud-based solutions [8]. This section of the chapter addresses the basic components of the IoT system in solar power monitoring, including sensors, protocols, and cloud-based data collection systems.

15.3.1 Internet of Things Architecture in Solar Energy Monitoring

The solar energy monitoring, which is created using IoT, involves different types of sensors to collect the measurable parameters such as solar irradiance, temperature, voltage, current, and the environmental status. The sensors provide real-time information, which is useful in the optimization of the solar panel activity and fault detection [9].

- **PV (Photovoltaic) Sensors:** A sensor used to measure the strength of the sun and the effectiveness of solar panels to maintain energy transformation in optimum conditions.
- **Temperature Sensors:** Temperatures in respective solar panels and the immediate surroundings should be monitored in a way that they avoid overheating and efficiency losses.

- **Current Sensors and Voltage sensors:** These devices detect the amount of electrical output of the solar panels and can notify the operators when this output changes, which could indicate a problem.
- **Weather Sensors:** Wind speed, humidity, and atmospheric pressure influence the solar energy production.
- **Dust and Dirty sensors:** Provide the ability to detect the amount of dust on the solar panels to activate automated cleaning services.
- **Vibration Sensors:** Identify mechanical issues within the support frameworks of the solar panels, which are subjected to forces like strong winds.
- **Humidity Sensors:** Identify humidity that can ruin the wiring of solar panels and/or the performance of the panels.

15.3.2 Edge Computing and Communication Protocols

The technology will go a long way in eradicating the latency and in processing the solar energy data in real time. Instead of sending all the information to a central point in the cloud, edge computing devices such as Internet of Things (IoT) gateways and microcontrollers process data in their immediate surroundings when required and reduce bandwidth consumption by an order of magnitude, as well as response rates [10].

- **Edge Devices:** Microcontrollers (including Raspberry Pi, ESP32), embedded systems performing sensor data processing and then sending it, and IoT gateways are edge devices.
- **Machine Learning at the Edge:** With machine learning at the edge, predictive analytics can be used to perform fault detection, predictive maintenance, energy forecasting, and energy efficiency gains.
- **Data Compression and Filtration:** Edge devices narrow down unnecessary data and minimize the data being uploaded to the cloud.
- **Decentralized Computing:** This reduces reliance on centralized cloud service providers by enabling edge nodes to analyze significant information in real time, leading to faster decision-making.

Strong communication protocols are applied to facilitate effortless communication between sensors, edge devices, and cloud platforms:

- **MQTT (Message Queuing Telemetry Transport):** This is a lightweight protocol that is specifically meant to be used by low-powered IoT devices to ensure quick data transfer.
- **CoAP (Constrained Application Protocol):** Developed to be used in constrained IoT applications and low-bandwidth applications.
- **LoRaWAN (Long Range Wide Area Network):** This is used to allow long-range, low-battery communication with solar farms situated in remote locations.
- **Zigbee and Bluetooth Low Energy (BLE):** It is employed in short-range wireless communication between the sensors and the controllers.
- **5G and LPWAN:** The two technologies have the capability of enhancing the rate of data transfer and providing connectivity during the execution of solar power plants on a large scale.
- **Wi-Fi and Ethernet:** Ensuring that there is a stable and high data transmission in solar monitoring setups that are local.

15.3.3 Data Management Cloud-Based Solutions

Cloud provides a centralized and scalable storage, processing, and analysis platform of solar energy-related information [11]. Cloud solutions enhance the use of the system, provide the possibility of remote observation, and contribute to predictive analytics used to maintain and optimize.

- **Big Data Analytics:** Trends: The analytics based on AI identify trends, predict the performance of the energy generation, and optimize the work of the systems.
- **Remote Monitoring Dashboards:** The users utilize both web and mobile applications that visualize real-time solar energy data, monitor performance, and identify abnormalities.
- **Predictive Maintenance:** AI algorithms are based on sensor data analysis, which helps predict equipment failure and reduce downtime and maintenance costs.
- **Cybersecurity Controls:** Cloud systems encrypt, have the capacity to identify a user, and apply blockchain to safeguard sensitive energy information.
- **Digital Twins Technology:** Cloud-based digital twins create simulations of a real-world solar farm to enable the task of simulation, testing, and optimization of solar energy systems.

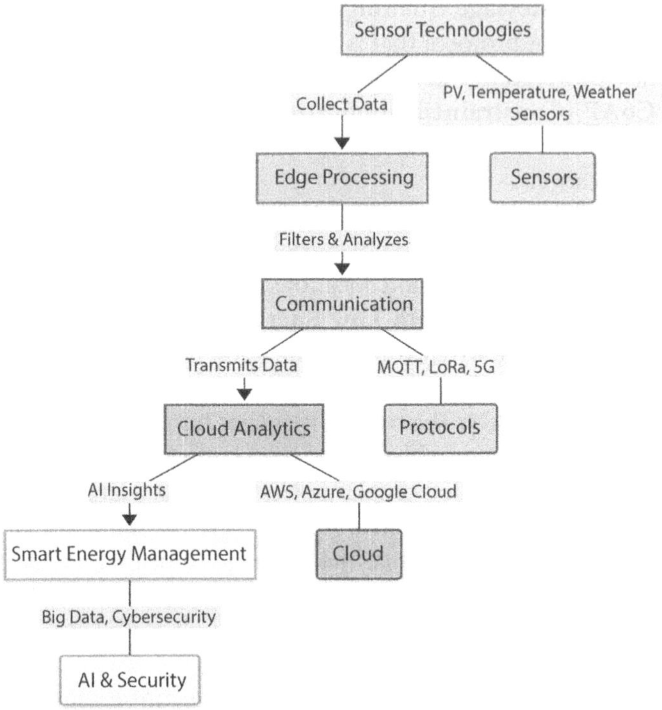

Figure 15.2 Smart solar energy monitoring with IoT: a harmonized implementation of sensors, edge computing, and AI to perform optimally.

- **Cloud-Powered Artificial Intelligence Protection:** Artificial intelligence systems should be used to create automated alerts and reports to enable the maintenance team take proactive measures.

Figure 15.2 illustrates the IoT system of solar energy monitoring, such as sensor technologies, edge computing, communication protocols, cloud analytics, and AI-based decision making. Sensors are used to obtain real-time data, which is processed at the edge and transferred using lightweight communication protocols. The cloud enables solar energy modules to store and process data, which could be used by AI-based analytics, predictive maintenance, and intelligent energy management to make it more efficient.

15.4 Solar Energy Optimization AI Technologies

Artificial Intelligence (AI) has made solar energy more efficient and reliable, and made it predictable [16]. The AI-based solutions have the ability to perform real-time monitoring, fault detection, and adaptive energy management. This section explores the major AI technologies, including machine learning, deep learning, generative AI, and reinforcement learning, which are critical in streamlining solar energy systems [13].

15.4.1 Predictive Maintenance Algorithms Based on Machine Learning

Machine learning (ML) algorithms are employed in predictive maintenance in solar energy systems to detect a possible failure, reduce downtime, and increase effectiveness [14]. ML models have the ability to analyze vast amounts of historical and real-time sensor data to determine trends that indicate a decline in the condition of the system or a failure of individual components.

- **Supervised Learning Algorithms:** Regression and classification-based models (e.g., Random Forest, Support Vector Machines (SVM)) are used to predict equipment failures when using past information on the performance of a machine.
- **Unsupervised Learning:** Find the anomalies and irregularities that do not conform to the usual pattern of the solar panel performance with the help of clustering algorithms (K-Means, DBSCAN).
- **Reinforcement Learning (RL):** RL can be used to optimize maintenance using the information it learns about the environment and equipment status.
- **Time-Series Forecasting:** ARIMA and Long Short-Term Memory (LSTM) models are methods that can predict trends in historical operations by using historical data on operations.
- **Computer Vision in Fault Detection of Solar Panels:** An image processing method shows cracks or the presence of damage with reference to an image analysis of the panels.

15.4.2 Deep Learning in Solar Panel Analysis

Deep learning refers to a branch of machine learning that employs algorithms based on the human brain to discover patterns and draw predictions on the basis of sizable datasets of complicated information [15].

- **Convolutional Neural Networks (CNNs):** CNNs involve the processing of infrared and visible light images to locate defects, micro-cracks, and dirt deposits on solar panels.
- **Anomaly Detection by Autoencoders:** Unsupervised models that are to be trained to gain regular operation patterns in order to detect a mistake or inefficiency as a deviation.
- **Recurrent Neural Networks (RNNs) in Energy Forecasting:** RNNs consider the series of energy production data and train to anticipate the future output of energy.
- **Solar Inspection Pre-processing:** Deep learning algorithms can be better applied to detect the defects on the solar panels.
- **Smart Process and Control:** AI ML in Quality Control: Automated (Deep Learning-based) AI ML Inspection to identify manufacturing errors prior to actual implementation.

15.4.3 Solar Irradiance Forecasting Using Generative AI

The field of solar irradiance prediction is being transformed by the generative AI technologies based on the synthetic dataset and the increased accuracy of the forecasting, as well as the assistance of a more accurate modeling of the weather dynamics [16].

- **GAN-based Synthetic Data Generation:** GANs can be used to generate authentic weather and irradiance data that can be utilized to train AI models to circumvent the issue of gathering historic data.
- **Generative Models:** General in climate modeling. Generative models, including VAEs (Variational Autoencoders), can also be applied to climate modeling, e.g., by training the probabilistic distributions of solar irradiance and generating forecasting situations.
- **Artificial Intelligence Improved Weather Forecasting:** Predicting Solar Power by Satellite Data, Atmospheric Variables, and Weather History.
- **Hybrid AI Models:** Hybrid models of AI by integrating generative and physics-based techniques into solar forecasting; it will be possible to get stronger predictions.
- **Synthetic Data Augmentation:** The effectiveness and accuracy of AI models in predicting solar energy can also be augmented by means of synthetic data augmentation.

15.4.4 Reinforcement Learning of Adaptive Energy Control

Solar energy harvesting and management methods can adapt to changing strategies in a short and effective period through reinforcement learning (RL) [17].

- Algorithms based on RL (Reinforcement Learning) regulate and modify the energy that is flowing through the grid in real-time depending on a number of factors, such as grid demand, weather patterns, and battery storage levels.
- Artificial intelligence controllers to maximize energy distribution policies.
- Solar tracking systems, which are RL-enabled, alter the orientation of the solar panels over time with a view to maximizing sunshine.
- The battery storage can be maximized to ensure that the RL models are used to calculate the appropriate balance between energy storage and grid supply to avoid the waste of energy.

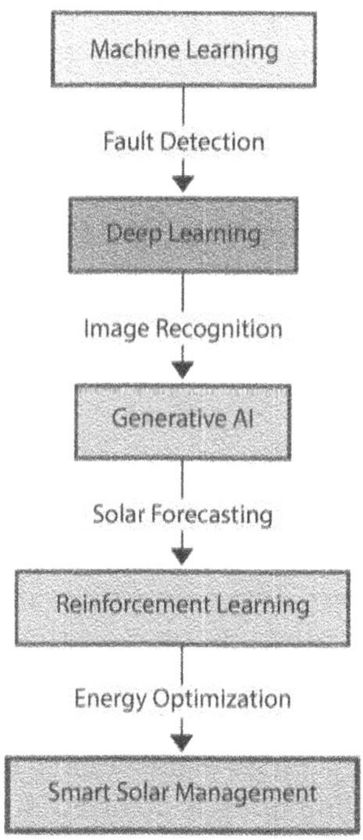

Figure 15.3 The AI-powered optimization: solar energy transformation with smart algorithms.

- Cooperative artificial intelligence agents streamline decentralized energy operator networks.

Figure 15.3 shows the uses of AI Technologies in the optimization of solar. There are a growing number of data-driven methodologies that are being used to enhance fault detection, analysis, and prediction, including machine learning and deep learning. They utilize it through solar irradiance using generative AI and control through reinforcement learning. A combination of these technologies results in a more efficient, self-adaptive, and sustainable solar energy ecosystem.

15.5 Solar Management IoT-AI Systems

Internet of Things (IoT) and Artificial Intelligence (AI) have revolutionized the process of producing, monitoring, and distributing solar energy. With the incorporation of real-time data collection and intelligent decision-making, it is possible that energy IoT-AI platforms will manage not only to enhance the efficiency of energy [18], but also reduce the cost of operation and distribute energy in the most optimal way. The foundations of such systems are rooted in the idea of interconnected elements, predictive analytics, and AI optimization that are aimed at making sure that solar energy is employed and used effectively and in a sustainable manner.

15.5.1 Systems Components and Architecture Design

The combination of solar management, IoT, and AI implies linking various units of sensors, devices, and analytical systems [19]. It is typically employed to allow real-time tracking, smart decision-making, and energy allocation.

1. **Smart Sensors and IoT Devices:** IoT Sensors are placed on the solar panels and the energy storage units to measure such parameters as temperature, voltage, current, irradiance, and weather conditions. These are devices that transmit data to the central processing unit on a continuous basis, and performance can be measured in real time.
2. **Edge Computing to Process Data:** To minimize the latency and achieve a higher level of operational efficiency, the application of edge computing is involved in solar management based on IoT. In edge computing, sensor data is sensed and then processed locally, after which only the information of relevance is sent to the cloud servers to be further analyzed.

This reduces the pressure on the network bandwidth and provides real-time analytics.

3. **Cloud Storage of Data:** A Cloud is a warehouse to which all data is stored in order to process solar energy on a large scale. AI models process this information on the cloud to formulate patterns, forecast failures, and determine the best energy management strategies.
4. **AI-Driven Decision Making:** AI gets deep into the past and present data of weather conditions and uses this data to enhance better decisions in terms of the production of solar energy, maintenance schedule, and grid interaction [19]. After that, it identifies inefficiencies within the system and suggests remedial measures with the aid of machine learning models.
5. **Integration with Smart Grid:** IoT-AI solar management systems are connected with Smart grids, and it is possible to deliver energy efficiently. The grids help achieve power supply and demand dynamically, whereby any surplus power is stored in batteries or sent back to the grid.

15.5.2 Integration of Real-Time Monitoring and Predictive Analytics

Real-time tracking of the performance of the solar panels would be necessary to ensure maximum efficiency and to detect any possible malfunction [16]. The IoT sensors will gather information on energy generation, the weather conditions, and equipment status regularly. AI-based predictive analytics have the potential to enhance monitoring, predict patterns, anomalies, and possible failures in advance.

1. **Anomaly Detection and Fault Prediction:** The AI models are used to track sensor data in order to detect anomalies in the functioning of solar panels. In case of a drop in efficiency, the maintenance team would be alerted automatically, reducing the downtimes and repair expenses.
2. **Machine Learning Algorithms:** The algorithm will analyze meteorological data and predict concentrations of solar irradiance [20]. This kind of information helps in the moderation of the energy storage and grid distribution schemes in the name of stability, even on cloudy days.

3. **Energy Analytics:** AI-based analytics keep track of energy usage patterns and suggest the best ways to optimize them. This can be very helpful in a commercial and residential environment where demand fluctuates during the day.
4. **Remote System Control:** The solar farms and rooftop solar systems can be controlled remotely through the use of IoT connectivity. Real-time modification of panel angles, energy storage settings, and grid connections is all based on the AI algorithm.

15.5.3 AI Energy Storage and Distribution Optimization

By using AI in Energy Storage and Distribution Optimization, there is a need to store and supply the solar power in an efficient way, so that power is available at all times [21]. Through this technology, energy storage and consumption are optimized based on the current demand and grid conditions.

1. **AI-Optimized Battery Management:** The AI models are used to optimize the use of the battery through the analysis of the charge-discharge cycle, battery health, and energy demand. This will avoid overcharging, increase the battery life, and make sure that the energy stored will be available when one needs it.
2. **A Robust Tool of Energy Storage is Reinforcement Learning of Smart Grid Adaptation:** AI-Optimized Battery Management. The data used to optimize the utilization of batteries are the charge-discharge cycles, health, and demand of the batteries analyzed by AI models. It assists in decreasing the overcharging, prolonging the battery life, and consuming energy upon need.
3. **Dynamic Energy Distribution:** AI-based reinforcement learning models may apply to the inputs of data associated with the variations in energy generated and used, and thus, the other energy sources can be properly adapted to satisfy energy requirements. These models predict the grid demands and dynamically redistribute the energy allocation scheme.
4. **Smart Energy Redistribution:** It means that the smart grid technology considers the energy requirements of various regions and redistributes energy resources as needed

through the power of AI algorithms. This prevents misdirection of the energy as well as provides effective utilization of the Sun-earned electricity.

5. **Demand Response Systems:** Demand-response systems are artificial intelligence systems that are used to manage the supply of energy based on the actual demand, thereby keeping the load balanced. AI is also being employed in giving suggestions to businesses and households on how to optimize energy usage and, hence, reduce the cost of electricity.

The interaction of the two technologies facilitates the use of more capable, more responsive, and stronger solar energy management [23]. These allow more efficient solar energy ecosystem monitoring, predictive maintenance, and optimization of energy distribution, leading to a more sustainable and efficient ecosystem of solar energy. The solar management systems will further develop and include artificial intelligence (AI) and the Internet of Things (IoT) so as to automatically regulate and optimize the energy production and consumption.

15.6 Applications and Case Studies

Through the IoT and AI, the solar energy industry has experienced various developments, particularly in efficiency, cost-effectiveness, and sustainability. From small residential systems to large utility farms, these technologies demonstrate maximum prospects in a number of applications of solar power generation on land [24]. Here we are going to address the three general uses, namely, 1- residential solar energy management systems, 2- commercial and industrial use cases, and 3- utility-scale solar farms, with the implementation of the integration of both IoT and AI.

15.6.1 Residential Solar Energy Management Systems

Net-metering programs are significant in ensuring that the solar panels become a cost-efficient alternative to homeowners wishing to save on their electric bill, but also contribute to saving the environment [25]. These are solar energy management systems that follow clever algorithms to monitor and optimize the production and utilization of solar energy within a home property.

1. **Smart Home Integration:** AI-powered HEMS are capable of smartly integrating and coordinating the power requirements of IoT-powered devices [26]. By using machine learning algorithms, the energy demand and usage can be predicted, and thus can be used to minimize peak load and efficiently use power. Machine learning applications forecast the energy demand and control the usage, which provides maximum load reduction and efficient power consumption.
2. **Predictive Maintenance:** AI-based analytics detects anomalies in performance, which leads to preventive maintenance and reduces any unexpected failures. In addition, as the panel performance is constantly analyzed, AI will be able to identify the inefficiencies caused by dirt, shade, or the condition of the panel itself and, therefore, clean it or replace it in time. Appendix: Data Augmentation to Neural Networks: Recently, AI has been utilized to reduce overfitting in the goal of enhancing generalization. They apply predictive algorithms to make use of stored energy in the event that solar generation is minimal, so that reliance on grid power is reduced.
3. **Remote Monitoring and Control:** Mobile applications that are linked to IoT sensors can help homeowners to observe the efficiency of their solar panels, the presence of energy, and the battery condition in real-time. Based on AI-driven analytics, the user is able to modify their energy usage behavior with the aim of achieving optimal savings and energy efficiency.
4. **Smart Grid Integration:** Smart grids have residential solar systems that create supply and demand balances with the help of AI. Demand response programs involve homeowners selling surplus energy to the grid or using stored energy to supply peak demand periods, which adds to the general stability of the grid.
5. **Dynamic Tariff Adaptation:** The solar price can vary, and AI-powered solar management systems monitor this and will automatically switch to solar power when solar energy is required and switch to grid power when it is not. It implies that savings are mostly realized through the use of on-site energy when tariffs are high and battery charging when tariffs are low.

15.6.2 Commercial and Industrial Implications

Companies and industries consume vast amounts of energy, and solar energy is one of the cost-effective means to satisfy these needs. AI and IoT facilitate the use of solar energy using efficiency, low operational costs, and reliability of the energy [27].

1. **Smart Distribution of Energy through AI:** Smart grids are using AI algorithms to dynamically distribute energy and supply to demand to deliver energy efficiently.
2. **Load Forecasting:** Load forecasting is an energy consumption modeling technique that forecasts energy usage patterns of various industries with the help of ML models, and thus it assists in the optimal timing of solar panels to satisfy this demand without relying on conventional grids. AI-based forecasting minimizes the loss of energy and assists companies in operating within reasonable energy parameters.
3. **Automated Maintenance Systems:** The IOT sensors monitor faults in panels, inverters, etc., and alerts are produced. Predictive analytics would also be able to anticipate likely failures before they occur, and thus, the downtime and repair expenses would be reduced.
4. **Carbon Footprint Reduction:** The AI-enabled monitoring systems enable companies to adhere to the sustainability goals and regulations through monitoring carbon savings. Sharing data-dependent insights based on trends of energy consumption assists companies in adopting strategic decision-making and reducing their carbon footprint.
5. **Microgrid Integration:** Microgrids can be big commercial solar arrays that supply power to commercial facilities or an industrial factory. This enables plush virtualization of microgrid performance, which makes sure that the maximum use of renewable energy sources is made with a stable solution stability of the grid.
6. **Energy Trading Platforms:** AI-based energy trading platforms based on blockchain technology assist companies in trading excess solar energy on a peer-to-peer commercial platform. This will enable more access to energy, a non-dependence on central energy organizations; it will also promote the use of green energy.

15.6.3 Solar Farms of Utility Scale with IoT-AI

The integration of IoT and AI is applicable at all levels, residential, commercial, and large-scale. Still, the most significant profit will be achieved in large-scale solar farms to make the process more productive, allow predictive maintenance, and provide grid stability [28].

1. **Drones with AI-Powered Solar Panel Inspection:** Thermal imaging combined with drones is used to identify faulty solar panels, resulting in faster inspection and more accuracy. Artificial intelligence is used to scan the images posted by drones and detect hot spots, cracks, and dust accumulation to perform preventive maintenance.
2. **Smart Inverters and Energy Storage:** This is an AI algorithm that processes weather data and grid parameters that contribute to the optimization of the power to be distributed, which helps in the prevention of energy loss due to fluctuations. Predictive analytics are used to ensure that solar farms do not overload or have shortages by matching the output to demand.
3. **Natural Language Processing:** Chatbots and virtual assistants apply AI to enhance customer services based on natural language processing that offers real-time information and support to the user. Being AI-driven, optimization is also used to optimize battery storage to release energy efficiently when there is a high demand.
4. **Solar Farm Management:** IoTs are also useful in managing the solar farms, whereby the IoT sensor records the conditions in the environment, and the AI model makes automated decisions regarding the optimization of the pieces merely to improve the results. The AI-based tracking systems are capable of changing the location of solar panels to expose them to a greater amount of sunlight.
5. **Weather-Adaptive Energy Management:** AI-based models can predict the energy production and maximize the use of storage based on real-time weather data. With the prediction of cloud cover, AI adjusts battery charging and distribution schemes to ensure that the supply of energy is constant.
6. **Connection to National Grids:** Large solar fields supply energy to national grids, and AI can make maximum use of the same by tracking changes in loads. The grid integration

software supported by AI will ensure that energy efficiency is maintained with minimal loss.

7. **Automated curtailment plans:** In the situation where the supply surpasses the demand in the electricity grid, AI-driven curtailment plans will result in minimum energy wastage. The output of the panels is dynamically controlled by smart controllers to synchronize it according to consumption patterns.
8. **Smart Security and Cyber Threat Prevention:** Since the systems of the solar farms are interconnected, AI-based tools of cybersecurity make sure that hackers do not attack them, suffer a data breach, or are misused by unauthorized individuals.

The simplified workflow that illustrates the collection of real-time data using the IoT sensors and processing it with the assistance of AI to make intelligent decisions is presented in Figure 15.4. The AI system is used to optimize domestic, commercial, and utility-scale solar systems, battery control, load forecasting, energy adjustment based on the weather, and other features. The inclusion of these intelligent systems enables the system to provide energy efficiency, predictive maintenance, and smart solar management.

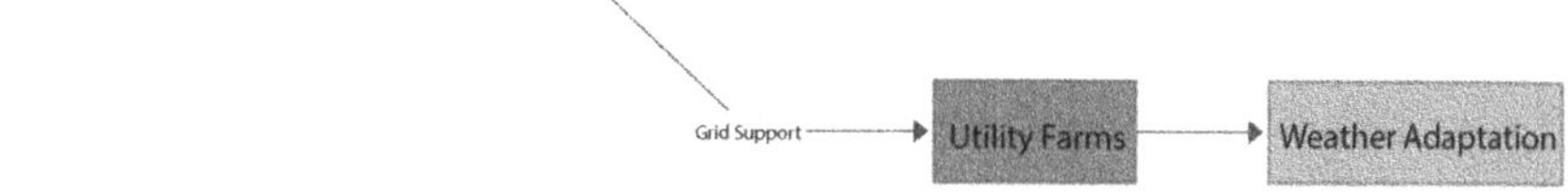

Figure 15.4 IoT-AI-based integrated solar management architecture: residential, commercial, and utility access and optimization.

15.7 Problems and Future Projections

The Internet of Things (IoT) AI in Solar Energy System: IoT-AI is transforming the solar energy landscape. IoT has provided an opportunity for AI to make a major contribution. Although this convergence has a very promising future, it also presents numerous technical, infrastructural, and security issues [29]. The future of smart solar is being transformed by the emerging technologies such as blockchain, digital twins, and new sensors. The section briefly mentions the possible obstacles to the introduction of the IoT-AI-based solar systems and also reviews future trends that will transform the world of solar energy.

15.7.1 Technical Challenges in IoT-AI Implementation

1. **Interoperability and Standardization:** The first problem that makes the implementation of IoT and AI in the solar system challenging is the absence of a standard form. Various vendors manufacture the IoT devices and use their proprietary network protocols and data formats. This means that the integration of systems becomes difficult and that, in many cases, there is a need to have custom interfaces and middleware. AI models also depend on data streams that are reliable and also on a similar data format. The variations in the hardware of IoT sensors, their sampling rates, or environmental noise may cause inconsistency in data, thereby resulting in less precise and predictive AI predictions.
2. **Volume of Data and Processing Speed:** The solar farms with IoT realizations generate huge data volumes, including real-time data on the irradiance levels, the temperature of the panels, the weather conditions, and the power output. This information cannot be quickly processed, especially when an AI algorithm must operate in real-time to predictively maintain or optimize things. In either case of no existing advanced edge computing facilities, or also where dense high-speed internet is not yet available, data processing latency would be extremely high since the latency would form a bottleneck thereby blocking most of the scenarios that require rapidity (which is why many of them have failed when trying to deal with surge of power, tanks overflow, equipment malfunction etc.).

3. **Power Constraints and Lifespan of Devices:** IoT devices can be low-power sensors and tend to be located remotely or outdoors, making it hard to replace the batteries and maintain the devices. Thus, we must have close control over the energy consumption of all of the system and sensors, including sensors, edge devices, and communication modules, so that they can be operational continuously. Dust and extreme temperatures, as well as moisture, are environmental factors that may degrade sensor performance with time and data input accuracy to AI algorithms.
4. **The Quality and Generalization of AI Models in Training Datasets:** The AI models applied to solar energy systems require extensive datasets with a large variance to work effectively. Conversely, the solar measurements recorded in the actual world can be highly differentiated depending on the location, weather, and configuration. An AI model really successful when trained on data in a specific area may not prove successful when used in a different area. It is also costly and computationally painful to make sure that AI models are retrained regularly to allow them to stay accurate in rapidly evolving environmental conditions.
5. **Cybersecurity Risks:** As solar energy systems become more connected, they become more vulnerable to cyberattacks. With IoT networks, hackers can intrude into the network possessing solar assets, interrupting the flow of energy, and end up stealing confidential data. Most AI algorithms lead to energy wastage or the unavailability of systems in case of any tampering or wrong setup. This underscores the security of AI models and IoT communication protocols by end-to-end encryption, authentication, and systems for detecting abnormalities.

15.7.2 Transactions Secure Transactions Integrated with Blockchain

There are significant solutions to the security and trust problems that are present in the IoT-AI solar systems using blockchain technology. Blockchain is a decentralized and unalterable registry in which all the transactions, interactions, and data between devices are stored safely.

1. **Integration of Blockchain:** IoT and AI, combined with blockchain technology, allow the formation of decentralized and safe data exchange systems that could assist in the safe storage of the obtained datasets. It comes in especially handy in decentralized energy systems, where the myriad actors, including households, utilities, and regulators, have to be more assured of the provenance of data.
2. **Peer-to-peer Energy Trading:** Blockchain would enable peer-to-peer or peer-to-grid solar energy trading between prosumers (such as solar panel owners) and consumers, based on smart contracts. With a smart home that has surplus solar and a neighbor who is interested in using it, the blockchain smart contracts can enable the surplus solar to be sold directly to the neighbor without involving a utility company to handle the surplus solar. Although AI algorithms can forecast the energy supply and demand, fewer transactions can be possible with the help of blockchain.
3. **Identity and Access Management:** An identity and permissions management of devices would also be possible on a solar IoT network using blockchain. By so doing, system parameters will only be accessed or manipulated by authenticated devices and users, thereby reducing the possibility of hacking.
4. **Blockchain Implementation:** The Problems. Blockchain, as a concept, is difficult to make energy-efficient and scalable. Ethereum is an open blockchain that is likely to consume a significant amount of computing power and is latent. The applications in the solar sector better fit the governance with the model of the private or consortium blockchain. This integrated architecture that incorporates AI, IoT, and blockchain involves large-scale coordination among various fields and so encompasses a great deal of development effort that can slow the deployment and the adoption.

15.7.3 IoT-AI Solar Systems: Emerging Technologies

The intelligent solar energy systems will advance to new cutting-edge technologies as they enter the future [30]. These are some of the innovations that are already in place or have huge potential to transform solar management.

1. **Digital Twins Solar Infrastructure:** This is a digital model of a solar system that is updated in real time on IoT sensor data. This enables high-level simulation, predictive maintenance, and performance optimization. AI can use the digital twin to simulate a scenario of what would happen for the best maintenance schedule, panel orientation, inverters, and others. It is cost-saving, minimizes downtimes, and enhances efficiencies.
2. **AIoT (Artificial Intelligence of Things):** AIoT is also a mere name of an idea, in which IoT devices are equipped with AI functionality, thus enabling local decisions to be made by devices. Solar domain AIoT devices are capable of setting and maintaining cleaning schedules of the panels, observing the presence of shading, and adjusting the slope of the solar panels without necessarily being connected to a cloud. The IoT reduces the latency, reliance on bandwidth, and makes the related system more resilient, which forms a solar system that is more autonomous and reliable in the remote or off-grid zone.
3. **6G and Low-Power Wide Area Networks (LPWANs):** With the growth in size and complexity of solar systems, they will require more reliable and quicker communication standards. The 6G networks with ultra-low latency and high bandwidth will enhance the functionality of AI-controlled solar systems. Conversely, more appropriate would be low-power wide-area network (LPWAN) technologies, e.g., LoRaWAN and NB-IoT, which do not require much power and have an extensive range. These networks enable the deployment of large-scale sensor arrays in utility-scale solar locations at a low cost.
4. **Long-Term Solar Optimization through Quantum Computing and AI:** Quantum computing may also derive rules or principles of highly optimized systems of the sun that a classical computer may not be able to compute, based on computational restrictions. Weather, energy, and Smart grid AI models also train and run exponentially faster. Quantum-enhanced machine learning can also allow the optimization of energy distribution in large regions in real-time, considering massive quantities of variables within milliseconds.

5. **Edge AI and Federated Learning:** The Intelligence is placed nearer to the data source. The small AI models created to analyze data near the source generate edge AI information instead of sending sensor data to the cloud. This reduces latency and improves privacy, and assists with cost reduction in the cloud. With Fed-learning, one can train AI models on multiple devices and make the data local, thus preventing the need to transfer sensitive data to a central hub. This will ensure the privacy-sensitive solar operations are safeguarded and also meet the upcoming regulations, such as GDPR.

15.8 Conclusion

Solar management with IoT and AI has transformed the mode of monitoring, optimization, and communication of solar energy. It can be accompanied by the Internet of Things (IoT) sensors that can provide you with real-time information about the weather conditions, panel performance, energy usage, and AI-driven analytics that will assist in ensuring predictive maintenance and achieving better energy prediction and smart grid control. A combination of these technologies will result in greater automation, energy savings, and cost efficiency, which will result in more dependable and sustainable solar energy.

15.8.1 Conclusion of Findings and Reflections

The IoT sensors play a crucial role in real-time control of the performance of solar panels, environmental factors, and battery state. These devices transmit data to edge computing and cloud computing platforms, where immediate processing and trend analysis in the past can be performed. This architecture allows detection of errors in early stages, performance improvement, and efficiency of energy distribution. Similar to the case of EVs, AI is making solar energy management smarter, predictive with analytics, load forecasting, and adapting its energy control. Even machine learning models are up to the task, using past data to forecast system outages and efficient power dispatch; deep learning methods can be used to identify defects in solar panels by satellite imagery and drones. Battery consumption is regulated by reinforcement learning algorithms, which then allow them to supply energy when necessary and reduce their dependence on the main grid. These transactions are executed with the help of smart contracts, and blockchain technology provides the possibility to add security and transparency to decentralized solar microgrids to manage energy. It enables energy transfer with no security and provides some degree of trust between consumers and producers to build a non-volatile and strong energy network. AI-IoT can be possible, and it has been proven by the fact that there are successful real-life applications. The residential solar energy management systems utilize AI-driven automation and scheduling of home consumption. With the power of machine learning, developers can optimize industrial solar installations in real-time, and utility-scale projects can stabilize the grid as well as become more responsive to the weather in an attempt to maximize the energy output.

15.8.2 Practice Implementation Recommendations

Scalable IoT-AI can be adopted successfully only with a modular architecture. In order to ensure the reliability, clarity, and safety of data transmission, the standardized communication protocols, such as MQTT and LoRaWAN, should be used. This means that the use of edge computing gateways to carry out real-time data processing is needed to reduce overreliance on cloud connectivity and improve the response time. Architecture of Strong and dependable IoT Sensor implementations: These are powerful encryption, authentication, and decentralized security systems to minimize cybersecurity vulnerabilities. Concerning efficiency, AI models can be trained most effectively in the case when they are constantly updated to suit the dynamics of the surrounding environment. The edge devices will have lightweight models that can be used to make real-time decisions, and more complicated decisions can be made on the cloud. Through digital twin technology applied during the development of solar systems, designers and engineers have an opportunity to create a virtual copy of the solar installation, which will allow predictive analytics and real-time operational analytics. Tech Acceptance: Government policy and incentives, regulatory support, subsidies, and research funding have to be used to promote the adoption of AI-IoT. In addition, the app-intuitive mobile applications and dashboard will make end consumers track, analyze, and optimize the use of solar power. AI-IoT Solar Energy: Trends in the Future. AI and IoT will allow solar energy to enter the new era of applications: self-educated energy grids, AI-controlled energy storage, and automatic optimization of the sun. New technologies are constantly being developed, and solar energy systems will continue to enhance a sustainable and decentralized energy future through increasingly intelligent, flexible, and efficient elements.

AI disclosure statement: The author acknowledges the use of AI-based tools for minor language editing or grammatical correction. However, all intellectual contributions, analyses, and conclusions presented in this chapter are entirely the author's own.

Bibliography

1. Sargiotis, D., Smart Infrastructure for Sustainable Energy Consumption: Leveraging AI and Big Data. *SSRN Electron. J.*, 2025, https://doi.org/10.2139/ssrn.4789747.
2. T, M., B, B., R, S., Naidu, R., M., R., Ramachandran, P., Rajkumar, S., Kumar, V., Aggarwal, G., Siddiqui, A., Intelligent Energy Management across Smart Grids Deploying 6G IoT, AI, and Blockchain in Sustainable Smart Cities. *IoT*, 2024, https://doi.org/10.3390/iot5030025.
3. Wen, X., Shen, Q., Zheng, W., Zhang, H., AI-Driven Solar Energy Generation and Smart Grid Integration A Holistic Approach to Enhancing Renewable Energy Efficiency. *Int. J. Innovative Res. Eng. Manage.*, 2024, https://doi.org/10.55524/ijirem.2024.11.4.8.
4. Kim, C., Synergizing Solar Cell Technology, Radio Wave Communication, AI Integration, and Business Opportunities: A Comprehensive Review. *Int. J. Multi. Sci. Arts*, 2024, https://doi.org/10.47709/ijmdsa.v3i01.3559.
5. Maurya, P., Artificial Intelligence to Enhance Energy Management and Distribution in Smart Grid Communication Networks. *Tuijin Jishu/J. Propul. Technol.*, 2024, https://doi.org/10.52783/tjjpt.v45.i02.6648.
6. SaberiKamarposhti, M., Kamyab, H., Krishnan, S., Yusuf, M., Rezania, S., Chelliapan, S., Khorami, M., A comprehensive review of AI-enhanced smart grid integration for hydrogen energy: Advances, challenges, and future prospects. *Int. J. Hydrogen Energy*, 2024, https://doi.org/10.1016/j.ijhydene.2024.01.129.
7. Khalid, M., Energy 4.0: AI-enabled digital transformation for sustainable power networks. *Comput. Ind. Eng.*, 193, 110253, 2024, https://doi.org/10.1016/j.cie.2024.110253.
8. Alahi, M., Sukkuea, A., Tina, F., Nag, A., Kurdthongmee, W., Suwannarat, K., Mukhopadhyay, S., Integration of IoT-Enabled Technologies and Artificial Intelligence (AI) for Smart City Scenario: Recent Advancements and Future Trends. *Sensors (Basel, Switzerland)*, 23, 2023, https://doi.org/10.3390/s23115206.
9. Yousef, L., Yousef, H., Rocha-Meneses, L., Artificial Intelligence for Management of Variable Renewable Energy Systems: A Review of Current Status and Future Directions. *Energies*, 2023, https://doi.org/10.3390/en16248057.

10. Bouquet, P., Jackson, I., Nick, M., Kaboli, A., AI-based forecasting for optimised solar energy management and smart grid efficiency. *Int. J. Prod. Res.*, 62, 4623–4644, 2023, https://doi.org/10.1080/00207543.2023.2269565.
11. Pateriya, N., Thakre, N., Kewat, P., Vishwakarma, A., IoT in the Energy Sector: Revolutionizing Energy Management and Consumption. *Int. J. Innovative Res. Comput. Commun. Eng.*, 2023, https://doi.org/10.15680/ijircce.2023.1110050.
12. Cicceri, G., Tricomi, G., D'Agati, L., Longo, F., Merlino, G., Puliafito, A., A Deep Learning-Driven Self-Conscious Distributed Cyber-Physical System for Renewable Energy Communities. *Sensors (Basel, Switzerland)*, 23, 2023, https://doi.org/10.3390/s23094549.
13. Udayakumar, R., Mahesh, B., Sathiyakala, R., Thandapani, K., Choubey, A., Khurramov, A., Alzubaidi, L., Sravanthi, J., An Integrated Deep Learning and Edge Computing Framework for Intelligent Energy Management in IoT-Based Smart Cities. *2023 International Conference for Technological Engineering and its Applications in Sustainable Development (ICTEASD)*, pp. 32–38, 2023, https://doi.org/10.1109/ICTEASD57136.2023.10585232.
14. Khediri, S., Benfradj, A., Thaljaoui, A., Moulahi, T., Khan, R., Alabdulatif, A., Lorenz, P., Integration of artificial intelligence (AI) with sensor networks: Trends, challenges, and future directions. *J. King Saud Univ. Comput. Inf. Sci.*, 36, 101892, 2023, https://doi.org/10.1016/j.jksuci.2023.101892.
15. Stecuła, K., Wolniak, R., Grebski, W., AI-Driven Urban Energy Solutions—From Individuals to Society: A Review. *Energies*, 2023, https://doi.org/10.3390/en16247988.
16. Moghaddam, S., Dashtdar, M., Jafari, H., AI applications in smart cities' energy systems automation. *Repa Proc. Ser.*, 2022, https://doi.org/10.37357/1068/crgs2022.3.1.01.
17. Minh, Q., Nguyen, V., Quy, V., Ngoc, L., Chehri, A., Jeon, G., Edge Computing for IoT-Enabled Smart Grid: The Future of Energy. *Energies*, 2022, https://doi.org/10.3390/en15176140.
18. Szczepaniuk, H. and Szczepaniuk, E., Applications of Artificial Intelligence Algorithms in the Energy Sector. *Energies*, 2022, https://doi.org/10.3390/en16010347.
19. Salama, A. and Abdellatif, M., AIoT-based Smart Home Energy Management System. *2022 IEEE Global Conference on Artificial Intelligence and Internet of Things (GCAIoT)*, pp. 177–181, 2022, https://doi.org/10.1109/GCAIoT57150.2022.10019091.
20. Esenogho, E., Djouani, K., Kurien, A., Integrating Artificial Intelligence, Internet of Things, and 5G for Next-Generation Smartgrid: A Survey of Trends, Challenges and Prospects. *IEEE Access*, 10, 4794–4831, 2022, https://doi.org/10.1109/access.2022.3140595.
21. Wu, S., Shirkey, G., Celik, I., Shao, C., Chen, J., A Review on the Adoption of AI, BC, and IoT in Sustainability Research. *Sustainability*, 2022, https://doi.org/10.3390/su14137851.

22. Kumar, A., Sharma, S., Goyal, N., Singh, A., Cheng, X., Singh, P., Secure and energy-efficient smart building architecture with emerging technology IoT. *Comput. Commun.*, 176, 207–217, 2021, https://doi.org/10.1016/J.COMCOM.2021.06.003.
23. Boza, P. and Evgeniou, T., Artificial intelligence to support the integration of variable renewable energy sources into the power system. *Appl. Energy*, 290, 116754, 2021, https://doi.org/10.1016/J.APENERGY.2021.116754.
24. Feng, C., Liu, Y., Zhang, J., A taxonomical review on recent artificial intelligence applications to PV integration into power grids. *Int. J. Electr. Power Energy Syst.*, 132, 107176, 2021, https://doi.org/10.1016/J.IJEPES.2021.107176.
25. Zhang, X., Manogaran, G., Muthu, B., IoT-enabled integrated system for green energy in smart cities. *Sustainable Energy Technol. Assess.*, 46, 101208, 2021, https://doi.org/10.1016/J.SETA.2021.101208.
26. Ahmad, T., Zhang, D., Huang, C., Zhang, H., Dai, N., Song, Y., Chen, H., Artificial intelligence in the sustainable energy industry: Status Quo, challenges and opportunities. *J. Cleaner Prod.*, 2021, https://doi.org/10.1016/J.JCLEPRO.2021.125834.
27. Kumar, N., Chand, A., Malvoni, M., Prasad, K., Mamun, K., Islam, F., Chopra, S., Distributed Energy Resources and the Application of AI, IoT, and Blockchain in Smart Grids. *Energies*, 2020, https://doi.org/10.3390/en13215739.
28. Kumari, A., Gupta, R., Tanwar, S., Kumar, N., Blockchain and AI amalgamation for energy cloud management: Challenges, solutions, and future directions. *J. Parallel Distrib. Comput.*, 143, 148–166, 2020, https://doi.org/10.1016/j.jpdc.2020.05.004.
29. Miglani, A., Kumar, N., Chamola, V., Zeadally, S., Blockchain for Internet of Energy management: Review, solutions, and challenges. *Comput. Commun.*, 151, 395–418, 2020, https://doi.org/10.1016/j.comcom.2020.01.014.
30. O'Dwyer, E., Pan, I., Acha, S., Shah, N., Smart energy systems for sustainable smart cities: Current developments, trends and future directions. *Appl. Energy*, 2019, https://doi.org/10.1016/J.APENERGY.2019.01.024.

Index

Also of Interest

Check out these other related titles from Scrivener Publishing

Solar Energy Concentrators, Edited by Inamuddin, ISBN: 9781394204328. Discover the latest techniques and applications for solar energy concentrators in this essential guide for academics, researchers, environmentalists, and professionals seeking to harness the power of solar energy while reducing environmental impact and costs.

Optimization in Sustainable Energy: Methods and Applications, Edited Prasenjit Chatterjee, Anita Khosla, Ashwani Kumar and Gülay Demir, ISBN: 9781394242108. This state-of-the-art book offers cutting-edge optimization techniques and practical decision making frameworks essential for enhancing the efficiency and reliability of sustainable energy systems, making it an invaluable resource for researchers, policymakers, and energy professionals.

Secure Energy Optimization: Leveraging Internet of Things and Artificial Intelligence for Enhanced Efficiency, Edited by Abhishek Kumar, Surbhi Bhatia Khan, Narayan Vyas, Vishal Dutt, and Shakila Basheer, ISBN: 9781394271818. *Secure Energy Optimization: Leveraging Internet of Things and Artificial Intelligence for Enhanced Efficiency* is essential for anyone looking to navigate the transformative landscape of energy management, as it expertly combines the principles of IoT and AI with real-world case studies to provide actionable insights for achieving sustainable and efficient energy optimization.

Materials for Solar Energy Conversion: Materials, Methods and Applications, Edited by R. Rajasekar, C. Moganapriya and A. Mohankumar, ISBN: 9781119750604. This book provides professionals and students with a resource on the basic principles and applications of solar energy materials and processes, as well as practicing engineers who want to understand how functional materials operate in solar energy conversion systems.

Thermal Battery Management System for Hybrid and Electric Vehicles, Edited by Ashwani Kumar, Mukesh Kumar Awasthi, Nitesh Dutt, Yogesh Kumar Singla, and Sivasakthivel Thangavel, ISBN: 9781394289202. *Thermal Battery Management System for Hybrid and Electric Vehicles* is essential for anyone seeking to understand the cutting-edge advancements and challenges in battery thermal management, providing valuable insights that drive innovation and improve the performance of electric and hybrid vehicles.

Solar Electric, Water and Air Tribrid Auto Engineering, Edited by Chandan Deep Singh, Kanwaljit Singh, Davinder Singh, Talwinder Singh, Er. Jasvinder Singh, and Er. Rajdeep Singh, ISBN: 9781394166169. *Solar Electric, Water and Air Tribrid Auto Engineering* is a must-have for anyone in the automotive industry, as it offers a comprehensive analysis of cutting-edge technologies that could revolutionize vehicle design and fuel efficiency, paving the way for a more sustainable future.

Digital Convergence in Intelligent Mobility Systems, Edited by Rathishchandra R. Gatti & Chandra Singh, ISBN: 9781394275243. *Digital Convergence in Intelligent Mobility Systems* gives a comprehensive understanding of how digital technologies are revolutionizing transportation, equipping you with the insights needed to navigate the future of intelligent mobility systems.

AI for Autonomous Vehicles: The Future of Driverless Technology, Edited by Sathiyaraj Rajendran, Munish Sabharwal, Yu-Chen Hu, Rajesh Kumar Dhanaraj, and Balamurugan Balusamy, ISBN: 9781119847465. This title presents the research prospects and security challenges present in the exciting new field of autonomous vehicles by comprehensively introducing advanced concepts of artificial intelligence (AI) in driverless technology.

Introduction to Automotive Engineering, By R. Sakthivel, Faisal O. Mahroogi, S. Narayan, S. Abubakar, M. U. Kaisan, and Youssef Alammari, ISBN: 9781119479802. A brief introduction to automotive engineering, this volume is a useful reference as well, covering not just the basics, but also some of the latest innovations, such as electric and self-driving vehicles.

AUTONOMOUS VEHICLES VOLUME 1: Using Machine Intelligence, Edited by Romil Rawat, A. Mary Sowjanya, Syed Imran Patel, Varshali Jaiswal, Imran Khan, and Allam Balaram. ISBN: 9781119871958. Addressing the current challenges, approaches and applications relating to autonomous vehicles, this groundbreaking new volume presents the research and techniques in this growing area, using Internet of Things, Machine Learning, Deep Learning, and Artificial Intelligence.

AUTONOMOUS VEHICLES VOLUME 2: Smart Vehicles for Communication, Edited by Romil Rawat, Purvee Bhardwaj, Upinder Kaur, Shrikant Telang, Mukesh Chouhan, and K. Sakthidasan Sankaran, ISBN: 9781394152254. The companion to *Autonomous Vehicles Volume 1: Using Machine Intelligence*, this second volume in the two-volume set covers intelligent techniques utilized for designing, controlling and managing vehicular systems based on advanced algorithms of computing like machine learning, artificial Intelligence, data analytics, and Internet of Things with prediction approaches to avoid accidental damages, security threats, and theft.

Hydrogen Electrical Vehicles, Edited by Mehmet Sankir and Nurdan Demirci Sankir, ISBN: 9781394166381. Hydrogen electrical vehicles are an essential component of the "Green New Deal" and this book covers cutting-edge technologies designed for fuel-cell-powered cars.

Smart Charging Solutions for Hybrid and Electric Vehicles, Edited by Sulabh Sachan, Sanjeevikumar Padmanaban, and Sanchari Deb, ISBN: 9781119768951. Written and edited by a team of experts in the field, this is the most comprehensive and up to date study of smart charging solutions for hybrid and electric vehicles for engineers, scientists, students, and other professionals.

Printed and bound by CPI Group (UK) Ltd, Croydon, CR0 4YY
17/09/2026
14964285-0004